The meaning of company accounts

Fifth Edition

Walter Reid and D R Myddelton

Gower

First published 1971
Second edition 1974
Third edition 1982
Fourth edition 1988

Fifth edition published by Gower Publishing Company Limited,
Gower House, Croft Road, Aldershot, Hants GU11 3HR, England

Gower Publishing Company, Old Post Road, Brookfield,
Vermont 05036, USA

CIP catalogue records for this book are available from the British Library and the US Library of Congress

ISBN 0–566–07349–8 Hardback
       0–566–07350–1 Paperback

Typeset in 10pt Times by Poole Typesetting (Wessex) Ltd, Bournemouth, Dorset and printed in Great Britain by Bath Press Ltd, Bath.

Contents

Preface

OBJECTIVES

This book is intended to help those who use company accounts to gain a solid grasp of what they mean and how they relate to business operations. Managers without formal accounting or financial training should find it useful, and it will also provide a thorough introduction to company accounts for those pursuing formal accounting or management studies programmes.

We have taken care to make the book as brief as possible, but we believe that a superficial approach to company accounts is not enough. It might cause readers, on the basis of flimsy analysis, to draw wrong conclusions from accounts. Further, it would almost certainly lead to frustration if readers were to discover in business a wide range of practical complications of whose nature and extent they had been unaware. There is thus a need for the book to be comprehensive as well as concise.

WORKBOOK DESIGN

The Meaning of Company Accounts brings together both basic and detailed material within a framework which can best be described as a 'workbook'. This comes somewhere between a conventional textbook and a programmed text. Like a programmed text it is structured and involves a high degree of participation by the reader; but it is also very flexible, and is designed for use as a reference book as well as for guided reading.

Throughout the book we have tried to develop ideas in a logical sequence and to present them in a form which makes a strong visual impact. In this respect the side-by-side page layout is a great help. To aid learning further, the text of most sections includes examples which we invite the reader to work through. We expect that many who use the workbook may find difficulty with at least some of the topics. The chance to work through examples at such points may be critical to achieving a suitable level of understanding.

Not all readers will have trouble with the same points, and this poses a problem for us as authors. If the workbook is comprehensive on all topics it will be too bulky for those with limited time available; while if it is too concise it may not provide the right support in areas of difficulty. To resolve this dilemma we have divided each section of the book into two parts: the text which provides a comprehensive study of the whole subject, but moves quickly from topic to topic; and additional exercises and problems (mostly with solutions), which readers are free to use as suits them best.

SEQUENCE OF SECTIONS

Broadly the book consists of two parts. Sections 1 and 2 cover general accounting issues, the structure of company accounts and some of the approaches to and formal techniques of financial analysis. They define the area which the rest of the book explores in greater depth and illustrate the total accounting package in published company accounts before we look at the underlying detail.

Sections 3 to 11 deal in more depth with the theoretical and practical problems of recording business transactions, measuring income and expense, assets and liabilities, and presenting information in the profit and loss account, balance sheet, and cash flow statement. This material forms a vital foundation on which to base an understanding of the meaning of company accounts. Section 12 then provides an overview of how to analyse and interpret financial accounts.

HOW TO USE THE BOOK

In some senses no part of this book can be fully understood on its own – the twelve sections form an integral structure. For this reason, readers who are not taking part in a formal programme may prefer to read quickly at first and to gain an overall view before tackling difficulties in detail. Two complete readings may well be more rewarding than a single study in depth. Ideas which seem difficult to begin with may often become clear later on, after covering other parts of the book.

The same approach may be useful even within sections. A quick look through the text to gain some idea of the areas to be covered may well make it easier to understand the relevance and context of the detailed topics on a more careful reading of the section. We emphasize the responsibility that rests on each reader to use the approach to the book which seems best to him or her.

Those with little previous knowledge who wish to acquire a substantial level of competence in analysis should follow study of the text of each section with extensive use of the additional examples. For those who already have some knowledge of accounting, only certain sections of the latter may be useful. The intention is that each reader should be able to move at his or her own pace throughout, building up strength where weaknesses exist and moving more quickly where further detailed work is not required.

PROBLEMS AND SOLUTIONS

The additional material at the end of each section consists of about a dozen exercises and problems. The first exercise in nearly all sections contains a number of definitions, for which we ask the readers to *write down* an answer in the space provided. Suggested definitions, often with additional comments, then appear on the following page. Some readers may find terminology a problem, and a careful tackling of each of the definitions in this book should well repay the trouble.

The remaining exercises and problems have been treated in three ways. First in each section come some fairly basic problems on matters covered in the text. Space is left in the book for the reader to use for his or her answer, and again we strongly recommend taking the trouble to *write out* an attempted answer to the problem being tackled. The suggested solution appears in detail on the next page, together with comments. In effect we are almost having a 'conversation' with each reader in respect of these early problems; and we do several times make extra points in our notes to the solutions which do not occur in the text itself.

Then come several rather more difficult problems, solutions to which appear at the end of the book. For most of these problems we ask readers to use their own paper, as it would require too much space to leave room in the book itself. These more difficult problems may be regarded as self-tests for readers on how well they have understood the material in the text. We have chosen to show solutions at the back of the book, rather than immediately after each problem. This is in order to minimize the temptation to look at the solutions too soon! More personal benefit will usually be gained from a serious attempt to work completely through each problem *before* studying our solution at the back of the book.

Finally, in most sections, we have included three or four problems for which we publish no solutions. These may be used as assignments on formal programmes in companies or business schools, or the reader may care to attempt them for personal satisfaction. Some of these problems are 'essay type' questions for which there is no single 'correct' answer.

In total the problems and exercises constitute nearly half of the book. The workbook design clearly places more demands on the reader than a normal textbook. But the extra effort required to select and tackle the particular material which satisfies each reader's own needs should be well rewarded by the rapid development of a real competence to interpret accounting statements. An understanding can be gained which extends significantly beyond the appraisal of results based merely on mechanical application of standard analytical techniques. The bibliography at the end of the book will help those who wish to extend further their studies of related and more advanced aspects of accounting theory and practice.

FIFTH EDITION

In the four years since the fourth edition was published, there have been a number of developments in accounting. Three new accounting standards have appeared; and the Companies Act 1985 has been amended by the Companies Act 1989. The Accounting Standards Committee has been replaced by a new Accounting Standards Board, within the new Financial Reporting Council framework.

The main changes in this fifth edition are as follows:

- the Introduction is now included within Section 1
- we have added material in Section 5 on revaluing fixed assets
- Section 6 on cash flow statements was formerly Section 9 on funds flow statements. (We have rewritten the section in the light of the new accounting standard FRS 1.)
- Sections 7, 8, and 9 were formerly numbered 6, 7, and 8. In Section 9 (Group accounts), we have added some more material on the consolidated profit and loss account; and we include a new sub-section on Brands
- Section 10 (International accounting) is new, though much of the text comes from the former section on group accounts. The problems are mostly new
- Sections 11 and 12 were formerly numbered 10 and 11
- We have added in Appendix 6 (pages 325 to 335) some skeleton forms for analysis, covering overview financial ratios, segment analysis, and cash/funds flow analysis. We would encourage readers to photocopy the forms in Appendix 6 for their own use, as convenient.

For the fifth edition there is an Instructor's Guide containing solutions to all the problems for which no solution is published in this book. This is available free to any teacher of accounting working in a recognized institution. Please write for a copy to:

Professor D. R. Myddelton,
Cranfield School of Management,
Cranfield,
Bedford MK43 0AL.

We have thoroughly revised the text wherever it has seemed possible to improve the clarity of our discussion by so doing; and we refer where appropriate to current accounting standards. We have also, of course, updated the 'real' company accounts used, as well as the material in the appendices. In some instances, for reasons of space, it has been necessary to edit and reset some of this data.

Walter Reid and D. R. Myddelton

The Authors

Walter Reid was Professor of Accounting and Financial Control at the London Business School from 1973 to 1988 and is now a Visiting Professor at the School. He is a Chartered Accountant. He was formerly Group Financial Controller at Edwards High Vacuum International Limited, and associate consultant with McKinsey and Company Inc. He was a member of the Sandilands Committee on Inflation Accounting. He is now extensively involved in education and training within companies as a founder Director of Management Development Associates Limited and is also a consultant to a number of large companies.

D. R. Myddelton is a Chartered Accountant and a graduate of the Harvard Business School. He has been Professor of Finance and Accounting at the Cranfield School of Management since 1972. He has written books on tax reform and on inflation accounting, and text books on accounting, economics and financial management.

Acknowledgements

We are grateful to all the companies from whose annual accounts we have reproduced extracts:

The Burton Group plc
Grand Metropolitan plc
Hanson plc
H.J. Heinz Company
Imperial Chemical Industries plc
Kwik Save plc
Northern Foods plc
Reed International plc
Whitbread plc

We should stress that we remain entirely responsible for the analysis and comments thereon.

We should like to thank the many students at the London Business School and at the Cranfield School of Management who have commented on various editions and drafts of the text and problems. Thanks are also due to our academic colleagues for their help over the years and in particular to Swee Im Ung, Lynne Teasdale and Antony Morris for their extensive help in the preparation of this edition.

Finally we owe our gratitude to Sheila Hart at Cranfield whose help has been essential to the production of this book.

Section 1
The background and structure of company accounts

DEVELOPMENT OF ACCOUNTING

In its simplest form, accounting recorded cash receipts and payments and measured the resulting balance at the end. This might be for a specific business venture or for a definite period of time. As some businesses grew larger and more complex, so did the number and variety of their transactions. Traders needed quite elaborate records to classify transactions according to type. In order to record revenues and expenses, assets and liabilities, a system evolved in the fifteenth century known as 'double-entry' bookkeeping. This system was not only able to classify transactions, but was also self-checking. Goethe called it 'the finest invention of the human mind'; and it remains the foundation of modern accounting.

The Industrial Revolution brought the next main step in accounting. For many years most trade involved either sole traders or partners, who bore the risks of the business up to the limit of their personal wealth. But by the late nineteenth century larger concerns needed more capital resources than all but a few individuals could muster. This led to the increasing use of 'limited liability' companies, whose affairs were regulated by Companies Acts. Their emergence began to separate a firm's ownership from its day-to-day management. This required regular formal stewardship reports from the managers to the dispersed owners.

At first it was feared that managers and part-owners enjoying the protection of limited liability might act with less prudence than wholly-liable sole traders and partners. As a result company directors were conservative in what they let accounts reveal, and balance sheets emphasised financial soundness while often concealing secret reserves. These reserves could easily be used to smooth out reported profits from year to year, which might mislead shareholders.

In the twentieth century, public trading of shares greatly expanded, especially on the UK and US stock exchanges. This led to the development of accounting standards to help investors and others compare company accounts. Secret reserves in both countries are now forbidden, though prudence remains a feature of accounting practice.

Since the 1950s the increasingly world-wide nature of business has spawned many large multinational companies. Combined with unprecedented rates of inflation in the developed countries, this has also led to complex problems of translating fluctuating foreign currencies. Recent developments include attempts to harmonize different national accounting practices by international agreement.

Modern requirements

In the UK successive post-war Companies Acts have required companies to divulge more and more details about their affairs. Schedule 4 of the Companies Act 1985 (as amended by the Companies Act 1989) now contains the main legal requirements for company accounts. Companies must prepare a profit and loss account and balance sheet each year in one of the permitted formats (set out on pages 317 to 324). Moreover, and of supreme importance, the accounts must show a 'true and fair view' of the profit or loss for the year, and of the company's position at the year-end.

In addition, companies are expected to follow Statements of Standard Accounting Practice (SSAPs). These contain principles and detailed rules governing the form and content of published UK financial statements. (A list of all twenty-two SSAPs in force at 31 July 1991 is set out on page 307.) They can broadly be classified into four general areas: disclosure (7), group accounting (5), taxation (4), and various specific topics (6).

In September 1991, the new Accounting Standards Board (ASB) issued the first of its Financial Reporting Standards (FRS), which will in time supersede SSAPs. FRS 1 requires all but the smallest companies to publish a cash flow statement which shows, in a standard format, the various sources from which a company has derived cash during the year, and how it has used the cash. (It replaces SSAP 10, issued in 1975, which required a somewhat similar statement listing sources and uses of 'funds'.)

The Companies Acts aim to protect shareholders and creditors, but there is a growing view that companies may also owe duties to other groups in society, such as: employees, suppliers, customers, government, and the public at large.

Pressures for more disclosure

The 1948 Companies Act required group accounts; the 1967 Act required companies to disclose total turnover, and to analyse sales and profits between different business segments and between geographical areas. The 1981 Act set out detailed EEC format requirements for accounts; the 1985 Companies Act mainly consolidated earlier Acts; and the 1989 Act enacted changes in respect of groups. Evidently we are going through a period of far-reaching changes, tending to refine and extend the reporting duties of companies.

Companies of different sizes must meet varying levels of required disclosure. The importance of large 'stewardship' companies, run by professional managers who are not, to any significant extent, also the owners, may justify extensive disclosure to help protect the interests of the shareholders. Companies whose shares are listed on the Stock Exchange must also comply with the detailed requirements of the Council of the Stock Exchange.

But in small 'proprietorship' companies, a few owners and their families own all the shares, and often act as managers too. Reporting burdens for them must not be too heavy. Thus small and medium-sized companies need not disclose certain details. The Companies Act 1985 (as amended in 1989) defines 'small' and 'medium' companies as those meeting two or more of the following maximum conditions:

	Small	Medium
Turnover	£2.0 million	£8.0 million
Total assets	£0.975 million	£3.9 million
Number of employees	50	250

Large and diversified groups of companies are under continuing pressure to disclose still more. Not only must they consolidate the accounts of the holding company and all its subsidiaries, to present the combined affairs of the whole group as if they were the business of a single entity (see Section 9); but they must also disclose segmental information about sales, profits and assets (SSAP 25). More details are sought concerning research, intangible assets, employees, etc. But clearly there must be a limit. Already annual reports of large companies comprise nearly 100 pages – the size of a small book every year. The general principle is that the costs of producing information should not outweigh its likely benefits. But those who might benefit often do not have to bear the costs, hence the pressure for more and more disclosure.

THE ACCOUNTING TASK

We have seen that, at its simplest, accounting deals with receipts and payments of cash. If all transactions are complete at the accounting date, it is easy to summarize receipts and payments and calculate the closing balance. But problems begin to emerge when an ongoing business needs 'interim' accounts. For now, whatever accounting date is chosen, some transactions will be incomplete. And the longer the time taken to complete transactions (the 'business cycle'), the more difficult will be the accounting task.

At least once a year companies must publish three accounting statements:

- a profit and loss account including the revenues and expenses for the accounting period, and showing the resulting profit or loss
- a balance sheet (statement of financial position), showing the assets a company owns or controls at the year-end, and how it has financed them
- a cash flow statement showing the various sources of cash received in the period and the uses of cash expended.

To prepare these statements, accountants must break into the continuous stream of transactions at regular intervals to:

- identify and measure the relevant revenues and expenses relating to an accounting period
- identify and measure the assets held, including those relating to incomplete transactions, and determine their means of finance
- compare the beginning and ending liabilities and assets, to discover where cash has come from and how it has been invested.

The accounting task (pictured opposite) is not simple. For a typical business the results can only be approximate. Some items of revenue and expense may be easy to assign to specific accounting periods, but incomplete transactions raise problems. For example, those preparing accounts need to decide in which period to charge costs intended to generate future benefits. It is not enough to identify the various assets and liabilities at the balance sheet date: accountants must also attach a definite value to them. This may involve partly completed stocks, partly worn-out equipment, or unexpired intangible assets.

Problems of this kind do not yield uniquely 'correct' solutions. They depend partly on uncertain future events, so measurement is often a matter of judgement. Accounting is an art not a science.

THE MAIN ACCOUNTING STATEMENTS

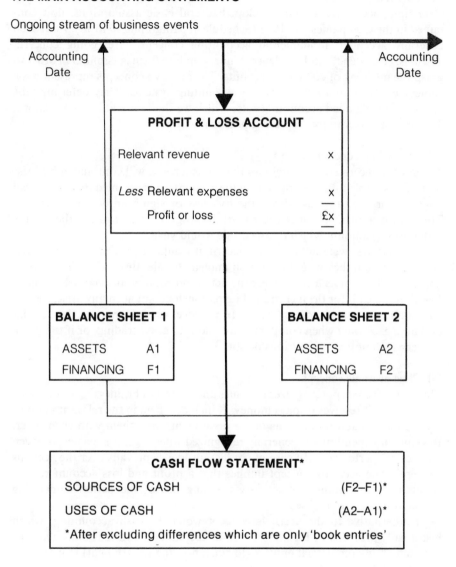

Ongoing stream of business events

Accounting Date   Accounting Date

PROFIT & LOSS ACCOUNT

Relevant revenue	x
Less Relevant expenses	x
Profit or loss	£x

BALANCE SHEET 1

ASSETS	A1
FINANCING	F1

BALANCE SHEET 2

ASSETS	A2
FINANCING	F2

CASH FLOW STATEMENT*

SOURCES OF CASH	(F2–F1)*
USES OF CASH	(A2–A1)*

*After excluding differences which are only 'book entries'

FUNDAMENTAL ACCOUNTING CONCEPTS

Over time, accountants have developed several basic assumptions, now contained in the Companies Act 1985 (Schedule 4, paragraphs 10 to 13). Four such generally accepted 'fundamental accounting concepts' are: going concern, accruals, consistency, and prudence. Understanding them is essential in order to grasp the meaning of company accounts. The first two concepts represent basic choices between alternative possible accounting systems. They determine the nature of the detailed accounting rules which we shall look at in later sections. The second two concepts represent practical wisdom.

(a)   The going concern concept

The going concern concept assumes that an enterprise will continue in business in the foreseeable future. In preparing the accounts, it is assumed that there is no intention or need to close down the business or significantly curtail its size. Thus, for example, accounts value work-in-progress at cost rather than at the (often lower) amount which a forced sale would yield.

If the business were not a going concern, it would be prudent to value assets at no more than they would realize on immediate sale. But such a 'liquidation' approach does not as a rule reflect the actual position of an ongoing business. Moreover, it calls for the inclusion of items which do not normally arise, such as redundancy payments to employees. In practice, accountants use the liquidation approach only when companies are about to cease trading, or if the going concern assumption is in serious doubt.

(b)   The accruals concept

The accruals concept recognizes revenues and costs as a business earns or incurs them, not as it receives or pays money. It includes them in the relevant period's profit and loss account, and as far as possible matches them with each other. Revenue or expenditure is generally recognized when legal title passes, or when services are performed. (In case of conflict, prudence prevails over the accruals concept.) The accruals concept implies that a profit and loss account reflects changes in the amount of net assets arising out of the period's operating transactions, as we shall see.

An alternative to the accruals concept would be cash accounting, which historically preceded it. Businesses reckon accrual accounting is more realistic, but some non-commercial entities (for instance, the government) still account on a cash basis.

(c)   The consistency concept

Accounting requires consistent treatment for similar items within each accounting period and from one period to the next. Otherwise comparing accounts between periods and between businesses would be meaningless. A company therefore needs to disclose fully any change in accounting treatment, and where suitable restate prior years' figures on the new basis.

(d)   The prudence concept

We have already seen that accounting is conservative. Under the prudence concept accounts do not anticipate revenues and profits. The profit and loss account includes revenues (and therefore profits) only when they are 'realized'. This may be either in cash, or else in the form of other assets whose ultimate cash proceeds are fairly certain. In contrast, accounts make full provision for all known expenses and losses, even where they are less certain and their amount has to be estimated.

These four fundamental accounting concepts are practical assumptions, not theoretical ideals. They may need to change as accounting practice develops. But at present they are generally accepted in the UK as providing the framework for financial statements.

Accounting bases and policies

Accounting bases are methods of applying fundamental concepts to deal with a wide variety of business transactions. Accounting policies are the specific accounting bases which an enterprise chooses as best suited to present its financial results fairly. Businesses have become so complex and diverse as to rule out complete uniformity; but where more than one accounting basis is available, the policy chosen can make a big difference. A company must therefore state what its accounting policies are, and stick to them, so that readers can understand its financial statements properly.

ACCOUNTING AND INFLATION

Between 1970 and 1989, the pound lost 85 per cent of its purchasing power. UK inflation over that period averaged 10 per cent a year – an unprecedented rate over such a long peacetime period. In such conditions historical cost accounts are seriously distorted: they give a misleading view of companies' real assets, and of their profits or losses after charging for the real cost of resources consumed.

Two different ways of coping with the problem have been suggested. The Current (or Constant) Purchasing Power (CPP) method applies a single general index of money prices to past money amounts. CPP changes the unit of measurement in accounts from money to a unit of constant purchasing power, while retaining historical costs. Current Cost Accounting (CCA), on the other hand, applies different specific price indices to past amounts. CCA substitutes 'current costs' for historical costs, while retaining money as the accounting unit of measurement.

SSAP 7 proposing CPP was issued in 1974 and withdrawn in 1978, while SSAP 16 proposing CCA was issued in 1980 and withdrawn in 1985. Both CPP and CCA were heavily criticized, on a number of different grounds. This bald summary omits much of the drama of this long-running, but still unsettled, debate. Section 11 describes each of the two methods in more detail.

The 'inflation accounting' debate has faded in the early 1990s, due to the decline in inflation. In the five years from 1987 to 1991 inclusive, the average rate of UK inflation was just over 5 per cent a year. Of course this is hardly negligible (though, in effect, accounts now neglect it!); but it is much less than the rates of around 10 per cent a year which prevailed in the previous two decades.

'TRUE AND FAIR VIEW'

Given alternative accounting bases, what does a 'true and fair view' imply? These words do not carry their everyday meaning. In accounting, 'true and fair' is a technical phrase meaning appropriate classification of items and the consistent application of generally accepted accounting principles.

Financial results for a single year are often less useful as a guide to a company's performance than accounts for several years. The Companies Act 1985 requires annual accounts to disclose figures not just for the latest year, but for the preceding year as well. A legal prospectus requires at least five years' past figures for most companies seeking to raise money in the stock market; and many companies now publish five- or ten-year summaries of the main items in the profit and loss account and balance sheet.

Responsibility for disclosing a 'true and fair view' in accounts rests legally with the directors of a company. They must decide on the form and content of accounts, which should of course comply with the Companies Act 1985. The company's auditors must then report whether or not, in their opinion, the accounts do give a 'true and fair view' (see page 13).

Under the going concern concept, balance sheet amounts seldom represent the sums which would be received on the 'break-up' of a company. Current assets appear at cost (unless net realizable value is lower); and, except where interests in land and buildings have been revalued, accounts normally show tangible fixed assets at historical cost less depreciation (see Section 5). This may be well below current market value.

So the phrase 'true and fair' should not tempt users of accounts to believe that a balance sheet discloses the 'true worth' of a company. It is not meant to. The balance sheet makes no attempt to value a business; and the American phrase 'net worth' used in balance sheets to refer to shareholders' interests is highly misleading. A balance sheet is merely a statement of those assets and liabilities of a business which the accounting rules recognize. Many significant assets are excluded, especially intangible assets such as business 'know-how' and the value of people. Thus the market value of a business often differs widely from the net book value of its assets.

THE ACCOUNTING MODEL
The principal operations in the model are:

- record transactions, whether for cash or on credit
- prepare cash flow statement
- assemble in the profit and loss account items relevant to the year
- analyse other items (not in the profit and loss account)
- prepare closing balance sheet.

We can now look at each of these more closely.

Recording transactions: cash and credit
Whether a company enters into transactions for cash or on credit terms depends on the nature of its business. A retail shop will normally buy goods on credit (paying for supplies a month or so after purchase) but sell for cash; while a company making cars enters into only a few cash transactions (such as for wages). It will buy *and* sell most goods and services on credit, and only after the credit period has elapsed will there be a cash outflow or inflow. We shall look more closely at how a company's accounting system records transactions when we consider (in Section 3) the use of cash books, ledgers and journals (day books).

To the extent that cash has not yet been received from a credit sale, the company possesses a legal right to receive cash, which the year-end balance sheet shows as a debtor (account receivable). Similarly, if the company owes money for goods or services bought on credit this will show in the balance sheet as a creditor (account payable). Any differences between credit transactions and related cash flows in a period will lead to an increase or decrease in outstanding debtors and creditors.

Cash flow statement
Cash transactions can be classified by type of receipt (sale, interest received, etc.) or by type of payment (wages, purchase of fixed asset, etc.). Thus a cash flow statement can be prepared, suitably classified, which will show and explain the change in the cash balance for a period.

Profit and loss account and other accounts
A main function of the profit and loss account for a period is to show the operating profit or loss. It does this, to a large extent, by 'matching' against the revenues relevant to a period the expenses incurred to generate the revenues.

Trading transactions, however, may not relate entirely to the current year (as we shall discuss in detail in Section 4). For example, rent may be payable on 30 September for six months ahead. If the accounting year-end is 31 December, then only half the rent payable is relevant for this year's profit and loss account. The rest will apply to next year's; and the amount of rent paid in advance will appear as a current asset ('prepayment') in the balance sheet at 31 December.

Not all business transactions are of a trading nature. Non-trading transactions such as borrowing money or purchasing an office building, for example, will appear as changes in balance sheet amounts for loans and fixed assets respectively.

Opening and closing balance sheets
Nearly all annual accounts relate to ongoing businesses, so that the annual report usually contains *two* balance sheets. One sets out the assets and liabilities at the beginning of the current year (that is, the end of the previous year), and the other shows the position at the end of the current year. Later in this section we shall see how balance sheets classify items. Changes which take place are the result of the company's trading and non-trading activities during the year.

The diagram opposite shows in detail the structure of the accounting 'model'. Please study it carefully. In particular, it sets out the links between transactions, cash flows, and the two main financial statements. We shall now consider the individual financial statements in more detail.

6

STRUCTURE OF THE ACCOUNTING MODEL

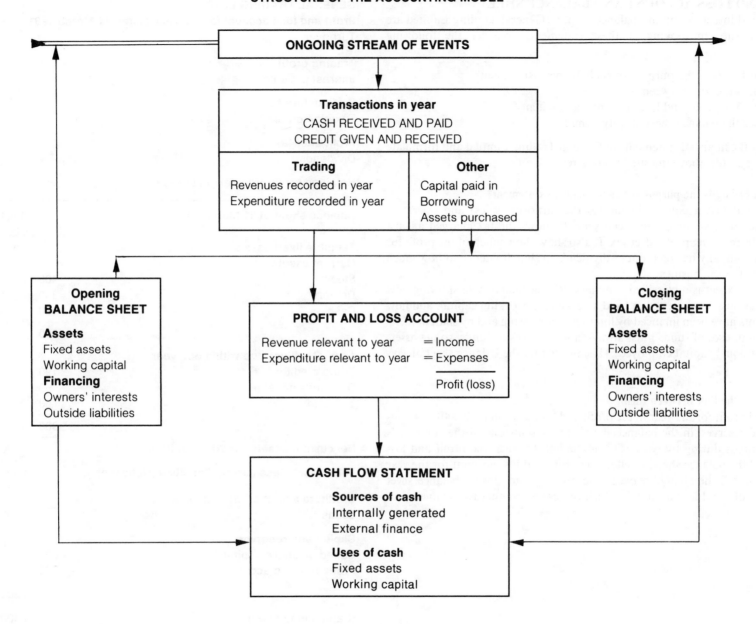

PROFIT AND LOSS ACCOUNT AND BALANCE SHEET

The profit and loss account and balance sheet of General Trading Limited are set out opposite. In looking at these statements consider the following questions:

1 (a) What briefly is the purpose of each financial statement?
   (b) What is the link between them?
2 How does the profit and loss account classify items?
3 How does the balance sheet classify items?

Please study the financial statements of General Trading Limited and formulate your answers to the above questions *before* reading on.

1(a) What briefly is the purpose of each financial statement?

The profit and loss account summarises the turnover (sales) and operating profit of the business for the financial year. It shows the tax charged against profit and the resulting profit after tax. It also shows how much of the profit for the year the company has paid out as dividends to shareholders and how much it has retained in the business.

The balance sheet is a classified summary at a particular date showing how much the business has invested in fixed assets and in working capital, and how these amounts have been financed by long-term borrowing and by shareholders' funds. In total, uses of funds must always equal sources of funds, so net assets must always equal capital employed. This means that the balance sheet always balances.

1(b) What is the link between them?

The retained profit for the year in the profit and loss account (£30 000) increases 'Capital and reserves' in the balance sheet. It represents one of the company's sources of funds during the year. This is the link between the profit and loss account and the balance sheet. In effect the profit and loss account for the year explains in detail the change between the opening and closing balance sheet figure for 'profit and loss account' (which represents cumulative retained profits).

GENERAL TRADING LIMITED

Profit and loss account for the year ended 31 March 1991	£'000
Turnover	2 400
Trading profit	160
Interest payable	20
Profit before tax	140
Taxation on profit	50
Profit after tax	90
Dividends	60
Retained profit, transferred to reserves	30

Balance sheet at 31 March 1991		1991 £'000		1990 £'000
Tangible fixed assets		800		700
Current assets				
Stocks	400		250	
Debtors	350		300	
Cash	150		100	
	900		650	
Less: **Creditors due within one year**				
Trade creditors	190		140	
Dividends payable	60		20	
Taxation	50		30	
	300		190	
Net current assets (working capital)		600		460
Total assets less current liabilities (Net assets)		1 400		1 160
Creditors due after more than one year				
Loans		200		140
Capital and reserves				
Called up share capital	1 000		850	
Profit and loss account	200		170	
		1 200		1 020
(Capital employed)		1 400		1 160

PROFIT AND LOSS ACCOUNT CLASSIFICATION

2 How does the profit and loss account classify items?

The usual published format of the profit and loss account would show the main expenses which are deducted from turnover (sales) to arrive at the operating profit. The statement is not normally divided but in fact contains three separate parts:

(a) Trading account

The trading account deals with turnover (sales revenue) and the costs of achieving sales. Cost of sales represents all the costs needed to bring the goods into a saleable condition and gross profit is the difference between sales and these costs. Distribution costs and administrative expenses are the costs incurred by the business in selling the goods and in running the business. The final figure in the trading account is the operating profit (or loss) for the period.

(b) Profit and loss account

The profit and loss account begins with the operating profit, and adds other income, such as dividends receivable. The law requires accounts to disclose various expenses separately, including depreciation, interest paid, audit fees and directors' remuneration. If the profit and loss account itself does not show such items, they will have to be disclosed in a note to the accounts.

The balance remaining is the profit before tax and deducting tax gives the profit for the year after tax. Extraordinary items, if any, appear in the statement after the 'profit for the year after tax' has been established, and are often referred to as 'below the line' items. We discuss them in Section 4.

(c) Appropriation account

The appropriation account shows how much of the profit for the year is distributed as dividends, how much transferred to special reserves and how much retained in the profit and loss account. The amount retained for the year is added to the cumulative amount retained from previous years. The new total is shown in the balance sheet under the heading 'profit and loss account' (which is part of the reserves).

GENERAL TRADING LIMITED
Trading, profit and loss, and appropriation account
for the year ended 31 March 1991

(a) Trading account	£'000
Turnover	2 400
Cost of sales	1 500
Gross profit	900
Distribution costs	600
Administrative expenses	140
Operating profit	160

(b) Profit and loss account	
Operating profit	160
Interest payable	20
Profit before tax	140
Taxation on profit	50
Profit after tax	90

(c) Appropriation account	
Profit after tax for the year	90
Dividends	60
Retained profit, transferred to reserves	30

BALANCE SHEET CLASSIFICATION

3   How does the balance sheet classify items?

NET ASSETS represent the way in which the long-term resources of the company have been employed, on fixed assets or working capital.

Fixed assets are intended for use on a continuing basis in the company's activities. They include tangible assets, such as land and buildings, plant and equipment, and intangible assets, such as goodwill.

Current assets are 'current' because they are expected to be turned into cash within twelve months from the balance sheet date (or within the operating cycle of the business, if it is longer). The items shown as current assets usually appear in reverse order of liquidity: first, stocks, then debtors, and finally cash itself (the most liquid).

Less: Creditors due within one year (current liabilities). These are due for payment within one year from the balance sheet date, and often much sooner. They include short-term borrowings, amounts due to suppliers (trade creditors), current tax liabilities, and any proposed dividends to shareholders.

Working capital (net current assets) is the 'circulating capital' of the business. It is the excess of current assets over current liabilities. Even though the constituent items, as we have just seen, are all short term, the net balance of working capital requires long-term capital to finance it.

CAPITAL EMPLOYED is divided between creditors due after more than one year (long-term liabilities) and capital and reserves (shareholders' funds).

Creditors due after more than one year (long-term liabilities). These mostly represent long-term borrowing (loans, mortgages, or debentures), which amounts to semi-permanent capital for a company. It is generally undertaken for fairly long periods, say five to ten years. When repayment becomes due, the item may often be replaced either by newly-issued shares or by more long-term borrowing.

Capital and reserves (shareholders' funds).
The called-up share capital, usually in the form of ordinary shares, is the permanent capital of the business. A company cannot reduce its share capital without special permission from the court.

The profit and loss account reserve represents cumulative retained profits which are legally available to pay dividends to shareholders. In practice, however, dividends are usually paid out of the current year's profits.

GENERAL TRADING LIMITED
Balance sheet at 31 March 1991

£'000

Net assets

Tangible fixed assets		
Land and buildings		300
Plant and machinery		500
		800
Current assets		
Stocks	400	
Debtors	350	
Cash	150	
	900	
Less: **Creditors due within one year** (current liabilities)		
Trade creditors	190	
Dividends payable	60	
Taxation	50	
	300	
Net current assets (working capital)		600
Net assets (total assets less current liabilities)		1 400

Capital employed

Creditors due after more than one year		200
Capital and reserves		
Called up share capital	1 000	
Profit and loss account	200	
		1 200
Capital employed		1 400

CASH FLOW STATEMENT

The third main financial statement in the annual accounts of companies is the cash flow statement required by FRS 1. Its purpose is to show the sources and amounts of cash arising in the year, from operations, sales of fixed assets, borrowing, issue of shares, and so on; and how the cash has been used in paying tax and dividends, investing in fixed assets, repaying borrowing, and so on. The cash flow statement supplements the profit and loss account and balance sheet, and we have already seen how the three statements are interlinked. (Section 6 looks at cash flow statements in more detail.)

At this stage we can compile a simple cash flow statement for General Trading Limited for the year ended 31 March 1991, by listing the changes in the balance sheet figures between 31 March 1990 and 31 March 1991, which were both shown on page 8. (The Companies Act 1985 requires companies to publish comparative figures for the previous year for both the profit and loss account and the balance sheet.)

The analysis needed to prepare a simple cash flow statement is in two steps:

Step 1 Calculate balance sheet differences

GENERAL TRADING LIMITED

	Balance sheet 1990 £'000	Balance sheet 1991 £'000	Differences Sources £'000	Differences Uses £'000
Fixed assets	700	800		100
Stocks	250	400		150
Debtors	300	350		50
Cash	100	150		50
Less: Trade creditors	140	190	50	
Dividends payable	20	60	40	
Taxation	30	50	20	
	1 160	1 400		
Loans	140	200	60	
Called up share capital	850	1000	150	
Profit and loss account	170	200	30	
	1 160	1 400	350	350

Step 2 Classify the sources and uses of cash

One figure of special interest in the cash flow statement is the net flow of cash from operating activities. In the balance sheet, the profit and loss account balance has increased by £30 000, the amount of retained profit for the year. But it is usual to include more detail from the profit and loss account itself (page 8). Operating profit before interest and tax is £160 000 (= £90 000 profit after tax + tax charged £50 000 + interest payable £20 000). Tax actually paid is £30 000 (the amount charged of £50 000 less the £20 000 increase in the end-of-year tax liability outstanding). Similarly, dividends actually paid in the year are £20 000 (the total dividends proposed for the year of £60 000 less the £40 000 increase in end-of-year dividends payable). In the format required by FRS 1, changes in working capital are also shown as part of cash flows resulting from operating activities; while interest and dividends, and tax paid, are shown below as separate classifications.

GENERAL TRADING LIMITED
Cash flow statement, Year ended 31 March 1991

£'000

Operating activities			
Profit before interest and tax		160	
Less: Increase in stocks	150		
Increase in debtors	50		
Less: Increase in trade creditors	(50)	150	
			10
Interest and dividends paid (20 + 20)			(40)
Taxation paid			(30)
Investing activities			
Fixed assets			(100)
Net cash outflow before financing			(160)
Financing activities			
Ordinary share capital issued		150	
Loans borrowed		60	210
Increase in cash			50

DISCLOSURE IN ANNUAL REPORTS

Accountants face many problems in reflecting complex business transactions in financial statements. How much detail should accounts present, and in what form? Larger companies now publish figures to the nearest million pounds only, and the accounts of even quite small companies normally go only to the nearest thousand pounds. Most accounting numbers cannot be exactly 'correct', and even if they could such precision would not be useful.

A public company's annual report and accounts must contain at least the following:

- directors' report
- balance sheet
- profit and loss account
- cash flow statement
- notes to the accounts
- auditors' report on the above.

The format and contents of accounts must comply with the Companies Act 1985. But the law does not always say whether certain details should appear in the accounts, in the notes or in the directors' report. The directors' report must deal with certain matters not all of an accounting nature, unless the annual report does so somewhere else. The list opposite (above) shows the main items.

In addition, most chairmen include in the annual report a statement discussing the year's results and commenting on future prospects. Many companies also publish financial statistics covering several past years, on a consistent basis. Anyone looking into a company's performance and financial position should carefully examine all these, as well as analysing the accounts themselves.

The modern trend is to simplify the items on the face of the accounts so that laymen can understand them. At the same time, extensive notes to the published accounts give the detail which financial analysts require. The notes form *part* of the 'accounts' (sometimes the most important part). They are *not* just an optional extra. The notes to the accounts must include all the items in the list opposite (below), which is not exhaustive.

The annual reports of large companies may contain fifty pages or more, with twenty pages on reviewing operations, three or four pages for the financial statements, and twelve pages or more for the notes to the accounts. All the rest may take another twelve to fifteen pages.

Directors' report (unless shown elsewhere)

1 Names of the directors and details of their shareholdings
2 Main classes of business and any major changes
3 Important changes in fixed assets
4 Research and development activities
5 A fair review of the year's business, and the end-of-year position
6 Likely future developments
7 Any important events since year-end
8 Details of any of its own shares a company has acquired during the year.

Notes to the accounts (not exhaustive)

1 Accounting policies
2 Authorized share capital
3 Details of any shares or debentures issued during the year
4 Transfers to or from reserves
5 Details of fixed assets: purchases, disposals, depreciation, valuations
6 Turnover, profit or loss and net assets for each separate class of business
7 Turnover, profit or loss, and net assets for different geographical markets
8 Details of directors' remuneration
9 The average number of employees, total wages, social security and pension costs
10 Auditors' fees
11 Details of tax
12 The basis on which foreign currencies have been translated into sterling
13 Where significant, the name of the each subsidiary or associated undertaking, its country of incorporation, and the proportion owned of each class of shares
14 The name of the company's ultimate holding company, if any
15 Where material, any items with Arabic numerals in the statutory formats (see pages 317 to 324) which have been combined in the accounts, for example debtors, stocks, creditors.

AUDITORS' REPORT

An audit is the independent examination of an enterprise's financial statements. The auditors' report covers the accounts, including the notes, and (to some extent) the directors' report as well. It is the directors of a company who are responsible for the accounts on which the auditors report.

The Companies Act 1985 requires the auditors of every company to report to its members on every balance sheet and profit and loss account laid before the company in general meeting. The report is made to the members of the company, that is, the shareholders. A standard form of audit report is as follows:

'We have audited the accounts in accordance with Auditing Standards. In our opinion the accounts give a true and fair view of the state of affairs of the company at (the year-end date) and of the profit (or loss) and cash flow for the year then ended, and have been properly prepared in accordance with the Companies Act 1985.'

Auditing standards prescribe the basic principles and practices for the conduct of an audit. There are two:

1 The auditors' operational standard
2 The audit report – revised.

In addition, there are auditing 'guidelines', which give guidance on:

- Procedures for applying auditing standards
- Their application to specific items in financial statements
- Current auditing techniques
- Audit problems in particular circumstances or industries.

Qualifications

Where auditors are unable to report that in their opinion the accounts give a true and fair view, then they must say so ('qualify' their report). The qualification may be due to uncertainty, or to a disagreement between the directors of a company and the auditors.

Nature of qualification	Material but not fundamental	Fundamental
UNCERTAINTY	'subject to' opinion	disclaimer of opinion
DISAGREEMENT	'except for' opinion	adverse opinion

In a 'subject to' opinion the auditors disclaim an opinion, and in an 'except for' opinion express disagreement, on a particular matter which is material but not fundamental.

Only something important will cause auditors to qualify their report. Since most company directors are anxious to avoid this if at all possible, a qualified audit report should *always* be a matter of serious concern to readers of accounts. They should try to assess carefully what every word in the audit report means and implies. Even serious qualifications sometimes use what may seem to be highly technical language; but it would be foolish to assume that an auditors' qualification is a mere technicality.

Circumstances leading to uncertainty may include:

(a) inability to carry out necessary audit procedures, or lack of proper accounting records;
(b) inherent uncertainties, for example in relation to major litigation or long-term contracts, or doubt about the company's ability to continue as a going concern.

Circumstances giving rise to disagreement may include:

(a) failure to follow one or more accounting standards (SSAPs or FRSs) and the auditors do not concur;
(b) disagreement as to facts or amounts in the accounts;
(c) disagreement as to the manner or extent of disclosure in the accounts.

SUMMARY

We have briefly reviewed the progress of accounting, from personal ventures by sole traders to complex world-wide operations by multinational groups. The basic 'double-entry' bookkeeping approach remains; and so does the essential requirement for accounts to show a 'true and fair view'. The Companies Act 1985 requires extensive financial disclosure, but less from a small 'proprietorship' limited company than from a large 'stewardship' public limited company (plc).

We have seen that there are three main annual accounting statements: the profit and loss account, the balance sheet, and the cash flow statement. Problems arise in preparing annual accounts for ongoing businesses, since many transactions will be incomplete at the balance sheet date. Accountants must attach values to assets, and try to 'match' expenditures against revenues in the relevant accounting period.

In recent years the authorities have taken steps to formalize accounting standards and narrow the range of acceptable accounting policies. They have emphasized four 'fundamental accounting concepts': going concern, accruals, consistency, and prudence. These reflect the practical wisdom of centuries, but we have seen how accounting practices have been changing to meet new needs. This evolution seems certain to continue.

The profit and loss account summarizes the revenues and expenses of a business for an accounting period. We studied its underlying three-part structure: the split between the trading account, profit and loss account, and appropriation account. We also noted the more usual brief form of the published profit and loss account; and we saw how retained profit for the period represents the link with the balance sheet.

The balance sheet is a classified summary at a particular date showing the fixed assets and working capital of the business and how they have been financed. We noted the main classification in the balance sheet between uses of funds and sources of funds, that is, between net assets and capital employed. We saw how the usual format deducts current liabilities from current assets, to present a figure for working capital (net current assets).

We looked at the preparation of a simple cash flow statement from differences between the opening and closing balance sheets. We noted which items the directors' report must deal with, if not shown elsewhere; and we saw that the notes form *part* of the 'accounts', and must cover a wide range of details. Finally we considered the auditors' report, its standard form of wording, and the nature of 'qualifications' to an audit report.

PROBLEMS

Now, with this basic understanding of the way in which published company accounts present information, we can go on to consider how financial statements can be used to appraise a company's performance and financial condition. This is the subject covered in Section 2. Before moving on to Section 2, however, we expect that many readers will wish to attempt some or all of the problems set out on the next few pages (pages 15 to 22).

We believe that working through problems is extremely helpful to most readers in consolidating their understanding of the text. In particular we recommend that you work the first 'problem' in each group following a chapter of text. It consists of ten definitions, and we ask you to take the trouble to *write down* your own attempt at each definition in the space provided *before* going on to look at our version of the definitions over the page.

The remaining problems after each section of text are of three kinds, gradually becoming more complex and difficult. The first few problems leave space in the book for you to write your answer (sometimes simply by amending a set of accounts in manuscript); and our solution is then shown overleaf. For the second group of questions you are asked to use your own paper for your answers, and then to compare them with our solutions at the end of the book (starting on page 336). Finally, in each section there are a few problems for which we do not publish solutions. You may like to attempt answers for your own satisfaction; or, if this book is being used as part of a formal training course, this third group of problems may, in part or in total, be used for class assignments. (Answers to this third group of problems are available on request to teachers in a recognized institution – see Preface, p. ix.)

1.1 Definitions

Please write down, in the space provided, your definition of the terms below. Then compare your answers with the definitions shown overleaf.

(a) Balance sheet

(f) Current assets

(b) Profit and loss account

(g) Working capital

(c) Fixed assets

(h) Retained profits

(d) Creditors due within one year

(i) Cash flow statement

(e) Capital and reserves

(j) Ordinary dividends

15

1.1 Definitions

(a) *Balance sheet* A financial statement summarizing as at a particular date the sources of funds provided to a business by shareholders and others, and how those funds have been used to invest in fixed assets and working capital.

(b) *Profit and loss account* The profit and loss account summarizes the turnover (sales), expenses and operating profit for the financial year. It shows the tax charged against profit and the profit after tax. It also shows how much of the profit for the year has been paid out in dividends and how much retained. The law requires accounts to disclose various expenses separately, including depreciation, interest paid, audit fees and directors' remuneration. If the profit and loss account itself does not show such items, they will have to be disclosed in a note to the accounts.

(c) *Fixed assets* Assets intended for use on a continuing basis in the company's activities. There are three categories of fixed assets: intangible, tangible, and investments.

(d) *Creditors due within one year* = current liabilities. Amounts owed by the business to others, due to be paid within twelve months from the balance sheet date; for example, bank overdrafts, trade creditors, dividends proposed, current tax liabilities. 'Trade creditors' may be defined as: persons or businesses to whom amounts are due for goods or services purchased on credit.

(e) *Capital and reserves* = shareholders' funds, owners' equity. Amounts which ultimately 'belong' to the shareholders; the interests of the owners in a company. They are not 'liabilities' in the same sense as other sources of funds, since they are not normally payable to shareholders unless the company ceases to exist (is 'wound up'), or the directors decide to pay dividends out of past retained profits. Shareholders' funds consist of called up share capital, retained profits and other reserves.

Assets less 'external' liabilities = shareholders' funds, which is thus a *residual* amount, depending on the book value attached to a company's assets.

(f) *Current assets* All assets other than fixed assets (see opposite). Either cash or assets expected to be converted into cash or consumed in the business within the normal operating cycle of the business; for example, stocks (both for resale and for use), debtors, prepaid expenses. Some industries (for example whisky distilling or construction) have a normal operating cycle longer than twelve months.

(g) *Working capital* = current assets minus current liabilities, net current assets. The net asset (vertical) balance sheet format reveals working capital as a subtotal.

(h) *Retained profits* = retained earnings. The excess of profits over (losses and) dividends paid out to shareholders. Can relate either to a particular period, or to the accumulated total over a company's whole life to date (after deducting any amounts 'capitalized' – see Section 8). The item 'retained profit for the year' is the *link* between the profit and loss account for the period and the balance sheet at the end of the period.

(i) *Cash flow statement* = classified statement of sources and uses of cash. A financial statement showing, in suitably classified form, the sources of cash of a business for an accounting period, and the ways in which that cash has been used during the period.

(j) *Ordinary dividends* The amount of profits distributed or proposed to be distributed to the ordinary shareholders (the owners of the ordinary share capital of a company). The directors of a company decide how much of the reported profits they will propose to distribute; and the shareholders are then asked to approve the proposal at the annual general meeting.

1.2 Classification of balance sheet and profit and loss account items

For each item shown below, place a cross in the appropriate column. (Some items may appear in more than one column; and at least one of the items is not explicitly shown in the financial statements.)

When you have completed the exercise, please compare your answers with those shown over the page.

	Balance sheet					Profit and loss account		
	Capital and reserves	Creditors due after more than one year	Creditors due within one year	Fixed assets	Current assets	Trading account	Profit and loss account	Appropriation account
(a) Stock								
(b) Trade creditors								
(c) Leasehold property								
(d) Taxation								
(e) Called up share capital								
(f) Auditors' report								
(g) Cash								
(h) Fixtures and equipment								
(i) Debenture interest								
(j) Ordinary dividend								
(k) Turnover								
(l) Management potential								
(m) Retained profits								
(n) Debtors								
(o) Long-term borrowing								

1.2 Classification of balance sheet and profit and loss account items

Solution

	Balance sheet					Profit and loss account		
	Capital and reserves	Creditors due after more than one year	Creditors due within one year	Fixed assets	Current assets	Trading account	Profit and loss account	Appropriation account
(a) Stock					x			
(b) Trade creditors			x					
(c) Leasehold property				x				
(d) Taxation			x liability				x expense	
(e) Called up share capital	x							
(f) Auditors' report								
(g) Cash					x			
(h) Fixtures and equipment				x				
(i) Debenture interest			?				x	
(j) Ordinary dividend			?					x
(k) Turnover						x		
(l) Management potential								
(m) Retained profits	x cumulative							x for period
(n) Debtors					x			
(o) Long-term borrowing		x						

Notes: Items (i) and (j), 'Debenture interest' and 'Ordinary dividend', may appear as 'Creditors due within one year', to the extent that they are wholly or partly outstanding at the balance sheet date.

Problems

The following problems involve the construction of company accounts. They range from the simple to the more complex.

A suggested answer to each of the two problems on this page can be seen overleaf. You are *strongly urged* not to look at them until you have written out your own answers in the spaces provided.

1.3 The Corner Shop Limited

Compile the balance sheet (in 'net asset' format) of The Corner Shop Limited at 30 June 1992 from the following information:

	£
Called up share capital	10 000
Leasehold shop	8 000
Cash	4 000
Profit and loss account	6 000
Trade creditors	2 000
Stock	6 000

THE CORNER SHOP LIMITED

£

Fixed asset

Current assets

Less: **Creditors due within one year**

Capital and reserves

1.4 Peterson Equipment Limited

Compile the balance sheet (in 'net asset' format) of Peterson Equipment Limited at 30 April 1991 from the following information:

	£'000
Land and buildings	156
Plant and machinery, net	114
Tax payable	14
Cash	17
Cumulative retained profits	107
Debtors	45
Long-term borrowing	80
Stock	38
Called up share capital	140
Trade creditors	29

PETERSON EQUIPMENT LIMITED

£'000

Fixed assets

Creditors due after more than one year

Capital and reserves

1.3 The Corner Shop Limited

Solution

THE CORNER SHOP LIMITED
Balance sheet at 30 June 1992

	£
Fixed asset	
Leasehold shop	8 000
Current assets	
Stock	6 000
Cash	4 000
	10 000
Less: **Creditors due within one year**	
Trade creditors	2 000
	8 000
	16 000
Capital and reserves	
Called up share capital	10 000
Profit and loss account	6 000
	16 000

Notes

1 The heading of the balance sheet shows:
   (a) the name of the company
   (b) the balance sheet date.
2 Current assets are shown in order of liquidity, with the least liquid assets at the top.

1.4 Peterson Equipment Limited

Solution

PETERSON EQUIPMENT LIMITED
Balance sheet at 30 April 1991

		£'000
Fixed assets		
Land and buildings		156
Plant and machinery, net		114
		270
Current assets		
Stock	38	
Debtors	45	
Cash	17	
	100	
Less: **Creditors due within one year**		
Trade creditors	29	
Tax payable	14	
	43	
Net current assets		57
Total assets less current liabilities (net assets)		327
Creditors due after more than one year		
Long-term borrowing		80
Capital and reserves		
Called up share capital	140	
Profit and loss account	107	
		247
(Capital employed)		327

Notes

1 Each main item has a separate subtotal.
2 The subtotal Net current assets (£57 000) may be entitled 'Working capital'.
3 The sub-total of capital and reserves is shown separately, and may be entitled 'Shareholders' funds'.

Please use separate sheets of paper for your answers to each of the following problems. Answers to these problems are shown at the end of the book, starting on page 336.

1.5 The Acme Company Limited

The Acme Company Limited prepares accounts to 30 June. From the following information compile the 1992 balance sheet, using the 'net asset' format:

	£'000
Cash	20
Current tax payable	20
Shop fixtures and equipment	30
Trade creditors	30
Profit and loss account	50
Called up share capital	200
Stock	60
Freehold shop	150
Debtors	40

1.6 General Contractors Limited

Prepare the profit and loss account for General Contractors Limited for the year ended 31 December 1992 from the following information:

	£'000
Trading profit before depreciation and interest	200
Tax on the profit for the year	40
Proposed dividends	60
Interest payable	10
Invoiced sales in the year	1 250
Cost of sales	1 050
Depreciation on plant and equipment*	50*

* = not included in cost of sales.

1.7 The Marvel Trading Company Limited

The Marvel Trading Company Limited prepares annual accounts to 30 June each year. The company made a trading profit of £100 000 in 1992 after deduction of all charges including depreciation, but before charging interest payable of £8 000. Income from investments during the year amounted to £12 000, and the estimated tax charge on the profit for the year was £26 000. Sales turnover in the year amounted to £1 200 000.

The company proposes to pay dividends of £40 000 in total in respect of its ordinary shares. You are asked to prepare the company's profit and loss account (including the appropriation account) for the year ended 30 June 1992.

1.8 The Fine Fare Catering Company Limited

The accounts of the Fine Fare Catering Company Limited for its first year, ended 31 March 1991, contain the following items. Compile the balance sheet and profit and loss account.

	£'000
Turnover	150
Proposed dividends	8
Called up share capital	60
Fixtures and fittings	10
Cash	10
Trade creditors	20
Leasehold restaurant	70
Stock	20
Tax due on profit for the year	10
Trading profit after depreciation	30

1.9 Andrew Hunt Limited

Andrew Hunt Limited's first accounts, for the nine months ended 30 September 1992, contain the following items. Prepare the balance sheet and profit and loss account.

	£'000
Cash	200
Trade creditors	320
10% Debenture 1997	400
Debtors	470
Depreciation charge for plant and machinery	50
Dividends proposed	150
Leasehold factory	600
Plant and machinery net (after deducting depreciation for the period)	450
Turnover	3 400
Called up share capital	750
Stock	330
Tax on profit	145
Cost of sales (excluding depreciation	2 740
Interest paid	30

No solutions are published for the following problems

1.10 Allen and Faber Limited

Allen and Faber Limited has been trading for many years. Its accounts for the year ended 31 December 1992 contain the following items. You are required to prepare, in suitably classified format, the balance sheet and profit and loss account for 1992.

	£'000
Called up share capital	1 500
15% Debentures	600
Cumulative retained profits, 1 January 1992	1 040
Stock	700
Plant and equipment, at cost	1 730
Debtors	510
Cost of sales (excluding depreciation)	4 250
Debenture interest paid	90
Cumulative depreciation on plant	890
Trade creditors	380
Freehold land and buildings	2 140
Proposed dividend	210
Tax on profit for the period	190
Cash	170
Trading profit before interest	790
Tax liability	330
Turnover	5 210
Depreciation for the period	170

1.11 Developing negatives

Could the items below ever be negative? If so, under what circumstances? How would you show each item on the balance sheet?

(a) Retained earnings
(b) Corporation tax payable
(c) Working capital
(d) Work-in-progress

1.12 The missing balance sheet

On 3 May 1992 a burglary took place at the head office of Swanton Publishing Limited. Among the items stolen was the only copy of the draft balance sheet at 31 March 1992, and books of account issued to prepare it.

Fortunately, Mr Edgerton, the company's assistant chief accountant, had noted on a separate piece of paper a number of balance sheet items and relationships.

See if you can reproduce the company's balance sheet at 31 March 1992 from Mr Edgerton's notes, which are shown below:

(a) Long-term liabilities	= 1½ times working capital
(b) Debtors	= Current liabilities
(c) Authorized share capital	= £180 000
(d) Cash	= ½ stock
(e) Net fixed assets	= Total liabilities + £100 000
(f) Called up share capital	= 2/3 × shareholders' funds
(g) Liquid assets	= Reserves
(h) Shares issued (50p each)	= 280 000 out of 360 000 authorized
(i) Acid test ratio	= 1.40

The acid test ratio represents $\dfrac{\text{debtors plus cash}}{\text{current liabilities}}$

1.13 Sultan Chemicals Limited

From the following information draw up the profit and loss account of Sultan Chemicals Limited for the year ended 30 April 1992.

	£'000
Administrative expenses	300
Cost of sales	3 700
Distribution costs	1 300
Dividends payable	300
Extraordinary items (expenses)	150
Interest payable	200
Retained profit for the year	(balancing item)
Share of profits of associated undertakings	100
Taxation	200
Turnover	6 000

Section 2
Analysing company accounts

INTRODUCTION

We have studied the structure of the main financial statements: the profit and loss account, balance sheet, and cash flow statement. In Section 3 we shall consider in more detail the steps by which transactions are summarized in books of account; and in Sections 4 and 5 we shall deal with the accounting rules for valuing assets and measuring profit or loss. But first we shall look at the accounts as a whole. In this section we consider how to extract the most useful facts for assessing performance and financial position.

The information disclosed in published accounts may relate to a single company or to a group of companies under common control. It will reveal the:

- level of sales and profit (or loss)
- earnings per share and dividends
- different kinds of assets and how they are financed
- relationship between debt and shareholders' funds
- relationship between current assets and current liabilities

At the end of this section (pages 53 to 57) we set out the financial statements of Northern Foods plc for the year ended 31 March 1991, and extracts from the notes to the accounts. The profit and loss account and balance sheet are 'consolidated' statements bringing together the results of all companies in the Northern Foods Group. (We discuss the process of 'consolidation' of group accounts in Section 9.) The financial statements include a cash flow statement for the group, and in addition to extracts from the notes there is a five-year financial record. Most companies disclose summary financial figures for at least five years, to show trends for a period of time as well as the current position.

In view of the constraints of space, we have not included the chairman's statement, the directors' review of operations, nor the directors' report. All these contain a great deal of information which is helpful in assessing the financial performance and status, and the outlook for the following year.

Analysis of financial statements can be broken down into four main steps: overview; ratio analysis; cash flow; and business segments. We deal with the first two in this section, with cash flow in Section 6, and with business segments in Section 12, where we return to the complete analysis of company accounts and interpretation of the results.

OVERVIEW

The main financial statements refer only to the current and previous year. But to place a detailed analysis in context we must look at the trends in key figures over a number of years. The key figures to select may depend on the specific nature of a company's business, but the most useful trends to note will often include the following:

- turnover (sales)
- net assets (total assets less current liabilities)
- operating profit (trading profit)
- profit after tax
- earnings per share.

Over a five-year period, we can calculate the annual percentage changes in each key figure, and compare them with an index of price changes such as the Retail Prices Index (RPI). For a company listed on the Stock Exchange, we can also compare changes in the share price with market index or with a suitable industry index.

The five-year trend summary will often also provide ratios covering a number of years. But it may be best to postpone detailed ratio analysis until the second stage. Companies will normally try to adjust the figures in their own five-year summaries on to a consistent basis. But it will often be necessary to make further adjustments in seeking to compare the ratios of different companies.

To illustrate, we show figures for Northern Foods plc, which is a broadly-based fresh food manufacturing group. Turnover dropped by a quarter in 1988, due to the disposal of the group's US operations. Since then turnover has increased somewhat less than inflation; but profit margins have improved. The share price has performed especially well in 1991.

NORTHERN FOODS plc
Five-year trend 1987–1991

Year ended 31 March	1987	1988	1989	1990	1991
Key figures (£ million)					
Turnover	1348	1019	1041	1094	1187
Shareholders' funds	263	276	296	314	305
Operating profit	79.1	77.4	88.5	94.0	111.6
Profit after tax	49.9	54.4	60.7	64.9	77.0
Earnings per share (pence)	22.7	24.7	27.4	29.3	34.7
Growth					
Turnover		(24)	2	5	9
Net assets		5	7	6	(3)
Operating profit		(2)	14	6	19
Profit after tax		9	12	7	19
Earnings per share		9	11	7	18
Change in RPI (%)		3.5	7.9	8.1	8.2
Stock market					
Share price (following June)		308	322	330	467
% change					
Share price		1	5	2	42
All Share Index		(14)	18	2	9
Industry Index (Food Manufacturing)		(4)	11	3	2

RATIO ANALYSIS

When approaching the detailed ratio analysis of a company's accounts, it is helpful to group the ratios under three broad headings to measure different facets of the business:

- performance ratios
- financial status ratios
- stock market ratios

The full list of ratios which we shall define and use is set out opposite.

Performance ratios

Performance ratios are intended to show how well a business is being run. They include ratios measuring return on investment, both return on shareholders' funds and return on net assets. If we wish to focus on operating performance both non-operating income and non-operating assets (such as long-term investments and the retained income) must be excluded from the return on net assets and related ratios. Return on net assets, as we shall see, breaks down into subordinate ratios including profit margin and net asset turnover.

Financial status ratios

Financial status ratios indicate a company's financial position; they distinguish between solvency and liquidity, between long-term and short-term capacity to meet liabilities.

Stock market ratios

Stock market ratios relate earnings (profits) and dividends to the number of ordinary shares in issue and to stock market prices.

On the next page we discuss return on investment, the most comprehensive of the performance ratios.

Performance ratios
Return on equity %
Tax ratio %
Return on net assets %
Profit margin %
Net asset turnover
Fixed asset turnover
Stock turnover
Debtor turnover
Creditor turnover

Financial status ratios
Debt/Capital employed %
Interest cover
Current ratio
Acid test

Stock market ratios
Earnings per share (pence)
Price/earnings ratio
Dividend yield %
Dividend cover

RETURN ON INVESTMENT

Two main measures of performance are:

$$\text{Return on Equity} = \frac{\text{Profit after tax}}{\text{Ordinary Shareholders' Funds} (= \text{Equity})}$$

$$\text{Return on Net Assets} = \frac{\text{Profit before interest payable and tax}}{\text{Net Assets} (= \text{Capital Employed})}$$

These are both return on investment (ROI) measures. The concept of return on investment is fundamental in the world of business. People with capital funds to invest will seek the highest possible return on their money, all else being equal. Investors wanting a regular stream of income may prefer a government security with half-yearly interest to an equity investment with irregular (or smaller) dividends. They may prefer the government stock even though, taking capital growth into account, the equity investment's expected long-run return may be higher.

Investment usually contains an element of risk, for the money is being invested today in the hope of yielding benefits in the uncertain future. Gauging the degree of risk is difficult, but the market tries to quantify it and adjusts the required rate of return accordingly.

A generalized way of picturing the trade-off between risk and return is shown opposite. The slope of the line represents the 'price of risk'. Notice that even a risk-free investment (the intercept I pt on the vertical axis) shows a positive rate of return. This 'risk-free rate of interest' represents the 'price of time'. Of course, like any market prices, interest rates and risk premiums may fluctuate as economic conditions change.

In analysing accounts it is important to remember that the level of risk of the business – both in its trading and its financial structure – will affect the returns which an investor should obtain. Even if a return on an investment seems high and represents an increase over the previous year, it may still be inadequate because of the very big risks involved.

RISK AND RETURN

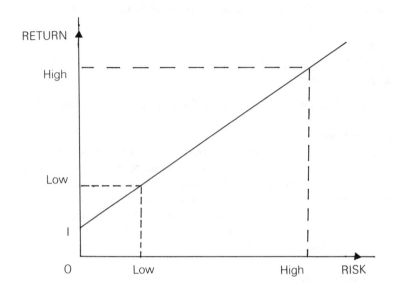

Return on Equity

Return on ordinary shareholders' funds (= return on equity) is the most comprehensive measure of the performance of a company and its management for a period. It takes into account all aspects of trading and financing, from the viewpoint of the ordinary (equity) shareholder.

Using the figures for ABC Trading Limited for the year ended 30 June 1992 (shown opposite), the ratio is calculated as follows:

$$\frac{\text{Return}}{\text{Equity}} = \frac{\text{Profit after tax}}{\text{Shareholders' funds}} = \frac{120}{800} = 15.0\%$$

Return on Net Assets

The other main return on investment ratio is return on net assets. It deals with return (= profit) *before* tax and *before* financing charges: and it looks at total capital employed (= net assets), not merely that part relating to shareholders' interests (= equity). The return on net assets ratio for ABC Trading Limited for 1992 is thus as follows:

$$\frac{\text{Return}}{\text{Net Assets}} = \frac{\text{Profit before interest payable and tax*}}{\text{Net Assets}} = \frac{210}{1000} = 21.0\%$$

(*This unwieldy expression is shortened to PBIT.)

This measure indicates the performance achieved *regardless* of the method of financing. As we shall see in Section 8, a company's capital structure (its financial 'gearing') can affect its return on equity; but it makes no difference to return on net assets. Since it can often be difficult in practice to split the capital employed in *part* of a business as between debt and equity, the return on net assets ratio is useful in measuring the performance of divisions within a company.

The two return on investment measures are linked as shown below:

RETURN ON NET ASSETS	=	Profit before interest payable and tax ÷ Debt + equity

adjust for

	Interest payable	Debt
	Tax	

RETURN ON EQUITY	=	Profit after tax ÷ Equity

ABC TRADING LIMITED
Profit and loss account for the year ended 30 June 1992

	£'000
Turnover	2 000
Operating profit	210
Interest payable	30
Profit before tax	180
Taxation	60
Profit after tax	120
Dividends	80
Retained profit	40

Balance sheet at 30 June 1992

Tangible fixed assets	600
Working capital	400
Total assets less current liabilities	1 000
Creditors due after more than one year	
Loans	(200)
	800
Capital and reserves	
Called up share capital	500
Profit and loss account	300
	800

The balance sheet format used in this book up to now lists fixed assets (600) and working capital (400) as 'Net assets' (1 000), and then long-term creditors (200) and capital and reserves (800) (= 'Capital employed' (1 000)). This is a useful format for learning, but is rare in practice. Far more common is the format shown for ABC Trading Limited above, which deducts 'Creditors due after more than one year' (200) from 'Total assets less current liabilities' (1 000), to give a figure equal to capital and reserves (800) (= 'Shareholders' funds').

PYRAMID OF RATIOS

Return on net assets is a useful measure for management control purposes because it can readily be broken down into a number of elements.

The first level of division is into two basic parts:

Return on Net Assets = Profit Margin × Net Asset Turnover

This may be more easily understood if expressed as follows:

$$\frac{\text{Profit}}{\text{Net Assets}} = \frac{\text{Profit}}{\text{Sales}} \times \frac{\text{Sales}}{\text{Net Assets}}$$

The 'profit' referred to here is the profit before interest payable and tax. Using the figures for ABC Trading Limited, the breakdown is:

$$\frac{210}{1\,000} = \frac{210}{2\,000} \times \frac{2\,000}{1\,000}$$

$$21.0\% = 10.5\% \times 2.0$$

The 10.5 per cent profit margin on sales is a familiar measure of performance. The concept of 'net asset turnover' may not be so familiar, but it is a useful way of thinking about capital utilization. The number '2.0' can be thought of literally as the number of times that capital is being turned over in sales revenue in a period. Perhaps more concretely, it is the number of pounds' worth of sales generated per pound of investment.

The basic division of return on net assets into profit margin and net asset turnover can be further broken down to form a 'pyramid' of ratios, as set out on the right. Changes in higher level ratios are 'explained' (or analysed) in terms of changes in a number of lower level ratios. This can be done as shown, in accounting terms: for example, splitting the ratio 'Operating Expenses as a percentage of Sales' between the various different kinds of operating expenses; or any given ratio for the whole company (say, gross profit margin on sales) can be split between various divisions or product lines of the company.

This is where the special potential of the return on net assets 'pyramid of ratios' as a management control tool arises. It enables the company's results to be studied in even greater detail: by splitting the accounting ratios (as in the diagram); by analysing ratios between divisions of the company; and finally, by splitting annual ratios into short time periods (say months).

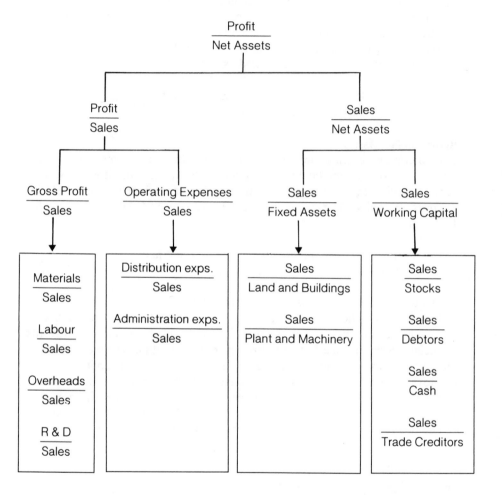

Another approach to the pyramid of ratios is shown on the right. The diagram shows how a company could increase its return on net assets either by increasing the profit (the 'return') or by reducing the net assets employed (the 'investment') for each £ of sales revenue. The latter is equivalent, of course, to increasing the net asset turnover.

How can the profit (before interest payable and tax) be increased, assuming the same investment in net assets? Either by increasing the revenue from sales of goods or services, or by reducing expenses for a given level of sales revenue.

In this book we shall not examine in detail how profit margins can be improved. Our use of ratios for external analysis can obviously be adapted for internal use by managers running their businesses. It is clear that product design, quality of manufacture, pricing, efficient delivery, packaging, advertising, credit terms and so on may help to increase sales. Similarly, skilful administration and the like may help to reduce expenses. Thus, while accounting can help business people and others to evaluate trading performance (both past and future), many other skills must be combined to earn maximum profits.

In the same way, reducing net assets per £ of sales revenue can be divided between reducing fixed assets and reducing working capital – both for a given level of sales. (In practice, in times of inflation this result may be achieved by increasing the investment in net assets *less than in proportion* to an increase in sales revenue.)

Fixed asset per £ of sales can be reduced in various ways: by more intensive utilization, by better plant layout, by good maintenance enabling replacements to be delayed, by efficient project management on new capital expenditure. Reducing working capital per £ of sales may mean either reducing current assets (stocks, debtors, and cash) or increasing trade creditors or other current liabilities. For many manufacturing companies the investment in stocks and debtors together amounts to roughly *half* of the total assets, so efficient management in this area can be very important.

Some of the ratios we have considered can be split into more detail, to examine whether there may be room for improvement in the investment in particular categories of assets. The essence of a commercial outlook is not merely to look for *technical* efficiency (for example a 'better' machine), but for *economic* efficiency (for example a 'better' machine that is *worth the extra cost*).

It is also possible to employ other ratios which we shall not examine in this book. In some businesses, sales, expenses, investment and profits can usefully be analysed on a 'per employee' basis or per £ of employees' costs. Or a retailing operation may want to look at sales revenue and expenses on a 'per square foot' basis. The results, as usual, can be compared either over time within a company, or against some external standard (for example foreign competition).

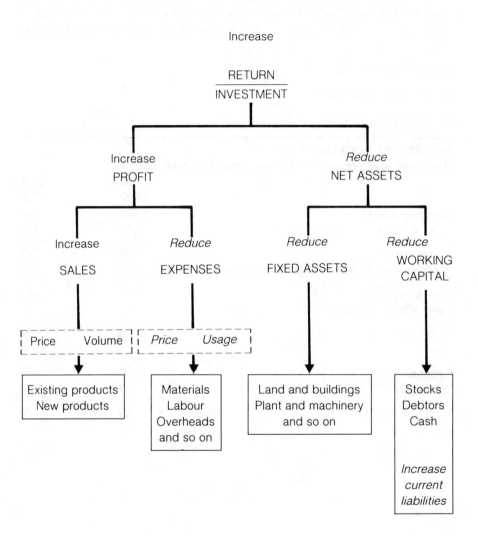

MANAGEMENT ACTION TO IMPROVE PERFORMANCE

RATIO CALCULATION

After you have studied the diagram showing a 'pyramid' of ratios, and noted the links between the various parts, the next step is to calculate a set of financial ratios for yourself.

The accounts of Precision Locks Limited for the year ended 30 June 1992 are set out below (together with comparative figures for 1991). You are asked to study the profit and loss account and balance sheet, and then to calculate in turn:

- performance ratios

- financial status ratios

- stock market ratios.

PRECISION LOCKS LIMITED

Profit and loss account for the year ended 30 June 1992

	1992 £'000	1991 £'000
Turnover (sales)	1 200	1 000
Cost of sales	800	700
Gross profit	400	300
Distribution and administrative expenses	250	200
Operating profit	150	100
Loan interest payable	10	10
Profit before tax	140	90
Tax	50	30
Profit after tax	90	60
Dividends	40	30
Retained profit	50	30

At each stage in the analysis you will be asked to calculate the appropriate ratios, and then to compare your answers with those set out on the pages immediately following. In each case the ratios for 1991 have already been calculated, and are set out alongside.

Please now study the Precision Locks accounts; then turn to the next page and begin the detailed analysis of the 1992 results. Assume that the company's share price was 200p on 30 June 1991, and 300p on 30 June 1992.

Balance sheet at 30 June 1992

		£'000		1991 £'000
Fixed assets				
Factory and machinery at cost		350		300
Less: Accumulated depreciation		140		100
		210		200
Current assets				
Stock	350		300	
Debtors	200		150	
Cash	40		50	
	590		500	
Less: **Creditors due within one year** (current liabilities)	250		200	
		340		300
Total Assets less current liabilities (Net Assets)		550		500
Creditors due after more than one year				
Long-term loan		100		100
Capital and reserves				
Called up share capital (£1 shares)	300		300	
Profit and loss account	150	450	100	400
(Capital employed)		550		500

PERFORMANCE RATIOS

Using the appropriate figures from Precision Locks Limited's accounts set out on the previous page, please calculate the following nine performance ratios for 1992. When you have completed the calculations, compare your answers with those shown overleaf, together with comments.

		1992	1991
Return on equity			
$\dfrac{\text{Profit after tax}}{\text{Shareholders' funds}}$ = _____ =			15.0%
Tax ratio			
$\dfrac{\text{Tax provided}}{\text{Profit before tax}}$ = _____ =			33.3%
Return on net assets			
$\dfrac{\text{Profit before interest payable and tax}}{\text{Net assets}}$ = _____ =			20.0%
Profit margin			
$\dfrac{\text{Profit before interest payable and tax}}{\text{Sales (Turnover)}}$ = _____ =			10.0%
Net asset turnover			
$\dfrac{\text{Sales}}{\text{Net assets}}$ = _____ =			2.0 times
Fixed asset turnover			
$\dfrac{\text{Sales}}{\text{Fixed assets}}$ = _____ =			5.0 times
Stock turnover			
$\dfrac{\text{Sales}}{\text{Stock}}$ = _____ =			3.3 times
Debtor turnover			
$\dfrac{\text{Sales}}{\text{Debtors}}$ = _____ =			6.7 times
Creditor turnover			
$\dfrac{\text{Sales}}{\text{Creditors due} < 1 \text{ year}}$ = _____ =			5.0 times

PERFORMANCE RATIOS

Return on equity: $\dfrac{\text{Profit after tax}}{\text{Shareholders' funds}} = \dfrac{90}{450} = 20.0\%$

This key measure of performance takes into account not only the results of operations, but also the effect of financing and the impact of tax.

Tax ratio: $\dfrac{\text{Tax provided}}{\text{Profit before tax}} = \dfrac{50}{140} = 35.7\%$

This ratio indicates the tax charge as a proportion of profit. Comparing the ratio over time and with other companies in the same industry may show whether tax is being well managed. (See also Section 7.)

Return on net assets: $\dfrac{\text{Profit before interest payable and tax}}{\text{Net assets}} = \dfrac{150}{550} = 27.3\%$

This measure of performance ignores both tax and the company's method of financing. It includes all the net assets, rather than just the funds provided by the ordinary shareholders. To repeat, return on net assets = profit margin × net asset turnover (27.3% = 12.5% × 2.2).

Profit margin: $\dfrac{\text{Profit before interest payable and tax}}{\text{Sales}} = \dfrac{150}{1\,200} = 12.5\%$

Analysts may also wish to calculate the percentage to sales of the different kinds of expense. In most companies some expenses vary (more or less) in proportion to sales, while others are (more or less) fixed. So the profit margin percentage does not represent the proportion of any *increase* in sales turnover that would come through as *extra* profit before tax.

Net asset turnover: $\dfrac{\text{Sales}}{\text{Net assets}} = \dfrac{1\,200}{550} = 2.2$ times

The net asset turnover ratio is one measure of how well a company has used its productive capacity. It needs to be interpreted with care where there have been changes in capacity during a period. It is useful to analyse this ratio into its main constituent parts – fixed assets and the elements of working capital.

Fixed asset turnover: $\dfrac{\text{Sales}}{\text{Fixed assets}} = \dfrac{1\,200}{210} = 5.7$ times

This ratio is a measure of how well the company is using its fixed assets (excluding intangibles and investments). It shows how many £s in sales each £1 of investment in tangible fixed assets has generated.

Stock turnover: $\dfrac{\text{Sales}}{\text{Stock}} = \dfrac{1\,200}{350} = 3.4$ times

This ratio indicates how quickly goods move through the business. Usually the quicker the better, though a high turnover rate may suggest a risk of shortages. Where possible stock turnover should be calculated by comparing stock (valued at cost) with cost of sales:

$$\frac{\text{Cost of sales}}{\text{Stock}} = \frac{800}{350} = 2.3 \text{ times}$$

Closing stock may not be the same as average stock during the year, so the stock turnover ratio may not represent the true rate of turnover. Moreover if there are seasonal variations in stock levels, merely averaging the opening and closing year-end figures will not reveal 'average' stock levels *during* the year.

An increase in stock levels (causing a fall in stock turnover) may result from stocks piling up because of falling sales during the year. Or it may represent a deliberate build-up in stocks to meet planned sales expansion. In controlling production and stocks, therefore, forecasting the level of future sales volume plays a vital role.

Debtor turnover: $\dfrac{\text{Sales}}{\text{Debtors}} = \dfrac{1\,200}{200} = 6.0$ times

Where companies sell for cash as well as on credit, only credit sales should be included in the ratio to compare with trade debtors. As with stock turnover, if there are seasonal variations in sales, the ratio needs to be interpreted carefully.

Some analysts prefer to calculate the 'number of days' sales' represented by the end-of-period trade debtors. One can either divide 365 days by the debtor turnover ratio (365/6.0 = 61 days) or one can calculate as follows:

$$\frac{\text{Debtors}}{\text{Daily sales}} = \frac{\text{Debtors} \times 365}{\text{Annual sales}} = \frac{200 \times 365}{1\,200} = 61 \text{ days}$$

Credit turnover: $\dfrac{\text{Sales}}{\text{Creditors}} = \dfrac{1\,200}{250} = 4.8$ times (76 days)

Again, using cost of sales may be more appropriate if possible; but changes in stock levels and the effect of other expenses and purchases can complicate the picture. The ratio shown above can give useful clues about trends.

FINANCIAL STATUS RATIOS

Ratios of financial status measure a company's ability to meet its liabilities. They can be divided between:

Solvency ratios – dealing with long-term liabilities
Liquidity ratios – dealing with short-term liabilities

Please refer back to the 1992 accounts of Precision Locks Limited (on page 30) and calculate the following financial status ratios. Then turn to the next page, and compare your answers with the ratios shown there.

As you calculate the ratios, consider what they mean and how they contribute to your appraisal of the company's financial status.

			1992	1991
Solvency ratios				
Debt ratio				
$\dfrac{\text{Debt}}{\text{Capital employed}}$ =	_____ =			20.0%
Interest cover				
$\dfrac{\text{Profit before interest payable and tax}}{\text{Loan interest}}$ =	_____ =			10.0 times
Liquidity ratios				
Current ratio				
$\dfrac{\text{Current assets}}{\text{Current liabilities}}$ =	_____ =			2.5 times
Acid test				
$\dfrac{\text{Liquid assets (debtors + cash)}}{\text{Current liabilities}}$ =	_____ =			1.0 times

FINANCIAL STATUS RATIOS
Solvency ratios

Debt ratio: $\dfrac{\text{Debt}}{\text{Capital employed}} = \dfrac{100}{550} = 18.2\%$

Debt is 18 per cent of the capital employed, which means (in this simple case) that equity is the other 82 per cent. This relatively low debt ratio ('gearing') gives lenders a fairly high level of safety ('equity cushion').

Another way of measuring the same thing is the 'debt/equity' ratio:

$$\dfrac{\text{Debt}}{\text{Shareholders' funds}} = \dfrac{\text{Debt}}{\text{Equity}} = \dfrac{100}{450} = 22.2\%$$

Bank overdrafts are legally repayable 'on demand', and, like instalments of long-term debt falling due for payment within less than twelve months, appear under 'Creditors due within one year'. But both bank overdrafts and any current portions of long-term debt may often be regarded as part of a company's interest-bearing long-term capital employed. They contrast with 'spontaneous' sources of funds, normally *not* bearing interest, such as trade credit or tax liabilities.

Interest cover: $\dfrac{\text{Profit before interest payable and tax}}{\text{Interest payable}} = \dfrac{150}{10} = 15.0 \text{ times}$

The 'interest cover' ratio relates profit before interest payable and tax (PBIT) to (before-tax) interest payable. Interest payable cannot normally be split between short-term and long-term. Interest receivable, which represents the 'return' on liquid assets, is included in profit before interest payable and tax: it should *not* normally be netted off against interest payable, in calculating interest cover.

This ratio shows the relative safety of loan interest, in the same way that the debt ratio aims to measure the loan capital cover. One ratio derives from the profit and loss account, the other from the balance sheet. Section 8, dealing with capital structure, considers these two ratios from another point of view.

Liquidity ratios

Current ratio: $\dfrac{\text{Current assets}}{\text{Current liabilities}} = \dfrac{590}{250} = 2.4 \text{ times}$

This ratio indicates to what extent short-term assets are adequate to settle short-term liabilities. ('Current' in accounting implies turning assets into cash, or paying creditors, within twelve months from the balance sheet date.) Should the ratio be less than 1.0, current assets would not fully cover short-term creditors. This would be all right in a company with a strong daily cash flow, such as a retailer or a brewer. But for a normal manufacturing company it would suggest looking closely at the acid test ratio (see below), because financial problems might be developing.

A 'normal' current ratio in a manufacturing business might be between 1.5 and 2.0. Too *low* a current ratio may mean liquidity problems, but a current ratio can also be too *high*. Funds tied up in working capital can be costly to finance.

Acid test: $\dfrac{\text{Liquid assets (debtors + cash)}}{\text{Current liabilities}} = \dfrac{240}{250} = 1.0 \text{ times}$

The acid test (sometimes called the 'quick ratio') is a strict test of liquidity. In measuring the resources available to meet current liabilities, it excludes stock which may take several months to turn into cash.

On the other hand, not all creditors need be due within a few months. Current taxation, for instance, may not actually be payable for up to nine months from the balance sheet date. Thus many companies might fairly safely have an acid test ratio of somewhat less than the 'norm' of 1.0.

A more accurate way to estimate cash sufficiency would be to forecast expected payments and receipts in detail month by month for the near future. A company would invariably do this as part of its own cash management; but an external analyst will lack the information needed to complete the forecast.

The current ratio and acid test 'norms' of 1.5 to 2.0, and about 1.0, are fair guides for many manufacturing and commercial companies. But different 'norms' may apply in other industries, which can be found by looking at the statistics for those specific industries.

Many analysts prefer to treat interest-bearing short-term borrowings as part of 'long-term' capital employed in calculating the solvency ratios. We ourselves adopted this approach earlier. But cautious analysts might still treat them as 'short term' for calculating the liquidity ratios! (After all, bank overdrafts usually *are* repayable on demand.) Thus the prudence concept in this case might override the consistency concept.

STOCK MARKET RATIOS

The following stock market ratios are used extensively in the financial markets in referring to the performance of a company. Please calculate the ratios for 1992, by referring back to the Precision Locks accounts on page 30. Then turn over the page to compare your solutions with those shown overleaf.

		1992		1991

Earnings per share

$$\frac{\text{Profit after tax}}{\text{Number of ordinary shares in issue}} = \underline{\hspace{3cm}} = \quad 20.0\text{p}$$

Price/earnings ratio

$$\frac{\text{Market price per share}}{\text{Earnings per share}} = \frac{300\text{p}}{} = \frac{200\text{p}}{20\text{p}} = 10.0$$

Dividend yield (net)

$$\frac{\text{Dividend per share (net)}}{\text{Market price per share}} = \frac{}{300\text{p}} = \frac{10\text{p}}{200\text{p}} = 5.0\%$$

Dividend cover

$$\frac{\text{Earnings per share}}{\text{Dividend per share}} = \underline{\hspace{3cm}} = \quad 2.0 \text{ times}$$

STOCK MARKET RATIOS

Earnings per share: $\dfrac{\text{Profit after tax}}{\text{Number of ordinary shares in issue}} = \dfrac{90}{300} = 30.0\text{p}$

The earnings (= profit) figure here is the same 'profit after tax' figure that we used to calculate return on equity. In more complex cases we should strictly use 'earnings attributable to ordinary shareholders' – this would be before extraordinary items (see Section 4), but after minority interests (see Section 9) and after preference dividends (see Section 8).

The earnings per share figure (EPS) is widely used in measuring changes from year to year. 'Per share' figures relate to *ordinary* shares: the number of shares *issued*, not the number *authorized*. If shares have been issued during a period, a weighted average should be used.

Price/earnings ratio: $\dfrac{\text{Market price per share}}{\text{Earnings per share}} = \dfrac{300\text{p}}{30.0\text{p}} = 10.0\text{ times}$

The price/earnings (P/E) 'ratio' is simply a multiple. Thus Precision Locks Limited 'has a P/E ratio of 10.0'.

The market price (MP) of the ordinary shares does not appear in the published accounts. It takes account of expected *future* profits, whereas the earnings per share figure is based (like the return on investment ratios) on reported *past* profits.

If a company makes a loss, earnings per share will be *negative*. But since the shares will still have a positive value in the stock market, the P/E ratio itself will be negative. Thus interpretation requires caution!

Dividend yield (net): $\dfrac{\text{Dividend per share}}{\text{Market price per share}} = \dfrac{13.3\text{p}}{300\text{p}} = 4.4\%$

This ratio deals only with the part of current earnings paid out in dividends. (The company 'retains' the rest.) Thus it represents only part of a shareholder's possible 'return' (since it does not include any 'capital gain' arising if the share price goes up). Published accounts disclose dividends per share; but for Precision Locks we have to calculate it:

$$\frac{40}{300} = 13.3\text{p}$$

The dividend per share above is shown *net* of tax. In fact it is normal to calculate dividend yield *gross* of basic rate income tax (see Section 7), but we ignore this complication here.

Dividend yield indicates an investor's current income yield in relation to the share's current market price. This is unlikely to be the same as the amount *paid* for the shares (the market price on the date the investor bought them).

Dividend cover: $\dfrac{\text{Earnings per share}}{\text{Dividends per share}} = \dfrac{30.0\text{p}}{13.3\text{p}} = 2.25\text{ times}$

This ratio measures the number of times that the actual dividend could have been paid out of the current year's earnings. The higher the dividend cover the 'safer' the dividend. This ratio, like dividend yield, is normally calculated *gross* of tax (see Section 7); but again we ignore this complication here.

The ratio is sometimes expressed the other way round, as the 'dividend payout ratio' (DPR):

$$\frac{\text{Dividends per share}}{\text{Earnings per share}} = \frac{13.3\text{p}}{30.0\text{p}} = 44.3\%$$

There are, of course, many other influences on the price of a company's shares in the market besides the dividend yield and dividend cover. As a rule, investors expect some dividends each year. However shareholders' returns come from dividends *plus* capital gains. If a company can use retained earnings profitably enough, investors may be willing to forego dividends. The share price should then tend to rise, to reflect the internally financed growth.

The four stock market ratios discussed here are linked as follows:

Net Dividend Yield		Dividend Cover		Net Earnings Yield		P/E Reciprocal
$\dfrac{\text{DPS}}{\text{MP}}$	$\times$	$\dfrac{\text{EPS}}{\text{DPS}}$	$=$	$\dfrac{\text{EPS}}{\text{MP}}$	$=$	$\dfrac{1}{\text{P/E Ratio}}$
4.4%	$\times$	2.25	$=$	$\dfrac{30.0}{300} = 10.0\%$	$=$	$\dfrac{1}{10.0}$

Unfortunately the relationship between earnings yield (which is normally expressed 'gross') and the price/earnings ratio (which uses 'net' EPS) is usually less simple than shown here.

PRECISION LOCKS LIMITED

Comments

Summary of results

You are asked now to enter the figures which you have calculated in the 1992 column below; to enter also the 1991 ratios which were set out in the earlier pages; then to summarize briefly (on the right) the main comments which you think should be made in appraising the company's 1992 performance and financial position compared with the results for the previous year.

When you have completed your summary of the ratios, and written out your comments, please turn to the next page where a suggested answer is shown.

		1992	1991
Performance ratios			
Return on equity	%		
Tax ratio	%		
Return on net assets	%		
Profit margin	%		
Net asset turnover			
Fixed asset turnover			
Stock turnover			
Debtor turnover			
Creditor turnover			
Financial status ratios			
Debt ratio	%		
Interest cover			
Current ratio			
Acid test			
Stock market ratios			
Earnings per share	pence		
Price/earnings ratio			
Dividend yield (net)	%		
Dividend cover			

PRECISION LOCKS LIMITED

Summary of results

	1992	1991
Performance ratios		
Return on equity	20.0%	15.0%
Tax ratio	35.7%	33.3%
Return on net assets	27.3%	20.0%
Profit margin	12.5%	10.0%
Net asset turnover	2.2 times	2.0 times
Fixed asset turnover	5.7 times	5.0 times
Stock turnover	3.4 times	3.3 times
Debtor turnover	6.0 times	6.7 times
Creditor turnover	4.8 times	5.0 times
Financial status ratios		
Debt ratio	18.2%	20.0%
Interest cover	15.0 times	10.0 times
Current ratio	2.4 times	2.5 times
Acid test	1.0 times	1.0 times
Stock market ratios		
Earnings per share	30.0p	20.0p
Price/earnings ratio	10.0	10.0
Dividend yield (net)	4.4%	5.0%
Dividend cover	2.25 times	2.0 times

Comments

1 1992's performance is better than 1991's, with return on equity and return on net assets both up by about one third.

2 Sales (turnover) rose by 20 per cent, and the profit margin increased from 10.0 to 12.5 per cent, leading to a 50 per cent increase in profit before interest.

3 The tax ratio in 1992 was similar to 1991, so profit after tax also increased by 50 per cent.

4 The ordinary dividend rose by one third, so the dividend cover and the retained profits both increased.

5 The price/earnings ratio has stayed at 10.0, as the market price per share rose from 200p to 300p (up 50 per cent), the same as earnings per share. But general market trends will have affected the share price, as well as Precision Locks Limited's own results.

6 Fixed asset utilization improved as sales increased faster than the net investment in fixed assets.

7 Stocks again seem rather high relative to sales volume (and even higher relative to cost of goods sold). But to suggest a 'correct' stock level we would need to know more about the nature of the company's business.

8 The average credit period taken by debtors has increased by 10 per cent. Combined with a higher sales volume, this has meant a 33 per cent rise in debtors. If credit policy has not changed, perhaps the administration of credit control needs looking at.

9 The company is financing some of its increased investment in stock and debtors by taking slightly longer credit. Creditor turnover has fallen from 5.0 times (73 days) to 4.8 times (76 days).

10 As trading activity grows the company will need more funds. With the acid test ratio just below 1.0 the cash position will have to be watched carefully. There seems to be room for more long-term borrowing if necessary.

STANDARDS FOR ANALYSIS

Computing the ratios examined in this section plays an essential part in financial analysis; but figures for a single accounting period may not be much use on their own. The results are far more revealing when compared with some kind of 'standard'. Similar ratios for earlier periods can indicate trends; budget ratios can show how well a company is achieving its financial objectives; or the results of other companies in the same industry can provide an external standard.

(a)   Earlier years' results

If accounting policies are consistent, previous periods' results may permit fair comparison with the current period (subject to changed conditions). An improvement over last year's performance may still be a bad result (just as a worse result than last year's may still be good).

(b)   Internal company budgets

Budgets show planned performance, so actual results in line with budget may well represent an adequate outcome. The more care taken in preparing budgets, the more reliable they are as standards. Changed conditions since budgets were agreed may call for explicit revisions to budgets, or they will cause unavoidable variances from original budgets. External analysts, of course, rarely have access to a company's own budgets; and any attempt to require publication would surely distort the budgeting process.

(c)   Results of other companies in the same industry

Differing accounting practices and business policies may hinder comparisons with other companies. Moreover defining an 'industry' may not be easy, and large companies often operate in more than one industry. But where these problems are not too serious, and suitably detailed figures are available, industry results can provide a useful external standard.

DIFFERENT VIEWPOINTS

Accounting controversies often stem from implicit differences of viewpoint. The 'entity' view, for example, makes the company itself the centre of attention, with management having to deal with a number of 'stakeholders' such as: employees, suppliers, customers, owners, lenders. Proponents emphasize total assets employed and trading profits; and they tend to welcome the value-added statement, which deducts from sales turnover the costs of bought-in goods and services (other than employees' wages). The traditional 'proprietary' view, in contrast, regards as paramount the interests of shareholders, the ultimate owners of a company. Supporters of this view focus on shareholders' funds (capital and reserves), and profit after tax and dividends.

A related distinction is between 'economic profit', relevant for decision-making within the business, and 'accounting profit', which is probably more suitable for stewardship to outside investors. Economic profit is sales turnover minus current 'opportunity cost' of goods and services consumed, while historical cost accounting charges only the actual expenses incurred. A significant difference relates to the cost of capital: economic profit charges interest on *total* capital employed (including notional interest on equity capital), whereas accounting profit charges only actual interest payable on debt capital.

Another difference in viewpoint concerns the relative functions and significance of the profit and loss account and the balance sheet. If the main focus is on the profit (or earnings per share) for the current period, then the matching concept may be of special importance. If, however, the emphasis is on financial soundness, as displayed by the balance sheet, then the concept of prudence may tend to prevail. The former approach may be of special interest to shareholders; the latter may be more suitable for creditors.

We can conclude that there is more than one possible viewpoint from which to analyse company accounts. Nor should we expect too much from computing a few simple financial ratios. The complex far-flung affairs of modern business groups are not so easy to sum up. Still, the sort of analysis introduced in this section can be valuable in focusing attention on key aspects of companies' performance and financial position. In conjunction with relevant standards, ratio analysis can give useful clues about suitable questions for an external analyst to pose. But we can hardly expect it to give all the answers.

COMPARING DIFFERENT COMPANIES' RESULTS

Problems can arise in comparing the results of one period with another for a single company. Matching expenses with revenues and valuing assets is difficult in a going concern. At least a single company will normally be consistent in its accounting treatment of various items; but even more care is needed when comparing the results of different companies.

Recent attempts to reduce the range of acceptable accounting policies have met with some success. Even so, two different companies' accounts may not deal with similar accounting items in quite the same way. Hence some of the figures may need adjustment to bring the two sets of accounts on to a common basis. Even if the analyst possesses enough detailed information to do this, great care is still needed in comparing the adjusted figures.

It is important for people who use accounting figures to understand what accounts really mean. They should know how companies record transactions and summarize them in financial statements; and they should appreciate the various possible ways to value assets and to measure profit or loss. Later sections aim to provide such understanding.

To introduce some of the issues dealt with later, we compare below two companies in the same industry, Brown Limited and Green Limited. To keep it simple, assume that at 30 June 1992 the two companies' accounts looked exactly the same on the surface. But we shall find that accounting figures which seem identical may reflect very different facts underneath. Subjective opinion and judgement can greatly affect a company's balance sheet and reported profit; and we shall see how misleading the unthinking use of financial statements can be.

The original accounts of Brown Limited and Green Limited are set out opposite, with certain items of further information on the next page.

BROWN LIMITED

GREEN LIMITED

Profit and loss account for the year ended 30 June 1992		£'000
Turnover		1 000
Cost of sales		600
		400
Operating expenses		200
Profit before tax		200
Tax (25%)		50
Profit after tax		150

Balance sheet at 30 June 1992

Tangible fixed assets		
Freehold factory at cost		150
Machinery at cost	240	
Less: Accumulated depreciation	140	
		100
		250
Current assets		
Stock	250	
Debtors	180	
Cash	20	
	450	
Less: **Creditors payable within one year**	200	
		250
Total assets less current liabilities (Net assets)		500
Capital and reserves		
Called up share capital		300
Profit and loss account		200
(Capital employed)		500

Analysis of results

An initial study of the accounts of Brown Limited and Green Limited would, of course, yield identical results. For example, the operating performance – of each company – might be summarized as follows:

$$\text{Return on net assets} = \frac{\text{Profit before tax}}{\text{Net assets}} = \frac{200}{500} = 40.0\%$$

$$\text{Profit margin} = \frac{\text{Profit before tax}}{\text{Sales}} = \frac{200}{1\,000} = 20.0\%$$

$$\text{Net asset turnover} = \frac{\text{Sales}}{\text{Net assets}} = \frac{1\,000}{500} = 2.0 \text{ times}$$

But the further information shown opposite modifies this first impression. Overleaf we take it into account and show adjusted accounts for Brown Limited and Green Limited. Before you turn over the page, we suggest it would be a useful exercise for you to do the same. Please now attempt to produce adjusted accounts yourself for each of the two companies, in the light of the further information presented opposite.

To highlight the changes, please also recalculate the three performance ratios above, and see how much difference your adjustments have made to them. Make all necessary adjustments, then compare your results with ours overleaf. Please note that our answers are not the only possible set of adjusted accounts. The point of the example is precisely to illustrate that accounts depend to a large extent on *opinion*; and reasonable, experienced business people may often hold different opinions about the best accounting treatment of particular items.

Further information

(a) Freehold factory

Brown acquired its freehold factory in 1980; expert valuers reckon its current market value is £300 000. The current market value of Green's factory, which was bought in 1989, is about the same as the purchase price.

(b) Depreciation of machinery

Brown expects most of its machines to last for some twelve years, and charges to cost of sales each year one-twelfth of the cost. Green reckons the life of similar machines to be eight years, and writes off one-eighth of the cost annually. The result is that Green charges £10 000 a year more depreciation than Brown.

(c) Stock valuation

Brown's policy is to write down stock which has not moved for twelve months to 50 per cent of cost. At 30 June 1992 the balance sheet included at £20 000 stock which cost £40 000. Green writes off the entire cost of stock which had not moved for a year, and charged £40 000 to cost of sales in 1992 in that respect.

(d) Debtors

Much of Brown's business is with a few large customers, one of which (Black Limited) is in financial trouble. Of the £50 000 which Black owed Brown at 30 June 1992, it seems unlikely that more than £40 000 will be recovered. Brown has made no provision for the possible loss, believing (perhaps optimistically) that Black will resolve its troubles and eventually pay the debt in full.

Green trades with a large number of smaller customers, and has provided an amount equal to 2 per cent of debts outstanding at the year-end. In previous years only 1 per cent was provided, which matched the actual average bad debt loss over a number of years. Green increased the level of provision for bad debts in 1992, feeling (perhaps pessimistically) that the coming months might find a number of customers in financial difficulty.

(e) Development costs

Both companies spent £90 000 on developing new products in the year. Brown carries forward as an asset £40 000 spent on one particular project, which is expected to generate revenue in the following year. Thus Brown charges only £50 000 for development costs in the current year; but plans to write off the remaining £40 000 next year. Green writes off all development costs in the year in which they are actually incurred, regardless of which period is expected to benefit.

Adjusted results

Clearly the different circumstances for the two companies make it misleading to compare their published accounts directly. The two companies' level of performance is *not* the same, as the original ratios suggested it was.

It is possible, using the further information provided, to adjust the two companies' accounts to bring them more closely on to the same basis. Our own adjusted figures appear on the right; but we emphasize that the 'further information' listed would also permit different adjustments. Moreover, there may still be other facts which are relevant but unknown. We have assumed that all the adjustments affect the tax charge.

Choosing between one basis of accounting and another means exercising judgement. There is no way to avoid subjective opinions affecting accounts. Who can tell for certain how long a particular asset will last, at what price stock will be sold, or whether an outstanding debt will ever be collected?

Our own adjusted accounts give rise to the following performance ratios, which we compare below with the original ratios:

	Original	Brown adjusted	Green adjusted
Return on net assets	40.0%	$\frac{140}{605} = 23.1\%$	$\frac{220}{515} = 42.7\%$
Profit margin	20.0%	$\frac{140}{1\,000} = 14.0\%$	$\frac{220}{1\,000} = 22.0\%$
Net asset turnover	2.00	$\frac{1\,000}{605} = 1.65$	$\frac{1\,000}{515} = 1.94$

The adjusted figures, especially Brown's, are now very different. Brown's return on net assets is nearly halved, profit margin on sales has fallen by nearly one-third, and asset turnover by one-fifth. The comparison with Green, whose return on net assets and profit margin have both improved slightly, now shows significant differences. But the ratios based on the published accounts were identical.

So readers of accounts should be cautious about making sweeping interpretations. Often the kind of ratio analysis we have worked through in this section does more to suggest particular *questions* the analyst should ask, than it does to provide definitive *answers*.

	BROWN LIMITED GREEN LIMITED		BROWN LIMITED		GREEN LIMITED	
	Original		Adjusted		Adjusted	
Profit and loss account **Year ended 30 June 1992**						
		£'000		£'000		£'000
Turnover		1 000		1 000		1 000
Cost of sales		600	b + 10 e + 40	650	c − 20	580
		400		350		420
Operating expenses		200	d + 10	210		200
Profit before tax		200		140		220
Tax (25%)		50		35		55
Profit after tax		150		105		165
Balance sheet **at 30 June 1992**						
		£'000		£'000		£'000
Fixed assets						
Freehold factory		150	a + 150	300		150
Machinery, net		100	b − 10	90		100
		250		390		250
Current assets						
Stock	250		e − 40	210	c + 20	270
Debtors	180		d − 10	170		180
Cash	20			20		20
	450			400		470
Less: Creditors	200		Tax − 15	185	Tax + 5	205
		250		215		265
Net assets		500		605		515
Share capital		300		300		300
Capital reserve		–	a + 150	150		–
Retained profits		200	− 45	155	+ 15	215
Capital employed		500		605		515

DEBT: SHORT-TERM OR LONG-TERM?

In our earlier discussion of the financial status ratios of Precision Locks Limited (page 34), we suggested a cautious approach to measuring debt ratio and interest cover. We included both short-term and long-term interest-bearing borrowings as 'debt' in calculating the debt ratio. (It is not usually possible to split interest payable between short-term and long-term, but even if it were, we would include both in computing 'interest cover' – along with any interest 'capitalized' in the accounts.) Thus for the purpose of computing both these solvency ratios, we suggest treating short-term borrowings (and interest thereon) *as if* they were long-term.

We were also conservative in our approach to the liquidity ratios. In computing both current ratio and acid test ratio, we included short-term borrowings as *current* liabilities (despite our different treatment in computing the solvency ratios). This may seem inconsistent, but we emphasize the *conservatism* of our approach. In financial ratio analysis, we want to see the position 'at its worst', in each case, in judging the soundness of a company's financial position.

To show how much difference it can make, let us reconsider the various financial status ratios for Precision Locks Limited, on the new assumption that the current liabilities of £250 000 include £100 000 of short-term bank overdraft. (We also assume, for the sake of this example, that bank overdraft interest of £12 000 was included in distribution and administrative expenses.)

The table opposite shows summarized accounts treating the bank overdraft first as a current liability (left), and then as long-term financing (right), both for purposes of the debt ratio and interest cover, and for the liquidity ratios. We also show the return on net assets ratio under the two different assumptions. We have marked with an asterisk the alternative we prefer in each case.

PRECISION LOCKS LIMITED	£100 000 overdraft shown as	
	Current liability	Long-term financing
Summarized balance sheet 30 June 1992	£'000	£'000
Fixed assets, net	210	210
Current assets (stock 350)	590	590
Less: current liabilities	250	150
	340	440
	550	650
Debt finance	100	200
Shareholders' funds	450	450
	550	650

Summarized profit and loss account year ended 30 June 1992		
Gross profit	400	400
Distribution etc. expenses	250	238
	150	162
Interest payable	10	22
Profit before tax	140	140

Selected ratios	Original	Revised
Debt ratio (%)	$\frac{100}{550} = 18.2$	$\frac{200}{650} = 30.8^*$
Interest cover (times)	$\frac{150}{10} = 15.0$	$\frac{162}{22} = 7.4^*$
Current ratio (times)	$\frac{590}{250} = 2.36^*$	$\frac{590}{150} = 3.93$
Acid test (times)	$\frac{240}{250} = 0.96^*$	$\frac{240}{150} = 1.60$
Return on net assets (%)	$\frac{150}{550} = 27.3$	$\frac{162}{650} = 24.9^*$

* = preferred treatment

THE NEED FOR CAUTION

In appraising the accounts of Precision Locks Limited, we compared the 1992 results with 1991's. This form of comparison assumes that the two years' figures have been prepared on a consistent basis, and can yield results both for external analysts and for managers within a company.

It is a legal requirement to disclose any material change in the basis of accounting which might impair a consistent presentation and, where the accounting treatment has changed, to adjust the comparative figures as well as the current year's. So one might reasonably expect to be able to rely on comparison of one year's accounts with another's.

One might assume, for example, that if two sets of accounts show the same totals for particular items such as fixed assets or stocks, the financial meaning of each item must be the same. But this need not be so. The totals appearing in financial statements usually summarize a whole series of transactions, or combine separate asset and liability balances, the nature and mixture of which can vary from one period to another. (We have already mentioned possible changes in the mix of cash and credit sales, and the problems that they can give rise to in calculating trade debtor turnover.)

Nor can one assume that accounting measures of performance are exact, or that the same transactions would inevitably lead to the same financial result whenever they occurred or whoever measured them. We shall see many examples in later sections, when we look more closely at the complex problems of income measurement.

In accounts for periods less than a year, seasonal factors may need special attention. They may complicate comparison of one period with another. And even with annual accounts, the balance sheet position may not be typical: for example, liquidity may seem very good if the balance sheet date occurs when stocks are extremely low, just after a heavy selling period.

In comparisons over time within a company, it can be hard to judge how adequate a level of performance earlier results represent. And business conditions may have changed.

The original published accounts of Brown Limited and Green Limited were identical; but when we examined further information in detail, we found that in some respects the two companies had prepared their accounts on very different bases. We were able to produce adjusted figures which (perhaps) allowed a more useful comparison, but such further information may not always be available.

SUMMARY

We started this section by outlining four main steps in a full financial analysis of company accounts. We have dealt with two in this section: first, an overview to give perspective and to identify trends in key figures over a period of several years; and then a detailed analysis of financial ratios. Later sections deal with analysis of cash flow and of business segments.

We examined the basic concept of return on investment, briefly discussed the relationship between 'risk' and 'return', and looked at the links between return on equity and return on net assets. We also saw two ways of dividing the return on net assets ratio into a 'pyramid' of ratios; and we noted the potential of this approach as a tool of internal management control.

Next we considered in some detail how to analyse company accounts by means of financial ratios. We worked through the 1992 accounts of Precision Locks Limited, calculated various financial ratios, and compared them with those of the previous year, in three groups: performance ratios, financial status ratios and stock market ratios.

Each of those groups of financial ratios helps to interpret different aspects of a company's affairs, and each is important. Most businesses face a continuing financial challenge to balance *liquidity* against *profitability*.

Following our work on Precision Locks, we observed the need for *standards* with which to compare a company's financial ratios for a particular period. We suggested: previous years; internal budgets; other companies in the same industry; and external industry averages. We also noted that accounts can be looked at from more than one viewpoint, perhaps the two most common (as far as external analysts are concerned) being that of the company as a whole (the 'entity' viewpoint), and that of the ordinary shareholders in the company (the 'proprietary' viewpoint).

We went on to consider the problems of trying to compare the results of two different companies, Brown Limited and Green Limited. We saw how important judgement and opinion can be in measuring profit or loss, and in attaching values to assets in a going concern.

We next discussed the treatment of bank overdrafts and current instalments of long-term debt. We saw that it can make a big difference whether they are treated as current liabilities (hence reducing working capital) or as longer-term liabilities (hence forming part of capital employed). Part of the problem here is the distinction between a debt that may be legally liable to be repaid 'on demand', and one which in reality is unlikely to be cleared within twelve months from the balance sheet date.

Finally, we mentioned a number of reasons for caution in analysing company accounts. In later sections we shall be looking in more detail at many of the matters touched on only briefly here.

2.1 Definitions

Please write out in the spaces provided below your definitions of the ratios listed. Then compare your definitions with those set out overleaf. *Unless you actually write down your answers you are missing much of the potential learning.*

(a) Return on net assets

(b) Current ratio

(c) Earnings yield

(d) Acid test

(e) Price/earnings ratio

(f) Dividend yield

(g) Debt ratio

(h) Interest cover

(i) Return on equity

(j) Dividend cover

2.1 Definitions

(a) *Return on net assets* is profit before interest payable and before tax (PBIT) divided by net assets.

(b) *Current ratio* is current assets divided by creditors due within one year (current liabilities).

(c) *Earnings yield* is earnings per share (EPS) divided by market price per share. The ratio is usually calculated gross of tax in the UK (see Section 7); but where it is calculated *net* of tax, it represents the reciprocal of the price/earnings ratio.

(d) *Acid test* (also called the 'quick ratio') is liquid assets divided by creditors due within one year (current liabilities). 'Liquid assets' are normally represented by cash plus short-term marketable securities plus debtors; but long-term debtors (if any) should be excluded.

(e) *Price/earnings ratio* (P/E ratio) is market price per ordinary share divided by earnings per share (EPS) for the most recent year.

(f) *Dividend yield* is dividend per share dividend by market price per share. In Section 2 this ratio has been calculated net of tax; but in fact it is usually calculated on a gross basis (see Section 7).

(g) *Debt ratio* is usually defined as total borrowings (that is, long-term debt plus recurring overdrafts and the current portion of long-term debt) divided by capital employed (that is, debt plus equity). Sometimes another definition of 'debt ratio' is calculated by dividing debt by shareholders' funds (in which case it may also be called the 'debt/equity' ratio).

(h) *Interest cover* is profit before interest payable on debt and before tax (PBIT) divided by interest payable on debt.

(i) *Return on equity* is profit after tax (and after preference dividends and minority interests if applicable (see Section 9)) divided by equity shareholders' funds. But 'extraordinary items' (see Section 4) would not normally be deducted in determining profit after tax here.

(j) *Dividend cover* is profit after tax (as above) divided by ordinary dividends for the year. It may simply be net EPS divided by net DPS; but ought strictly to be calculated gross (the 'maximum' basis), as described in Section 7.

2.2 James Smith Limited: basic ratios

The 1992 accounts of James Smith are set out below. You are asked to complete the descriptions and ratios as shown for return on equity. When you have finished, check your answers with those shown overleaf.

JAMES SMITH LIMITED
Profit and loss account for year ended 30 September 1992

	£'000
Turnover	1 500
Cost of sales	1 130
Gross profit	370
Operating expenses	150
Operating profit	220
Interest payable	20
Profit before tax	200
Tax	70
Profit after tax	130
Dividends (net)	80
Retained profit	50

				£'000	
(a)	Return on equity	$=$	$\dfrac{\text{Profit after tax}}{\text{Shareholders' funds}}$	$=\dfrac{130}{350}$	$= 37.1\%$
(b)	Return on net assets	$=$		$=$	$=$
(c)	Profit margin	$=$		$=$	$=$
(d)	Aset turnover	$=$		$=$	$=$
(e)	Debt ratio	$=$		$=$	$=$
(f)	Interest cover	$=$		$=$	$=$

JAMES SMITH LIMITED
Balance sheet at 30 September 1992

		£'000
Tangible fixed assets		
Factory and equipment		400
Current assets		
Stocks	300	
Debtors	200	
Cash	50	
	550	
Less: **Creditors due within one year**		
Creditors	200	
Dividend	80	
Tax	70	
	350	
		200
Total assets less current liabilities (Net assets)		600
Creditors due after more than one year		
Loans		250
Capital and reserves		
Called up share capital	200	
Profit and loss account	150	
		350
(Capital employed)		600

(g)	Current ratio	$=$		$=$	$=$
(h)	Acid test	$=$		$=$	$=$

2.2 James Smith Limited

Solution

£'000

(a)	Return on equity	=	$\dfrac{\text{Profit after tax}}{\text{Shareholders' funds}}$	=	$\dfrac{130}{350}$	=	37.1%
(b)	Return on net assets	=	$\dfrac{\text{Profit before interest payable and tax}}{\text{Capital employed}}$	=	$\dfrac{220}{600}$	=	36.7%
(c)	Profit margin	=	$\dfrac{\text{Profit before interest payable and tax}}{\text{Sales}}$	=	$\dfrac{220}{1\,500}$	=	14.7%
(d)	Asset turnover	=	$\dfrac{\text{Sales}}{\text{Net assets}}$	=	$\dfrac{1\,500}{600}$	=	2.50 times
(e)	Debt ratio	=	$\dfrac{\text{Debt}}{\text{Capital employed}}$	=	$\dfrac{250}{600}$	=	41.7%
(f)	Interest cover	=	$\dfrac{\text{Profit before interest payable and tax}}{\text{Interest}}$	=	$\dfrac{220}{20}$	=	11.0 times
(g)	Current ratio	=	$\dfrac{\text{Current assets}}{\text{Current liabilities}}$	=	$\dfrac{550}{350}$	=	1.57 times
(h)	Acid test	=	$\dfrac{\text{Liquid assets}}{\text{Current liabilities}}$	=	$\dfrac{250}{350}$	=	0.71 times

48

2.3 Worldchem plc

A summarized version of the 1992 accounts of Worldchem plc is shown below and on the right, together with comparative figures for the previous year. Most of the notes to the accounts, which give further details about nearly every item, are omitted here.

You are asked to:

1 Calculate the financial ratios set out in the following pages for the two years ended 31 March 1991 and 1992. (Use 142p and 136p respectively as the market price per ordinary share for 1991 and 1992. These were the prices at 30 June 1991 and 30 June 1992.)
2 Compare the detailed results for 1992 with those for 1991 and comment on any aspects or changes you think significant.

Suggested answers are given on page 52.

WORLDCHEM PLC
Consolidated profit and loss account
Year ended 31 March 1992

		1992	1991
		£m	£m
Turnover		1 028	923
Operating costs		889	773
Operating profit		139	150
Interest	(1)	2	6
Profit before taxation		137	144
Taxation		46	48
Profit after taxation		91	96
Dividends		41	33
Profit retained		50	63

(1)	Interest payable	15	14
	Interest receivable	(13)	(8)
		2	6

WORLDCHEM PLC
Consolidated balance sheet at 31 March 1992

	1992		1991	
	£m		£m	
Tangible fixed assets				
Land and buildings		237		205
Plant and machinery		152		127
		389		332
Current assets				
Stocks	205		178	
Debtors and prepayments	211		182	
Liquid resources	115		176	
	531		536	
Less: **Creditors due within one year**				
Bank loans and overdrafts	16		26	
Trade creditors and accruals	157		139	
Taxation	45		46	
Dividends	21		19	
	239		230	
Net current assets (working capital)		292		306
Total assets less current liabilities (Net assets)		681		638
Creditors due after more than one year				
Loans		161		148
Capital and reserves				
Called up share capital (25p shares)	163		163	
Reserves	357		327	
		520		490
(Capital employed)		681		638

	1992	1991

Performance ratios

(a)   Return on equity (%)

(b)   Tax ratio (%)

(c)   Return on net assets (%)

(d)   Profit margin (%)

(e)   Net asset turnover (times)

(f)   Fixed asset turnover (times)

(g)   Stock turnover (times)

(h)   Days' sales in debtors (days)

(i)   Days' sales in creditors (days)

Financial status ratios

(j)   Debt ratio (%)

(k)   Interest cover (times)

(l)   Current ratio (times)

(m) Acid test (times)

Stock market ratios

	1992	1991

(n) Earnings per share (pence)

(o) Price/earnings ratio (times)

(p) Dividend yield (net) (%)

(q) Dividend cover (times)

Comments

After completing your calculation of the financial ratios set out above, please be sure to examine the results together with the accounts and *write out* some comments on the 1992 results.

WORLDCHEM PLC

Solution

Performance ratios

		1992		1991	
(a)	Return on equity	$\frac{91}{520}$	$= 17.5\%$	$\frac{96}{490}$	$= 19.6\%$
(b)	Tax ratio	$\frac{46}{137}$	$= 33.6$	$\frac{48}{144}$	$= 33.3\%$
(c)	Return on net assets	$\frac{137 + 15}{681 + 16}$	$= 21.8\%$	$\frac{144 + 14}{638 + 26}$	$= 23.8\%$
(d)	Profit margin	$\frac{152}{1\,028}$	$= 14.8\%$	$\frac{158}{923}$	$= 17.1\%$
(e)	Net asset turnover	$\frac{1\,028}{697}$	$= 1.47$ times	$\frac{923}{664}$	$= 1.39$ times
(f)	Fixed asset turnover	$\frac{1\,028}{389}$	$= 2.64$ times	$\frac{923}{332}$	$= 2.78$ times
(g)	Stock turnover	$\frac{1\,028}{205}$	$= 5.01$ times	$\frac{923}{178}$	$= 5.19$ times
(h)	Days' sales in debtors	$\frac{211 \times 365}{1\,028}$	$= 74.9$ days	$\frac{182 \times 365}{923}$	$= 72.0$ days
(i)	Days' sales in creditors	$\frac{157 \times 365}{1\,028}$	$= 55.7$ days	$\frac{139 \times 365}{923}$	$= 55.0$ days

Financial status ratios

		1992		1991	
(j)	Debt ratio	$\frac{161 + 16}{697}$	$= 25.4\%$	$\frac{148 + 26}{664}$	$= 26.2\%$
(k)	Interest cover	$\frac{152}{15}$	$= 10.1$ times	$\frac{158}{14}$	$= 11.3$ times
(l)	Current ratio	$\frac{531}{239}$	$= 2.22$ times	$\frac{536}{230}$	$= 2.33$ times
(m)	Acid test	$\frac{326}{239}$	$= 1.36$ times	$\frac{358}{230}$	$= 1.56$ times

Stock market ratios

		1992		1991	
(n)	Earnings per share	$\frac{91}{(163 \times 4)}$	$= 14.0$p	$\frac{96}{(163 \times 4)}$	$= 14.7$p
(o)	Price/earnings ratio	$\frac{136}{14.0}$	$= 9.7$	$\frac{142}{14.7}$	$= 9.7$
(p)	Dividend yield (net)	$\frac{6.3}{136}$	$= 4.6\%$	$\frac{5.1}{142}$	$= 3.6\%$
(q)	Dividend cover	$\frac{14.0}{6.3}$	$= 2.22$ times	$\frac{14.7}{5.1}$	$= 2.88$ times

Worldchem plc

Notes

(c)   Bank loans and overdrafts are shown as creditors due within one year in the balance sheet; but in practice they may be regarded as part of the longer-term financing of the business. Hence we show 'net assets' as 681 + 16 (638 + 26 for the previous year).

(l)   Despite what is said above, we prefer to take the conservative approach, and include bank loans and overdrafts as 'current' liabilities for the purpose of computing the liquidity ratios.

(p)   Dividend per share = £41M ÷ (163M × 4) = 6.3p.

Comments

1   Return on equity of Worldchem plc has declined due to a lower return on net assets.

2   The main problem facing the company is much lower profit margins – down from 17.1% to 14.8%.

3   Net asset turnover has improved due to lower liquid resources, and an 11% increase in sales turnover. The turnover of fixed assets, stock and debtors have all declined slightly.

4   Gearing is slightly lower, but with lower profit the interest cover has declined.

5   The current and acid test ratios are both lower, reflecting the reduced liquid resources, but still look high for a chemical company.

6   With profit after tax down and dividends up, the dividend cover has declined.

2.4 Northern Foods plc (A): Financial ratio analysis

The accounts of Northern Foods plc for the year ended 31 March 1991, together with extracts from the notes relating to them, are shown on pages 53 to 57.

You are asked to study the accounts and then to calculate the financial ratios set out in the following pages for the two years ended 31 March 1991 and 31 March 1990. (Use the June 1991 share price of 467p for year-end 1991, and the June 1990 share price of 330p for year-end 1990. These prices will incorporate all of the information disclosed in the accounts.) Please also compare the 1991 and 1990 results, and write down on a separate sheet your comments on any significant changes.

Suggested solutions and comments are shown on pages 60 to 62.

Consolidated profit and loss account for the year ended 31st March 1991

	Notes	1991 £m	1990 £m
Turnover	1	**1,187.0**	1,094.4
Cost of sales		**(874.9)**	(827.4)
Gross profit		**312.1**	267.0
Distribution costs		**(144.9)**	(125.5)
Administrative expenses		**(57.8)**	(50.0)
Other operating income		**2.2**	2.5
Operating profit	2	**111.6**	94.0
Investment income		**2.6**	1.7
Interest payable	4	**(6.1)**	(3.1)
Allocated to profit sharing		**(2.7)**	(2.4)
Profit on ordinary activities before taxation	1	105.4	90.2
Taxation on profit on ordinary activities	7	**(28.4)**	(25.3)
Profit on ordinary activities after taxation		**77.0**	64.9
Extraordinary items	8	**1.1**	(5.9)
Profit for the financial year	9	**78.1**	59.0
Dividends	10	**(32.2)**	(27.8)
Retained profit for the year	24	**45.9**	31.2
Earnings per ordinary share		**34.66p**	29.25p

Movements on reserves are set out in notes 21 to 24.

Consolidated balance sheet at 31st March 1991

	Notes	1991 £m	1991 £m	1990 £m	1990 £m
Fixed assets					
Tangible fixed assets	13		**400.2**		346.1
Current assets					
Stocks	15	**54.2**		51.4	
Debtors	16	**142.9**		138.8	
Investments	17	**0.5**		—	
Cash at bank and in hand		**19.6**		17.6	
		217.2		207.8	
Creditors: amounts falling due within one year	18	**292.5**		229.5	
Net current liabilities			**(75.3)**		(21.7)
Total assets less current liabilities			**324.9**		324.4
Creditors: amounts falling due after more than one year	18		**7.0**		3.5
			317.9		320.9
Provisions for liabilities and charges	19		**12.5**		6.7
			305.4		314.2
Capital and reserves					
Called up share capital	20		**55.6**		55.5
Share premium account	21		**61.3**		60.6
Revaluation reserve	22		**12.3**		12.7
Other reserves	23		**4.1**		4.1
Profit and loss account	24		**172.1**		181.3
Shareholders' funds			**305.4**		314.2

C.R. Haskins *director*

M. Clark *director*

11th June 1991

Statement of source and application of funds for the year ended 31st March 1991

	1991 £m	1990 £m
Source of funds		
Profit on ordinary activities before taxation	**105.4**	90.2
Item not involving movement of funds:		
Depreciation	**33.7**	28.9
Extraordinary items involving movement of funds	**(4.1)**	(5.7)
Total generated from operations	**135.0**	113.4
Issue of shares	**0.8**	1.1
Sale of fixed assets	**3.0**	7.4
Total funds generated	**138.8**	121.9
Application of funds		
Purchase of fixed assets	**60.7**	75.9
Acquisitions (note 25)	**69.1**	17.1
Dividends paid	**29.5**	26.0
Taxation paid	**13.5**	7.8
	172.8	126.8
Working capital requirements:		
Stocks	**(1.9)**	1.6
Debtors	**1.5**	11.1
Creditors	**(1.1)**	(2.4)
	(1.5)	10.3
Total funds utilised	**171.3**	137.1
Increase in net borrowings	**32.5**	15.2
Represented by:		
Increase in borrowings	**35.0**	21.1
Increase in cash at bank and short term investments	**2.5**	5.9
	32.5	15.2

The effect of currency movements has been eliminated from this statement.

Accounting policies (Selected)

Accounting convention
The accounts are prepared under the historical cost convention except for the revaluation of properties which is incorporated in the accounts.
The accounts are prepared in accordance with applicable accounting standards.

Foreign currencies
Assets and liabilities in foreign currencies are expressed in sterling at the rates of exchange ruling at the balance sheet date.
Results of overseas subsidiary undertakings are translated at an average rate for the year. All exchange differences arising on consolidation are taken to reserves. Any other exchange differences are dealt with in the profit and loss account.

Stocks
These are valued at the lower of cost and net realisable value. Cost includes an addition for production overheads where appropriate.

Goodwill
Goodwill, being the excess of the consideration over the fair value of the separable net tangible assets at the date of acquisition of newly acquired businesses or subsidiary undertakings, is charged directly to reserves in the year of acquisition.

Fixed assets
Surpluses arising from the revaluation of properties are taken direct to reserves. Net revaluation surpluses realised in respect of properties sold are transferred from the revaluation reserve to the profit and loss account.
Assets acquired under finance leases are capitalised as tangible fixed assets and the outstanding instalments, exclusive of interest, are included in loans. Interest is charged against profits in proportion to the amount of loan outstanding.
Interest incurred on borrowings to finance construction of fixed assets is capitalised up to the date of commissioning.

Depreciation
Freehold land is not depreciated. Other fixed assets are written off in equal instalments over their expected useful lives as follows:

Buildings	20–50 years (or over the remaining life of the lease if shorter)
Plant and equipment	5–15 years
Motor vehicles	3–14 years

Notes to the accounts

1 Analysis of activities

	1991 £m	1990 £m
Turnover		
Dairy	**446.9**	438.3
Convenience Foods	**283.7**	233.2
Meat	**281.9**	253.5
Grocery	**174.5**	163.6
UK turnover	**1,187.0**	1,088.6
North America	**—**	5.8
Group turnover	**1,187.0**	1,094.4
Profit		
Dairy	**49.9**	45.3
Convenience Foods	**21.8**	15.6
Meat	**22.1**	18.2
Grocery	**17.8**	15.2
UK operating profit	**111.6**	94.3
UK finance charges	**(4.1)**	(2.1)
Profit sharing	**(2.7)**	(2.4)
UK profit before tax	**104.8**	89.8
North America	**0.6**	0.4
Group profit before tax	**105.4**	90.2

2 Operating profit

	1991 £m	1990 £m
This is stated after charging:		
Depreciation (including £0.6m (1990 – £0.7m) on finance leases)	**33.7**	28.9
Auditors' remuneration	**0.5**	0.4
Directors' remuneration	**0.5**	0.4
Operating lease charges	**15.0**	12.5

4 Interest payable

	1991 £m	1990 £m
Debenture stocks	**0.1**	0.2
Loans wholly repayable within 5 years	**5.9**	2.6
Loans not wholly repayable within 5 years	**—**	0.1
Finance leases	**0.1**	0.2
	6.1	3.1

The interest charge for the year has been reduced by £1.2m (1990 – £3.1m) in respect of interest capitalised on major projects.

7 Taxation on profit on ordinary activities

	1991 £m	1990 £m
UK corporation tax at 34 per cent (1990 – 35 per cent)	**21.4**	25.3
Deferred taxation	**7.8**	(0.4)
Prior year adjustments	**(1.1)**	0.3
	28.1	25.2
Overseas taxation	**0.3**	0.1
	28.4	25.3

The charge for UK corporation tax for the year has been reduced by £2.5m (1990 – £3.8m) in respect of excess capital allowances over depreciation.

8 Extraordinary items

	1991 £m	1990 £m
Discontinuance costs after taxation relief of £0.2m (1990 – £2.4m)	**(9.1)**	(5.9)
Release of provisions	**10.2**	—
	1.1	(5.9)

12 Intangible fixed assets

At 31st March 1991 the accumulated amount of goodwill written off against the consolidated profit and loss account was £163.7m (1990 – £109.6m). The write-off is also reflected in the parent company profit and loss account.

14 Fixed asset investments

	Company 1991 £m	Company 1990 £m
Subsidiary undertakings		
Shares at cost		
At 31st March 1990	**92.7**	80.4
Cost of acquisition	**—**	12.3
At 31st March 1991	**92.7**	92.7
Loans due from subsidiary undertakings	**150.0**	121.2
Loans due to subsidiary undertakings	**(31.8)**	(35.5)
	210.9	178.4
Less: accumulated goodwill written off	**(163.7)**	(109.6)
	47.2	68.8

15 Stocks

	Group 1991 £m	Group 1990 £m
Raw materials	**26.5**	25.5
Work in progress	**3.8**	3.5
Finished goods	**23.9**	22.4
	54.2	51.4

13 Tangible fixed assets

Group

	Freehold property £m	Long leases £m	Short leases £m	Plant fixtures & vehicles £m	Total £m
Cost or valuation					
At 31st March 1990	134.8	54.3	2.9	323.6	515.6
Exchange adjustments	—	(0.1)	—	(0.6)	(0.7)
Additions	8.3	1.6	0.8	50.0	60.7
Arising on acquisitions	9.2	—	3.0	18.4	30.6
Disposals	(1.4)	(0.1)	(0.2)	(12.4)	(14.1)
At 31st March 1991	**150.9**	**55.7**	**6.5**	**379.0**	**592.1**
Analysis					
Valuation – 1978	21.4	12.5	0.3	—	34.2
– 1982	1.5	—	—	—	1.5
Cost	128.0	43.2	6.2	379.0	556.4
Depreciation					
At 31st March 1990	12.7	7.4	0.6	148.8	169.5
Exchange adjustments	—	—	—	(0.4)	(0.4)
Charge for the year	2.5	1.7	0.3	29.2	33.7
On disposals	(0.5)	—	(0.1)	(10.3)	(10.9)
At 31st March 1991	**14.7**	**9.1**	**0.8**	**167.3**	**191.9**
Net book amounts					
At 31st March 1991	**136.2**	**46.6**	**5.7**	**211.7**	**400.2**
At 31st March 1990	122.1	46.9	2.3	174.8	346.1

The additions for the year include £8.1m (1990 – £23.4m) in respect of assets in the course of construction.

16 Debtors

	Group 1991 £m	Group 1990 £m	Company 1991 £m	Company 1990 £m
Amounts falling due within one year:				
Trade debtors	108.9	91.9	—	—
Taxation recoverable	—	—	—	7.8
Other debtors	22.0	24.1	15.8	14.4
Prepayments	6.7	9.2	1.2	0.6
Amounts due from subsidiary undertakings	—	—	223.0	133.0
	137.6	125.2	240.0	155.8
Amounts falling due after more than one year:				
Taxation recoverable	—	—	6.3	5.4
Other debtors	5.3	13.2	8.4	1.7
Prepayments	—	0.4	—	—
	5.3	13.6	14.7	7.1
	142.9	138.8	254.7	162.9

18 Creditors

	Group 1991 £m	Group 1990 £m	Company 1991 £m	Company 1990 £m
Amounts falling due within one year:				
Bank loans	17.9	18.6	17.9	18.6
Debenture loans	—	2.1	—	2.1
Overdrafts	4.4	2.4	25.6	4.9
Bills payable	45.0	14.0	45.0	14.0
Other loans	0.9	0.5	—	—
Total short-term borrowings	68.2	37.6	88.5	39.6
Trade creditors	97.4	90.9	0.6	0.6
Other creditors including social security	37.4	21.3	6.2	1.7
Accruals and deferred income	17.3	17.4	1.8	1.1
Taxation	53.3	46.1	35.1	37.3
Proposed dividend	18.9	16.2	18.9	16.2
Amounts due to subsidiary undertakings	—	—	121.4	16.8
	292.5	229.5	272.5	113.3

19 Provisions for liabilities and charges

Group

	Deferred taxation 1991 £m	Other provisions 1991 £m	Total 1991 £m	Deferred taxation 1990 £m
Amount provided at 31st March 1991 in respect of:				
Accelerated capital allowances	3.1	—	3.1	13.9
Other timing differences	6.4	—	6.4	(1.8)
Acquisitions	(2.9)	12.2	9.3	—
Advance corporation tax recoverable	(6.3)	—	(6.3)	(5.4)
	0.3	12.2	12.5	6.7

20 Called up share capital

	Authorised		Allotted and fully paid	
	1991	1990	**1991**	1990
	£m	£m	**£m**	£m
Ordinary shares of 25p each	**67.5**	67.5	**55.6**	55.5

24 Profit and loss account

	Group **1991** **£m**	Company **1991** **£m**
At 31st March 1990	**181.3**	**97.0**
Retained profit for the year	**45.9**	**5.4**
Exchange differences	**(1.1)**	**(0.7)**
Transfer from revaluation reserve	**0.1**	**0.1**
Goodwill written off on acquisitions	**(54.1)**	**(54.1)**
At 31st March 1991	**172.1**	**47.7**

25 Acquisitions

During the year the group made a number of acquisitions, the principal of which are listed in the directors' report.

The fair value to the group of assets purchased, together with the consideration paid, can be summarised as follows:

	Local book values £m	Acquisition provisions £m	Fair value adjustments £m	Fair value on acquisition £m
Tangible fixed assets	31.8	—	(1.2)	30.6
Stocks	4.7	—	—	4.7
Debtors	3.9	—	—	3.9
Creditors and provisions	(14.9)	(9.3)	—	(24.2)
	25.5	(9.3)	(1.2)	15.0
Goodwill				54.1
Consideration – cash				69.1

Five-year record: year ended 31st March

£m where applicable	1987	1988	1989	1990	**1991**
Turnover	1,348	1,019	1,041	1,094	**1,187**
Profit before tax	75.2	77.3	85.3	90.2	**105.4**
Earned for ordinary shareholders from operations	49.9	54.4	60.7	64.9	**77.0**
Extraordinary items	20.1	(13.6)	(9.2)	(5.9)	**1.1**
Ordinary dividends	(19.8)	(22.1)	(24.9)	(27.8)	**(32.2)**
Retained in the business	50.2	18.7	26.6	31.2	**45.9**
Number of ordinary shares in issue (millions)	220.3	221.0	221.5	222.0	**222.4**
Earnings per ordinary share (pence)	22.70	24.69	27.43	29.25	**34.66**
Dividends per ordinary share (pence)	9.00	10.00	11.25	12.50	**14.50**
Dividend cover (times)	2.5	2.5	2.4	2.3	**2.4**
Retained profit plus depreciation	80.6	42.0	52.7	60.1	**79.6**
Capital expenditure	55.6	49.0	66.0	75.9	**60.7**
Shareholders' funds	263.3	276.4	296.3	314.2	**305.4**

Report of the auditors to the members of Northern Foods plc

We have audited the accounts on pages 28 to 44 in accordance with Auditing Standards.

In our opinion the accounts give a true and fair view of the state of affairs of the Company and of the Group at 31st March 1991 and of the profit and source and application of funds of the Group for the year then ended and have been properly prepared in accordance with the Companies Act 1985.

Ernst & Young
Chartered Accountants
Hull

11th June 1991

NORTHERN FOODS plc: Analysis of results for years ended 31 March 1990 and 1991

Performance ratios

	1991	1990
Return on equity %		
Tax ratio %		
Return on net assets %		
Profit margin %		
Net asset turnover (times)		
Fixed asset turnover (times)		
Stock days (cost of sales basis)		
Trade debtor days (sales basis)		
Trade creditor days (cost of sales basis)		

58

NORTHERN FOODS plc: Analysis of results for years ended 31 March 1991 and 1990

Financial status ratios

	1991	1990
Solvency		
Debt ratio %		
Interest cover (times)		
Liquidity		
Current ratio (times)		
Acid test (times)		
Stock market ratios		
Earnings per share (p)		
Price/earnings ratio (times) (June price)	467	330
Dividend yield (gross) %	467	330
Dividend cover (times)		

NORTHERN FOODS plc: Analysis of results for years ended 31 March 1991 and 1990

Performance ratios

		1991			1990		
Return on equity %		$\dfrac{77.0}{305.4}$	=	25.2	$\dfrac{64.9}{314.2}$	=	20.7
Tax ratio %		$\dfrac{28.4}{105.4}$	=	26.9	$\dfrac{25.3}{90.2}$	=	28.0
Return on net assets %	(a)	$\dfrac{105.4 + 6.1}{324.9 + 68.2}$	=	28.4	$\dfrac{90.2 + 3.1}{324.4 + 37.6}$	=	25.8
Profit margin %		$\dfrac{111.5}{1187.0}$	=	9.4	$\dfrac{93.3}{1094.4}$	=	8.5
Net asset turnover (times)		$\dfrac{1187.0}{393.1}$	=	3.02	$\dfrac{1094.4}{362.0}$	=	3.02
Fixed asset turnover (times)	(b)	$\dfrac{1187.0}{400.2 - 8.1}$	=	3.03	$\dfrac{1094.4}{346.1 - 23.4}$	=	3.39
Stock days (cost of sales basis)	(c)	$\dfrac{874.9}{54.2}$	=	16.1 22.6 days	$\dfrac{827.4}{51.4}$	=	16.1 22.7 days
Trade debtor days (sales basis)	(d)	$\dfrac{1187.0}{108.9}$	=	10.9 33.5 days	$\dfrac{1094.4}{91.9}$	=	11.9 30.7 days
Creditors days (cost of sales basis)	(d)	$\dfrac{874.9}{97.4}$	=	9.0 40.6 days	$\dfrac{827.4}{90.9}$	=	9.1 40.1 days

(a)   Add back interest (note 4). Net assets equals £324.9m shown in the balance sheet plus short-term borrowing (£68.2m) shown in note 18.

(b)   Fixed asset turnover is intended to show how well the company is using operating assets. Assets in course of construction (note 13) are excluded.

(c)   This is an alternative way to calculate stock days. First calculate stock turnover and then divide the resulting figure into 365. Because it can be hard to compare ratios of other companies using 'cost of sales', some analysts prefer to calculate 'stock turnover' based on sales revenue.

(d)   As the accounts provide a detailed split of debtors and creditors, trade debtors' and trade creditors' turnover ratios have been calculated, rather than turnover for total debtors (£142.9m) and total creditors (£224.3m).

NORTHERN FOODS plc: Analysis of results for years ended 31 March 1991 and 1990

Financial status ratios

	1991		1990	
Solvency				
Asset ratio %	$\dfrac{7.0+68.2}{324.9+68.2}$ =	19.1%	$\dfrac{3.5+37.6}{324.4+37.6}$ =	11.4%
Interest cover (times)	$\dfrac{105.4+6.1}{6.1+1.2}$ =	15.3	$\dfrac{90.2+3.1}{3.1+3.1}$ =	15.1
Liquidity				
Current ratio (times)	$\dfrac{217.2}{292.5}$ =	0.74	$\dfrac{207.8}{229.5}$ =	0.91
Acid test (times)	$\dfrac{163.0}{292.5}$ =	0.56	$\dfrac{156.4}{229.5}$ =	0.68

Stock market ratios

	1991		1990	
Earnings per share (p)	$\dfrac{77.0}{222.4}$ =	34.6p	$\dfrac{64.9}{222.0}$ =	29.2p
Price/earnings ratio (times) (June price)	$\dfrac{467}{34.6}$ =	13.5	$\dfrac{330}{29.2}$ =	11.3
Dividend yield (gross) %	$\dfrac{14.5}{467\times.75}$ =	4.1%	$\dfrac{12.5}{330\times.75}$ =	5.1%
Dividend cover (times)	$\dfrac{34.6}{14.5}$ =	2.4	$\dfrac{29.2}{12.5}$ =	2.3

NORTHERN FOODS plc
Summary of ratios

	1991	1990
Performance ratios		
Return on equity	25.2%	20.7%
Tax ratio	26.9%	28.0%
Return on net assets	28.4%	25.8%
Profit margin	9.4%	8.5%
Net asset turnover (times)	3.02	3.02
Fixed asset turnover (times)	3.03	3.39
Stock days (cost of sales basis)	22.6	22.7
Trade debtor days (sales basis)	33.5	30.7
Trade creditor days (cost of sales basis)	40.6	40.1
Financial status ratios		
Solvency		
Debt ratio	19.1%	11.4%
Interest cover (times)	15.3	15.1
Liquidity		
Current ratio (times)	0.74	0.91
Acid test (times)	0.56	0.68
Stock market ratios		
Earnings per share (pence)	34.6	29.2
Price/earnings ratio (times)	13.5	11.3
Dividend yield	4.1%	5.1%
Dividend cover (times)	2.4	2.3

Comments

1 From the five-year financial record, it is clear that Northern Foods plc has performed well since 1987, with profits growing at a steady rate. Turnover has grown somewhat less than the rate of inflation since 1988.

2 Returns on equity and net assets are increasing, mainly due to improving profit margins (8.5 per cent to 9.4 per cent). The company attributes this to 'tight controls and the elimination of low margin business'.

3 Stock days have remained steady at 22.6 days which is reasonable considering the nature of the business. Debtor days, although increasing slightly in 1991 to 33.5 days, appear to be well under control.

4 Creditor days remain slightly higher than debtor days indicating that the business is partly supporting its working capital requirements through its creditors.

5 The debt ratio increased in 1991 to 19.1 per cent but is still very low, as also indicated by the interest cover of 15 times. Northern Foods plc is financing its modest growth through self-generated cash rather than borrowings.

6 The current ratio and acid test, although low, are normal for businesses with such highly liquid assets, and are in line with other food manufacturers and retailers.

7 Earnings per share shows a marked increase to 34.6 pence in 1991. The dividend cover ratio of 2.4 shows the company pays out just under half of its earnings each year to its shareholders.

8 The company's share price has increased by 52 per cent since 1987 running ahead of the Stock Market as a whole, as well as other food manufacturers. The share price performed especially well in 1991. The Market's confidence in the company is reflected in its high P/E ratio of 13.5.

No answers are published for the following problems.

2.5 Northern Foods plc (B): Restating balance sheets

Restate the Northern Foods group balance sheets as at 31 March 1991 and 31 March 1990, set out on page 53, on a 'common size' basis, by expressing all the money amounts as a percentage of shareholders' funds at the end of each year. Comment on your results.

2.6 The Secret Seven

Set out opposite are 'balance sheet percentages' of seven companies in different industries. Can you identify each column of figures with a particular industry? (It will probably be useful to write down the reasons for your answers.) The percentages shown relate each of the balance sheet items to net assets (= to capital employed). A percentage for turnover calculated on the same basis is also shown.

In alphabetical order, the seven industries represented are: aerospace and automotive engineering, chemicals, defence and motor vehicles, food and drink manufacturers, food retailer, mining, property holding.

2.7 Cobham plc: Financial ratios, filling in the details

Set out overleaf, in summarized form, are the balance sheet of Cobham plc at 31 December 1991, and the profit and loss account for the year ended 31 December 1991. Also set out are some key ratios, already calculated. You are asked to fill in the numbers showing how each of the financial ratios has been calculated. A share price of 600p has been used, and there were 450 million ordinary shares outstanding throughout the year 1991.

THE SECRET SEVEN

	A	B	C	D	E	F	G
Tangible fixed assets							
Cost or valuation	106	103	127	130	75	65	98
Less: Accum. dep'n.	44	38	15	63	26	10	–
Net book value	62	65	112	67	49	55	98
of which: Land & bldgs.	32	27	94	15	7	39	98
Plant etc.	30	38	18	52	42	16	–
Intangible fixed assets	–	–	–	–	1	34	–
Investments	8	3	–	6	21	3	–
	70	68	112	73	71	92	98
Current assets							
Stocks	61	39	9	30	16	19	–
Debtors	28	48	1	35	14	22	2
Cash etc.	40	19	21	8	18	4	5
	129	106	31	73	48	45	7
Less: **Current liabilities**							
Short-term borrowings	5	28	6	7	4	3	–
Creditors	94	46	37	39	15	34	5
	99	74	43	46	19	37	5
Net current assets	30	32	(12)	27	29	8	2
NET ASSETS	100	100	100	100	100	100	100
Long-term loans	25	24	14	25	31	45	22
Provisions	14	7	2	8	12	5	–
Shareholders' funds	54	68	84	63	50	50	78
Minority interests	7	1	–	4	7	–	–
CAPITAL EMPLOYED	100	100	100	100	100	100	100
Turnover	226	199	248	175	78	137	6

COBHAM plc
Balance sheet at 31 December 1991

£ million

Fixed assets

Tangible assets, net	1 540
Investments	230
	1 770

Current assets

Stocks	260
Debtors (trade 400; other 100)	500
Cash	240
	1,000

Less: **Current liabilities**

Short-term borrowings	(460)
Trade and other creditors	(510)
	(970)
Total assets less current liabilities	1 800
Long term liabilities	(480)
Provisions for liabilities and charges	(120)
Shareholders' funds	1 200

Profit and loss account for the year ended 31 December 1991

Turnover		2 340
Cost of sales		1 200
Gross profit		1 140
Distribution, administration and research costs		740
Operating profit		400
Interest payable	100	
Less: Interest receivable	(30)	70
Profit before tax		330
Taxation		90
Profit after tax		240
Dividends		80
Retained profit for the year		160

COBHAM plc
Financial ratios
Performance ratios

Return on net assets	=	‾‾‾‾‾	=	19.0%
Profit margin	=	‾‾‾‾‾	=	18.4%
Net asset turnover	=	‾‾‾‾‾	=	1.04 times
Stock days	=	‾‾‾‾‾	=	79.1 days
Trade debtor days	=	‾‾‾‾‾	=	62.4 days

Financial status ratios

Debt ratio	=	‾‾‾‾‾	=	41.6%
Interest cover	=	‾‾‾‾‾	=	4.3 times
Current ratio	=	‾‾‾‾‾	=	1.03
Acid test ratio	=	‾‾‾‾‾	=	0.76

Shareholder ratios

Return on equity	=	‾‾‾‾‾	=	20.0%
Earnings per share	=	‾‾‾‾‾	=	53.3p
Price/earnings ratio	=	‾‾‾‾‾	=	11.25 times
Dividend cover	=	‾‾‾‾‾	=	3.0 times
Dividend yield (net)	=	‾‾‾‾‾	=	3.0%

Section 3
Recording business transactions

BASIC TRANSACTIONS AND COMPANY ACCOUNTS

A company's accounts are summary statements embracing a wide variety of transactions and including only items which can be expressed in financial terms. But how do individual transactions become incorporated in accounts? What is the link between the everyday activities of a business and its published financial statements?

Users of accounting statements need to understand how they relate to identifiable business activities. Managers, for example, should be able to foresee how actions which they are planning will be reflected in the company's financial statements, both in the short and longer term.

To secure this understanding, and to provide the accounting 'language' skills which are needed to comprehend accounting processes, we shall consider in this section:

1 The impact of individual transactions on a company's balance sheet and profit and loss account.
2 The recording of individual transactions in the books of account.
3 The link between the books of account and published financial statements.

In subsequent sections of the book we shall consider in some detail:

- valuation rules for fixed and current assets
- accounting procedures for preparing more complex sets of accounts.

Finally, in Section 12, we shall be able to look in detail at examples of published accounts, knowing what they represent and how they have been drawn up. By that stage we shall have made substantial advances in our understanding of the meaning of company accounts.

The later part of this section starting on page 78 deals in more detail with the accounting records, with the flows of information in recording multiple transactions, and with double-entry bookkeeping. Readers who want to gain a quick general appreciation of how business events affect accounts may prefer to skim the later pages of this section.

IMPACT OF INDIVIDUAL TRANSACTIONS ON ACCOUNTS

The changes which take place in the accounting statements of a company when transactions are recorded will most clearly be seen from a simple example. Let us look therefore at a company which is just starting business, and consider the changes made in its accounts to reflect the main transactions undertaken in the first three months of its existence.

These can be grouped into seven stages:

1 The issue of ordinary shares for cash.
2 Buying fixed and current assets for cash.
3 Selling goods at a profit.
4 Buying stock for cash and on credit.
5 Selling on credit.
6 Paying suppliers.
7 Paying operating expenses and incurring a long-term loan.

In seeing how the above transactions are reflected in accounts, we shall look at the balance sheet and profit and loss account after each stage. The notes underneath each set of accounts explain various matters of interest. To ensure that you understand the procedures, you will be asked to complete the adjustments for one of the later stages.

Stage 1 The issue of ordinary shares

On 1 April 1991 a number of investors subscribed £50 000 to incorporate Initial Enterprises Limited (IE Limited), a small trading company. The balance sheet immediately afterwards is shown below.

IE LIMITED
Balance sheet at 1 April 1991
(Use of funds) ASSETS

Current asset

Cash	£50 000

(Source of funds) LIABILITIES
Capital and reserves

Called up share capital	£50 000

Notes

1 *The company has a separate legal identity*
   Incorporating IE Limited establishes it with a legal identity quite distinct from that of its shareholders. Its memorandum and articles of association define its nature and powers. Ultimate control belongs to the company's shareholders, but to exercise day-to-day control they elect directors.

2 *The company views shareholders' capital as an ultimate 'liability'*
   There is no intention that the company, which is assumed to be a 'going concern', will ever repay the £50 000 it received from its shareholders in return for ordinary shares in the company. Share capital will normally be repaid only when a company ceases to exist (is 'wound up'). From the company's viewpoint, however, such 'permanent' capital is still a 'liability'. Cases have occurred where companies, lacking suitable investment opportunities, have repaid part of their share capital (but such 'reconstructions' require legal approval).

3 *Holding cash is a 'use' of funds*
   At this early stage in its existence, the company holds its funds in the form of cash. It is important to note that holding cash is a *use* of funds, for it emphasizes that resources are always employed *somehow*. There is no way in which a company (or indeed an individual) can be completely isolated from the market.

4 *Assets equal liabilities*
   The balance sheet balances because the company's assets equal its liabilities (counting shareholders' funds as 'liabilities'). They must, because uses of funds necessarily equal sources of funds. This is simply another way of expressing double-entry accounting.

Stage 2 Buying fixed and current assets for cash

During April the company takes steps to set up business:

(a) It buys a small freehold shop for £20 000 cash

(b) It buys stock for £20 000 cash.

At the end of April the balance sheet reflects the changes. The letters against certain items refer to these two transactions.

IE LIMITED
Balance sheet at 30 April 1991

(Uses of funds) ASSETS

		£
Fixed asset		
Freehold shop		20 000[a]
Current asset		
Stock		20 000[b]
Cash	(50 000 − 20 000[a] − 20 000[b])	10 000
		30 000
		50 000

(Source of funds) LIABILITIES

	£
Capital and reserves	
Called up share capital	50 000

Notes

1 The balance sheet still balances. Uses of funds equal sources.
2 No new source of funds has been introduced; but the nature of the assets has changed, although the total has remained the same.

	£	£
Cash	− 40 000	
Freehold shop		+ 20 000
Stock		+ 20 000
	− 40 000	+ 40 000

Stage 3 Selling goods at a profit

The company begins to trade, and during May:

(a) It sells stock for £6 000 in cash

(b) The stock originally cost £5 000.

IE LIMITED
Balance sheet at 31 May 1991
ASSETS

		£'000
Fixed asset		
Freehold shop		20
Current assets		
Stock	20 − 5[b]	15
Cash	10 + 6[a]	16
		31
		51
LIABILITIES		
Capital and reserves		
Called up share capital		50
Profit and loss account		1
Turnover	6[a]	
Less: Cost of sales	5[b]	
		51

Notes

1 Assets originally costing £5 000 have been sold for £6 000, giving the company a *profit* of £1 000. (The figures are now shown in thousands.) This is a new source of capital and is included as part of 'capital and reserves'.
2 Sales, or turnover, are shown in the profit and loss account as a source of revenue.
3 Physical stock has been reduced, so the balance sheet figure is also reduced. The *cost* of stock sold is deducted from the sales revenue in the profit and loss account, to show the profit on the transaction.

Stage 4 Buying stock for cash and on credit

In the first week of June the company:

(a) Buys stock costing £10 000 for cash
(b) Buys stock costing £5 000 on credit.

IE LIMITED
Balance sheet at 5 June 1991   £'000
ASSETS
Fixed asset
Freehold shop   20

Current assets

Stock	$15 + 10^a + 5^b$	30
Cash	$16 - 10^a$	6

                                                                 ——
                                                                 36
                                                                 ——
                                                                 56
                                                                 ══

LIABILITIES
Capital and reserves
Called up share capital   50

Profit and loss account   1

Turnover	6
Less: Cost of sales	5

                                                                 ——
Shareholders' funds   51

Creditor due within one year
Trade creditor 5^b
                                                                 ——
                                                                 56
                                                                 ══

Notes

1 A further source of funds has become available to the business – that allowed by short-term trade credit.
2 A subtotal 'Shareholders' funds £51 000' has been introduced.
3 As in Stage 2, no profit or loss arises on the above transactions. A profit or loss arises only when goods or services are *sold* ('realized').

Stage 5 Selling on credit

In the second week of June, the company sells goods as follows:

(a) Sells for £12 000 cash stock which had cost £10 000
(b) Sells on credit for £6 000 stock which had cost £5 000.

IE LIMITED
Balance sheet at 12 June 1991   £'000
ASSETS
Fixed asset
Freehold shop   20

Current assets

Stock	$30 - 10^a - 5^b$	15
Debtors	$0 + 6^b$	6
Cash	$6 + 12^a$	18

                                                                 ——
                                                                 39
                                                                 ——
                                                                 59
                                                                 ══

LIABILITIES
Capital and reserves
Called up share capital   50

Profit and loss account   4

Turnover	$6 + 12^a + 6^b$	24
Less: Cost of sales $5 + 10^a + 5^b$	20

                                                                 ——
Shareholders' funds   54

Creditor due within one year
Trade creditor   5
                                                                 ——
                                                                 59
                                                                 ══

Notes

1 Sales (turnover) of £6 000 on credit rather than for cash involves the introduction of a new item – debtors.

Stage 6 Paying suppliers

In the remainder of the month the company buys further stock, and pays the amount due to its existing creditor:

(a)   Buys stock for cash £10 000

(b)   Buys stock on credit £3 000

(c)   Pays existing creditor £5 000.

At this stage, you should be able to make the necessary adjustments to record the above transactions. Please alter the figures in the balance sheet at 12 June 1991 (shown opposite). Make sure your amended balance sheet balances!

Then compare your solution with that shown overleaf.

IE LIMITED

Balance sheet at 12 June 1991		£'000
ASSETS		
Fixed asset		
Freehold shop		20
Current assets		
Stock	15	
Debtors	6	
Cash	18	
		39
		59
LIABILITIES		
Capital and reserves		
Called up share capital		50
Profit and loss account		4

Turnover	24
Less: Cost of sales	20

Shareholders' funds		54
Creditor falling due within one year		
Trade creditor		5
		59

IE LIMITED *30* (*working copy*)
Balance sheet at ~~12~~ June 1991 £'000
ASSETS
Fixed asset £'000
Freehold shop 20

Current assets

Stock $+10a +3b + 15 = 28$
Debtors $6 = 6$
Cash $-10a - 5c + 18 = 3$

37

~~57~~ 59

LIABILITIES
Capital and reserves
Called up share capital 50

Profit and loss account

| Turnover | 24 |
| *Less:* Cost of sales | 20 |

4

Shareholders' funds 54

Creditor falling due within one year
Trade creditor $5 + 3b - 5c$ 3 ~~8~~

~~57~~ 59

Notes

1 The payment of a creditor reduces the amount due within one year (trade creditor) and current assets (cash) by the same amount (£5 000).

2 Notice that the two stages of a credit purchase amount, in the end, to the same thing as a cash purchase:

	Liabilities	*Assets*
Cash purchase		Stock up
		Cash down
Credit purchase		
(i) Purchase	Creditor up	Stock up
(ii) Payment	Creditor down	Cash down

IE LIMITED (*final statement*)
Balance sheet at 30 June 1991 £'000
ASSETS
Fixed asset
Freehold shop 20

Current assets
Stock 28
Debtors 6
Cash 3

37

57

LIABILITIES
Capital and reserves
Called up share capital 50

Profit and loss account 4

| Turnover | 24 |
| *Less:* Cost of sales | 20 |

Shareholders' funds 54

Creditor due within one year
Trade creditor 3

57

Stage 7 Paying operating expenses and incurring a long-term loan

Before the accounts of the company for the first quarter can be drawn up, two further transactions must be incorporated:

(a) The company pays £2 000 operating expenses incurred during the quarter
(b) The company borrows £10 000 at 10 per cent a year.

The balance sheet after making these adjustments is set out below.

IE LIMITED
Balance sheet at 30 June 1991   £'000
ASSETS
Fixed asset
Freehold shop   20

Current assets

Stock	28	28
Debtors	6	6
Cash	$3 - 2^a + 10^b$	11

                                                                                                45
                                                                                                65

LIABILITIES
Capital and reserves
Called up share capital   50

Profit and loss account

Turnover	24
Less: Cost of sales	20
	4
Less: Operating expenses	2^a
Operating profit	2

Shareholders' funds   52

Creditor due after more than one year
10% Debenture stock $0 + 10^b$ 10

Creditor due within one year
Trade creditor   3
                                                                                                65

IE LIMITED
Balance sheet, 30 June 1991   £'000
ASSETS
Fixed asset   £'000
Freehold shop   20

Current assets
Stock   28
Debtors   6
Cash   11
                                                                                                45
                                                                                                65

LIABILITIES
Share capital
Called up share capital   50

Profit and loss account*   2*

Shareholders' funds   52

Creditor due after more than one year
10% Debenture stock   10

Creditor due within one year
Trade creditor   3
                                                                                                65

IE LIMITED
Profit and loss account for the three months ended 30 June 1991

                                                                                             £'000
Turnover   24
Less: Cost of goods sold   20

Gross profit   4
Less: Operating expenses   2

Operating profit   2

*Now shown as a separate account (below)

BALANCE SHEET CHANGES: COLUMNAR ANALYSIS

So far we have been content to record, one by one, the effect of each transaction on the profit and loss account and balance sheet. Clearly, this approach could not serve for the numerous transactions which affect even quite small companies in the course of a year.

What is needed is a way for the accountant to collect together transactions of a similar kind, to summarize them, and then to enter them in aggregate in the financial statements. Such a system is still generally referred to as the bookkeeping system, even though, today, the records may not be in the form of 'books', but may be magnetic disks, magnetic tape, or other forms of computer storage.

Before looking at the contents of the 'books of account', however, it will be helpful to establish the links between transactions and financial statements more clearly.

We can extend our ability to undertake transaction analysis by using columnar worksheets, rather than simply altering the financial statements. Set out below is a worksheet which shows the figures for IE Limited at Stage 6:

1 Opening balances.
2 Transactions.

- buy stock for cash £10 000
- buy stock on credit £3 000
- pay existing creditor £5 000.

3 Closing balances.

IE LIMITED – STAGE 6

Shop	Stock	Debtors	Cash		Share capital	P & L	Creditors
20	15	6	18	Opening Balances	50	4	5
	10		(10)	Buy stock for cash			
	3			Buy stock on credit			3
			(5)	Pay creditor			(5)
20	28	6	3	Closing Balances	50	4	3

You will see that the closing figures are those needed to compile the balance sheet for IE Limited at the end of Stage 6. The columnar worksheet provides a flexible way of dealing with transactions which form the link between the opening and closing balance sheet figures. The system can be extended by using more columns, and can deal with many transactions.

You can test this for yourself by preparing the balance sheet and profit and loss account for Cheviot Enterprises Limited for the year ended 31 December

1991 in the spaces provided below. The figures in the balance sheet at 31 December 1990 are set out in the top line of the columnar worksheet on the opposite page. You are asked:

(a) to record in the worksheet the following transactions
(b) to add the columns and compile the closing balances
(c) to extract figures for completing the outline financial statements shown below on this page.

The solution is shown on page 74.

Transactions during 1991:

		£	
1	Sell on credit goods for	2 500	(entered)
2	The goods had cost	1 200	
3	Pay expenses in cash	500	
4	Purchase stock on credit	1 400	
5	Receive cash from customers	2 400	
6	Pay cash to suppliers	1 100	
7	Purchase additional fixed assets for cash	600	

CHEVIOT ENTERPRISES LIMITED
Balance sheet at 31 December 1991
Profit and loss account, year ended 31 December 1991

	£		£
Fixed assets		Turnover	
Plant and machinery		Cost of sales	___
Current assets		Gross profit	
Stock		Expenses	___
Debtors			
Cash	___	Profit for the year	
			═══
	___		
	═══		
Capital and reserves			
Called up share capital			
Profit and loss account	___		
Creditors due within one year			
Creditors	___		
	═══		

CHEVIOT ENTERPRISES LIMITED
Columnar analysis – 1991

Plant and machinery	Stock	Debtors	Cash		Share capital	Profit and loss account	Creditors
2 500	1 300	200	650	Opening balances	4 500		150
		2 500		Sold goods on credit		2 500	
				Cost of goods sold			
				Closing balances			

CHEVIOT ENTERPRISES LIMITED
Columnar analysis – 1991

Plant and machinery	Stock	Debtors	Cash		Share capital	Profit and loss account	Creditors
2 500	1 300	200	650	Opening balances	4 500		150
		2 500		Sold goods on credit		2 500	
	(1 200)			Cost of goods sold		(1 200)	
			(500)	Expenses		(500)	
	1 400			Purchases on credit			1 400
		(2 400)	2 400	Cash received from customers			
			(1 100)	Cash paid to suppliers			(1 100)
600			(600)	Fixed assets purchased			
3 100	1 500	300	850	Closing balances	4 500	800	450

Balance sheet at 31 December 1991

		£
Fixed assets		
Plant and machinery		3 100
Current assets		
Stock	1 500	
Debtors	300	
Cash	850	
		2 650
		5 750
Capital and reserves		
Called up share capital		4 500
Profit and loss account		800
		5 300
Creditor due within one year		
Creditors		450
		5 750

Profit and loss account
year ended 31 December 1991

	£
Turnover	2 500
Cost of sales	1 200
Gross profit	1 300
Expenses	500
Profit for the year	800

Distinguishing additions and deductions

A longer list of transactions would have caused problems in adding up the columns, since plus and minus figures appear together. We can avoid this by dividing each column into two, and showing pluses and minuses on separate sides of the central line within each column. As we shall see, this is what happens in the bookkeeping system used by companies to record transactions.

We shall find also that asset balances appear on one side of the central line and liabilities on the other. Using this approach for Cheviot Enterprises, we shall show asset balances on the left of each column and liability balances on the right. The transactions can then be entered, which may add to, or reduce, the opening asset and liability balances. The closing balances can then be determined by adding up the two sides of each column as shown below.

CHEVIOT ENTERPRISES LIMITED
Columnar analysis – 1991

Plant and machinery		Stock		Debtors		Cash			Share capital		Profit and loss account		Creditors	
+	−	+	−	+	−	+	−		−	+	−	+	−	+
2 500		1 300		200		650		Opening balances		4 500				150
				2 500				Sold goods on credit				2 500		
			1 200					Cost of goods sold			1 200			
							500	Expenses			500			
		1 400						Purchases on credit						1 400
					2 400	2 400		Cash received from customers						
							1 100	Cash paid to suppliers					1 100	
600							600	Fixed assets purchased						
3 100	−	2 700 −1 200	◄ 1 200	2 700 −2 400	◄ 2 400	3 050 −2 200	◄ 2 200			4 500	1 700 ◄ −1 700	2 500	1 100 ◄ −1 100	1 550
3 100		1 500		300		850		Closing balances		4 500		800		450

BOOKS OF ACCOUNT: CASH AND LEDGER ACCOUNTS

Columnar worksheet analysis, while more flexible than a system of altering figures on the face of the balance sheet and profit and loss account, is still not flexible enough. The number of columns which can be recorded across a page is clearly limited; but for even a small company many different headings will be needed – for different revenue and expense items as well as different asset and liability accounts.

In the evolution of accounting this was dealt with by treating each column separately. It became an 'account' in the 'books of account' to give separate accounts for each kind of asset, liability, income and expense. The asset and expense balances are shown on the left of each account, and the liability and income balances on the right. Thus:

Assets	+ on left	− on right
Liabilities	− on left	+ on right
Income	− on left	+ on right
Expenses	+ on left	− on right

The separate accounts can be listed underneath each other, as shown opposite. In total the books of account 'balance' when the opening balances have been entered on each account. This can be checked by taking out a 'Trial Balance', which is a test listing of all the balances in the books of account to see whether they *do* balance.

CHEVIOT ENTERPRISES LIMITED
Trial balance at 1 January 1991

	£	£
Cash	650	
Fixed asset	2 500	
Stock	1 300	
Debtors	200	
Share capital		4 500
Profit and loss		–
Creditors		150
	4 650	4 650

On the next page the transactions for Cheviot Enterprises Limited have been entered in the ledger accounts. The cash account has been separated from the other accounts, and has been described as the 'Cash Book'. The other accounts are grouped together and referred to as 'Ledger Accounts' (sometimes referred to as 'T-accounts').

CHEVIOT ENTERPRISES LIMITED
Separate accounts at 1 January 1991

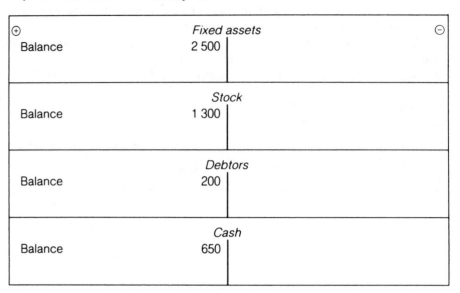

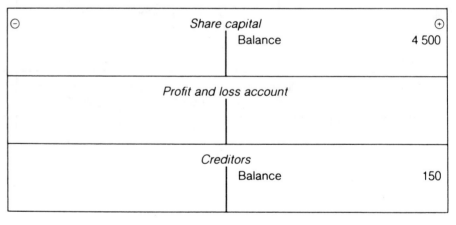

Recording transactions in the books of account

The opening balances have been entered in the cash book (the record containing the cash account) and the ledger (the record containing other accounts). The transactions have then been entered and at each stage the balances on each side of the central line still balance because an entry has been made on each side. This is the *double-entry* system of keeping records.

Looking at each transaction in turn

1	Sell goods on credit	2 500
	+ Profit (sale)	
	+ Debtors	

The entries are on opposite sides of the central line, so both are +. Liabilities increase. Assets increase.

Note when entries are made in the accounts a cross-reference is made to the account which contains the other side of the entry.

2	The goods sold had cost	1 200
	− Stock	
	− Profit (increase expense 'cost of goods sold')	
3	Pay expenses in cash	500
	− Cash	
	− Profit (increase expenses)	
4	Purchase stock on credit	1 400
	+ Stock	
	+ Creditors	
5	Receive cash from customers	2 400
	+ Cash	
	− Debtors	

The two entries are on the *same* side of the central line so they must balance + and −.

6	Pay cash to suppliers	1 100
	− Cash	
	− Creditors	
7	Purchase additional fixed assets	600
	− Cash	
	+ Fixed assets	

Once all the transactions have been entered, the accounts can be 'balanced'; and the balance 'carried down' (c/d) to the next period into which it is 'brought down' (b/d). The balances brought down appear in the closing balance sheet.

You may like to check that the books as a whole still 'balance' after entering the transactions, by listing all the individual balances on the various accounts and taking out a closing trial balance.

Cash book

		⊕			⊖
	Balance	650	3	Profit & loss account =	
5	Debtors	2 400		Expenses	500
			6	Creditors	1 100
			7	Fixed assets	600
				Balance c/d	850
		3 050			3 050
	Balance b/d	850			

Ledger

Share capital

⊖			⊕		
				Balance	4 500

Profit and loss

2	Cost of stock sold	1 200	1	Credit sales	2 500
3	Cash − expenses	500			
	Balance c/d	800			
		2 500			2 500
				Balance b/d	800

Creditors

6	Cash	1 100		Balance	150
	Balance c/d	450	4	Stock	1 400
		1 550			1 550
				Balance b/d	450

Fixed assets

⊕			⊖		
	Balance	2 500		Balance c/d	3 100
7	Cash	600			
		3 100			3 100
	Balance b/d	3 100			

Stock

	Balance	1 300	2	Profit & loss a/c	1 200
4	Creditors	1 400		Balance c/d	1 500
		2 700			2 700
	Balance b/d	1 500			

Debtors

	Balance	200	5	Cash	2 400
1	Sale	2 500		Balance c/d	300
		2 700			2 700
	Balance b/d	300			

THE ACCOUNTING RECORDS AND DOUBLE-ENTRY BOOKKEEPING

We have noted already that the principal elements in the accounting records are the cash book and the ledger. Other subsidiary records needed to make the system operational are 'day books' (or 'journals').

Cash book

The cash book is the accounting record which shows receipts and payments of cash. The kind of information generally included is indicated below. (The actual details come from Problem 3.10: Plumridge Engineering Limited.)

Receipts are entered on the left-hand side (increases in an asset account), and payments on the right-hand side. Accountants refer to the left-hand side as the 'debit' side (abbreviated to Dr), and call the right-hand side the 'credit' side (Cr).

In addition to the date and amount of each cash transaction, the cash book shows the ledger account in which the *other* side of the transaction has been entered as part of the double-entry system (for example: Loan – Fo(lio) 10). The word 'Folio' means 'page', and each ledger account will have a page or folio reference number. It does not matter whether the accounting records are kept in actual books, or on cards maintained by accounting machines, or in computer files: the bookkeeping system is essentially the same.

The cash book records all receipts and payments of cash in the sequence in which they occur, and is thus a 'day book' (or 'journal') record. It is also, as we have seen, in effect a 'ledger account for Cash' – though for convenience it is invariably maintained as a separate record.

Ledger

The ledger is the record which contains the ledger accounts, comprising the various liability and asset accounts; and also the individual accounts for revenues and expenses, the balances on which are transferred, at the end of the accounting period, to the profit and loss account.

A typical ledger account (for debtors) is shown below. Again you will see a reference to the account in which the opposite side of each transaction can be found. Thus the two sides of the transaction 'receipt of £50 000 cash from debtors' have been recorded. In bookkeeping terms the £50 000 receipt would first be entered in the cash book. It would then be 'posted' to (entered in) the debtors ledger account.

It is usual for accounts to appear in the ledger in some sort of classified sequence such as the following, for convenience. (Gaps may be left in the sequence, to allow for new ledger accounts to be opened as required: for example Fo 41 Motor vehicles, Fo 82 Royalty income.)

Shareholders' funds
1 Share capital
2 Capital reserves
3 Profit and loss

Liabilities
10 Loan
11 Creditors

Assets
39 Land and buildings
40 Machinery

50 Debtors

Revenue
80 Sales
81 Investment income

Expenses
90 Wages
91 Purchases

etc.

Dr			**Cash book**			CB Fo 10		Cr
Date	Description	Fo	Amount	Date	Description	Fo	Amount	
			Dr.					Cr.
1.7.90	Balance	b/d	30 000	1.2.91	Machine	40	80 000	
1.11.90	Sale	80	50 000	8.6.91	Wages	90	30 000	
31.12.90	Loan	10	100 000	20.6.91	Creditors	11	40 000	
7.6.91	Debtors	50	50 000					
				30.6.91	Balance	c/d	80 000	
			230 000				230 000	
1.7.91	Balance	b/d	80 000					

Dr			**Debtors book**			Ledger Fo 50		Cr
Date	Description	Fo	Amount	Date	Description	Fo	Amount	
			Dr.					Cr.
1.7.90	Balance	b/d	40 000	7.6.91	Cash	CB10	50 000	
				30.6.91	Balance	c/d	30 000	
30.11.90	Sale	80	40 000					
			80 000				80 000	
1.7.91	Balance	b/d	30 000					

Bookkeeping system

Even a small company may need hundreds of different ledger accounts. The principal asset and liability accounts will be few but the company could have fifty or more suppliers and hundreds of credit customers. Each supplier (creditor) and customer (debtor) will have a separate ledger account, to record his or her position with the company. Obviously, the ledger can soon become very large. Another reason for numerous ledger accounts is the need to analyse expenditure in some detail. Depending on the degree of analysis required for management purposes, there could easily be fifty or more separate expense accounts. Generally the analysis of income requires fewer ledger accounts.

To aid accounting administration, and to avoid unmanageable numbers of ledger accounts in one place, it is general practice to divide the ledger into a number of parts, as illustrated opposite:

	containing accounts for
Creditors (or purchase or bought) ledger	individual suppliers
Debtors (or sales or sold) ledger	individual customers
Nominal ledger	income and expenses
Private ledger	liabilities and assets also "control" accounts for other parts of the ledger

The use of 'control' accounts makes the private ledger, together with the cash book, a self-balancing system. The control accounts will contain the totals of all the detailed entries in the other parts of the ledger. Thus the debtors control account entries for a week will be the totals of all credit sales and all cash receipts from credit customers which have been entered in the individual customer accounts. At any accounting date, therefore, the balance on the debtors control account will equal the sum of all the balances in the individual customers' accounts in the debtors ledger.

With this system, any number of accounts can be maintained, and any number of transactions can be dealt with. By suitable classification of the various accounts, and subdivision for more extensive analysis where suitable, the ledger accounts in the 'books of account' become almost infinitely flexible.

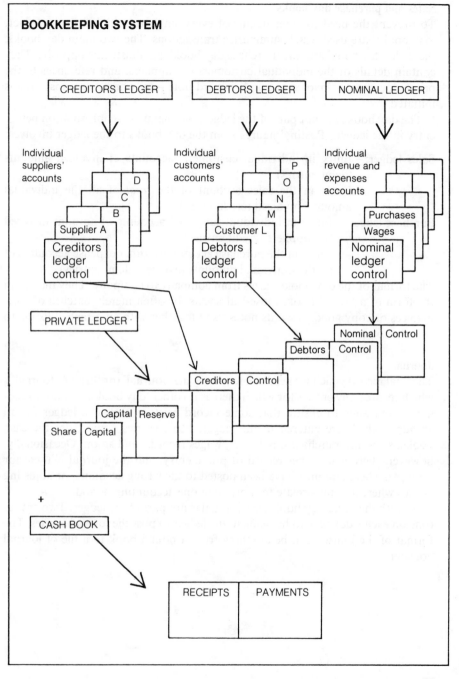

BOOKKEEPING SYSTEM

Sales and purchase day books

To prevent the need to enter details of every single transaction in the ledger, 'day books' are used which summarize transactions. The two main day books, the 'Sales day book' and the 'Purchase day book', are illustrated opposite. They contain details of the individual customers or suppliers, and references to the prime document – invoice or goods inward note – by which the transaction is initiated.

The day books are not part of the ledger: they summarize information before entry in the ledger. 'Posting' figures from the day books to the ledger involves:

Sales ledger: – Entry in individual customers' accounts of invoiced amounts (debit entries)
– Entry in the sales account of the *total* of all the individual amounts invoiced (credit entry).
Purchase ledger: – Entry in individual suppliers' accounts of amount invoiced by suppliers (credit entries).
– Entry in the purchase account (or other expense accounts) of all the individual amounts invoiced (debit entries).

The format of the day books varies from company to company. They may be in the form of a bound book, loose-leaf sheets, or often merely batches of copy invoices or copy goods inwards notes fixed together with an attached listing to give the total.

Journal

The final record which we need to mention is the 'Journal' (or 'Private Journal'), which records any entries for which there is no other 'day book'. The bookkeeping system aims to ensure that some record exists outside the ledger for all amounts which are entered in the ledger. Most entries come from the cash books, sales and purchase day books, wages records, and so on. Occasionally, however, there is no other record of prime entry, and the journal is used: for example, where amounts have been posted to the wrong accounts, or adjusting entries where amounts relate to more than one accounting period.

As with the other day books, the journal is not part of the ledger. Two entries (one on each side) have to be made in the ledger to post the journal entries. The format of the journal can be anything from a bound book to a file of journal vouchers.

Sales day book

Date	Customer	Invoice No.	DL Fo	Invoice amount £
1 March	A Brown	013672	B 12	125
1 March	B Cook	013673	C 8	60
2 March	Jones & Co.	013674	J 17	420
				–
				–
				–
	Total			£2 600

Posted to the *debit* of individual debtors' accounts in the debtors' ledger.

Posted in total to the *credit* of the sales account in the ledger.

Purchase day book

Date	Supplier	Goods inwards note	CL Fo	Invoice amount £
1 March	T Lawson & Co	732105	L 9	261
2 March	E Thompson Ltd	732106	T 7	481
3 March	Electrix Ltd	732107	E 11	160
				–
				–
				–
	Total (for week)			£1 900

Posted to the *credit* of individual creditors' accounts in the creditor's ledger.

Posted in total to the *debit* of the purchases account in the ledger.

Journal

Date		Fo	Debit	Credit
30 June	Land and buildings	39	27 000	
	To capital reserve	2		27 000
	Being revaluation of land and buildings from cost £83 000 to £110 000			

INFORMATION FLOWS

We have considered the various parts of the total accounting system. Set out below is a diagram representing the complete system.

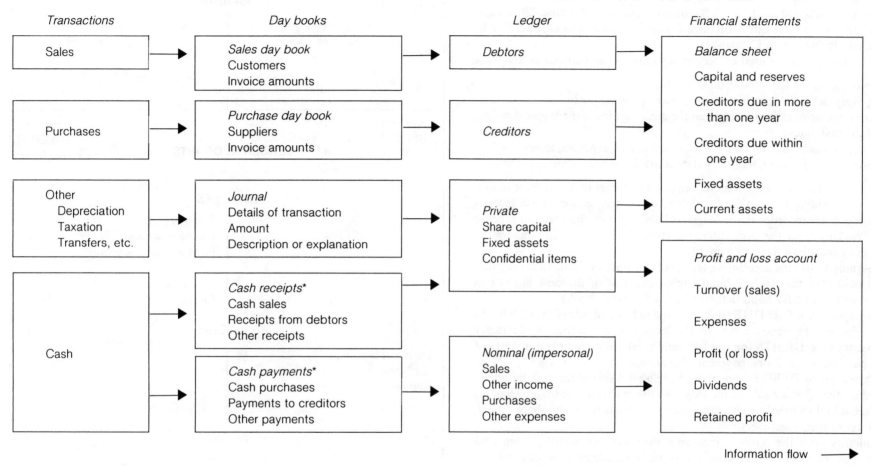

*The cash book constitutes the ledger account for cash, as well as a book of prime entry.

DOUBLE-ENTRY BOOKKEEPING

We have seen that accountants refer to the left-hand side of an account as the 'debit' side, and the right-hand side as the 'credit' side. Thus, for Cheviot Enterprises, which sold stock for £2 500 on credit, instead of saying: 'Plus Sales, Plus Debtors' (as we did earlier on page 77), in practice one would say: 'Credit Sales, Debit Debtors with £2 500'.

The double-entry rules used by accountants can be summarized as follows:

1 Debits are on the left, credits on the right.
2 For every debit entry there must be a corresponding credit.
3 In total the debit entries must equal the credit entries in the ledger accounts and the cash book.
4 Accounts which have DEBIT balances are: assets, expenses, losses.
5 Accounts which have CREDIT balances are: liabilities, income, profits.

The diagram set out opposite may be helpful. The ledger may be regarded as a method of providing an analysis of cash (and credit) transactions. Cash receipts and payments are recorded in the ledger as liability, asset, income, and expense items. Working from the cash entry, therefore, it is easy to tell whether the ledger entry must be a debit or a credit.

In learning to use the accounting terms we can start by thinking simply that cash is paid with the RIGHT hand (right-hand side of the cash book) and received with the LEFT hand (left-hand side of the cash book).

Cash payments or CREDITS (shown on the right-hand side of the cash book) are detailed on the opposite side of the ledger, so the entries in the ledger accounts must be DEBITS (on the left-hand side) – for example purchases of assets, payment to creditors, payment of expenses.

Cash receipts or DEBITS (shown on the left-hand side of the cash book) are detailed on the opposite side of the ledger so the entries in the ledger accounts must be CREDITS (on the right-hand side) – for example issuing share capital, sales, receipts from customers.

Familiarity with the terms comes only with use; but starting from *cash* transactions wherever possible should help you to handle most of the commonest transactions without much trouble.

At first, the use of the neutral accounting terms 'debit' and 'credit' sometimes confuses non-accountants, who tend to attach emotional values to them. Debit is thought to be 'bad', and credit 'good', so that it becomes difficult to think of an asset balance as a debit. It is essential to regard the words merely as technical terms, with no connotation whatever of 'good' or 'bad'. Simply, a debit balance or entry is on the left, a credit on the right.

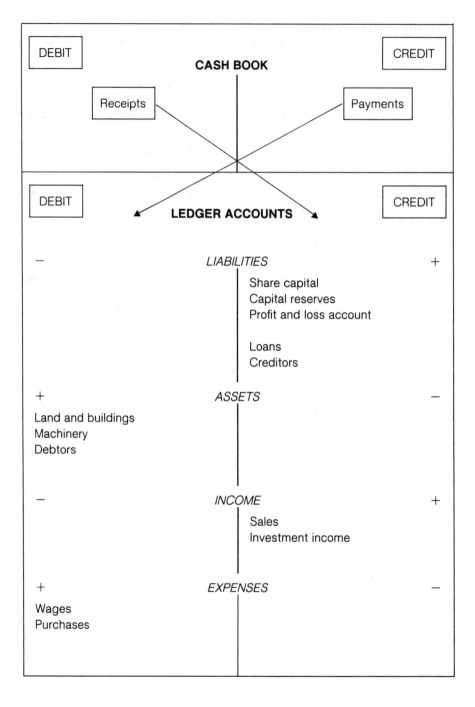

STAGES IN PREPARING PUBLISHED FINANCIAL STATEMENTS

One of the requirements of the Companies Act 1985 is that published financial statements must agree with the books of account. It may be helpful now to summarize the process by which:

- business transactions are recorded in the books of account
- published financial statements are prepared from the books of account.

The major sequence of steps is as follows:

1 Record all transactions for a period in the books of account by means of the double-entry system, either in the cash book and ledger accounts, or in one of the day books and the ledger accounts.
2 Total the entries for a period in the cash book and in each ledger account, and determine the 'balance' at the end of the period on each account.
3 Extract a 'trial balance', by listing all the debit and credit balances at the end of the period on the ledger accounts and on the cash book. If the double-entry process has been followed correctly, the total of the debit balances should always equal the total of the credit balances.
4 Make any necessary adjustments to the trial balance schedule (we shall be describing these in Section 4). We show opposite the *format* of a 'trial balance schedule', using the figures for Initial Enterprises Limited at Stage 7 as an example; but with no entries in the 'Adjustments' columns.
5 Draw up the profit and loss account for the period, and the balance sheet at the end of the period, in suitably classified formats. After all necessary 'adjustments' in the trial balance schedule have been entered in the books of account, every ledger account balance should appear in the balance sheet; either separately, or aggregated with other balances for similar items. (Income and expense account totals for a period will have been transferred, 'closed off', to the profit and loss account for the period.)

IE LIMITED
Trial balance at 30 June 1991

Folio		Trial balance Dr £	Trial balance Cr £	Adjustments Dr £	Adjustments Cr £	Profit and loss Dr £	Profit and loss Cr £	Balance sheet Dr £	Balance sheet Cr £
1	Share capital		50 000						50 000
4	10% Debenture		10 000						10 000
8	Trade creditors		3 000						3 000
10	Freehold shop	20 000						20 000	
20	Stock	28 000						28 000	
21	Debtors	6 000						6 000	
50	Sales		24 000				24 000		
60	Cost of sales	20 000				20 000			
70	Operating expenses	2 000				2 000			
CB	Cash	11 000						11 000	
						22 000	24 000		
	Profit and loss					2 000			2 000
		87 000	87 000			24 000	24 000	65 000	65 000

Note:

The credit entries in the profit and loss column (£24 000) exceed the debit entries (£22 000), so there is a 'credit balance' of £2 000. This is included as such in the balance sheet. In the ledger account for 'profit and loss', the £2 000 would be entered on the debit side as 'balance carried down' in the old period; and it would then be 'brought down' as a credit balance at the opening of the new period.

SUMMARY

In this section we have considered three methods of recording the effect of business transactions on company accounts.

The simplest method, which we used in looking at Initial Enterprises, is to enter each transaction directly on to the face of the balance sheet and profit and loss account. This is a convenient way to demonstrate the basic notion of double-entry, but it is clearly not practicable for any operating business.

The second method, which we adopted for Cheviot Enterprises, is to use columnar analysis to show how individual transactions combine to link the opening balances with the closing balances for a period. Although this adds flexibility, and helps to show the logic of double-entry in terms of 'plus' and 'minus' in the various asset and liability accounts, again it is not practicable for any but the very smallest business.

The third method – 'double-entry bookkeeping' – is the system actually used in business. It consists of entering all transactions first in 'day books' (or 'journals'), and thence in 'ledger accounts'. The possibility of indefinite extension, subdivision, and classification makes this system highly flexible and practical. The development of sophisticated computers in recent years has not affected the underlying principles of double-entry bookkeeping – though, of course, it has substantially changed the physical nature of the 'books of account'.

We saw how the cash book and ledger accounts together form a self-balancing system, because each transaction requires a *double* entry – both a debit entry and a credit entry. Thus the books should always balance. We also briefly considered how preparing financial statements from the books of account involves extracting a 'trial balance', and then making any necessary adjustments.

We shall not repeat here the summary of the rules of double-entry bookkeeping (on page 82), or the description of the sequence of steps from recording business transactions in the books of account to preparing the financial statements (set out on page 83).

Those readers who wish to consolidate their understanding of basic accounting procedures should now turn to the problems (and worked solutions), which will give some practice in working through bookkeeping exercises.

3.1 Definitions

Please write down below your definitions of each of the terms shown. Then compare your answers with those shown overleaf.

(a)   A credit entry

(b)   The cash book

(c)   A journal entry

(d)   Ledger posting

(e)   The 'balance' on a ledger account

(f)   A trial balance

(g)   Debtors' control account

(h)   Double-entry bookkeeping

(i)   Debit

(j)   Write-off

3.1 Definitions

(a) *A credit entry* is an entry on the right-hand side of a ledger account (or cash book). (A debit entry is one on the left-hand side.) It may increase a credit balance on a liability or income account, or *decrease* a debit balance on an asset or expense account. In accounting, the word 'credit' carries no favourable connotation.

(b) *The cash book* is the accounting 'book' (or other record) in which all cash receipts and payments are entered (either individually or in summary). The cash book may be thought of as representing the 'ledger account' for cash; though it *also* represents a 'day book' or 'journal'. Thus if cash of £2 500 is paid out for wages, a credit entry of £2 500 is made in the cash book; and a debit entry of £2 500 is made in the ledger account for wages.

(c) *A journal entry* sets out the debit and credit entries to be made in the ledger (= in ledger accounts) in respect of a business transaction, and describes the nature of the transaction. A journal entry always 'balances', in that the sum of debit entries to be made always equals that of credit entries. Where many transactions of a similar kind occur, they are usually entered in a 'day book' or 'journal', and posted to the ledger in total rather than as separate journal entries.

(d) *Ledger posting* is the process of making entries in the ledger from either the journal (or other day books) or the cash book.

(e) *The 'balance' on a ledger account* is the difference between the total amount of the credit entries and the total of the debits. Where the former are greater, there is said to be 'a credit balance'. Balances are periodically 'carried down' from an earlier period (and 'brought down' in the later period) to simplify the ledger account and to facilitate regular accounting. But the process of carrying down and bringing down merely tidies up the ledger account: it does not (in the double-entry sense) amount to making a ledger posting; and theoretically it would be possible to keep books in which balances were never formally carried down. (Balances are said to be brought *down* when they appear lower down the same page of the ledger, and brought *forward* when they appear at the top of the next page: the process is the same.)

(f) *A trial balance* is a list (in debit and credit columns) of all the balances on ledger accounts (including cash). It forms the basis for preparing published accounts; and it is on the trial balance working schedule that final adjustments are made (see problem 4.5 Wheeler Limited). Since there should be a debit for every credit (or, more accurately, since the sum of debit entries made in ledger accounts should equal the amount of credit entries), the total of debit balances on ledger accounts should equal the total of credit entries at any time. That the trial balance 'balances' does not prove that all the accounting entries in the ledger accounts are correct: but if the trial balance does not 'balance', an error *has* been made somewhere – either in making entries in the ledger accounts, or in extracting the balances and listing them. (Probably the commonest error for beginners is simply forgetting to include the *cash* balance in the trial balance: the 'cash book' is strictly a 'ledger account' for cash, and therefore it is part of the double-entry system.)

(g) *Debtors' control account* is a ledger account in which are entered (in total) all items posted to the accounts of individual debtors. The balance on the control account (which is sometimes called the 'debtors' total account') should then equal the total of the individual balances. As with a trial balance, if the control account balance equals the total of all the individual balances, that does not necessarily mean that all the accounting entries are correct; but disagreement between the two does prove an error has been made somewhere, either in the posting or in the listing. (For example, if a cash receipt from a debtor is wrongly posted to the *debit* of an individual debtor's account, and to the debit of the control account, the control account may agree with the individual accounts: but both are *wrong*, since a cash receipt ought to be *credited* to the debtor's account. In such a case will the trial balance 'balance'? No: because there will be a debit in the cash book for the cash receipt, and another debit in the debtors' control account where there should be a credit. So in the trial balance, the debit balances will exceed the credit balances by twice the amount of the cash receipt.)

(h) *Double-entry bookkeeping* is a system of accounting for business transactions which recognizes the dual aspect, that sources of funds must equal uses of funds. Thus the amount of debit entries in ledger accounts must equal the total amount of credit entries in ledger accounts; and the total of all ledger account balances must be equal as between debit and credit.

(i) *Debit* may be a *noun* (= 'a debit entry') which is the opposite of a credit entry; and which means an entry on the left-hand side of a ledger account. It carries no unfavourable connotation (for instance, assets are debits). Alternatively, 'debit' may be a *verb*, meaning 'to make a debit entry in a ledger account'.

(j) *Write-off* means charging an amount as an expense in the profit and loss account. A 'write-off' means an amount so treated. This appears to be a fairly unusual case of accounting terminology carrying a similar meaning to everyday language. 'All our money spent on pure research turned out to be a complete write-off.'

3.2 Abacus Book Shop Limited (A): Balance sheet

The balances appearing in the books of the Abacus Book Shop Limited at 1 January 1991 were as follows. You are asked to draw up a balance sheet as at that date: Use the Asset:Liability format used in this chapter

	£
Cash	2 000
Trade creditors	1 000
Debtors	2 000
Called up share capital	3 000
Profit and loss account	4 000
Stock	4 000

The answer is shown on the next page (left).

ABACUS BOOK SHOP LIMITED
Balance sheet, 1 January 1991

3.3 Broadhurst Timber Limited: Balance sheet preparation

Here are the balances in the ledger of Broadhurst Timber Limited at 30 September 1991. Please prepare the company's balance sheet at that date. Use the Asset:Liability format used in this chapter

	£'000
Bank overdraft	17
Cash	4
Trade creditors	46
Debtors	38
Dividend	6
Leasehold property	74
Long-term loan	35
Plant and equipment	133
Reserves	83
Share capital	100
Stocks and work-in-progress	49
Tax payable	11

The answer is shown on the next page (right).

3.2 Abacus Book Shop Limited (A)

Solution

ABACUS BOOK SHOP LIMITED
Balance sheet at 1 January 1991

ASSETS		£
Current assets		
Stock	4 000	
Debtors	2 000	
Cash	2 000	
	8 000	
		8 000
LIABILITIES		
Capital and reserves		
Called up share capital	3 000	
Profit and loss account	4 000	
	7 000	
Creditors due within one year		
Trade creditors	1 000	
	8 000	

Notes

1   Did you remember to include the correct headings?:
    Capital and reserves
    Creditors due within one year*
    Current assets
    *The Companies Act 1985 contains formats with the heading 'Creditors: amounts falling due within one year'; but for purposes of simplifying presentation we have used the abbreviated version. (This used to be called Current Liabilities.)

2   Did you insert a subtotal to show the total shareholders' funds? (This is not always explicitly named on the face of the balance sheet.)

3.3 Broadhurst Timber Limited

Solution

BROADHURST TIMBER LIMITED
Balance sheet at 30 September 1991

ASSETS		£'000
Fixed assets		
Leasehold property		74
Plant and equipment		133
		207
Current assets		
Stocks and work-in-progress	49	
Debtors	38	
Cash	4	
	91	
		298
LIABILITIES		
Capital and reserves		
Called up share capital		100
Reserves		83
		183
Creditors due after more than one year		
Long-term loan		35
Creditors due within one year		
Bank overdraft	17	
Creditors	46	
Dividend	6	
Tax payable	11	
		80
		298

3.4 Abacus Book Shop Limited (B): Amending balance sheet

The balance sheet of the Abacus Book Shop Limited on 1 January 1991 is set out below.

During the month of January, the company:

(a) Received £1 000 cash from credit customers
(b) Bought new books for £2 000 in cash
(c) Sold for £3 000 cash, books which had cost £2 000.

You are asked to amend the balance sheet to show the position at 31 January 1991. When you have done so, please compare your answer with that shown overleaf.

ABACUS BOOK SHOP LIMITED
Balance sheet at 1 January 1991

ASSETS		£
Current assets		
Stock	4 000	
Debtors	2 000	
Cash	2 000	
		8 000
		8 000
LIABILITIES		
Capital and reserves		
Called up share capital	3 000	
Profit and loss account	4 000	
		7 000
Creditors due within one year		
Trade creditors	1 000	
		8 000

The answer to this problem is shown at the end of the book.

3.5 Chemical Engineering Company Limited (A): Amending the balance sheet

During August 1991, the Chemical Engineering Company Limited:

(a) Bought for cash new plant costing £10 000
(b) Received £8 000 from debtors
(c) Paid creditors £5 000
(d) Sold on credit for £15 000 goods which had cost £18 000.

You are asked to amend the balance sheet as at 31 July 1991 shown below. (*Note:* For simplicity, all figures are shown in thousands.)

CHEMICAL ENGINEERING COMPANY LIMITED
Balance sheet at 31 July 1991

ASSETS		£'000
Fixed assets		
Plant at cost		28
Current assets		
Stock	25	
Debtors	15	
Cash	12	
		52
		80
LIABILITIES		
Capital and reserves		
Called up share capital		50
Profit and loss account		20
		70
Creditors due within one year		
Trade creditors		10
		80

3.4 Abacus Book Shop Limited (B)

Solution

The amended balance sheet of Abacus Book Shop Limited at 31 January 1991 is shown below. The final balance sheet is shown opposite.

ABACUS BOOK SHOP LIMITED   (*working copy*)
Balance sheet at *31* January 1991
ASSETS   £
Current assets
Stock   *+2000 b −2000 c*   4 000
Debtors   *−1000 a*   *1000* 2000~~2 000~~
Cash   *+1000 a   −2000 b + 3000 c*   *4000* 2000~~2 000~~
                                                  9000 ~~8 000~~
                                                  9000 ~~8 000~~

LIABILITIES
Capital and reserves
Called up share capital   3 000
Profit and loss account   *+1000 c*   *5000* ~~4 000~~
                                                  8000 ~~7 000~~

Creditors due within one year
Trade creditors   1 000
                                                  9000 ~~8 000~~

ABACUS BOOK SHOP LIMITED   (*final statement*)
Balance sheet at 31 January 1991
ASSETS   £
Current assets
Stock   4 000
Debtors   1 000
Cash   4 000
                                                      ———
                                                      9 000
                                                      9 000
                                                      ═══

LIABILITIES
Capital and reserves
Called up share capital   3 000
Profit and loss account   5 000
                                                      ———
                                                      8 000

Creditors due within one year
Trade creditors   1 000
                                                      ———
                                                      9 000
                                                      ═══

Notes

1 Did you remember to alter the *date* of the balance sheet?

2 It may help to identify each transaction with the appropriate letter of the alphabet.

3.6 Identifying debit and credit balances

Indicate for each of the items shown below whether it would normally appear in the ledger as a debit balance or as a credit balance.

When you have entered the amounts in the correct column on the right, please compare your answers with those overleaf.

Note

The twelve items listed are only *some* of the ledger balances: there are others not listed, so that the twelve items in their correct columns will not necessarily 'balance'.

	£	Dr £	Cr £
1 Cash held on deposit	1 000		
2 Payment of telephone expenses	200		
3 Called up share capital	50 000		
4 Debtors	5 000		
5 Cash received on sale of fixed assets	2 000		
6 Stock held for resale	8 000		
7 Received from debtors	1 000		
8 Trade creditors	7 000		
9 Purchase of motor car	5 100		
10 Share premium account	10 000		
11 Paid to suppliers (creditors)	3 000		
12 Payment of loan from bank	1 000		

A solution to this problem is shown overleaf.

3.7 Midmarsh Golf Club: Trial balance errors

The bookkeeper of the Midmarsh Golf Club has been trying for some time to draw up the accounts of the Club for the year ended 31 March 1991. As a preliminary step before making certain final adjustments, he has taken out a 'trial balance' from his ledger accounts and cash book – but it does not balance!

You are asked to examine the result of his efforts, and, on the basis of what you would normally expect, to alter his list to make the two sides balance.

	Bookkeeper's trial balance		Correct trial balance	
	Dr £	Cr £	Dr £	Cr £
Subscription income		3 000		
Cash in hand	200			
Bar stock		950		
Sports equipment for resale	450			
Subscriptions due not received		100		
Electricity bills paid	250			
Staff wages		2 300		
Profit on annual dance		400		
Creditors	300			
Fixtures and fittings	1 400			
Profit on bar sales	500			
Surplus, start of year	2 500			
Repair bills paid		450		
Cleaning expenses	600			
	6 200	7 200		

A solution to this problem is shown overleaf.

3.6 Identifying debit and credit balances

Solution

		£	Dr £	Cr £
1	Cash held on deposit	1 000	1 000	
2	Payment of telephone expenses	200	200	
3	Called up share capital	50 000		50 000
4	Debtors	5 000	5 000	
5	Cash received on sale of fixed assets	2 000		2 000
6	Stock held for resale	8 000	8 000	
7	Received from debtors	1 000		1 000
8	Trade creditors	7 000		7 000
9	Purchase of motor car	5 100	5 100	
10	Share premium account	10 000		10 000
11	Paid to suppliers (creditors)	3 000	3 000	
12	Payment of loan from bank	1 000	1 000	

Notes

1	Asset	Cash previously received
2	Expense	Opposite to cash payment
3	Liability	Opposite to cash receipt
4	Asset	Opposite to sale, which is a credit
5	Reduction of asset	Opposite to cash receipt
6	Asset	Opposite to cash payment or creditor
7	Reduction in asset	Opposite to cash receipt
8	Liabilities	Opposite to expenses or assets
9	Asset	Opposite to cash payment
10	Liability	Opposite to cash receipt
11	Reduction in liability	Opposite to cash payment
12	Reduction in liability	Opposite to cash payment

Once you remember that a cash receipt is a debit in the cash book (and a cash payment a credit), it is obvious that the 'other side' of the transaction in a ledger account must be a credit (or a debit for a cash payment). That automatically solves most of the problems.

3.7 Midmarsh Golf Club

Solution

	Bookkeeper's trial balance		Correct trial balance	
	Dr £	Cr £	Dr £	Cr £
Subscription income		3 000		3 000
Cash in hand	200		200	
Bar stock		950*	950	
Sports equipment for resale	450		450	
Subscriptions due not received		100*	100	
Electricity bills paid	250		250	
Staff wages		2 300*	2 300	
Profit on annual dance		400		400
Creditors	300*			300
Fixtures and fittings	1 400		1 400	
Profit on bar sales	500*			500
Surplus, start of year	2 500*			2 500
Repair bills paid		450*	450	
Cleaning expenses	600		600	
	6 200	7 200	6 700	6 700

Note

Errors are marked with an asterisk (*). Three balances which should be credits are shown as debits (300 + 500 + 2 500), totalling £3 300. And four balances which should be debits are shown as credits (950 + 100 + 2 300 + 450), totalling £3 800. Hence the net effect of correcting the errors is to increase the total of the debit balances by £500 and to reduce the total of the credit balances by the same amount. When a trial balance fails to 'balance', one obvious possible error is that a balance amounting to *half* the difference has been listed on the wrong side.

Answers to these two problems are shown at the end of the book.

3.8 Abacus Book Shop Limited (C): Amending balance sheet

In February, the Abacus Book Shop Limited was given the opportunity to buy a long lease on the shop for £6 000. It decided to do so, and to borrow £3 000 on the security of the lease. It also carried out the following transactions in February. You are asked to amend the balance sheet shown below to reflect these transactions.

		£
(a)	Receipt of loan at 10 per cent p.a.	3 000
(b)	Payment for lease	6 000
(c)	Sales for cash of books which had cost £2000	3 000
(d)	Sales on credit of books which had cost £1500	2 000
(e)	Purchases of books for cash	2 500
(f)	Purchases of books for credit	2 000

ABACUS BOOK SHOP LIMITED
Balance sheet at 31 January 1991

ASSETS		£
Current assets		
Stock	4 000	
Debtors	1 000	
Cash	4 000	
	─────	
	9 000	
	9 000	
LIABILITIES		
Capital and reserves		
Called up share capital	3 000	
Profit and loss account	5 000	
	─────	
	8 000	
Creditors due within one year		
Trade creditors	1 000	
	─────	
	9 000	

3.9 Whitewash Laundry Limited: Preparing accounts

The transactions of the Whitewash Laundry Limited in the quarter ended 31 March 1991 were:

		£'000
(a)	Total invoiced sales in quarter	60
(b)	Cash payments for supplies used in laundry	6
(c)	Cash received from credit customers	55
(d)	Operating costs: wages, fuel, etc. paid in cash	30
(e)	Selling and administrative costs paid in cash	15

The balance sheet at 1 January 1991 is shown below. You are asked to compile a profit and loss account for the quarter to 31 March 1991 (on a separate sheet of paper), and to prepare the balance sheet at the end of the quarter.

WHITEWASH LAUNDRY LIMITED
Balance sheet at 1 January 1991

ASSETS		£'000
Fixed assets		
Laundry and equipment		50
Current assets		
Debtors	30	
Cash	10	
	──	
		40
		──
		90
		══
LIABILITIES		
Capital and reserves		
Called up share capital		75
Profit and loss account		15
		──
		90
		══

3.10 Plumridge Engineering Limited: Transaction analysis

The opening balances of Plumridge Engineering Limited on 1 July 1991 were:

	£'000
Share capital	300
Trade creditors	50
Plant and machinery	200
Stock	80
Debtors	40
Cash	30

These have already been entered in the columnar analysis sheet and ledger accounts shown on the next page.

You are asked to enter the details of the company's transactions in the year ended 30 June 1992 which are set out below, both in the columnar analysis sheet and in the ledger accounts. When you have done this, please transfer the balances to the profit and loss account and balance sheet outline shown on the right-hand side of this page. Since you will be entering the same figures in both, the balances on the ledger accounts should be the same as those shown on the columnar analysis sheet.

Transactions in the year to 30 June 1992 were as follows:

		£'000
(a)	Sold stock for cash	50
(b)	The stock had cost	30
(c)	Borrowed from bank	100
(d)	Bought new machine for cash	80
(e)	Sold stock on credit	40
(f)	The stock had cost	20
(g)	Paid wages and other expenses	30
(h)	Paid suppliers (creditors)	40
(i)	Received from customers (debtors)	50

Note

To simplify your workings, we suggest you enter figures only in thousands of pounds. Ignore depreciation of fixed assets.

The solution to this problem is shown on pages 96 and 97.

PLUMRIDGE ENGINEERING LIMITED
Profit and loss account for year ended 30 June 1992

	£'000
Turnover	
Cost of sales	———
Wages and other expenses	———
Net profit for the year	═══

Balance sheet at 30 June 1992

	£'000
ASSETS	
Fixed assets	
Plant and machinery	
Current assets	
Stock	
Debtors	
Cash	——— ———
	═══
LIABILITIES	
Capital and reserves	
Called up share capital	
Profit and loss account	———
Creditors due after more than one year	
Loan	
Creditors due within one year	
Trade creditors	———
	═══

PLUMRIDGE ENGINEERING LIMITED
Columnar analysis

Plant etc.		Stock		Debtors		Cash		£'000	Share capital		Profit and loss		Loan		Creditors	
+	−	+	−	+	−	+	−		−	+	−	+	−	+	−	+
200		80		40		30		Opening balances		300						50

T-accounts (ledger accounts)

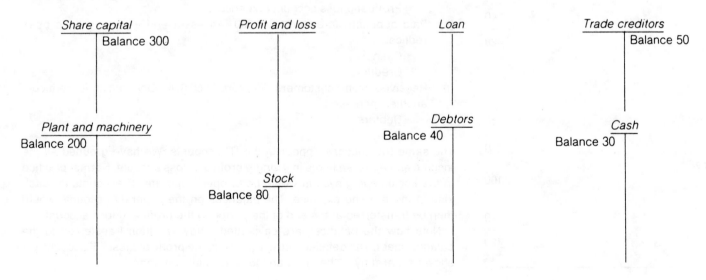

3.10 Plumridge Engineering Limited

Solution

PLUMRIDGE ENGINEERING LIMITED
Profit and loss account for year ended 30 June 1992

	£'000
Turnover	90
Cost of sales	50
	40
Wages and other expenses	30
Trading profit	10

Balance sheet at 30 June 1992

		£'000
ASSETS		
Fixed assets		
Plant and machinery		280
Current assets		
Stock	30	
Debtors	30	
Cash	80	
		140
		420
LIABILITIES		
Capital and reserves		
Called up share capital		300
Profit and loss account		10
		310
Creditors due after more than one year		
Loan		100
Creditors due within one year		
Trade creditors		10
		420

Transaction analysis

The link between the opening balances, the transactions and closing balances is clear in the columnar worksheets.

(a) Sold stock for cash £50 000. Income has increased and so has cash.
  +Profit and loss account (sale)
  +Cash

(b) The stock had cost £30 000. An asset account has been reduced and so has profit.
  −Stock
  −Profit and loss account (cost of sales)

(c) Borrowed from bank £100 000. An asset has increased. A corresponding liability has arisen.
  +Cash
  +Loan

(d) Bought new machine for cash £80 000. One asset goes up, another down.
  +Plant etc.
  −Cash

(e) Sold stock on credit £40 000. Income has increased and so have debtors.
  +Profit and loss account (sale)
  +Debtors

(f) The stock had cost £20 000.
  As in (b).

(g) Paid wages and other expenses £30 000. Cash has decreased and so has income.
  −Cash
  −Profit and loss account (expenses)

(h) Paid suppliers (creditors) £40 000. An asset and a liability have been reduced.
  −Cash
  −Creditors

(i) Received from customers (debtors) £50 000. One asset is reduced, another increased.
  −Debtors
  +Cash

The same transactions appear in the 'T' accounts. We have grouped all the income and expense items in a single profit and loss account. Normal practice in the bookkeeping system would be to open separate 'T' accounts for each kind of income and expense. The balances on the separate accounts would then be transferred at the end of the period to the profit and loss account.

Note how the balances are calculated. They are then transferred to the balance sheet. The detailed entries shown in the profit and loss 'T' account are shown separately in the profit and loss account statement.

3.10 Plumridge Engineering Limited

Solution

Columnar analysis

Plant etc. +	Plant etc. −	Stock +	Stock −	Debtors +	Debtors −	Cash +	Cash −	£'000	Share capital −	Share capital +	Profit and loss −	Profit and loss +	Loan −	Loan +	Creditors −	Creditors +
200		80		40		30		Opening balances		300						50
						50		(a) Sold stock for cash				50				
			30					(b) Cost of sale			30					
						100		(c) Borrowed from bank						100		
80							80	(d) Bought machine								
								(e) Sale on credit				40				
				40												
			20					(f) Cost of sale			20					
							30	(g) Paid wages & expenses			30					
							40	(h) Paid creditors							40	
					50	50		(i) Rec'd from customers								
280	−	80	50	80	50	230	150		−	300	80	90		100	40	50
−50		−50		−50		−150						−80				−40
280		30		30		80		Closing balances		300		10		100		10

T-accounts

Share capital

		Balance	300

Plant and machinery

Balance	200		
Cash	80^d		
	280		

Profit and loss

Stock	30^b	Cash sale	50^a
"	20^f	Credit sale	40^e
Wages etc.	30^g		90
	80		
Balance c/d	10		
	90		90
		Balance b/d	10

Stock

Balance	80	Cost of sale	30^b
		" " "	20^f
			50
		Balance c/d	30
	80		80
Balance b/d	30		

Loan

		Cash	100^c

Debtors

Balance	40	Cash	50^i
Sale	40^e	Balance c/d	30
	80		80
Balance b/d	30		

Trade creditors

Cash	40^h	Balance	50
Balance c/d	10		
	50		50
		Balance b/d	10

Cash

Balance	30	Machine	80^d
Sale	50^a	Wages etc.	30^g
Loan	100^c	Creditors	40^h
Debtors	50^i		
	230		150
		Balance c/d	80
	230		230
Balance b/d	80		

Answers to the next two problems are shown at the end of the book.

3.11 A Green Limited

The balance sheet of A Green Limited (vegetable wholesalers) at 31 March 1991 is shown below. In the three-month period to 30 June the following transactions took place:

		£
(a)	Purchases of vegetables on credit	16 000
(b)	Sales for cash of vegetables which had cost £12 000	15 000
(c)	Sales on credit of vegetables which had cost £4 000	5 000
(d)	Operating expenses paid in cash – wages, vans etc.	2 000
(e)	Cash payments to suppliers	14 000
(f)	Cash receipts from debtors	3 000

You are asked (on separate paper) to:

1 Open up cash book and ledger accounts and enter the opening balances (shown in the 31 March balance sheet).
2 Record the transactions shown above, and balance the accounts.
3 Extract a trial balance.
4 Prepare a profit and loss account for the three months ended 30 June 1991, and a balance sheet as at that date.

A GREEN LIMITED
Balance sheet at 31 March 1991
ASSETS
Fixed assets £
Vans 4 000

Current assets

Debtors	1 000	
Cash	3 000	
		4 000
		8 000

LIABILITIES
Capital and reserves

Called up share capital	3 000
Profit and loss account	2 000
	5 000

Creditors due within one year

Trade creditors	3 000
	8 000

3.12 Precision Engineering Limited

The balance sheet and profit and loss account of Precision Engineering Limited for the half-year ended 30 June 1991 are set out below. During the second half of 1991 the following transactions occurred:

		£'000	
(a)	Sales for cash	350	(cost £250)
(b)	Sales on credit	150	(cost £110)
(c)	Purchases of goods for cash	250	
(d)	Purchases of goods on credit	80	
Additional cash payments:			
(e)	Expenses	100	
(f)	Payments to creditors	90	
Additional cash receipts:			
(g)	Receipts from debtors	130	

Required: On separate paper, open up a cash book and ledger accounts incorporating balances at 30 June 1991. Then:

1 Record the transactions in the books of account for the second half of 1991 and balance the accounts as necessary (work in £'000).
2 Extract a trial balance.
3 Prepare a profit and loss account for the year ended 31 December 1991 and a balance sheet at that date. (Leave the tax provision at £10 000.)

PRECISION ENGINEERING LIMITED
Balance sheet at 30 June 1991

Fixed assets	£'000	
Factory and machinery	250	

Current assets		
Stock	200	
Debtors	60	
Cash	40	
		300
		550

Capital and reserves		
Called up share capital	300	
Profit and loss account	150	
		450

Creditors due within one year		
Trade creditors	100	
		550

Profit and loss account for half-year to 30 June 1991

	£'000
Turnover	400
Cost of sales	300
Gross profit	100
Expenses	70
Profit before tax	30
Tax	10
Profit after tax	20

3.13 Stamford Manufacturing Company Limited

On the basis of the information below you are asked to prepare:

(a) the balance sheet at 31 December 1992

(b) the profit and loss account for the year ended 31 December 1992

A   On 1 January 1992 the Stamford Manufacturing Company Limited was formed to make and sell widgets:
1   Ordinary shares were sold to provide £200 000 capital;
2   £160 000 was borrowed short-term from a bank at 10 per cent a year interest.

B   During the year 1992 the following cash payments were made:
1   Premises rented for £12 000 (Commercial expense);
2   Machines purchased for £240 000 (Fixed assets);
3   6 000 widget castings bought for £10 each (Stocks) – £48 000 cash paid, £12 000 still owing at year-end;
4   Operator's wages of £12 000 (Stocks). During 1992 all 6 000 widget castings were machined by the operator into finished widgets;
5   Manager's salary £24 000 (General expense).

C   Depreciation on the machines is charged at 10 per cent a year (Stocks).

D   During 1992 5 000 finished widgets were sold at £40 each – £180 000 cash received, £20 000 still receivable at year-end.

E   At the end of 1992 the bank loan was repaid, plus £16 000 interest.

F   Tax for 1992 was assessed at £10 000. £4 000 was paid in cash during the year, and £6 000 remained payable at the year-end.

G   An interim dividend of £16 000 was paid in cash to shareholders during 1992, and a final dividend of £20 000 was proposed in respect of the year 1992, to be paid in April 1993.

Please prepare the 1992 accounts by filling in the *pro forma* balance sheet and profit and loss account shown.

STAMFORD MANUFACTURING COMPANY LTD
Balance sheet at 31 December 1992

	£'000	£'000
Net Fixed Assets		
Fixed assets, at cost		
Less: accumulated depreciation	———	
Current Assets		
Stocks (inventory)		
Debtors (accounts receivable)		
Cash	———	
		———
		═══
Current Liabilities		
Bank Loan		
Creditors (accounts payable)		
Taxation payable	———	
Capital and Reserves		
Called-up Share Capital		
Retained Earnings	———	
		———
		═══

STAMFORD MANUFACTURING COMPANY LTD
Profit and loss account for the year 1992

	£'000
Sales	
Cost of Sales	____
Gross Profit	
Commercial Expenses	____
Operating Profit	
Interest Expense	____
Profit Before Tax	
Taxation Expense	____
Net Profit After Tax	====

Statement of retained earnings

	£'000
(Balance at 1 January 1992)	
Net Profit for 1992	____
Available for Distribution	
Less: Dividends payable in respect of 1992	
Interim	
Final	____
Retained Earnings, end of year	====

3.14 Basil Trading Limited: preparing accounts

There has been a small fire in the offices of Basil Trading Limited in which you have been working. You have managed to recover the following data for the year ended 31 December 1990.

	DR £m	CR £m
Wages	18.4	
Issued Share Capital		7.0
Accumulated depreciation (at 1.1.90)		6.0
Sales		72.0
Rent and rates expense	3.6	
Cash	2.5	
Dividend	4.0	
Dividend payable		2.0
Audit fee expense	0.2	
Stock (at 1.1.90)	6.0	
Debtors	8.0	
Salaries expenses	3.4	
Plant and machinery	17.0	
Land and buildings	13.0	
Creditors		3.6
Accumulated Profit (at 1.1.90)		10.0
Purchases expense	32.0	
Lighting and heating expense	2.0	
Loan payable		10.0
Loan interest expense	0.5	
	110.6	110.6

In addition the figures above need adjustment for the following items.
    Closing stock is to be valued at £4 million.
    Loan interest of £300 000 is payable but has not been allowed for in the accounts.
    Depreciation of £1.5 million is chargeable for 1990.
    Tax is to be charged on the profits for the year at 35%.
    Provision of £600 000 is to be made against debtors.
    £1 000 000 of the loan is repayable on 1 July 1991.
The task now is to prepare
a)   a profit and loss account for 1990
b)   a balance sheet as at 31 December 1990.

Section 4

Measuring profit or loss

PROFIT DETERMINATION AND THE ACCOUNTING PROCESS

So far we have not discussed problems of calculating profit. We have simply assumed that revenue and expenses can be measured, and that revenue less expenses equals profit (or loss when expenses exceed revenue). In practice, however, elaborate accounting rules are needed to deal with some of the complexities that often make measurement difficult.

Even with such rules, the profit reported for a given period is often subject to a wide margin of uncertainty. Problems arise which necessarily involve subjective judgements. (In this section we deal only with historical cost accounting. Section 11 discusses the additional problems which arise in trying to allow for the effects of inflation on accounting.)

Consider the results of the accounting process for a typical business. Businesses are normally ongoing concerns, and to calculate profit requires 'freezing' their financial position at regular intervals (say annually) in order to measure (value) all the constituent parts. The diagram below shows this.

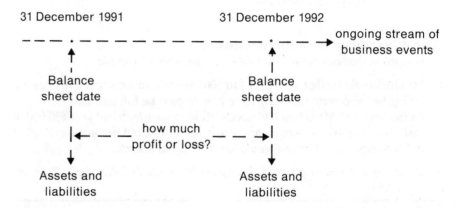

Measuring transactions which are incomplete at the accounting date presents problems. Their nature may become clearer by looking at two simple examples overleaf. In the first example, all transactions occur within a single accounting period; the second involves *incomplete* transactions.

Profit determination: all items within one accounting period

A Green runs a wholesale greengrocery business. In the year ended 31 December 1992 his cash transactions were:

	£'000
Sales	1 000
Purchases of goods	800
Operating expenses	120

There were no other transactions; and there was no opening or closing stock.

The revenue and expenses figures are known amounts which clearly relate to 1992, and the net profit before tax is £80 000.

	£'000
Sales	1 000
Cost of sales (purchases)	800
Gross profit	200
Operating expenses	120
Net profit before tax	80

Profit determination: incomplete transactions

Now suppose that *in addition* to the facts in the above example:

1 Mr Green sold further goods for £10 000 on credit to a customer in financial difficulties who seems unlikely to be able to pay the full amount.
2 At the year-end Mr Green had goods left in stock which had cost £20 000 in cash. Half the goods were highly perishable and would become worthless if not sold next day. The rest would keep for up to a week.

Now there is a range of possible figures for Mr Green's 1992 profit. Two are shown below:

Version A

	£'000	£'000
Sales		1 010
Purchases	800	
Less: Closing stock	20	
		780
Gross profit		230
Operating expenses		120
Net profit		110

Version B

	£'000	£'000
Sales		1 010
Less: Bad debt		10
		1 000
Purchases		800
Gross profit		200
Operating expenses		120
Net profit		80

The difference between the two profit figures results from the different views taken about the outstanding debtor of £10 000 and the remaining stock which had cost £20 000. Both views depend on *assumptions about uncertain future events.*

Version A assumes that Mr Green will collect the whole £10 000 debt and sell the entire remaining stock. Thus the 1992 profit is £110 000. If the debt proves to be bad and the stock is not sold, then under Version A profits in 1993 will have to be reduced by £30 000 as these amounts are written off.

Version B takes a gloomy view about both matters; and reports 1992 profits of only £80 000. If in the end Mr Green does collect the debt and sell the stock, then under Version B the accounts for 1993 will show an extra profit of £30 000.

The 'true' 1992 profit varies between £80 000 and £110 000, depending on one's views about the debtor and the stock at the year-end. Such judgements affect the reported profits of *two* periods, not just one. Notice that profit for a period need not be the same as the cash inflow from operations.

Profit measurement as a valuation process

We can extend our conception of profit by defining it not only as 'revenue less expenses' but also as 'the change in book value of shareholders' funds' during an accounting period. The next example shows a profit after tax in 1992 of £100 000, a figure which is both 'sales less expenses' and also 'closing shareholders' funds less opening shareholders' funds'.

In calculating profit as the difference between the closing and opening shareholders' funds figures, we assume that we adjust for any capital transactions during the period. Thus if £150 000 new capital had been introduced during the year, the difference in shareholders' funds would amount to £250 000, of which only £100 000 is profit. We would also have to add back any dividends paid, and make any other appropriate adjustments.

Valuation may be simple or difficult depending on the nature of the asset. There will be no problem with cash. But if (as is usual) current assets include stocks or debtors, judgements will have to be made concerning their value at the balance sheet date. The position is still more complex with fixed assets, as we shall see in Section 5.

Defining profit in these two interrelated ways may make it easier to understand why, in calculating profit or loss, the methods of valuation used for balance sheet amounts are just as relevant as determining the amount of income or expenses to report. They are two aspects of the same process dealing with incomplete transactions. Changes in balance sheet figures may affect those for profit or loss, and vice versa.

Profit and loss account for the year ended 31 December 1992

	1992 £'000	1991 £'000
Sales	1 200	1 000
Cost of sales	900	800
Gross profit	300	200
Operating expenses	150	120
Profit before tax	150	80
Taxation	50	30
Profit after tax	100	50

Balance sheet at 31 December 1992

	1992 £'000	1991 £'000
Fixed assets	250	200
Net current assets	300	250
Net assets	550	450
Share capital	300	300
Profit and loss account	250	150
Shareholders' funds	550	450

Profit = sales less expenses
       = closing less opening shareholders' funds

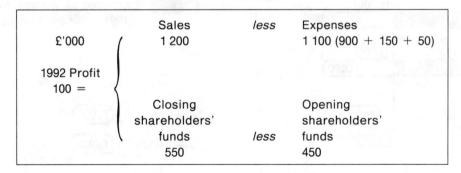

ACCRUAL ACCOUNTING

In looking at measurement of profit, we want to get a clear idea of what the figures in company accounts mean, how they have been calculated, and what is the margin of error. We shall see that the accuracy of published results will vary according to the nature of the business. The larger the number of incomplete transactions, the longer their timespan, and the greater their significance, the wider will be the range of possible profit figures.

We shall consider the problems of measuring profit and loss under two main headings: net current assets and fixed assets. The next section will deal with fixed assets and depreciation provisions. In this section we shall look at accrual accounting, the measurement of sales revenue and of certain expenses, the valuation of stock and long-term contracts in progress, and finally at so-called 'extraordinary' items.

We have seen that the accounting process seeks to 'freeze' the business as at the balance sheet date. But, in the normal course of events, many transactions will be in progress at this date and calculating the profit or loss for a period will require adjustments. Indeed, many of the problems in accounting stem from the 'chopping up' of a business's whole life into a series of much shorter accounting periods.

Example

Accrual accounting recognizes income and expenses when they accrue due, not when cash receipts or payments actually occur. It is therefore important to distinguish between cash receipts and 'income', and between cash expenditures and 'expenses'.

In analysing the accounts of a small property company for the year ended 31 December 1991, for example, one might find the income and expense adjustments as set out on the following pages. These illustrate the differences between cash amounts received and paid in a period and those amounts reported as accounting income and expenses.

Cash receipts and accrual accounting income

The following transactions are illustrated below:

(a) annual rent of £1 000 received in advance in July 1990, half of which relates to 1991

(b) annual rent of £500 received in advance in January 1991, all of which relates to 1991

(c) annual rent of £800 received in advance in April 1991, one quarter of which relates to 1992

(d) half-yearly rent of £600 received in arrear in March 1992, half of which relates to 1991.

Note that in accounts prepared on an accrual basis, income is allocated to the period to which it *relates* as opposed to that in which *cash is received*. Thus 'rent income' for 1991 is £1 900, although only £1 300 cash was actually received in 1991.

1991 income

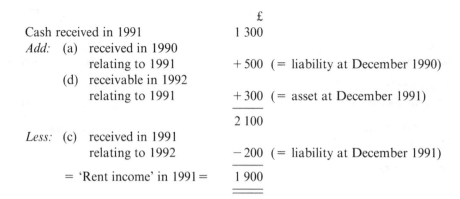

		£	
Cash received in 1991		1 300	
Add: (a)	received in 1990 relating to 1991	+ 500	(= liability at December 1990)
(d)	receivable in 1992 relating to 1991	+ 300	(= asset at December 1991)
		2 100	
Less: (c)	received in 1991 relating to 1992	− 200	(= liability at December 1991)
= 'Rent income' in 1991 =		1 900	

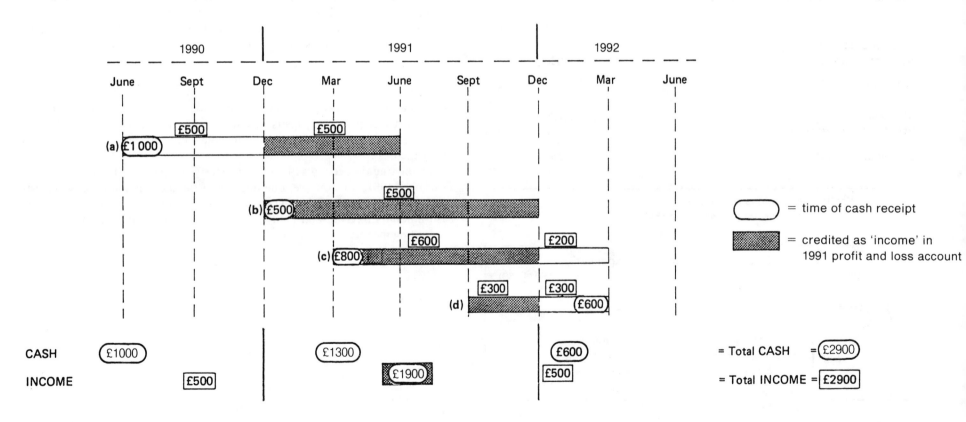

104

Cash expenditure and accrual accounting expense

The following transactions are illustrated below:

(e) annual rent of £800 paid in advance in October 1990, three-quarters of which relates to 1991

(f) half-yearly rent of £600 paid in advance in October 1991, half of which relates to 1992

(g) annual rent of £500 paid in arrear in December 1991, all of which relates to 1991

(h) annual rent of £400 paid in arrear in June 1992, half of which relates to 1991

Note that in an accrual accounting system rent payable is charged in the period to which it *relates*, not in the period in which *cash is paid*. Thus 'rent expense' for 1991 is £1 600 although only £1 100 cash was actually paid in 1991.

1991 expense

			£	
Cash paid in 1991			1 100	
Add:	(e)	paid in 1990 relating to 1991	+600	(= asset at December 1990)
	(h)	payable in 1992 relating to 1991	+200	(= liability at December 1991)
			1 900	
Less:	(f)	paid in 1991 relating to 1992	−300	(= asset at December 1991)
	= 'Rent expense' in 1991 =		1 600	

On the next page are shown the entries in the books of account to record the rent items receivable and payable.

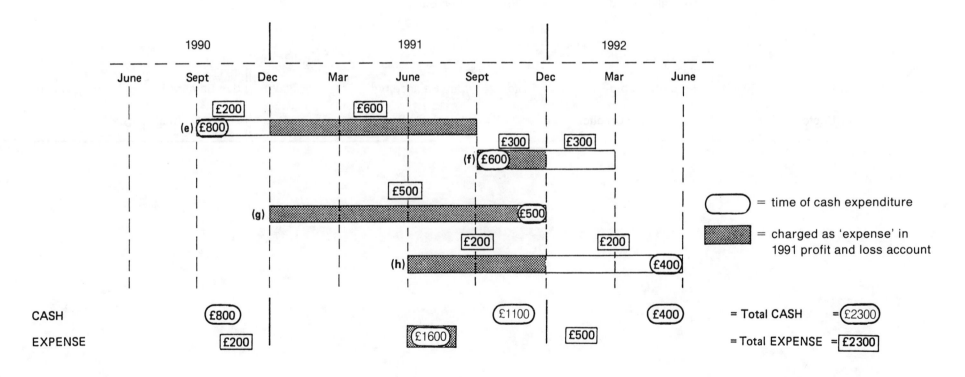

ENTRIES IN THE BOOKS OF ACCOUNT

Receipts and income	Expenditure and expense

Cash

1991		£		£
Jan (b) Rent received		500		
Apr (c) Rent received		800		
		1 300		

Cash

	£	1991		£
		Oct (f) Rent paid		600
		Dec (g) Rent paid		500
				1 100

Rents receivable

1991	£	1991	£
Dec Profit and loss account:		Jan Balance b/d	500(a)
1991 'income'	1 900	Jan Cash	500(b)
Dec Balance c/d	200(c)	Apr Cash	800(c)
		Dec Balance c/d	300(d)
	2 100		2 100
1992		1992	
Jan Balance b/d	300(d)	Jan Balance b/d	200(c)
'Debtor'		'Creditor'	

Rents payable

1991	£	1991	£
Jan Balance b/d	600(e)	Dec Profit and loss account:	
Oct Cash	600(f)	1991 'expense'	1 600
Dec Cash	500(g)	Dec Balance c/d	300(f)
Dec Balance c/d	200(h)		
	1 900		1 900
1992		1992	
Jan Balance b/d	300(f)	Jan Balance b/d	200(h)
'Prepayment'		'Accrued charge'	

Rentwell Limited: accrual accounting adjustments

Rentwell Limited's bookkeeper had drawn up the profit and loss account and balance sheet shown opposite. (Tax is ignored to simplify the example.)

The company's auditor found that adjustments were required to cover the following transactions:

(a) annual rent received of £40 000 for one property, relating to the year ending in September, had all been included in the accounts to 30 June

(b) no adjustment had been made in the accounts for rent payable by Rentwell on Blackacre. This property was held on a long lease at £20 000 per annum, with rent payable six-monthly in arrears on 31 March and 30 September

(c) rates of £4 000 per annum on another property had been paid for a year in advance on 1 April. No allowance had been made for the amount paid in advance at 30 June

(d) repair work for which Rentwell was liable was being carried out at 30 June on one of the company's properties. The work, which cost £2 000, was not finished until 31 July, and was estimated to be half finished at 30 June.

You are asked to amend the draft profit and loss account and balance sheet opposite to show the correct final figures for the year ending 30 June 1992. Strike out any figures which need changing and insert the correct ones. The answer is shown overleaf.

RENTWELL LIMITED

Profit and loss account for the year ended 30 June 1992		£'000
Rents receivable		600
Less: Rents payable	400	
Rates	50	
Other expenses	40	
		490
Net profit		110

Balance sheet at 30 June 1992		£'000
Fixed assets		
Leasehold properties		450
Current assets		
Debtors and prepayments	50	
Cash	10	
	60	
Less: **Creditors due within one year**	10	
		50
Total assets less current liabilities (Net assets)		500
Capital and reserves		
Called up share capital		300
Profit and loss account		200
(Capital employed)		500

107

RENTWELL LIMITED – Working paper

Profit and loss account for the year ended 30 June 1992

			£'000
Rent receivable	−10 a		590 ~~600~~
Less: Rents payable	+5 b	405 ~~400~~	
Rates	−3 c	47 ~~50~~	
Other expenses	+1 d	41 ~~40~~	493 ~~490~~
Net profit			97 ~~110~~

Balance sheet at 30 June 1992

			£'000
Fixed assets			
Leasehold Properties			450
Current assets			
Debtors and prepayments	+3c	53 ~~50~~	
Cash		10	
		63 ~~60~~	
Less: **Creditors due within one year**			
Creditors and accrued charges	+5b	16 ~~10~~	
	+1d	10	
		26	
Amount received in advance +10 a			37 ~~50~~
Total assets less current liabilities (Net assets)			487 ~~500~~
Capital and reserves			
Called up share capital			300
Profit and loss account			187 ~~200~~
Capital employed	$\frac{90}{110}$ = 200	B/F 90 to $\frac{97}{187}$ = −13	487 ~~500~~

RENTWELL LIMITED – Final accounts

Profit and loss account for the year ended 30 June 1992

		£'000
Rents receivable		590
Less: Rents payable	405	
Rates	47	
Other expenses	41	493
Net profit		97

Balance sheet at 30 June 1992

		£'000
Fixed assets		
Leasehold Properties		450
Current assets		
Debtors and prepayments	53	
Cash	10	
	63	
Less: **Creditors due within one year**		
Creditors and accrued charges	16	
Amount received in advance	10	
	26	
		37
Total assets less current liabilities (Net assets)		487
Capital and reserves		
Called up share capital		300
Profit and loss account		187
(Capital employed)		487

Rentwell Limited – adjusted trial balance

This case illustrates how the adjustments affect both the profit and loss account and the balance sheet. Obviously the changes would not normally be made on the face of the accounts. It is for adjustments of this kind that one would use the 'adjustments' column we saw in the trial balance in Section 3. The adjustments would then be incorporated in the books of account when the 'final' accounts had been completed.

The entries would appear on the trial balance schedule as follows:

	Trial balance		Adjustments		Profit and loss		Balance sheet	
	Dr	Cr	Dr	Cr	Dr	Cr	Dr	Cr
	£'000	£'000	£'000	£'000	£'000	£'000	£'000	£'000
Called up share capital		300						300
Profit and loss, balance b/f		90[1]						90[1]
Leasehold properties	450						450	
Debtors and prepayments	50		3[c]				53	
Cash	10						10	
Creditors		10		5[b] / 1[d]				16
Received in advance				10[a]				10
Rents receivable		600	10[a]			590		
Rents payable	400		5[b]		405			
Rates	50			3[c]	47			
Other expenses	40		1[d]		41			
					493			
Profit for the year[2]					97[2]			97[2]
	1 000	1 000	19[3]	19[3]	590	590	513	513

1   This is the opening balance. The items which make up the net profit for the year are shown individually.
2   The profit for the year, £97 000, is added to the balance brought forward on the profit and loss account, £90 000, to give the figure carried forward on the balance sheet, £187 000.
3   Notice that the adjustments 'balance', since they follow the double-entry principle.

Accrual accounting: a summary

We have seen that we must distinguish cash receipts from income, and cash expenditure from expense. Accounts recognize income and expense when they accrue due, not when they are actually received or paid in cash. Amounts paid or received in advance or in arrears are the subject of adjustments in preparing accounts, and give rise to debtor or creditor balances in the balance sheet.

Merely because a company has made a profit does not imply that it has the same amount of cash on hand. The profit may result from credit sales for which it has not yet received cash; or it may already have spent the cash, for example on promoting future products, or on investment in fixed assets.

It is often easy to apportion income and expense on a time basis, including amounts in the period to which they relate.

Another basis for making adjustments, which we shall consider later in this section, is to charge expense in the accounting period in which related revenue is recognized. Thus the balance sheet may carry forward expenditure from the period in which it is incurred to 'match' it in a later period against the revenue which it has helped to generate. Here there are much greater problems, for this kind of 'deferred revenue expenditure' may sometimes represent an 'asset' of dubious value. How can anyone tell, for example, whether a film costing £20 million is ever going to recover its cost? Yet a judgement must be made for accounting purposes, which will affect the results of more than one accounting period.

We should emphasize that not all expenses *can* be directly matched against specific revenue. Against which sales, for instance, should the audit fee be matched? Or what about the cost of a flight to Brazil in an (unsuccessful) attempt to win a large sales order? Nevertheless the only basis for carrying forward costs (as assets) on the balance sheet is a reasonable expectation of sufficient *future* revenues against which to match them.

Summary of accrual accounting adjustments

We can distinguish seven different kinds of expenditure/expense (or receipt/income) mix, as shown below, of which five relate in some way to this year.

EXPENDITURE	'EXPENSE'		
1 Last year	Last year	=	Last year
2 Last year	This year	=	Asset start of year
3 This year	Last year	=	Liability start of year
4 This year	This year	=	This year
5 This year	Next year	=	Asset end of year
6 Next year	This year	=	Liability end of year
7 Next year	Next year	=	Next year

RECEIPTS	'INCOME'		
1 Last year	Last year	=	Last year
2 Last year	This year	=	Liability start of year
3 This year	Last year	=	Asset start of year
4 This year	This year	=	This year
5 This year	Next year	=	Liability end of year
6 Next year	This year	=	Asset end of year
7 Next year	Next year	=	Next year

MEASURING TURNOVER (SALES REVENUE)

The turnover (sales) figure is crucial in calculating profit for a period. Until the moment accounts recognize sales revenue, they treat any costs incurred in providing goods for sale as 'stock', and carry them forward as an asset on the balance sheet. Only when accounts recognize sales revenue does 'cost of goods sold' become an expense. Until that point there can be no profit.

The diagram below represents events in a manufacturing business. The business purchases raw materials, and then uses labour and capital equipment to convert them into finished goods (point A). When the business sells the finished goods on credit, legal title passes to the purchaser, who becomes a debtor (point B). Finally the customer pays cash (point C) to settle his account.

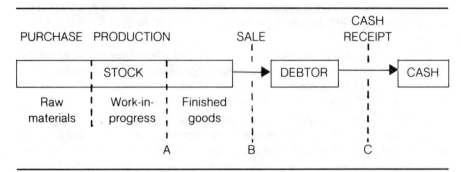

FLOW OF ACTIVITY

Accounts could possibly recognize sales revenue at any of the three points A, B, or C in the diagram. The process of adding value begins when raw materials are purchased; but it is hard to tell how much of the ultimate sales value has really been earned, either at this stage or later, when the manufacturing process has begun but not yet ended. (The various interim stages of partly-completed goods are known as work-in-progress.) Production of the goods is complete at point A, but prudence forbids accounts to include any profit yet.

When the goods are delivered, the seller sends the buyer an invoice, and legal title passes. It is at this stage (point B) that accounts recognize sales revenue (and hence profit). Sales revenue for a period thus represents the total value of goods and services invoiced to customers (excluding VAT).

A seller makes no profit unless he gets paid, but accrual accounting does not wait until a business actually receives cash (point C) before treating sales as income. That would be *too* conservative, since customers who fail to pay without good reason can legally be sued for the full sales price. And there are ways to provide for possible bad debts (see page 113).

Where goods are delivered 'on approval' or 'on sale or return', legal ownership does not pass. The 'selling' company's accounts must continue to show the goods as stock (at cost), and not yet record any profit until the sale is agreed.

Where customers, by agreement, return goods after a genuine sale, any such 'cancelled sales' should be deducted from total turnover. The goods returned are added to stock at cost (thus eliminating any profit); but if they are damaged or have otherwise lost value, the cost may need to be written down.

With hire-purchase transactions, profit is spread over time, and only part is recognized on the signing of the contract. With instalment sales, however, total profit on the sale is normally recognized at once, since title to the goods passes straight away. But any profit deriving from finance charges on outstanding instalments is spread over the contract period.

Sales turnover is often regarded as a key sign of business activity. Of course, it may not match *production* if the level of stocks is changing. Even if stock levels remain constant, the net turnover in accounts may not reflect changes in the physical volume of activity, since selling prices may have changed. The basic formula is:

$$\text{Sales Turnover} = \text{Price} \times \text{Volume}$$

SSAP 25 requires accounts to analyse turnover, profit, and net assets between separate classes of business and between geographical areas (see Section 12).

A common problem in interpreting turnover figures, and their effect on profit over time, is a change in 'sales mix' in a multi-product company. Even if profit margins on each item have fallen, total profit (and the apparent average profit margin) can increase over the previous period if more of a high-profit item is sold and less of a low-profit item. An example is shown below.

	Last year			This year		
	Profit margin	Weight		Profit margin	Weight	
Product A	18%	$\times \frac{1}{6}$	= 3	16%	$\times \frac{1}{2}$	= 8
Product B	$13\frac{1}{2}$%	$\times \frac{1}{3}$	= $4\frac{1}{2}$	12%	$\times \frac{1}{3}$	= 4
Product C	7%	$\times \frac{1}{2}$	= $3\frac{1}{2}$	6%	$\times \frac{1}{6}$	= 1
Average			11%			13%

111

MEASURING EXPENSES

Having dealt with cost of sales, let us now consider briefly four other kinds of expense that can cause problems of allocation between accounting periods:

(a) research and development costs
(b) marketing costs
(c) bad debts
(d) pensions.

(a) Research and development costs

Many companies invest large sums of money in basic and applied research and in developing new products. Writing off regular fairly small amounts of R&D spending in the year in which it is incurred causes few problems. But what if large investments in product development arise at irregular intervals? Recording expenses in one period and related revenues in later periods could seriously affect the company's profit pattern.

Although the dividing line may not always be very clear, we can recognize three separate categories of research and development: basic (or 'pure') research, mainly for the general advancement of scientific or technical knowledge; applied research, mainly for exploiting basic research; and product development, for introducing or improving specific products or processes.

SSAP 13 treats investment in basic and applied research as normal spending required to maintain a company's business and competitive position. No specific period will benefit, so it is best to write these research costs off as expenses as they are incurred. (A similar argument also applies to staff training costs.)

Many development projects have uncertain future benefits, so their costs will also be written off as incurred. However companies may (not 'must') carry forward development expenditure as an intangible fixed asset on the balance sheet, and amortise it over the periods expected to benefit, if: (a) there is a clearly defined project with separately identifiable expenditure; (b) the project is technically feasible and commercially viable; and (c) there is reasonable expectation of sufficient future benefits at least to cover all the costs. Few UK companies choose to avail themselves of this option, preferring to let the concept of 'prudence' outweigh that of 'matching'.

SSAP 13 requires companies to disclose the total amount of R&D expenditure charged against profit, analysed between current year spending and amounts amortised from deferred expenditure, including the amortisation of R&D tangible fixed assets.

(b) Marketing costs

The treatment of selling expenses is generally straightforward, the amount incurred in a year being charged as an expense in that year. One obvious example is sales commission which directly relates to items of revenue. (Of course, future selling expenses are not added to the 'cost' of finished goods in stock. But future selling expenses are deducted in estimating the likely 'net realisable value' in case it is *lower* than cost.)

Certain kinds of marketing costs raise similar problems to product development. Consider, for example, a company which launches an important product roughly every third year, when it updates the previous model. Let us assume that the company's year ends on 31 December. Between September and December 1992 it spends £20 million on media advertising for a product launch due in February 1993. In which period should the £20 million be charged as an expense?

The general rule is to charge costs in the year in which they are incurred; but this would fail to 'match' the costs against related sales revenues. How much, if anything, *should* be carried forward as an asset in the balance sheet at 31 December 1992? A wide range of answers is possible, which illustrates once again the subjective nature of the process for determining profit or loss. In fact the concept of 'prudence' would normally override that of 'matching' in this context; and it would be unusual for a company to carry forward *any* such costs ('revenue investments') as an asset in the December 1992 balance sheet.

A particular instance of capitalizing marketing costs arises with respect to accounting for brand names, which is discussed in Section 9 in connection with Goodwill.

(c) Bad debts

Accounts recognize revenue from credit sales when services are performed or when legal title to goods passes (which is usually when suppliers invoice customers). But if not all customers pay the full amounts due, a business has to charge 'bad debt' expenses against profits. There are three ways to do this: completely writing off specific bad debts; making provisions for specific 'doubtful' debts; and making general provisions.

A bad debt may occur because a customer cannot pay, or because of some dispute (for example, if goods never arrived, or were faulty). As soon as it becomes evident that a debt is bad, for whatever reason, there must at once be a complete write-off against profit. ('Bad debts' are treated as separate expenses: they do not simply reduce gross sales turnover.) 'Writing off' a bad debt also removes it from the 'debtors' total in the balance sheet.

But what happens if a debtor is very slow to pay, or if his financial position worsens? Or what if it is not clear how much the assets of a bankrupt debtor will realize for the creditors to share? The books of account will continue to include in 'debtors' the total amount legally due; but the business may wish to provide for possible specific bad debts ('doubtful debts'). It does so by charging a provision for bad debts expense in the profit and loss account, and setting up a separate 'provision for bad debts' liability account. This will be deducted from total debtors in the balance sheet.

Here is another area where management's subjective views can affect the level of reported profit. For instance not all banks took the same view about the true 'value' of the huge debts due from Brazil, Mexico, etc. in the mid-1980s; though when Citicorp led the way by making very large provisions for bad debts in 1987, many other banks at once followed suit.

Third, there may be a *general* provision for bad debts, on the basis of past average experience. For example, a company might maintain a provision amounting to 1 per cent of domestic debtors and 2 per cent of overseas debtors. In addition to any specific write-offs and provisions, it would then charge each year against profit the sum needed to adjust the general provision to these percentages of outstanding end-of-year debtors.

(d) Pensions

Most companies operate pension schemes, which may require employees to contribute to them. Pension schemes can be unfunded or funded, with different accounting implications.

Unfunded pension schemes are of three kinds. Under *terminal funding*, when each employee leaves, the company arranges to pay into an external fund an amount sufficient to finance the retiring employee's pension. The other two methods are completely unfunded. The *balance sheet provision* method sets up a provision for pensions year by year as the pension 'liability' accrues; while under the *pay-as-you-go* method, the company simply pays pensioners during their retirement. If a company goes bankrupt, pensioners in unfunded schemes may lose their pensions; though if their rights are 'vested' they will at least rank as creditors ahead of shareholders.

Funded pension schemes may be 'defined contribution' or 'defined benefit' schemes. The former involves no special problems: each year the company charges the contribution as pension expense in the profit and loss account. The pensioners eventually get whatever their contributions have earned in the fund, with no extra liability falling on the company. Defined benefit schemes, however, can give rise to accounting problems. Due to the uncertainties of investment, the amount in the fund at any time may differ from the company's actuarial liability for future pensions. This is normally re-calculated every three years, and depends on mortality rates, retirements, and so on.

SSAP 24 regards pensions as deferred pay. Under the accruals concept, therefore, companies should match the cost of pensions against the benefit of employees' services over their working lives. They may no longer simply treat as an expense the annual pension contributions to a defined benefit scheme. In the late 1980s that gave rise to large fluctuations, as over-funding resulted in 'pension holidays' for many companies. (Inadequate disclosure often made the problem even worse.)

SSAP 24 emphasizes the need to smooth the charge against profit over time. The regular cost is to be charged as a level percentage of payroll; and variations from regular cost (which may arise for a number of reasons, such as changes in the defined benefit levels) should normally be spread over the remaining service lives of the current employees. They should *not* be treated as prior year adjustments (see page 121). (A different approach might have required the balance sheet to show the company's total 'liability', perhaps discounted.)

VALUING STOCK: IN A TRADING COMPANY

A trading company's 'cost of sales' includes all expenses necessary 'to bring the goods into a saleable condition'. This covers the cost of purchasing the goods, and the related expenses of transport inwards, purchasing, warehousing, etc.

The heading 'operating expenses' includes all expenses needed to sell the goods and to run the business. Such expenses include advertising, packing, transport outwards, sales salaries, office rent, electricity, administrative salaries, and so on.

Where a trading company sells identifiable separate items of stock, such as cars or furniture, the cost of sales figure is simply the cost of the items which have been sold. Any items left in stock are valued at their cost, and (subject to adjustments) this amount appears as an asset in the end-of-period balance sheet.

Where, however, the goods sold are too numerous or too small to keep records showing the cost of each item (as, for example, in a grocery store), the cost of sales figure must be calculated *indirectly*.

The cost of sales in any period equals the cost of all goods made available for sale in the period (opening stock plus purchases) less the cost of any goods left unsold at the end.

Example

The accountant of Self Service Stores Limited is preparing the annual accounts to 31 March 1992 and wishes to calculate the cost of sales figure. He knows the opening stock figure was £610 000, based on a stock check carried out on 31 March 1991. The purchases figure for the year, shown in the books of account, was £4 730 000. From stock sheets prepared on 31 March 1992 he calculates that the closing stock at that date was £750 000. He can now calculate the cost of sales for the year to be £4 590 000, as shown below.

	£'000
Opening stock, 31 March 1991	610
Add: Purchases	4 730
	5 340
Less: Closing stock, 31 March 1992	750
= Cost of sales	4 590

Thus cost of sales equals purchases (£4 730K) *less* the *increase* in stock during the period (£750K − £610K = 140K) − or *plus* any *decrease* in stock. Opening stock and purchases are shown in the books of account, but it is more difficult to obtain a closing stock figure. This may require a physical stock check, which involves:

1 Physically locating and counting each item of stock.
2 Valuing each item (normally at the lower of cost or net realizable value).

Possible errors in stock figures

Physical stock checking can be tedious and time-consuming (and may even involve temporary restrictions on trading). As a result, many businesses take a physical stock check only once a year, probably at a time when stocks are at a seasonal low. An alternative to checking all items in stock at a single date is to keep 'perpetual' stock records. These are checked physically against actual stock regularly throughout the year, though not all at one time. Such records can supply 'closing stock' figures at the end of any accounting period.

Clearly the 'cost of sales' figure (and hence reported profit) is heavily dependent on the opening and closing stock valuations, which are subject to various possible errors. There may be an accidental omission or double count of physical stock items during the stock check, or errors in pricing items on the stock sheets, in calculating stock value, or in adding and summarizing stock sheet totals. These errors can occur in either the opening or the closing stock figures. Audit checks will lay heavy emphasis on verifying the stock balances.

The figure of £4 590 000 is intended to represent the cost of goods actually sold; but this total will also include the cost of stock losses, thefts and wastages, since these, too, will result in a lower closing stock figure. If individual items of stock are large or of high value it may be possible to control them separately. Otherwise the calculated cost of sales figure based on a stock check will have to be compared with some standard in order to discover any significant stock losses.

Where the company's pricing policy is to add a fixed percentage mark-up to the purchased cost of goods, it is easy to measure the accuracy of the cost of sales figures based on the stock check.

Example

Self Service Stores Limited adds a 25 per cent mark-up on cost. In the year to 31 March 1992 sales were £5 500 000.

	£'000
Cost of sales, based on stock check	4 590
Cost of sales 'should be' 100/125 × £5 500 000	4 400
Unexplained stock loss	190

On the basis of this variance, steps can be taken to find explanations for the difference. It looks as if Self Service Stores may have a shoplifting problem!

Since few companies maintain the same level of mark-up on all goods, it is seldom so easy to arrive at an accurate standard. It may often be best to use a cost of sales percentage based on past experience. If conditions change, however, it may not be clear whether it is the standard or the stock check figure which is wrong. Still, such a check can give an indication of substantial errors or losses.

Obsolescent and slow-moving stock

The accounting rule is that for balance sheet purposes stock should be shown 'at the *lower* of cost or net realizable value'. This applies in principle to each separate item of stock: it does not mean simply taking the lower of aggregate cost and aggregate net realizable value. This conservative rule prompts the question: 'Under what conditions should the book value of stock be written down below cost, or written off altogether?'

Where stock items are damaged or missing an adjustment is clearly needed to eliminate the lost investment from the accounts by making a charge against current profits. This will have the effect of *increasing* cost of sales (thus reducing profit) and *reducing* the amount of stock shown as an asset in the balance sheet.

Where, however, the stock exists in good condition, but is moving slowly or becoming out of date, how much, if anything, should be written off? Here is a very difficult area of decision, involving a judgement about the likely market demand for the stock in future periods.

Example

Bargain Motors Limited started business on 1 January 1991, buying and selling cars. Retained profit in the first year amounted to £200 000 and stock at the end of 1991 amounted to £400 000. During 1992 the company bought cars costing £5 000 000; and it sold for £6 400 000 cars which had cost £4 800 000. Operating expenses (ignoring tax) were £1 400 000. The draft profit and loss account and balance sheet for 1992, showing a profit of £200 000 and net assets of £1 400 000, are set out opposite in the left-hand columns.

The balance sheet stock figure was calculated as follows:

	£'000
Opening stock at cost	400
Add: Purchases at cost	5 000
	5 400
Less: Cars sold, at cost	4 800
Calculated closing stock, at cost	600

A detailed investigation of the items left in stock revealed that:

1 The stock included a number of discontinued accessories, which had cost £200 000 but which could now be sold for only 20 per cent of cost.

2 Cars which had cost £120 000 had been damaged and were now thought to be worth only about £70 000.

Revised accounts for 1992 are set out opposite (in the right-hand columns), incorporating the necessary stock adjustments. Notice that these affect both the profit and loss account and the balance sheet.

BARGAIN MOTORS LIMITED
Profit and loss account for 1992

	Draft £'000	Revised £'000
Turnover	6 400	6 400
Cost of sales	4 800	5 010
Gross profit	1 600	1 390
Operating expenses	1 400	1 400
Net profit (loss)	200	(10)

Balance sheet at 31 December 1992

	Draft £'000	Revised £'000
Stock	600	390
Other net assets	800	800
Net assets	1 400	1 190
Share capital	1 000	1 000
Profit and loss	400	190
Capital employed	1 400	1 190

Methods of stock valuation

So far we have assumed that there are no problems in attaching a 'cost' to each stock item. Companies generally keep records showing the invoice price of each item purchased. The values shown on the most recent invoice may be used for stock valuation purposes, but what if the stock level on hand at the end of a period exceeds the quantity of items purchased on the most recent invoice? Or what if the price of an item fluctuates sharply or continually increases, as happens in periods of rapid inflation? To deal with these issues a company policy must be established which will affect both the balance sheet stock figure and the profit or loss reported.

Example

The Glass Bottle Company Limited buys and sells a standard glass bottle. In the year to 30 September 1992 12 500 bottles were sold for £100 000. The stock and purchases accounts showed the following figures:

		Units	Unit cost	Total
			£	£
1 October 1991	Opening stock	5 000	4.00	20 000
1 January 1992	Purchases	4 000	5.00	20 000
1 April 1992	Purchases	4 500	6.00	27 000
1 August 1992	Purchases	5 000	7.00	35 000
		18 500		102 000

To determine the cost of sales in the year, we need to know the value of the closing stock of 6 000 bottles at 30 September 1992. But on what basis should the stock be valued?

The two most likely methods (in the UK) are:

(a) the 'First In First Out' basis (FIFO)
(b) the 'Average cost' basis.

In America a third method is also common:

(c) the 'Last in First Out' basis (LIFO).

These methods, illustrated opposite, give quite different results.

(a) 'First In First Out' basis (FIFO)

This assumes that the oldest items are sold first, leaving in stock those items which were purchased most recently. On this basis, the cost of the 12 500 bottles sold and of the 6 000 bottles in closing stock would be:

Cost of sales			Closing stock		
		£			£
5 000 @ £4.00	=	20 000	1 000 @ £6.00	=	6 000
4 000 @ £5.00	=	20 000	5 000 @ £7.00	=	35 000
3 500 @ £6.00	=	21 000			
			6 000	=	41 000
12 500	=	61 000			

(b) 'Average cost' basis

This assumes that average cost, recalculated (*) on every purchase, forms the basis for cost of sales and closing stock valuation. On the dates of the three replenishments during the year stock levels were respectively 3 000, 4 000, and 4 500 bottles.

		Units	Average cost	Total	Cost of sales
			£	£	£
1 October 1991	Stock	5 000	4.00	20 000	
	Issues	1 500	4.00	6 000	6 000
		3 500	4.00	14 000	
1 January 1992	Purchases	4 000	5.00	20 000	
		7 500	4.53*	34 000	
	Issues	3 500	4.53	15 867	15 867
		4 000	4.53	18 133	
1 April 1992	Purchases	4 500	6.00	27 000	
		8 500	5.31*	45 133	
	Issues	4 000	5.31	21 239	21 239
		4 500	5.31	23 894	
1 August 1992	Purchases	5 000	7.00	35 000	
		9 500	6.20*	58 894	
	Issues	3 500	6.20	21 698	21 698
30 September 1992	Stock	6 000	6.20	37 196	64 804

(c) 'Last In First Out' basis (LIFO)

This assumes that the most recent items are sold first, leaving in stock those items purchased earliest. On this basis the cost of sales and of the closing stock would be:

	Cost of sales			Closing stock	
		£			£
5 000 @ £7.00	=	35 000	5 000 @ £4.00 =		20 000
4 500 @ £6.00	=	27 000	1 000 @ £5.00 =		5 000
3 000 @ £5.00	=	15 000			
			6 000	=	25 000
12 500		77 000			

The LIFO method, in which the cost of sales figure is based on purchases at the most recent prices, tends in times of inflation to produce a particularly low cost of stock in the balance sheet. This can lead to serious distortions in reported profit if the volume of stock ever falls, since the charge against profit in that period relates to goods which are priced at exceptionally low and out-of-date costs. This problem is overcome by the Current Cost Accounting method (discussed in Section 11), which both charges cost of sales at 'current' costs and also revalues closing stock on the balance sheet to current costs as well.

LIFO is unusual in the UK, partly because the Inland Revenue will normally not allow it for tax purposes.

Clearly the results reported in the profit and loss account and balance sheet will vary depending on the method of stock valuation used. Applying the three bases above, the figures for the Glass Bottle Company Limited would be:

	FIFO	Average cost	LIFO
	£	£	£
Sales	100 000	100 000	100 000
Cost of sales	61 000	64 804	77 000
Gross profit	39 000	35 196	23 000
Closing stock	41 000	37 196	25 000

In such a case there is no 'right' answer. Different methods of stock valuation give different results; though, of course, whichever method is chosen it needs to be used consistently.

FIFO versus LIFO

	Profit and loss account	Closing balance sheet
FIFO	Out-of-date costs	Cost of most recent purchases
LIFO	Cost of most recent purchases	Very out-of-date costs

VALUING STOCK: IN A MANUFACTURING COMPANY

We have seen that problems arise in valuing a trading company's stock because of changes in purchase prices during a year, but at least purchase invoices show the cost of an item at certain points in time. But what is the 'cost' of an item which a company manufactures itself? At the end of each period varying quantities of stock are usually left in various stages of completion, and one needs to value 'work-in-progress', as well as stocks of raw materials and of finished goods.

All that we can attempt here is a general look at one system – batch costing – which is widely used in industry. From this we can see the kind of problems which will arise under any system used to calculate total cost. Two categories of cost are involved: the *direct costs* of material and labour which went into the stock and work-in-progress and the *indirect costs* incurred in the factory.

Direct material and direct labour can be directly identified with individual batches of products. Unit costs can be calculated by dividing total batch costs by the number of units produced.

Factory indirect expenses include the costs of supervision, depreciation and maintenance of machinery, factory rent, light and heat, and so on. In capital-intensive industries the indirect costs ('overheads'), which are often difficult to allocate to individual batches, may be much higher than the direct costs.

Apportioning indirect costs

The cost records will usually show the 'prime costs' (material and direct labour), but it is hard to tell how much of the total indirect costs relate to a particular product. Who can say how the works manager's time or the factory rent should be apportioned over all the products made in a period?

Example

Timber Box Limited makes wooden boxes and owns a small factory and some machinery. It employs a works manager and other staff, some of whom are engaged directly in making boxes, while others are concerned with purchases, stores, maintenance, cleaning, and so on. On 31 December 1991 the following balances appeared in the company's books:

	£'000
Sales	14 000
Direct material	6 000
Direct labour	1 500
Factory overheads	4 500
Administrative expenses	2 500

At the end of the year the company had in stock finished boxes for which the direct costs were: material £700 000, direct labour £200 000. At what valuation should the finished stock be shown in the accounts?

Absorption costing

One common method is to add factory overheads as a percentage of direct labour costs. Timber Box Limited's overhead rate would be 300 per cent:

$$\frac{\text{Overheads}}{\text{Direct labour}} = \frac{£4\ 500}{£1\ 500} = 300\%$$

On this basis, finished stock would be valued as follows:

	£'000
Direct material	700
Direct labour	200
Factory overheads*	600
Finished goods stock	= 1 500

*300% × direct labour £200 000

In practice, overhead absorption rates – like the 300 per cent on direct labour for Timber Box Limited – would normally be determined *in advance*. Forecast overhead costs would be divided by forecast production volume to determine the overhead absorption (or 'recovery') rate for the ensuing period. So total indirect costs 'absorbed' by products could differ from the actual indirect costs incurred for two reasons:

1 Actual overheads could differ from forecast overheads (spending variance).
2 Actual production volume could differ from forecast volume (volume variance).

Any overheads 'overabsorbed' (or 'underabsorbed') will have to be written off as a variance in the current period's profit and loss account – increasing (or reducing) reported profit.

If no variance arises under either heading, the products manufactured will exactly 'absorb' the actual total indirect costs. But even then a problem will arise if the level of stock varies. For example, if Timber Box Limited had no stock at the beginning of 1991, only £3 900 000 overheads will be charged as an expense in 1991, although overheads totalling £4 500 000 were actually incurred. The remaining £600 000 of overheads have been added to the value of closing stock, and will presumably be charged against profit as part of cost of goods sold in 1992.

Marginal costing

Some accountants argue that fixed overhead costs represent the necessary provision of capacity to produce, and should be regarded as 'period costs', incurred on a *time* basis, and not as 'product costs' (as implied by absorption costing). This approach is called 'marginal costing' and on this basis Timber Box Limited's finished stock value will be £900 000, that is, direct material £700 000 plus direct labour £200 000. The implications for treatment of costs are summarized in the table below:

	Product costs	Period costs
Expense (P & L)	In period when product sold	If related to current period
Asset (BS)	If product unsold at end of period	If related to future period

Those who favour marginal costing point out that it avoids the trouble of calculating arbitrary allocations of overheads. It also avoids the sharp fluctuations in reported profit which varying stock levels can lead to under absorption costing, and which many managers find hard to understand. Under marginal costing, profit tends to vary with sales not with production.

The contrary argument is that stock values are understated if nothing is included for the use of machinery and for indirect labour costs which were needed to convert raw materials into finished products.

SSAP 9, the accounting standard dealing with stock and work-in-progress, provides for some indirect costs to be carried forward. It requires stock and work-in-progress in published accounts to be valued 'at the lower of cost and net realizable value of the separate items of stock', where 'cost' *includes* production overheads based on a normal level of activity. 'Net realizable value' means the anticipated selling price less any further costs to completion and less any related selling and distribution costs. SSAP 9 also requires the total of stocks to be analysed into categories, for example raw materials, work-in-progress, finished goods, consumable stores, and so on.

Here are Timber Box Limited's 1991 profit and loss accounts summarized on the alternative bases:

	Absorption costing £'000		Marginal costing £'000
Sales		14 000	14 000
Direct material	6 000		6 000
Direct labour	1 500		1 500
Factory overheads	4 500		4 500
	12 000		12 000
Less: Closing stock	1 500		900
		10 500	11 100
Gross profit		3 500	2 900
Administrative expenses		2 500	2 500
Profit before tax		1 000	400
Closing stock in balance sheet		1 500	900

The two methods of valuing stock which we have considered led to very different results. In the first method all indirect manufacturing costs were taken into account (absorption costing), and in the second all were ignored (marginal costing). It is true that the amount gained or lost in one period is reflected in the accounts for the next, but a particular period's results could be significantly affected, especially where stock levels fluctuate.

In some businesses the ratio of indirect to direct costs might be higher, and the difference in profit even greater. Moreover, where direct labour is tending to become a fixed 'period cost', strict application of marginal costing could result in finished goods stock valuations consisting almost entirely of material costs.

Clearly two managements using different methods could arrive at very different stock valuations, and hence profit or loss figures. Comparisons between different companies can be hazardous in the absence of detailed information about methods of valuing stock.

FLOW OF MATERIAL THROUGH PRODUCTION PROCESS

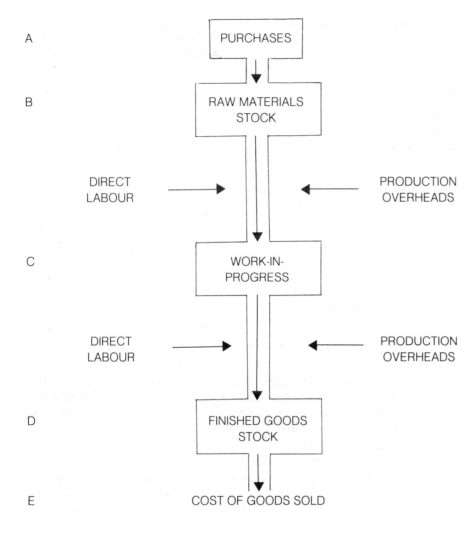

A   PURCHASES

B   RAW MATERIALS STOCK

DIRECT LABOUR →   ← PRODUCTION OVERHEADS

C   WORK-IN-PROGRESS

DIRECT LABOUR →   ← PRODUCTION OVERHEADS

D   FINISHED GOODS STOCK

E   COST OF GOODS SOLD

A and B   Value at the cost of material
C, D and E   Value at the incurred cost of material and direct labour (marginal cost) plus allocated production overheads (absorption cost).

VALUING STOCK: LONG-TERM CONTRACTS

We have seen that when a transaction covers more than one period decisions must be made as to when revenue should be recognized and expenses charged. The difficulties are increased when more than two accounting periods are involved, as with long-term contracts.

SSAP 9 requires work on long-term contracts to be included on the balance sheet at cost plus attributable profit less foreseeable losses (and less any progress payments already received). 'Attributable profit' is defined as the profit fairly attributable to work performed at the balance sheet date (assuming the final outcome of the contract can be estimated with reasonable certainty). 'Foreseeable losses' are losses estimated to arise over the duration of the contract. Thus again there is a conflict between 'prudence' and the 'matching' concept. Accounts must include only a 'fair share' of profits on the *completed* part of a contract, but the *whole* of any losses estimated on the entire contract.

Example

Alpha Construction Limited agrees to build an office block for Omega Property Limited for £3 million. Alpha estimates that the project will cost £2.1 million and that construction will take three years. At the end of the first year the job is one-third finished, and costs incurred, at £700 000, are on target.

What profit has Alpha made in the first year? How can the expected total profit be allocated over the three years? It is fairly obvious that not all the profit was 'earned' the day the contract was signed, and similarly that such profit as may be made will not all accrue on the final day when the last work is completed. Some other basis is required, to spread the total anticipated profit 'fairly' over the three years.

Because of the uncertainty inevitably involved in a further two years of construction, prudence will probably result in the profit recognized in year 1 being zero. The total cost may exceed £2.1 million; it may take more than two further years to complete construction, and so on. However, what if Alpha is showing a loss on its other transactions? What if the contract involves a different kind of work from that normally carried out? How will these factors affect the decision?

The scope open to the directors of companies such as Alpha to show varying levels of profit cannot be denied. The company's auditors can ensure that a consistent accounting basis is adopted from one year to another. But the directors are in the best position to make the necessary commercial judgements; and unless their conclusions are clearly unreasonable, it may be difficult for the auditors to disagree with them.

Under these conditions profit measurement is only approximate; accounting measures indicate a *range* within which profit falls but do not define an exact figure. Where the element of uncertainty is substantial, judgements are crucial; and even honest and competent judgements will sometimes prove wrong.

EXTRAORDINARY ITEMS

One accounting approach is to include only regular 'normal' items in the profit and loss account, and transfer 'non-recurring' items (whether positive or negative) directly to reserves. Such items would then never appear at all in the profit and loss account. But many accountants argue that the profit and loss account ought to report last year's actual profit or loss, rather than try to indicate a likely level of future 'maintainable' profit (or loss).

Modern UK practice comes between the two. It tends to include nearly all revenue items in the profit and loss account, following the 'all-inclusive' concept of profit. But it places 'extraordinary items' *below* the line showing profit or loss on ordinary activities after taxation (which forms the basis for computing earnings per share).

SSAP 6 defines 'extraordinary items' as 'material items which derive from events or transactions that fall outside the ordinary activities of the company, and which are therefore expected not to recur frequently or regularly'. Examples might include:

1 Discontinuance of a major part of the business.
2 Writing off intangibles because of unusual events during the period.
3 Expropriation of assets.

Extraordinary items should be disclosed separately, net of related tax, below the line. (An outline of a detailed profit and loss account is set out opposite.) Extraordinary items do not include prior year items; nor do they include items which are unusual only on account of their size, such as very large stock write-offs or bad debts. These are called 'exceptional items': companies should include them *above* the profit before tax line, and disclose them separately, either on the face of the profit and loss account, or in a note thereto. The distinction between 'exceptional' and 'extraordinary' items is somewhat fuzzy, and practice varies among leading companies.

Prior year adjustments can arise from changes in accounting policies or from correction of fundamental errors. They do not include normal recurring corrections and adjustments of accounting estimates made in prior years (for example, relating to depreciation or tax). SSAP 6 requires that, where prior year adjustments occur, companies should restate prior years' figures, and adjust the opening balance of retained profits. In those cases the analyst may want to carry back material adjustments into their proper periods, to reveal less inaccurate trends over time.

Profit and loss account for year ended 31 December 1992

Turnover

Operating profit
Exceptional item

Operating profit after exceptional item
Interest payable

Profit on ordinary activities before tax
Taxation

Profit on ordinary activities after tax   *
Extraordinary items (net of tax)

Profit for the year
Dividends

Retained profit for the year

*basis for computing earnings per share

SUMMARY

At the beginning of this section we pointed out that the larger the number of incomplete transactions, the longer their timespan, and the greater their significance, the wider will be the range of possible profit figures. The force of this statement should now be obvious.

We have seen that accrual accounting distinguishes cash receipts from 'income' and cash expenditures from 'expenses'. Income and expenses are recognized in the relevant period when they accrue, and not when they happen to be received or paid in cash.

The basis for many accounting adjustments is *time*, amounts being included in the period to which they relate. Another basis, using the *matching* concept, is to charge expenses in the accounting period which recognizes related revenue. This may be difficult in respect of spending on intangibles such as research, marketing or training, where future related revenues are often uncertain. Prudence then normally prevails over matching. We also looked at measuring bad debt expenses and pension costs.

Valuing stock is important in measuring the 'cost of sales'. Problems include obsolescence, the method of valuation (whether FIFO or average cost), the treatment of production overheads, and long-term contracts. Different accounting treatments in these areas can affect reported profit in more than one accounting period.

Finally we discussed 'extraordinary' items, and their inclusion in the profit and loss account, net of tax, 'below the line'.

Throughout this section we have emphasized that the process of measuring profit or loss usually contains an important element of judgement. The requirement to show a 'true and fair view' is overriding; but it would be quite wrong to suppose that most reported profit or loss figures are in any sense uniquely 'correct'. They are really only 'best guesses'.

4.1 Definition

Write down on this page your definitions of the terms shown. Then compare your answers with the definitions overleaf.

(a) Matching

(f) Work-in-progress

(b) An accrued charge

(g) Marginal costing

(c) Turnover

(h) Bad debts

(d) Sales mix

(i) Extraordinary items

(e) FIFO

(j) Overheads

4.1 Definitions

(a) *Matching* is the process of charging expenses in the same accounting period as that in which related revenue is recognized. Expenses which cannot be 'matched' are written off as soon as incurred. The only expenditure which is carried forward as an asset on the balance sheet is that which is reasonably certain to be matchable against related revenues in some *future* period.

(b) *An accrued charge* is an expense (often relating to a period of time, for example rent due) which has become legally payable as at a particular date, but which has not yet been invoiced or paid.

(c) *Turnover* is a synonym for sales (or sales revenue). It includes both cash and credit sales of goods and services, but does *not* include the sale of fixed assets. Nor, in published accounts, does it include VAT.

(d) *Sales mix* describes, in a multi-product company, the particular combination in a given accounting period of the sales revenue of all the company's different products. The mix can change while total sales revenue remains constant.

(e) *FIFO* (First In First Out) is a method of calculating cost of sales and valuing stock which assumes for accounting purposes that goods are sold or issued in the same order as that in which they were purchased or received. This method may be used even if it is not physically true. FIFO results in stock being included in end-of-period balance sheets at the most recent costs, while the cost of sales in the profit and loss account consists of (somewhat) earlier purchases. It is to be contrasted with LIFO (Last In First Out), which is rarely used in the UK.

(f) *Work-in-progress* (WIP) is a category of stock in a manufacturing company, representing products on which, as at the balance sheet date, the manufacturing process has begun (otherwise they would still be raw materials) but is not yet complete (otherwise they would be finished goods). It is reduced by any advances or progress payments received from the customer in the course of manufacture.

(g) *Marginal costing* is a method of allocating costs to products which takes into account only variable costs directly associated with a product, ignoring indirect (overhead) costs. It is to be contrasted with 'absorption' (full) costing, which SSAP 9 requires for the purposes of financial accounting.

(h) *Bad debts* are amounts owing to a business (debts) which are valueless, either because the debtor *cannot* pay (for example through bankruptcy), or because he *will* not (for instance through some dispute over quality or delivery).

(i) *Extraordinary items* arise from events or transactions outside the ordinary activities of the business, which are expected not to recur regularly or frequently. They would *not* include prior year adjustments, or items which are exceptional merely on account of their size. They are reported, net of related tax, in the profit and loss account below the figure for profit on ordinary activities after taxation for the year.

(j) *Overheads* are indirect costs which it may not be easy to identify with particular products. For accounting purposes (for example valuing stock) they are often allocated to products on some fairly general basis, such as a percentage of direct labour costs.

4.2 Hermes Travel Limited: Accruals and prepayments

Hermes Travel Limited started business as a travel agency on 1 November 1991. The company's first accounting period ended on 31 October 1992, by which time £38 000 had been paid in cash in respect of telephone expenses. This amount was made up as follows:

	£
Rent	
2 months to 31 December 1991	800
3 months to 31 March 1992	1 200
3 months to 30 June 1992	1 200
3 months to 30 September 1992	1 200
Calls	
2 months to 31 December 1991	6 400
3 months to 31 March 1992	15 200
3 months to 30 June 1992	12 000
Total cash paid	38 000

At 31 October 1992, there was an unpaid account for £16 000 in respect of calls for the three months to 30 September 1992 (£14 800) and rent for the three months to 31 December 1992 (£1 200). Calls for the month of October 1992 were estimated to have amounted to £5 400.

Calculate how much should be charged as telephone expense for the year ended 31 October 1992, and show the ledger account for the year.

The answer is shown on the next page.

4.3 Joshua Antiques Limited: Stock adjustments

Joshua Antiques Limited ended its financial year on the first Friday after 31 March in each year. Details were available of each antique dealt in, showing date of purchase, name of supplier, and cost; and (when sold) date of sale, name of customer (usually), and proceeds. From these records the manager prepared stock sheets at 3 April 1992 showing items apparently unsold with a total cost of £57 600. This was the figure shown as closing stock in the draft accounts for the year ended 3 April 1992.

In the course of audit work the following queries arose. Please identify for each item below what adjustment, if any, is needed to the closing stock figure; and calculate what the total closing stock should be in the final accounts.

(a) Three items of china, with a total cost of £240, were cracked. The manager thought they could be sold for £150 in total, instead of at the normal 100 per cent mark-up on cost.

(b) A picture of Westminster Bridge, which the manager had thought to be by Hogarth, had turned out to be by an unknown artist. Its selling value was accordingly reduced from £4 000 to £500 (which compared with a cost of £1 700).

(c) Offsetting the 'Hogarth' blunder, the firm had in stock a pair of water colours, which together had cost only £100. They were now attributed to Constable; and as a result their selling price had been raised from £250 to £6 000.

(d) A number of items of jewellery, which the records showed to have cost £430 in total, ought to have been in stock according to the records, but no trace could be found of them (nor had they been recorded as sold since 3 April). The manager reckoned the total sales proceeds would have been about £860.

(e) A rather dented silver coffee pot, which had cost £150, had been in stock for over a year. Because of its poor condition, it had been written down to £80 in the 1991 accounts but it appeared on 3 April 1992 in the stock records at £150. Its selling price was currently set at £180, but the manager doubted if he would get more than £90 for it.

An answer is shown on the next page.

125

4.2 Hermes Travel Limited

Solution

In addition to the £38 000 cash paid, the following amounts should also be included in telephone expense for the year ended 31 October 1992:

	£
Rent October 1992	400
Calls 3 months to 30 September 1992	14 800
October 1992	5 400
'Accrued charges' at 31 October 1992	20 600

Thus total telephone expense for the year ended 31 October 1992 is £58 600.

Ledger account

Telephone expense

Year 1991/92	£	Year 1991/92	£
Cash	38 000	Profit and loss account	58 600
Accrued charges c/d	20 600		
	58 600		58 600
		Year 1992/93	
		Accrued charges b/d	20 600

Notice how the £20 600 accrued charges are brought down as a credit in year 1992/93. The effect will be to reduce the expense in 1992/93 (the year in which the amounts concerned will actually be paid).

4.3 Joshua Antiques Limited

Solution

(a) The china should be shown at £150 (net realizable value) instead of at £240 (cost).

(b) The 'Hogarth' picture should be reduced from £1 700 (cost) to £500 (net realizable value).

(c) The water colours should continue to be shown at cost, £100. (This illustrates the 'prudence' concept: losses tend to be recognized at once, but profits only when actually earned.)

(d) The jewellery items should not be included in the closing stock, which should therefore be reduced by £430.

(e) The coffee pot should be shown at estimated net realizable value, which appears to be below cost. There is sufficient uncertainty that it might be best to show the item at £80 (the same as last year); even though, if the write-down were being made for the first time in 1992, the estimated sales proceeds of £90 would be the correct figure. Accordingly, a deduction of £70 needs to be made from the total stock figure.

Summary:

	£	£
Original closing stock total		57 600
(a)	− 90	
(b)	− 1 200	
(c)	−	
(d)	− 430	
(e)	− 70	
		1 790
Revised closing stock		55 810

4.4 Urban Properties Limited: Year-end adjustments

The accounts of Urban Properties Limited for the year ended 30 June 1992 are set out opposite, in draft form. The following items are to be taken into account:

(a) No adjustment has been made in respect of business rates for the year to 31 March 1993 paid in advance, amounting to £16 000 a year.

(b) Rent receivable of £3 000 for the June quarter has not been included.

(c) Rent received for the half-year to 30 September 1992 (£8 000) has all been included in the accounts to 30 June 1992.

(d) There is a dispute about the rent payable on one property. No rent has been paid since £6 000 was paid in advance in October 1991, in respect of the quarter to December 1991. It is estimated that as from the end of 1991 only half the level of rent previously payable will ultimately be due.

Please amend the draft balance sheet and profit and loss account shown opposite to incorporate any necessary adjustments in respect of the above items. To avoid undue complexity, we show current liabilities below capital and reserves. The answer is shown on the next page. Work in £'000. Alter the tax charge to 33 per cent of your amended profit.

URBAN PROPERTIES LIMITED
Draft profit and loss account
Year ended 30 June 1992

		£'000
Rent receivable		286
Other income		28
		314
Rent payable	64	
Business rates payable	41	
Other expenses	31	
		136
Profit before tax		178
Tax (@ 33 per cent)		59
Profit after tax		119

Draft balance sheet at 30 June 1992

		£'000
Fixed assets		
Properties		660
Current assets		
Debtors	6	
Cash	127	
		133
		793
Capital and reserves		
Called up share capital		500
Reserves		225
Shareholders' funds		725
Current liabilities		
Creditors	9	
Tax	59	68
		793

4.4 Urban Properties Limited: *Solution*

URBAN PROPERTIES LIMITED
Profit and loss account
Year ended 30 June 1992

			£'000
Rent receivable	+3b −4c		286̶ *285*
Other income			28
			314̶ *313*
Rent payable	+6d	70 64̶	
Business rates payable	−12a	29 41̶	
Other expenses		31	
			136̶ *130*
Profit before tax			178̶ *183*
Tax (@ 33 per cent)			59̶ *61*
Profit after tax			119̶ *122*

Draft balance sheet at 30 June 1992

			£'000
Fixed assets			
Properties			660
Current assets			
Debtors	+3b	9 6̶	
Prepayment	+12a	12	
Cash		127	
			133̶ *148*
			793̶ *808*
Capital and reserves			
Called up share capital			500
Reserves	(+3 − SEE P&L)		225̶ *228*
Shareholders' funds			725̶ *728*
Current liabilities			
Creditors	+4c +6d	9̶ *19*	
Tax	(+2)	59̶ *61*	
			68̶ *80*
			793̶ *808*

URBAN PROPERTIES LIMITED
Profit and loss account
Year ended 30 June 1992

		£'000
Rent receivable		285
Other income		28
		313
Rent payable	70	
Business rates payable	29	
Other expenses	31	
		130
Profit before tax		183
Tax (@ 33 per cent)		61
Profit after tax		122

Balance sheet at 30 June 1992

		£'000
Fixed assets		
Properties		660
Current assets		
Debtors	9	
Prepayments	12	
Cash	127	
		148
		808
Capital and reserves		
Called up share capital		500
Reserves		228
Shareholders' funds		728
Current liabilities		
Creditors	19	
Tax	61	
		80
		808

Answers to the following six problems in this section are given at the end of the book.

4.5 Wheeler Limited: Adjusting trial balance and preparing final accounts

The trial balance of Wheeler Limited extracted from the books at the end of the year ended 31 March 1992 is shown below.

The following items have not been taken into account:

(a) An audit fee (administrative expenses) of £5 000 is to be provided for.
(b) Loan interest is payable half yearly at 30 June and 31 December. The last payment was on 31 December 1991.
(c) Finished goods stock in the books at £12 000 is obsolete, and is to be written off as cost of goods sold in the current year.
(d) Tax of £95 000 is to be provided for.
(e) An ordinary dividend of 40p per share is proposed.

1 You are asked to make the necessary adjustments in the adjustments column of the trial balance schedule, and extend the figures into the profit and loss account and balance sheet columns. Each pair of columns should balance.

2 From the trial balance schedule as adjusted, please now prepare in final form the profit and loss account and balance sheet of Wheeler Limited for the year ended 31 March 1992.

	Trial balance		Adjustments		Profit and loss		Balance sheet	
	Dr £'000	Cr £'000	Dr £'000	Cr £'000	Dr £'000	Cr £'000	Dr £'000	Cr £'000
Cash book	201							
Ordinary £1 share capital		200						
Profit and loss account 1 April 1991		283						
12% loan		300						
Fixed assets: cost	942							
Fixed assets: accumulated depreciation		347						
Sales ledger control	183							
Stock	141							
Purchase ledger control		39						
Accrued charges								
Tax liability								
Dividend payable								
Sales		1 442						
Cost of goods sold	818							
Selling and administrative expenses	299							
Loan interest	27							
Tax expense								
Ordinary dividend								
Profit for year retained								
	2 611	2 611						

129

4.6 Canning and Sons Limited: Writing down stock

CANNING AND SONS LIMITED
Balance Sheet at 31 December 1991 — £'000
Fixed assets, net — 330

Current assets

Stock	213	
Debtors	254	
Cash	26	
	493	

Less Creditors falling due within one year

Trade creditors	132	
Tax	50	
	182	
		311
		641

Capital and reserves

Called up share capital	400
Profit and loss account	241
	641

Profit and loss account for the year ended 31 December 1991

Turnover	1 127
Cost of sales	871
Gross profit	256
Selling and administrative expenses	113
	143
Tax	36
Profit after tax	107

The 1991 accounts of Canning and Sons Limited, sellers of toys, are shown above as they were prepared for audit. The auditors raised only one significant point, to do with valuing stock. They recommended that a consignment of electric cars which had cost £40 000 and had not sold well over the Christmas period should be written down to 50 per cent of cost.

The company's directors reluctantly felt they had no choice but to accept the auditors' recommendation. You are asked to amend the draft accounts accordingly, making any necessary change to the provision for tax (which is based on a rate of 25 per cent).

4.7 Anderson Tiles Limited: FIFO stock valuation

At 1 April 1991, Anderson Tiles had 3 000 cases of a particular kind of tile in stock. They were shown as costing £4 a case.

In the year to 31 March 1992, three batches of cases were purchased. In June 4 000 cases @ £4.25 per case; in October 2 000 cases @ £4.75; and in December 3 000 cases @ £5.00.

Using the FIFO method of stock valuation, calculate the closing stock valuation at 31 March 1992, when there were 6 000 cases in stock. Then compute the cost of sales for the year. Verify your computation by identifying the volume of tiles and related costs per case assumed to be sold.

4.8 Berwick Paper Limited: Average cost stock valuation

Berwick Paper Limited replenished its stock of a certain type of paper at the end of each quarter. For the year 1991, opening stock was 1 200 tonnes, and the quantities purchased were 1 800 tonnes in March; 2 400 tonnes in June; 1 200 tonnes in September; and 1 800 tonnes in December. The cost attributable to the opening stock was £21 per tonne. Purchase prices per tonne through the year were £18 (March), £15 (June), £25 (September), and £20 (December).

The quantities issued each quarter were as follows:

March quarter	900 tonnes
June quarter	1 700 tonnes
September quarter	1 400 tonnes
December quarter	1 900 tonnes

Thus closing stock amounted to 2 500 tonnes (= opening stock 1 200 tonnes plus purchases 7 200 tonnes less issues in year 5 900 tonnes).

Assuming that purchases are made at the end of each quarter, and that the average cost method of valuing stock is used for issues, calculate the value of closing stock at 31 December 1991, and the cost of paper used during the year.

4.9 Newport Machines Limited: Absorption and marginal costing

In the year ended 30 June 1991, Newport Machines incurred the following factory costs:

	£'000
Direct material	450
Direct labour	300
Overheads	540

At 30 June stock was on hand on which had been incurred £30 000 direct material costs and £20 000 direct labour costs. This meant that if marginal costing were adopted, the stock would be valued at £50 000 for accounting purposes.

Calculate the overhead percentage on direct labour, and value the stock on the absorption cost basis.

4.10 Tiptop Office Supplies: Bad debts

Tiptop Office Supplies sold to many small customers who, in total, owed £426 000 at 30 September 1992 (not including £17 000 bad debts which had been written off during the year). Tiptop's policy was to provide 4 per cent of outstanding debtors at the year-end in respect of anticipated bad debts. Credit policy in 1992, however, had been somewhat laxer than in previous years, in an attempt to boost sales volume, so Tiptop decided to provide 5 per cent in respect of debtors at 30 September 1992.

The provision for bad debts account had a balance of £10 000 brought forward at 1 October 1991. This represented 4 per cent of £250 000, the total amount of debtors outstanding at 30 September 1992.

(a) what should the provision for bad debts be at 30 September 1992?
(b) how much will the 1992 charge for bad debts expense be?
(c) write up ledger accounts for 1992 (i) for provision for bad debts, and (ii) for bad debts expense.

No solutions are published for the following problems.

4.11 Shiny Snappers Limited: Stock valuation

Shiny Snappers Limited was formed to produce cameras. Sales were estimated at about 5 000 units per quarter, at an average price of £30 per unit; so production was set at this level. Stocks were planned to build up at the start, since the first quarter's sales were not expected to exceed 3 500 units. But even that sales estimate was too optimistic, and production was accordingly cut back to 2 000 units for the second quarter.

Direct costs of production averaged £20 per unit, and fixed production overheads amounted to £20 000 per quarter. The company sold 2 000 units in the first quarter and 4 000 (at a price reduced by 5 per cent) in the second. When the managing director saw the company's profit and loss accounts (set out below) for the first two quarters, he was astonished to see that profits were the same in each quarter, although sales had doubled in the second.

	1st quarter £'000	1st quarter £'000	2nd quarter £'000	2nd quarter £'000
Sales revenue		60		114
Opening stocks	–		72	
Cost of production	120		60	
	120		132	
Less: Closing stocks	72		30	
Cost of goods sold		48		102
Gross profit		12		12

Explain the results for the two quarters. How might different methods of accounting affect profits (FIFO v. LIFO; marginal v. full costing)?

4.12 Extraordinarily doubtful

How would you treat each of the following transactions:

(a) as ordinary revenue or expense items in the profit and loss account?
(b) as exceptional items separately disclosed in the profit and loss account?
(c) as extraordinary items 'below the line' in the profit and loss account?
(d) as items to be directly added to or subtracted from reserves in the balance sheet, without passing through the profit and loss account?
(e) in some other way?

Assume each item is large enough to be 'material'.

1 Damages awarded against a small restaurant for poisoning a customer.
2 Recent technical advances lead to significant lengthening of estimates of the lives of many of a company's fixed assets: hence future depreciation charges need to be reduced. What should be done with already accumulated 'excess' depreciation?
3 An unexpected tax refund relating to a transaction four years ago.
4 Non-recurring costs of closing one of six factories operated.
5 Loss arising from fire in an under-insured warehouse.
6 Elimination of goodwill arising from an acquisition during the year.
7 Special write-offs of obsolescent stock.
8 Loss arising from cocoa dealings by a manufacturer of chocolate, due to fluctuations in the commodity market.
9 Annual revaluation of property reveals a fall from last year's value.
10 Loss on nationalization of office abroad with compensation.

4.13 Magazine money

Toad, a new monthly magazine, attracts a large number of annual subscriptions by advertising. The company's first accounting period ends on 30 June 1992; but before that date many subscriptions have been received entitling subscribers to issues of *Toad* as far ahead (in some cases) as June 1993.

How should such 'advance subscriptions' be treated?:

(a) shown as a current liability on the balance sheet, on the grounds that the publishers 'owe' these subscribers, not money, but future issues of the magazine?
(b) included in sales, on the grounds that *selling* the magazine is the critical event, and that marginal (editorial and paper) costs are very low?
(c) omitted from sales and from cash, on the grounds that the subscriptions relate to post-balance-sheet events?

4.14 Roger Ancastle

In April 1992 Roger Ancastle was considering how to value the unsold copies of a book his firm of financial consultants had just published: 2 000 copies of the book had been printed, of which 1 000 copies had been bound. In the year ended 31 March 1992 400 copies had been sold for cash @ £45 each, of which the firm received £30 a copy. Stock on 31 March 1992 was 500 bound copies (plus 1 000 unbound), 100 bound copies having been sent out to reviewers to publicize the book. No other advertising was planned.

The main cost of printing a book is the set-up cost, in this case £20 000. The marginal cost, mainly the cost of paper, was £2 per copy. Thus while printing 2 000 copies had actually cost £24 000, printing 5 000 copies would in total have cost only £30 000. In addition it cost £4 to bind each copy. The firm had decided initially to bind only 1 000 copies of the 2 000 printed, to see if sales justified spending a further £4 000 on binding the second 1 000 copies.

Mr Ancastle's first thought was to value the stock of 1 500 unsold copies of the book at £20 000, as follows:

Method A £

500 bound copies	@ £16	= 8 000	} £20 000
1 000 unbound copies	@ £12	= 12 000	

Mr Ancastle was unsure whether it was correct to spread the set-up cost over the total number of copies printed, especially in view of the small marginal cost of printing more copies. He wondered if the firm ought to spread the set-up cost over the first 1 000 copies only, since only that number had been bound. The stock at 31 March 1992 would then be valued at only £15 000.

Method B £

$$\text{Set-up cost: } \frac{500}{1\,000} \times £20\,000 = 10\,000$$

Marginal printing cost: 1 500 @ £2	= 3 000	} £15 000
Binding cost: 500 @ £4	= 2 000	

Although Method B would result in showing a small loss of £1 000 on the book in the year ended 31 March 1992 (compared with a profit of £4 000 under Method A), Mr Ancastle thought it might be better accounting practice. The table shows what the stock value at 31 March 1992 would be under both Method A and Method B if the number of copies printed had been: (a) 1 000 copies, (b) 2 000 copies (the actual number), (c) 5 000 copies.

Mr Ancastle thought it strange that printing 5 000 copies rather than 1 000 would show £7 000 profit under Method A instead of £1 000 loss. Method A would produce £8 000 more profit under those circumstances even though the firm would have paid out £8 000 more cash. Method B would show the same £1 000 loss in all three cases.

Table

	1 000 copies £'000	2 000 copies £'000	5 000 copies £'000
Binding 1 000 copies	4	4	4
Cost of printing	22	24	30
Total expenditure	26	28	34
Less: Sales revenue	12	12	12
Net cash out-of-pocket	14	16	22
Method A			
Binding 500 copies @ £4	2	2	2
Unbound copies (proportion)	11	18	27
= Closing stock	13	20	29
Method B			
Binding 500 copies @ £4	2	2	2
500 balance of first 1 000 (printing set-up)	10	10	10
500 balance of first 1 000 (marginal cost)	1	1	1
Excess over 1 000 (marginal cost)	–	2	8
= Closing stock	13	15	21

Questions:

1 Assume that in the year ending 31 March 1993 a further 600 copies of the book are sold. Calculate what stock value would be shown at 31 March 1993 under both Method A and Method B; and what profit or loss would be reported in the year ended 31 March 1993.

2 How much profit or loss do you think Roger Ancastle's firm made on the book in the year ended 31 March 1992?

3 How would it affect your answer to (2) if Mr Ancastle's views on future sales after 31 March 1992 were as follows (in April 1992):

(a) Doubtful if as many as 200 more copies would be sold?
(b) Confident that at least 800 more copies would be sold?
(c) No idea how many more copies would be sold?

Section 5
Fixed assets and depreciation

CAPITAL EXPENDITURE

We have seen that an accrual accounting system distinguishes between expenditure and expense. So far we have been dealing only with spending related to day-to-day running of the business. Our concern has been to allocate this kind of 'revenue' spending between two successive accounting periods. Now we must look at 'capital' expenditure on acquiring fixed assets which have a life stretching over several accounting periods.

A business holds fixed assets not for resale, but to provide goods or services, for use on a continuing basis. Typical examples are land and buildings, machinery and equipment, office furniture, and so on. *Purpose*, rather than physical nature, determines whether a particular item represents capital or revenue; and whether it should appear in the balance sheet as a fixed or current asset. Cars, for example, which are fixed assets for many companies, are mostly current assets (stock) for Ford – which sells cars. (But some cars will be fixed assets even for that company.)

Determining the cost of fixed assets is generally fairly easy. For purchased items it will be the total invoiced cost of acquiring fixed assets and preparing them for use. This will include, for example, legal costs incurred in acquiring a lease, or costs of installing new plant or equipment.

Where a company manufactures fixed assets for its own use, the amount capitalized is often simply the direct outlay for labour and materials. This avoids difficult decisions about the extent of related overheads. Production cost may also include interest on capital borrowed to finance production, to the extent that it accrues in respect of the period of production.

SSAP 4 requires that government grants relating to fixed assets be credited to revenue over the asset's expected useful life. Companies show the asset at its total cost and credit a separate reserve account with the amount of the grant (*not* to be shown as part of shareholders' funds). They then release a suitable portion of the grant to profit each year and thus offset the grant against (gross) depreciation.

If substantial repairs merely restore a building or machine to its original condition, they are chargeable as revenue expenses. But to the extent that they 'improve' on the asset's original condition, they should strictly be capitalized. An improvement may consist of increasing the asset's capacity, lengthening its productive life, reducing its running costs, or improving the quality of its output.

DEPRECIATION

Fixed assets are gradually 'used up' in providing goods or services over time, and accounts recognize this by providing for 'depreciation' each year. This involves charging part of the fixed asset's cost as an expense in the profit and loss account and reducing its balance sheet book value by the same amount. We have already seen that companies may carry forward as an asset on the balance sheet 'revenue' spending which is expected to benefit future periods. In that sense, the net book value of a fixed asset could be regarded simply as equivalent to 'deferred depreciation expense'.

The purpose of providing for depreciation is to spread the net cost of a fixed asset over its expected useful life. During its life, a fixed asset's net book value (cost less total depreciation to date) will decline as its cost is steadily written off. By the time it stops being useful its book value should have fallen either to zero or to its remaining scrap or second-hand value.

The 'matching' concept strictly implies charging a fraction of a full year's depreciation expense both in the year of purchase and in the year of disposal. But some companies charge no depreciation in the year in which they acquire a fixed asset, while others charge a full year's expense. As long as they are consistent in their treatment, there is no need for concern.

In historical cost accounting, a fixed asset's net book value represents the unallocated residue of its original cost. It is *not* intended to represent the asset's market value at the balance sheet date (neither its replacement cost nor its realizable value). Thus providing for depreciation allocates cost: it does not attempt to *value* fixed assets. It spreads out the net cost of a fixed asset over its effective life, in order to match depreciation expense against related revenue.

If the depreciation charge is inadequate the profit reported for a period will be too high as will the net book value shown for fixed assets in the balance sheet. There may also be a danger that the company might distribute capital in the mistaken belief that it is income.

As we shall see in Section 7 the Inland Revenue has its own rules for calculating depreciation ('capital allowances') for tax purposes. So a company cannot reduce its tax liability by charging more depreciation in its accounts.

How depreciation works can be illustrated simply by looking at an example involving a short lease.

Example

On 1 January 1992 Electrical Instruments Limited purchased a three-year lease of a shop for £60 000. The accounts over the next three years would include the following items related to the lease:

Profit and loss account			
Year ended 31 December	1992	1993	1994
	£'000	£'000	£'000
Lease: depreciation expense	20	20	20
Balance sheet at 31 December			
Lease at cost	60	60	60
Less: Accumulated depreciation	20	40	60
Net book value	40	20	—

At the end of the third year, when the lease expires, it will be fully written off. This means that accumulated depreciation will amount to the original £60 000 outlay. Over the three-year life of the lease its entire cost will have been charged as depreciation expense in the profit and loss account.

The effect of charging depreciation is to reduce gross profit by an amount which would otherwise have appeared free for distribution in dividends. At the end of three years a total of £60 000 would have been thus withheld. This amount is then available to purchase another lease; or to invest in other assets.

The lease example is quite straightforward; but complex questions can arise in determining depreciation of fixed assets. Decisions made on these issues can significantly affect reported profit and asset figures over a number of years.

We shall consider the issues involved in depreciation under the following headings:

1 Estimating useful life and residual value.
2 Methods of depreciation.
3 Varying depreciation charges: effect on reported results.

ESTIMATING USEFUL LIFE AND RESIDUAL VALUE

Let us now look at a slightly more complicated example, the case of Furniture Removals Limited.

Example

Furniture Removals Limited was set up on 1 January 1991, purchased vans for £60 000, and started to trade. During the year cash receipts from sales were £100 000 and cash expenses for wages, petrol, and so on, were £60 000.

The draft accounts for the year before making any provision for depreciation are shown opposite (in the left-hand column). (To keep it simple, we ignore tax.) Obviously these accounts do not reflect the true picture. Profits are overstated in the absence of a charge for using the vans; and the vans are shown in the balance sheet at a figure which makes no allowance for deterioration through use.

How much should be provided for depreciation? In order to decide this, two questions must be answered *in advance*:

1 For how many years will the vans be used by the company?
2 What will they be worth at the end of that time?

These questions may be difficult to answer. In any event they clearly involve subjective judgements by the company's management. The likely useful life of an asset may be limited, depending on its nature, by:

(a) the passing of time
(b) physical wear and tear
(c) technical or market obsolescence.

Let us assume that Furniture Removal's managers estimate that:

1 The vans will be used for five years; and
2 at the end of that time they will be worth £10 000.

On this basis, the net cost of the vans to the company, over their whole useful life, will be: £60 000 − £10 000 = £50 000. This is the original cash cost less the expected ultimate cash proceeds from sale; it represents the total amount which must be provided for depreciation over the five years.

The next question is: how much of this £50 000 total depreciation to charge in the first year, how much in the second, and so on? As we shall see, there are a number of possible answers to this question; but let us assume for the moment that it is decided to make an *equal* charge in each year.

Thus the annual depreciation expense will be: $\dfrac{£50\,000}{5} = £10\,000$.

The 1991 accounts including this expense are shown opposite (in the right-hand column). Notice that the *cash balance has not changed* as a result of charging depreciation. The vans' net book value has fallen by £10 000; and this is reflected in a reduction of £10 000 in profit.

FURNITURE REMOVALS LIMITED
Balance sheet at 31 December 1991

	Draft £'000	Final £'000
Vans at cost	60	60
Less: Accumulated depreciation	—	10
Net book value	60	50
Cash	40	40
	100	90
Share capital	60	60
Retained profit	40	30
	100	90

Profit and loss account for 1991

	Draft £'000	Final £'000
Turnover	100	100
Cash expenses	60	60
Depreciation	—	10
	60	70
Profit for the year	40	30

Distribution of profit

Continuing the Furniture Removals example, let us now make a further assumption: that the directors decide to distribute all the available profit (£30 000) as dividends. (For simplicity we are ignoring tax.) The balance sheet below shows the position after paying the dividends.

FURNITURE REMOVALS LIMITED
Balance sheet after payment of dividends

	£'000
Vans at cost	60
Less: Accumulated depreciation	10
Net book value	50
Cash	10
	60
Share capital	60
Retained profit	–
	60

It can be seen that the effect of charging depreciation is to reduce the amount of profit available for dividends. The cash thus indirectly withheld may be used to replace the expired assets at the end of their life. In the absence of an adequate depreciation charge, too little may be retained and the company may in effect be distributing part of its capital in the guise of dividends.

At the end of year 5, when the fixed assets have been written down to £10 000, the cash available through accumulated depreciation (unless already used for some other purpose) will be £50 000. If the old vans then realize the predicted amount of £10 000 on disposal, the company will once again have its original capital (£60 000) in money terms. (Of course in periods of inflation this may no longer be enough to buy similar vans. We shall be discussing the problems caused by inflation in Section 11.)

In any event, the *accounting* purpose of determining the profit or loss earned by a business should be distinguished from the possible *financial* purpose of accumulating funds with which to replace a fixed asset. Not all fixed assets are replaced; certainly not always with identical assets. But depreciation is still a necessary accounting expense, in order to 'maintain capital'.

Alternative asset lives and residual values

We were able to complete the accounts of Furniture Removals Limited for 1991 by making specific assumptions about the expected useful life and residual value of the vans which had cost £60 000.

Let us now consider what difference it would have made to the reported results had the directors taken a different view of the uncertain future. What would have been the effect, for instance, of estimating a four-year useful life with a residual value of £12 000?

The calculation of the depreciation charge, the net profit (assuming constant £40 000 profits each year before depreciation), and the balance sheet net book value figures for each year of the anticipated life of the vans are set out below (left) on the basis of the original assumptions.

You are asked to calculate and enter (below right) the equivalent figures based on the assumption of a four-year life and £16 000 residual value. Continue to assume that an equal charge should be made each year.

Please complete your calculations *before* looking across at the next page.

Assumption 1			Assumption 2		
Cost		£60 000	Cost		£60 000
Estimated asset life		5 years	Estimated asset life		4 years
Estimated residual value £10 000			Estimated residual value £16 000		
Annual depreciation (£'000):	$\frac{60-10}{5}=10$		Annual depreciation (£'000)		

	Depreciation expense £'000	Net profit £'000	Net book value £'000		Depreciation expense £'000	Net profit £'000	Net book value £'000
Year 1	10	30	50*	Year 1			
Year 2	10	30	40	Year 2			
Year 3	10	30	40	Year 3			
Year 4	10	30	20	Year 4			
Year 5	10	30	10	Year 5			

---

*Net book value = Cost less accumulated depreciation (end of year).

Furniture Removals Limited

Set out opposite are figures (in £'000) based on the alternative assumptions about asset life and residual value. Both the profit and loss account and the balance sheet figures are affected – even though the *same* assets and the *same* businesses are involved!

Disposal of vans
for £14 000 at the end of year 4

Had the vans in fact been sold for £18 000 at the end of year 4, the entries opposite would have appeared in the profit and loss account in year 4.

Notice that the total net amount (in (£'000) charged over the fixed assets' life in each case is £42 (cost £60 less proceeds £18).

Assumption 1

Cost £60 000
Asset life 5 years
Residual value £10 000

Annual depreciation (£'000): $\dfrac{60-10}{5} = 10$

	Depreciation expense £'000	Net profit £'000	Net book value £'000
Year 1	10	30	50
Year 2	10	30	40
Year 3	10	30	30
Year 4	10	30	20
Year 5	10	30	10

Year 4

		£'000
Profit before depreciation		40
Less: Depreciation	10	
Loss on sale (a)	2	
		12
Net profit for year		28

(a) NBV £20 less proceeds £18

4 × £10 per year	=	40
Plus: loss on sale	=	2
Total net charge		42

Assumption 2

Cost £60 000
Asset life 4 years
Residual value £16 000

Annual depreciation (£'000): $\dfrac{60-16}{4} = 11$

	Depreciation expense £'000	Net profit £'000	Net book value £'000
Year 1	11	29	49
Year 2	11	29	38
Year 3	11	29	27
Year 4	11	29	16
Year 5			

Year 4

		£'000
Profit before depreciation		40
Less: Depreciation	11	
Profit on sale (b)	(2)	
		9
Net profit for year		31

(b) Proceeds £18 less NBV £16

4 × £11 per year	=	44
Less: profit on sale	=	(2)
Total net charge		42

METHODS OF DEPRECIATION

We have seen that estimates of likely lives and residual values of fixed assets can affect reported results. So can the choice of depreciation *method*. So far we have assumed that the company would want to charge an equal amount of depreciation expense in each year of a fixed asset's life; but this is only one of a number of possible methods.

The two most common methods of providing for depreciation are:

(a) straight line (the method we have used so far)
(b) declining balance.

(a) The straight line method

The straight line method of depreciation is the simplest of all. In the UK it is by far the commonest method. It involves writing off an equal charge each year based on the asset's estimated cost (original cost less residual value) and its estimated life.

This was the method used by Furniture Removals Limited:

$$\frac{60\,000 - 10\,000}{5} = \frac{£50\,000}{5} = £10\,000 \text{ a year depreciation}$$

$$= 16.7 \text{ per cent of cost } (= 1/6\text{th})$$

The effect is represented graphically opposite, showing the 'straight line' of the falling net book value year by year, and the 'straight line' annual depreciation charge.

Depreciation calculated on the straight line basis can always be expressed as a constant percentage of original cost.

The straight line method

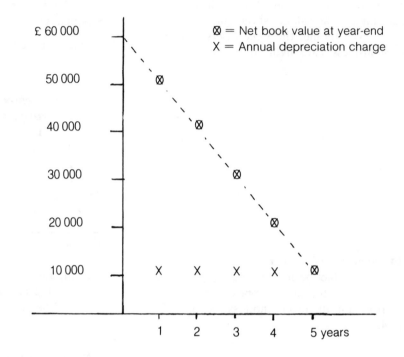

	Depreciation expense		Accumulated depreciation	Net book value
		£	£	£
Year 1	1/6 × £60 000 = 10 000		10 000	50 000
Year 2	1/6 × £60 000 = 10 000		20 000	40 000
Year 3	1/6 × £60 000 = 10 000		30 000	30 000
Year 4	1/6 × £60 000 = 10 000		40 000	20 000
Year 5	1/6 × £60 000 = 10 000		50 000	10 000

(b) The declining balance method

The declining balance method of ('accelerated') depreciation charges larger amounts in earlier years of an asset's life than in later years. The annual charge is calculated by applying to the asset's net book value at the start of each accounting period a constant percentage intended to reduce the net book value to (approximately) its residual value at the end of its estimated useful life.

Had Furniture Removals Limited used the declining balance method, the required percentage rate to reduce the net book value of the vans to their expected residual value of £10 000 at the end of year 5 would have been 30 per cent.* The net book value and annual depreciation is shown graphically opposite. Notice how quickly the asset's net book value falls, and how much the annual depreciation charge itself has declined after the first year or two.

It is not surprising that to write an asset off in a given time the declining balance method needs a higher percentage rate (usually about twice as high) than the straight line method. This is because the declining balance percentage is applied to the declining net book value, whereas the straight line percentage is applied to original cost. For the same reason, the declining balance method will never reduce an asset to zero net book value. But when the net book value becomes very small in relation to cost, it can be written off entirely in a single year.

Had Furniture Removals Limited used the declining balance method of depreciation instead of the straight line method, profits in earlier years would have been reduced and those in later years would have been higher. In total the two methods aim to write off exactly the *same* amount in depreciation over an asset's whole useful life; but the pattern of spreading the net cost between years over the asset's life is different.

Accelerated depreciation reduces the risk of heavier charges in later years (or a loss on disposal) should it prove that insufficient allowance has been made for obsolescence in estimating the asset's useful life. And it often produces a balance sheet net book value of fixed assets more closely in line with their declining market value than straight line depreciation. On the other hand, this is irrelevant in historical cost accounting if there is no intention of selling a fixed asset before the end of its useful life.

*The declining balance depreciation percentage uses the following formula:

$$r = \left[1 - (R/c)^{\frac{1}{n}}\right] \times 100$$

where: r = rate of depreciation per period
      c = original cost
      R = Residual value
      n = number of periods of useful life.

The declining balance method

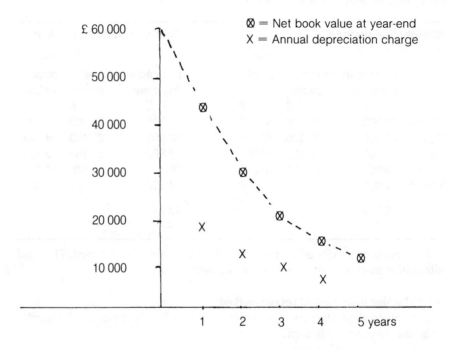

⊗ = Net book value at year-end
X = Annual depreciation charge

	Depreciation expense		Accumulated depreciation	Net book value
		£	£	£
Year 1	30% × £60 000 =	18 000	18 000	42 000
Year 2	30% × £42 000 =	12 600	30 600	29 400
Year 3	30% × £29 400 =	8 820	39 420	20 580
Year 4	30% × £20 580 =	6 174	45 594	14 406
Year 5	30% × £14 406 =	4 322	49 916	10 084

Straight line and declining balance methods compared

Whichever method of depreciation is used, and for whatever reasons, the significant differences between straight line and declining balance depreciation will reflect in both the net profit reported and the fixed asset net book values year by year. This is shown by the Furniture Removals figures:

Profit before depreciation = £40 000

	Straight line method			**Declining balance method**		
	Depreciation expense	Net profit	Net book value	Depreciation expense	Net profit	Net book value
	£	£	£	£	£	£
Year 1	10 000	30 000	50 000	18 000	22 000	42 000
Year 2	10 000	30 000	40 000	12 600	27 400	29 400
Year 3	10 000	30 000	30 000	8 820	31 180	20 580
Year 4	10 000	30 000	20 000	6 174	33 826	14 406
Year 5	10 000	30 000	10 000	4 322	35 678	10 084
	50 000			49 916		

In appropriate cases other methods of depreciation can be used. One such alternative method is discussed briefly below.

(c) Machine hour method (usage method)

Under this method, the depreciation charge for a period is based on the number of hours the machine is used.

Example

A company purchased a special processing machine for £55 000. The technical director estimated that the machine could be used for 10 000 hours before it would be virtually worn out, with £5 000 residual value. The net cost of £50 000 is to be charged over the total expected life of 10 000 hours at a rate of £5 depreciation per hour. If the company uses the machine for 2 000 hours in the first year, and for 3 500 hours in the second, the charges for depreciation will be respectively £10 000 and £17 500.

The machine hour method bases the depreciation charge on usage rather than on time. Thus the depreciation expense *varies* with production volume. (A similar approach, based on mileage, can be used for cars.)

The four variables in depreciation

We have seen that three variables need to be measured in calculating depreciation of fixed assets:

A Cost
B Estimated residual value } = net cost
C Estimated useful life

More than one *method* of depreciation (D) is then possible in order to write off a fixed asset's estimated net cost over its estimated useful life.

Because both the residual value and the useful life of a fixed asset are unknown in advance, as a rule depreciation charged in company accounts can only be an estimate, not a precisely accurate amount.

The diagram below summarizes the position.

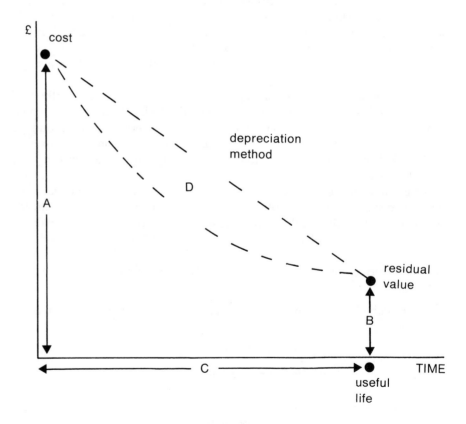

VARYING DEPRECIATION CHARGES: EFFECT ON REPORTED RESULTS

Enough has been said about the different possible methods of depreciation to show that great care is needed in trying to compare the results of two companies. The force of this warning can be appreciated by working through an example where large differences arise in the figures.

Let us take a case where possible technical obsolescence affects the estimates of a fixed asset's likely useful life. While engineers can often forecast physical wear and tear fairly accurately, the effects of technical or market obsolescence are much harder to foresee. In calculating depreciation we are concerned with an asset's *economically* useful life, not solely with its physical life in working order.

Example

Let us assume that two companies, Green Limited and Brown Limited, are in the same type of business, and that they are both regularly making profits before depreciation of £200 000 a year. (Ignore tax to simplify the example.) Let us further assume that they both acquire identical machines for use in production at a cost of £100 000 each.

Green's technical director believes that the machine could soon be replaced by a more sophisticated machine. He proposes that the company should write it off over three years, allowing for a residual value of only £12 500; and use accelerated depreciation in case the machine becomes obsolete even sooner than expected. This requires using a 50 per cent rate of declining balance depreciation.

The technical director of Brown, on the other hand, regards the machine as being of a standard design. He thinks it will continue in effective use for at least five years, after which time it should be possible to sell it for about £25 000. The company accepts his estimates, and uses straight line depreciation as usual.

You are asked to show the results of implementing these technical and commercial judgements in the accounts of Green Limited and Brown Limited. Space is provided opposite for you to *write in* your answers.

GREEN LIMITED

Cost of machine: £100 000
Estimated life: 3 years
Residual value: £12 500
Depreciation method: Declining balance
(Percentage to reduce net book value to £12 500 in 3 years = 50 per cent.)

	Profit before depreciation £'000	Annual depreciation £'000	Net profit £'000	Accumulated depreciation £'000	Net book value £'000
Year 1	200				
Year 2	200				
Year 3	200				

BROWN LIMITED

Cost of machine: £100 000
Estimated life: 5 years
Residual value: £25 000
Depreciation method: Straight line

	Profit before depreciation £'000	Annual depreciation £'000	Net profit £'000	Accumulated depreciation £'000	Net book value £'000
Year 1	200				
Year 2	200				
Year 3	200				
Year 4	200				
Year 5	200				

Please now compare your answers with those shown on the next page.

Green Limited and Brown Limited

This example illustrates the impact of opinion on reported results, for the widely different figures shown for the two companies represent the same physical facts. When the depreciation methods and rates were chosen there was no way to tell which would produce the more 'correct' answer.

If Green's anticipation of swift obsolescence proved true, then Brown would have shown profit figures which were too high in years 1 to 3. And at the end of year 3, Brown's net book value of £55 000 might be £42 500 higher than the residual value at that time. The asset balance might have to be written off against profits which it was no longer able to generate. But if Brown's judgement proved to be correct, then both the profits and asset book values shown in Green's accounts in years 1 to 3 are understated.

Revising initial estimates

Since both the economic life and the ultimate residual value of fixed assets can only be estimated at the beginning of their lives, there are bound to be errors in the light of events. One way to deal with such errors is simply to record a profit or loss on disposal when the asset's useful life ends. In effect this represents an adjustment of prior year depreciation charges.

Insignificant differences – small profits or losses on disposal – are usually absorbed in the figure shown for depreciation expense. Substantial profits or losses on disposal, however, may require separate disclosure in the year of sale. Significant regular profits (or regular losses) on disposals of fixed assets may indicate a definite tendency to overprovide (or underprovide) for depreciation.

Another possible policy when dealing with large differences is from time to time to revise the original estimates of fixed asset lives (or the estimated residual values). Imperial Chemical Industries plc's annual report, for example, includes the following statement about accounting policy on depreciation.
'The Group's policy is to write off the book value of each tangible fixed asset evenly over its estimated remaining life. Reviews are made periodically of the estimated remaining lives of individual productive assets, taking account of commercial and technological obsolescence as well as normal wear and tear.'

SSAP 12 requires that where there is a revision of the estimated useful life of a fixed asset, the undepreciated cost should be charged over the revised remaining useful life. But if the original estimate of an asset's life was too *short*, a company may find it has completely written off the cost of fixed assets which continue in productive use. The original cost is still included in the total cost of fixed assets, and the accumulated depreciation total includes that same amount. Cost and accumulated depreciation are 'written out' (eliminated) from the books only when a fully written-off fixed asset is actually disposed of or retired from active use.

GREEN LIMITED

Cost of machine: £100 000
Estimated life: 3 years
Residual value: £12 500
Depreciation method: Declining balance
(Percentage to reduce net book value to £12 500 in 3 years = 50 per cent.)

	Profit before depreciation £'000	Annual depreciation £'000	Net profit £'000	Accumulated depreciation £'000	Net book value £'000
Year 1	200	50	150	50	50
Year 2	200	25	175	75	25
Year 3	200	12.5	187.5	87.5	12.5

BROWN LIMITED

Cost of machine: £100 000
Estimated life: 5 years
Residual value: £25 000

Depreciation method: Straight line $\dfrac{100-25}{5} = 15$

	Profit before depreciation £'000	Annual depreciation £'000	Net profit £'000	Accumulated depreciation £'000	Net book value £'000
Year 1	200	15	185	15	85
Year 2	200	15	185	30	70
Year 3	200	15	185	45	55
Year 4	200	15	185	60	40
Year 5	200	15	185	75	25

LEASING FIXED ASSETS

Leasing assets is a way for the lessee to enjoy the use of assets without owning them. It is usual to distinguish between 'operating' leases and 'finance' leases:

	Operating lease	Finance lease
Period	May be very short; far less than the asset's useful life	Nearly all the asset's useful life
Payments	May be very small	The asset's full cost plus interest on the finance provided by the lessor
Commitment	Cancellable	Non-cancellable
Repairs	Done by lessor	Responsibility of lessee

In short, in an operating lease the lessor retains most of the risks and rewards of ownership of an asset, whereas in a finance lease these are transferred to the lessee.

In an operating lease, the lessee will simply charge the lease rental payments as an expense in the profit and loss account. No asset will appear in the balance sheet (unless there is a prepayment of rent).

Where a capital amount has been paid for a leasehold property, the lessee's balance sheet will show that 'premium' as a fixed asset, which will need to be amortized. The treatment of the regular lease rentals will depend on whether it is an operating lease or a finance lease.

SSAP 21 requires lessees to capitalize finance leases and show them as fixed assets on the balance sheet. The discounted value of the total unpaid lease rental payments will appear as a creditor. (The same applies to hire-purchase contracts which are of a financing nature.)

The result is virtually the same as if the asset had been purchased outright. Finance leases are treated, in effect, as an alternative way of financing the purchase of an asset. Much of the annual rental charge is treated as equivalent to an instalment of the asset's purchase price, and is deducted from the 'creditor' account on the balance sheet.

The balance of the rental charge represents 'interest' payable on the unpaid instalments, and is charged to the profit and loss account as an expense.

This is a clear example of reporting 'economic substance' rather than 'legal form'. The business *controls* the asset leased under a finance lease, even though it does not legally *own* it.

The profit and loss account will also be charged with annual depreciation on the capitalized fixed asset, calculated in the usual way. This will reduce the net book value of the fixed asset over time. The asset should be depreciated over its estimated useful life, or the lease term if shorter.

Depreciation and interest together may not differ much from the rental charge, so the net effect of capitalizing finance leases on the profit and loss account will be fairly small (though 'interest cover' will be reduced). But the effect on the balance sheet of adding a fixed asset and a creditor could be important: it will clearly reduce the apparent rate of return on net assets, and increase the debt ratio.

A hypothetical example is set out below.

	Operating lease £'000	Finance lease £'000
Balance sheet summary		
Leased assets	—	40
Other fixed assets	100	100
Net working capital	60	56*
Net assets	160	196
Creditors due after more than one year	50	86*
Shareholders' funds	110	110
Capital employed	160	196
Profit and loss account summary		
Depreciation expense	10	14
Lease rental expense	8	—
Profit before interest payable and tax	32	36
Interest payable	5	9
Profit before tax	27	27
Financial ratios		
Return on net assets	20.0%	18.0%
Debt ratio	31.3%	45.0%
Interest cover	6.4	4.0

*It is assumed that of the £40 000 capitalized, £4 000 represents creditors due within one year and £36 000 creditors due after more than one year.

REVALUATION OF FIXED ASSETS

The UK differs in one important respect from other countries which use historical cost accounting (such as the US, Germany and Japan). The Companies Act 1985 permits UK companies to show tangible fixed assets at *more* than historical cost. Companies may continue to use historical cost (less amounts written off); but they may use either 'current cost' (see Section 11) or market value (which need not be at the balance sheet date) instead. Intangible fixed assets other than goodwill may be shown at current cost; fixed asset investments either at market value or at directors' valuation.

The reason for allowing companies to depart from historical cost may be the very high UK rates of inflation over the past twenty years (see Section 11). In any event, many UK companies do revalue certain fixed assets upwards, especially land and buildings. The surplus goes to a revaluation reserve under shareholders' funds. The effect is to increase the book value, both of net assets and of shareholders' funds. Hence revaluation reduces the reported percentages for (a) return on net assets, (b) return on equity, and (c) debt ratio; and reduces the ratios for net asset turnover and fixed asset turnover.

SSAP 12 requires companies to base depreciation on any revalued amount, rather than on cost. The effect is usually small in respect of buildings, because their life is long. But most UK companies choose not to revalue plant and equipment, which could significantly increase the amount of depreciation and hence reduce profits.

The current position is that some UK companies continue to use historical cost only; but many have revalued some of their fixed assets at some time in the past. Very few companies, however, regularly revalue all their fixed assets, or even all their land and buildings. The result is that comparability among companies or over time is extremely difficult.

PRESENTATION IN PUBLISHED ACCOUNTS

The Companies Act 1985 requires companies to disclose three different kinds of fixed assets:

1 Intangible assets.
2 Investments.
3 Tangible assets.

Intangible assets

The permitted balance sheet formats (see pages 319 and 321) list four different kinds of intangible assets:

1 Development costs.
2 Concessions, patents, licences, trade marks, and similar rights and assets.
3 Goodwill.
4 Payments on account.

Accounts may show intangible fixed assets either at original cost or at cost less accumulated depreciation ('amortization') to date. Many companies prefer not to include intangible assets on the balance sheet: they may choose not to capitalize development costs, or patents and trade marks; and they may write off purchased goodwill immediately against reserves.

Where a company does capitalize development costs (see page 112), it must say why, and state the period over which it is writing off the costs. Where a company includes goodwill as an asset in the balance sheet, it must state the amortization period and give the reasons for choosing that period (see Section 9).

Investments

The Companies Act 1985 requires balance sheets to disclose the following different kinds of investments:

1 Shares in or loans to subsidiary undertakings (see Section 9).
2 Shares in or loans to associated undertakings (see Section 9).
3 Other shares.
4 Other loans.

Investments in subsidiary undertakings would not normally be shown as such in consolidated (group) accounts, for reasons explained in Section 9. The aggregate market value of listed investments must be disclosed. The accounts must provide for and disclose any permanent diminution in value of an investment. Investments of a short-term nature would be shown as current assets.

Tangible assets

Four different kinds of tangible assets are listed in the permitted balance sheet formats (though it is common for items (2) and (3) to be combined):

1 Land and buildings.
2 Plant and machinery.
3 Fixtures, fittings, tools and equipment.
4 Payments on account and assets in course of construction.

These are the kinds of assets we have mainly been discussing so far in this section; and, where appropriate, they include finance leases capitalized (the total amount of which must be disclosed).

Because of the extensive detailed disclosure required by the Companies Act 1985, a balance sheet normally shows on the face only the total net book value of tangible fixed assets. The detail is then set out in a note to the accounts. An example of detailed presentation is given below.

	Land and buildings £ million	Plant and equipment £ million	Total £ million
Cost			
At start of year, 1.1.91	120	585	705
Currency variations	4	11	15
New subsidiaries acquired	7	17	24
Capital expenditure	8	56	64
Disposals	(2)	(12)	(14)
At end of year, 31.12.91	137	657	794
Depreciation			
At start of year, 1.1.91	45	307	352
Currency variations	2	7	9
Disposals	(1)	(10)	(11)
Charge for year	5	48	53
At end of year, 31.12.91	51	352	403
Net book value, 31.12.91	86	305	391
Net book value, 31.12.90	*75*	*278*	*353*

Notes
1 The net book value of land and buildings comprises freehold properties £71 million, long leaseholds £15 million.
2 The net book value of plant and equipment includes £17 million in respect of finance leases capitalized.

SUMMARY

Fixed assets are used on a continuing basis in the company's business; they are not intended for resale. Intentions, not physical characteristics, determine whether a particular asset is fixed or current.

The cost of a fixed asset includes related legal, installation costs, and so on. Once the cost has been determined, there are three main problems in computing depreciation:

1   Estimating the fixed asset's useful life, which may be limited by the passing of time, wear and tear, or by technical or market obsolescence.
2   Estimating residual value, which in practice is often ignored if it is small.
3   Choosing a depreciation method, the main two being (a) straight line or (b) declining balance.

Depreciation allocates original cost against profit over time, in an attempt to match expense against revenue. It is not a valuation process.

Straight line depreciation writes off a constant percentage of cost each year, while the declining balance method writes off a constant percentage of the (declining) net book value at the beginning of each year.

Different methods all write off the same total amount over a fixed asset's life (namely, original cost less residual value); but the pattern differs between accounting periods, which affects both reported profit (or loss) and net assets. On disposal of a fixed asset, any profit or loss usually represents, in effect, an adjustment to prior years' depreciation charges.

Finance leases which transfer most of the risks and rewards of ownership of an asset must be capitalized and depreciated in the usual way. The discounted liability to pay future rentals is shown as a creditor.

Many UK companies revalue the land and buildings from time to time (but not plant and equipment). The result is to significantly affect a number of performance ratios, and to impair comparability between companies.

5.1 Definitions

Write down below your definition of the terms shown. Then compare your answers with the definitions overleaf.

(a) A tangible fixed asset	(f) The declining balance method
(b) Depreciation	(g) Accelerated depreciation
(c) Net book value	(h) Finance lease
(d) Residual value	(i) Amortization
(e) The straight line method	(j) Capital commitments

5.1 Definitions

(a) *A tangible fixed asset* is a resource with a relatively long economic life acquired not for resale in the ordinary course of business but for use in producing other goods and services.

(b) *Depreciation* (of fixed assets) is the process of allocating part of the cost of fixed assets (or, in some cases, the amount of their valuation) as expense to a particular accounting period. Accumulated depreciation is the total amount so provided to date for assets still held by the company; it must be shown separately in the balance sheet or in the notes to the accounts.

(c) *Net book value* (NBV) is the difference between the cost of a fixed asset (or, in some cases, the amount of its valuation) and the accumulated depreciation in respect of that asset. It is not normally intended to represent market value.

(d) *Residual value* is the amount for which a fixed asset can be sold at the end of its useful life. The expected residual value is taken into account in calculating depreciation during the asset's life (often it is treated as zero).

(e) *The straight line method* of depreciation charges an equal amount of depreciation in each year of an asset's life, by writing off a constant percentage of the asset's original cost.

(f) *The declining balance method* of depreciation writes off a constant percentage of the declining net book value of a fixed asset shown at the start of each accounting period. The percentage rate used is higher than for the straight line method.

(g) *Accelerated depreciation* is any depreciation method which charges higher amounts in the early years of an asset's life than in the later years. Declining balance is one such method.

(h) *A finance lease* is a non-cancellable commitment, usually lasting for nearly all the asset's economic life, where total lease payments usually exceed the total cash purchase price and repairs are the responsibility of the lessee. It transfers substantially all the risks and rewards of ownership of the asset to the lessee; and SSAP 21 requires companies to capitalize finance leases.

(i) *Amortization* is the name often given to depreciation of intangible fixed assets.

(j) *Capital commitments* are significant amounts of capital expenditure which a company is contractually bound to pay in the future, or which have been approved for expenditure (but not actually contracted for) at the balance sheet date.

148

5.2 Jonas Limited (A): Straight line depreciation

Jonas Limited buys a fixed asset for £8 400, expects it to last for six years (after which it will have no value) and proposes to write off depreciation on the straight line basis. Calculate the depreciation charge each year, and the net book value at the end of each year.

The solution to this problem is given overleaf.

Space for answer

		£
	Cost	8 400
Year 1	Depreciation	
	Net book value, end of year 1	
Year 2	Depreciation	
	Net book value, end of year 2	
Year 3	Depreciation	
	Net book value, end of year 3	
Year 4	Depreciation	
	Net book value, end of year 4	
Year 5	Depreciation	
	Net book value, end of year 5	
Year 6	Depreciation	
	Net book value, end of year 6	

5.3 Potter Publishing Limited: Changing from straight line to declining balance

Potter Publishing Limited is considering changing from the straight line method of depreciation to the declining balance method. Neither residual values nor estimated asset lives would change, but the percentage depreciation rate would be doubled. Assuming that Potter Publishing expects to replace its existing fixed assets fairly regularly over a ten-year cycle without marked fluctuations from year to year, how would you expect such a change to affect the company's accounts?

A solution to this problem is given overleaf.

5.4 Lawson Limited (A): Profit or loss on disposal

Lawson Limited paid £7 200 for a fixed asset which is expected to last for six years. It is to be written off on the straight line basis, assuming ultimate salvage proceeds of £600.

Calculate the depreciation charged each year, and the profit or loss on disposal, if the asset is actually sold for:

(a)   £3 500 at the end of year 4
(b)   £1 400 at the end of year 5
(c)   how would the asset be shown in the balance sheet at the end of year 3?

The solution to this problem is given overleaf.

Space for answer

		(a) £	(b) £
	Cost		
Year 1	Depreciation		
	Net book value, end of year 1		
Year 2	Depreciation		
	Net book value, end of year 2		
Year 3	Depreciation		
	Net book value, end of year 3		
Year 4	Depreciation		
	Net book value, end of year 4		
Year 5			

(a)   profit/loss on disposal
(b)   profit/loss on disposal
(c)   end of year 3 balance sheet:

5.2 Jonas Limited (A)

Solution

		£
	Cost	8 400
Year 1	Depreciation	1 400
	Net book value, end of year 1	7 000
Year 2	Depreciation	1 400
	Net book value, end of year 2	5 600
Year 3	Depreciation	1 400
	Net book value, end of year 3	4 200
Year 4	Depreciation	1 400
	Net book value, end of year 4	2 800
Year 5	Depreciation	1 400
	Net book value, end of year 5	1 400
Year 6	Depreciation	1 400
	Net book value, end of year 6	—

5.3 Potter Publishing Limited

Solution

In the first few years after the change, the depreciation expense charged against profit would be higher under the declining balance method and the reported profit therefore lower. After about ten years the new total annual depreciation charge should be about the same under both methods; but the extra declining balance depreciation charged in years 1 to 10 after the change will result in higher accumulated depreciation (and therefore lower balance sheet net book values of fixed assets) than under the straight line method.

Thus the immediate effect of the change will be to reduce reported profits and return on investment; but the ultimate effect will be to reduce reported capital employed without affecting profit (much), and thus to *increase* reported return on investment. (This might not be true if the total cost of fixed assets were to increase year by year, but it is assumed here that the total remains more or less constant over time.)

5.4 Lawson Limited (A)

Solution

		(a) £	(b) £
	Cost	7 200	7 200
Year 1	Depreciation	1 100	1 100
	Net book value, end of year 1	6 100	6 100
Year 2	Depreciation	1 100	1 100
	Net book value, end of year 2	5 000	5 000
Year 3	Depreciation	1 100	1 100
	Net book value, end of year 3	3 900	3 900
Year 4	Depreciation	1 100	1 100
	Net book value, end of year 4	2 800	2 800
	Sale proceeds	3 500	
	Profit on sale	700	
Year 5	Depreciation		1 100
	Net book value, end of year 5		1 700
	Sale proceeds		1 400
	Loss on sale		300

(a) Profit on disposal = £700
(b) Loss on disposal = £300

(c) End of year 3 balance sheet:		£
	Fixed asset at cost	7 200
	Less: Accumulated depreciation	3 300
	Net book value	3 900

Notes

1 Where a residual value is taken into account in calculating depreciation the straight line method does *not* charge simply one-sixth of cost each year (1/6 × £7 200 = £1 200). Instead, the charge is one-sixth of the expected *net* cost (1/6 × £6 600 = £1 100).

2 In both case (a) and case (b) the total amount written off over the life of the asset is its total net cost (original cost less residual value):
   (a) £7 200 − £3 500 = £3 700 = (4 × £1 100) − £700 profit
   (b) £7 200 − £1 400 = £5 800 = (5 × £1 100) + £300 loss

5.5 Jonas Limited (B): Different lives

Jonas Limited buys a fixed for £8 400, expects it to last for 6 years, and proposes to write off depreciation on the straight line basis. (See 5.2 Jonas Limited (A)).

(a)   what happens if the asset is sold for £2 000 after only 4 years?
(b)   what happens if the asset lasts for 8 years?

Please write your answers in the space below, trying to cover all the important accounting issues involved.

A solution to this problem is given overleaf.

(a)

(b)

5.6 Lawson Limited (B): Early disposal

Lawson Limited paid £7 200 for a fixed asset which is expected to last for six years. It is to be written off on the straight line basis, assuming ultimate salvage proceeds of £600 (see 5.4 Lawson Limited (A)).

The asset is actually sold for £3 500 at the end of year 4 (as in part (a) of Lawson Limited (A)).

Please set out the Disposal of fixed assets account.

A solution to this problem is given overleaf.

5.7 Whizzo Buses Limited

Whizzo Buses Limited decides to depreciate its buses on the basis of miles travelled. A particular vehicle costs £80 000; its residual value is expected to be £8 000; and its expected mileage during its life with Whizzo is expected to be 120 000 miles.

How much depreciation should be charged in the first three years of its life if it travels 12 000 miles, 20 000 miles, and 15 000 miles in years 1, 2, and 3 respectively?

A solution to this problem is shown overleaf.

5.8   Dingle Brothers

Dingle Brothers installed equipment costing £60 000 in a development zone. The equipment is expected to last 6 years, and to have no residual value. It is to be written off by the straight line method. Dingle Brothers receive a government grant of £24 000 which they credit to a reserve account.

What items will appear in the profit and loss account each year in respect of the equipment? What will the balance sheet at the end of year 2 show?

A solution to this problem is shown overleaf.

5.5 Jonas Limited (B)

Solution

(a) At the end of the fourth year, the £800 difference between the £2 800 net book value and the £2 000 sales proceeds will have to be written off as a loss on disposal. This will be treated as an expense in the profit and loss account in year 4, in addition to the normal annual depreciation of £1 400 in year 4.

Thus over the 4-year life of the asset the total amount written off will be:

	£
Depreciation = 4 × £1 400 =	5 600
Loss on sale =	800
	6 400

Notice that the £6 400 total amount written off over the asset's life is exactly equal to the original £8 400 cost less the £2 000 sale proceeds.

(b) No depreciation will be charged in years 7 and 8, since the asset has already been completely written off by the end of year 6. Any sales proceeds at the end of year 8 will be treated as a profit on sale.

In the balance sheet at the end of years 6 and 7 the asset will appear as follows:

	£
Fixed asset at cost	8 400
Less: Accumulated depreciation	8 400
Net book value	—

5.6 Lawson Limited (B)

Solution

Disposal of fixed assets

	Dr £		Cr £
Cost	7 200	Accumulated depreciation	4 400
P & L profit on sale	700	Cash received	3 500
	7 900		7 900

5.7 Whizzo Buses Limited

Solution

Depreciation will be charged at 60p per mile $(= \frac{£80\ 000 - £8\ 000}{120\ 000})$. Hence in the first three years depreciation will be 60p times 12 000 miles, 20 000 miles, and 15 000 miles; that is, £7 200, £12 000, and £9 000 respectively.

5.8 Dingle Brothers

Solution

Depreciation charges will amount to £60 000/6 = £10 000 a year; but this will be reduced by a credit to the profit and loss account each year of £24 000/6 = £4 000 a year. Thus the *net* charge will amount to £6 000 a year (= (£60 000 − £24 000)/6).

At the end of year 2 the balance sheet will show:

Fixed asset.	Equipment at cost	£60 000
	Less: Accumulated depreciation	£20 000
	Net book value	£40 000
Reserve.	Government grant	£24 000
	Less: Credited to profit	£ 8 000
	Balance	£16 000

Answers to the following six problems are given at the end of the book:

5.9 Jonas Limited (C): Changes in net cost
Jonas Limited buys a fixed asset for £8 400, expects it to last for 6 years, and plans to write off depreciation on the straight line basis. (See 5.2 Jonas Limited (A).)

(a) what difference would it make to the annual depreciation charges and net book values if Jonas Limited wanted to allow for salvage proceeds of £600 at the end of year 6 (instead of the original estimate of zero)

(b) how would you take into account an improvement costing £1 200 at the start of year 4, which is not expected to affect the asset's life or residual value? What would the asset's net book value be at the end of years 4, 5, and 6?

5.10 James Hillier Limited (A): Declining balance
James Hillier Limited buys a fixed asset for £8 000, and expects salvage proceeds of £750 at the end of its anticipated 4-year life. The asset is to be written off by the declining balance method, using a 50 per cent rate.

(a) calculate the depreciation charge and the net book value each year. What profit or loss is expected on disposal?

(b) if expected salvage proceeds at the end of year 4 were £1 300, what declining balance percentage depreciation rate would be appropriate?

5.11 James Hillier Limited (B): Declining balance disposal
The asset (in 5.10(a) James Hillier (A)) actually lasts for 6 years, at the end of which time it is sold for £600.

(a) starting with the net book value at the end of year 4 (calculated in James Hillier (A(a)), complete the depreciation schedule

(b) compile journal entries relating to the disposal of the fixed asset in year 6

(c) draw up ledger accounts relating to the fixed asset for year 6, starting with the balances brought forward from the end of year 5.

5.12 Gilbert Limited and Sullivan Limited: Different depreciation policies
Gilbert Limited and Sullivan Limited are identical companies except for their depreciation polices. In respect of a fixed asset costing £7 200, Gilbert estimates a useful life of 10 years, a salvage value of £1 200, and proposes to use the straight line method of depreciation. Sullivan estimates a life of 6 years, no salvage value, and proposes to use one-third as the annual proportion of the declining net book value to be written off each year.

The asset becomes technically obsolete at the end of year 4, and has to be scrapped with salvage proceeds of only £200. Calculate for each of the two companies the depreciation charge each year, the net book value at the end of each year, and the profit or loss on disposal.

5.13 Talmen Limited (A): Reduced economic life estimate
Talmen Limited spent £30 000 on 1 January 1991 on machine A, which was expected to last for 10 years and to have a residual value of £6 000 on 31 December 2000. Accordingly, for the first 3 years of its life straight line depreciation of £2 400 per annum was charged.

On 31 December 1993 a routine review reckons the remaining life is now only 4 years, and the residual value on 31 December 1997 will be only £2 000. What, if anything, should the company do to account for the revised estimate?

5.14 Talmen Limited (B): Increased economic life estimate
On 1 January 1991 Talmen Limited spent £30 000 on machine B, which was expected to last for 10 years and to have a residual value of £6 000 on 31 December 2000. As for machine A, therefore, £2 400 a year straight line depreciation was charged for the first 3 years.

A routine review on 31 December 1993 reckons that machine B still has a remaining life of 10 years; and that its residual value on 31 December 2003 will be £10 000. What, if anything, should the company do to account for the revised estimate?

No answers are given for the following problems.

5.15 Raphael Machines Limited
Soon after the end of the year to 31 March 1992, Mr Gabriel, an accountant working for Raphael Machines Limited, was preparing the company's final accounts for the year just ended. Among many fixed asset transactions for the year were:

(a) New equipment was installed during the year. The invoice cost had been £125 000, although only £120 000 cash had actually been paid to the suppliers since a 4 per cent cash discount for payment within 15 days had been offered.

(b) In addition to the invoice cost, £4 500 had been paid to have the equipment transported to the factory; and a further £7 000 to have it installed in working order. During its first week of operation, abnormal material scrap amounting to £6 000 was incurred while the new equipment was adjusted to perfect running order.

(c) The firm exchanged one of its used motor vehicles for a new van during the year. The book value of the old vehicle was £2 400 (cost £7 600 less accumulated depreciation £5 200); and the list price of the new van was £10 400. The garage concerned offered a trade-in price of £3 600 for the old van, which it was reckoned could have been sold for £3 000 cash.

Mr Gabriel was not sure how the above transactions should be treated in the accounts. You are required to advise him of the most appropriate treatment in each case, identifying the main alternatives and explaining the reason for your recommendation for each of the items.

5.16 Maintaining improvement

Which of the following items would you capitalize (and depreciate over time), and which would you write off as expenses in the current period? Why?

(a) cost of moving equipment from one factory in the group to another, and installing it
(b) special overhaul costs to bring existing equipment up to recently enacted government safety standards
(c) cost of acquiring newly offered range of typewriter accessories for the firm's 400 electric typewriters
(d) raw material wastage due to inevitable 'teething problems' of new equipment
(e) replacement of worn-out principal component of a cutting machine with a modern improved version which costs *less* than the original component did.

5.17 Revaluing plant

Assuming that everything else stayed the same, what would be the effect on a company's return on capital employed of:

(a) revaluing land upwards
(b) revaluing plant and equipment upwards
(c) increasing the estimated remaining lives of fixed assets.

5.18 Negative depreciation?

Greenhouse Monstrosities Limited owns and leases out office buildings in the City of London. As a rule it expects its buildings to last for 50 years; and regards straight line depreciation as less inappropriate than any other method. But since it anticipates that the market value of its buildings will increase over each of the next several years, the company is wondering whether it is really sensible to provide for any depreciation at all in its published historical cost accounts. Indeed, it has even considered 'charging' negative depreciation! Prepare as brief an explanation as you can of what you consider the correct accounting treatment in the circumstances, and for what reasons.

5.19 Nick Saint plc

Nick Saint plc's group tangible fixed assets at 30 September 1991 were shown as follows in the notes to the accounts:

	Land and buildings £m	Plant and equipment £m
Cost or valuation		
At 1 October 1990	320	785
Additions	39	109
(Disposals)	(3)	(32)
Adjustments for revaluations	4	4
At 30 September 1991	360	866
Depreciation		
At 1 October 1990	32	367
Provided in the year	8	75
(Disposals)	—	(27)
At 30 September 1991	40	415
Net book values		
At 1 October 1990	288	418
At 30 September 1991	320	451

Questions:

1 What was the total net book value of disposals in the year ended 30 September 1991? If the proceeds from disposals were £9m in total, how would the difference be accounted for?
2 If plant and equipment is depreciated on the straight line basis, what is the average useful life implied by the table above? What assumptions have you made?
3 If land and buildings in total were revalued at 30 September 1991 at £470m, how would the above figures change? What would happen to the difference?
4 Ignoring question (3) above, incorporate the following transactions occurring during the year ended 30 September 1992 in preparing a table of fixed asset details (similar to the one above) as at the end of that year:
    (a) additions: land and buildings £28m; plant and equipment £84m
    (b) disposals: plant and equipment £5m net book value (£21m accumulated depreciation)
    (c) depreciation average life (straight line): land and buildings 50 years; plant and equipment 12 years.

Section 6
Cash flow statements

INTRODUCTION

We saw in Section 1 the links between the financial statements. The balance sheet gives a static picture of a company's financial position at a single point in time, while the profit and loss account and cash flow statement summarize flows during the year. In addition we have seen that computing relationships between figures – financial ratios – can provide insights into company performance and financial position. A close study of the cash flow statement can also be revealing, especially with respect to finance.

FRS 1 requires medium and large UK companies (see page 2) to publish a cash flow statement as part of their annual accounts. Its aim is to show cash flows in and out of a company under three main headings: operations, investing, and financing. Cash flow statements reveal the extent to which a company has generated cash by operations, by selling fixed assets, or by borrowing or issuing ordinary share capital. They also show how the company has used cash to pay interest, dividends, and taxation, and to acquire fixed assets and make other investments. As with financial ratios, a trend in cash flow figures over time is of more interest than the results for a single year.

FRS 1, the first Financial Reporting Standard from the new Accounting Standards Board, supersedes the requirement in SSAP 10 for a funds flow statement. That was never a complete success, partly because there was no standard format (as there is for the cash flow statement). It is still too early, at the time of writing, to know how companies will comply with FRS 1, but we expect that most companies will use the 'indirect method'. As with funds flows, this method uses balance sheet differences to arrive at flows; but in the cash flow statement these differences are adjusted to eliminate accruals, debtors and creditors. Funds flows, which represent movements in both cash and credit, are thus converted into cash flows by eliminating the credit and accrual elements. The alternative *direct* method of preparing cash flow statements, provides in effect, a classified summary of the cash book.

In this section we shall first note the aim of FRS 1 and then the presentation of Kwik Save plc's consolidated cash flow statement in the new format. We then look at an alternative format which preserves some key elements of the funds flow format which we have previously recommended while also using the new cash flow information. Finally, we shall see how to derive a cash flow statement from the other financial statements and the notes to the accounts.

CASH FLOW STATEMENTS

According to the Accounting Standards Board (ASB), the aim of FRS 1 is 'to require reporting entities . . . to report on a standard basis their cash generation and absorption for a period. [They] are required to provide a primary financial statement analysing cash flows under [five] standard headings . . . in order to assist users of the financial statements in their assessment of the reporting entity's liquidity, viability and financial adaptability. The objective of the standard headings is to ensure that cash flows are reported in a form that highlights the significant components of cash flow and facilitates comparison of the cash flow performance of different businesses.'

A published cash flow statement therefore shows net cash inflows and outflows under the five specified headings, ending with the movement in cash and cash equivalents. An example is shown opposite for Kwik Save plc for 1990 and 1991 (somewhat simplified, and rounded to the nearest million pounds).

In designing a standard layout, the ASB had to make a number of decisions relating to the standard headings, and the items to be shown under each. One such decision concerned the treatment of working capital. The focus throughout FRS 1 is on 'cash': in effect it excludes sales and purchases from 'net cash from operations' to the extent that they are supported at the year end by *credit*. This treatment means that changes in the policy on taking or giving trade credit may lead to apparent changes in operating cash flows. As we show later (page 157), an alternative treatment enables changes in investment in working capital to be considered separately from longer term operating funds generation.

Published notes (*continued from right hand column*)

Analysis of cash and cash equivalents

	Balances	Balances	Balances	Change in year	
	1989 £m	1990 £m	1991 £m	1990 £m	1991 £m
Cash investments	32	26	3	(6)	(23)
Cash at bank and in hand	7	8	10	1	2
Bank overdrafts	(−)	(1)	(11)	(1)	(10)
	39	33	2	(6)	(31)

KWIK SAVE plc

Published consolidated cash flow statement, year ended 31 August

	1990 £m	1991 £m
Operating activities		
Cash received from customers	1 446	1 784
Cash payments to suppliers	(1 260)	(1 541)
Cash paid to and on behalf of employees	(97)	(116)
Other	15	13
Net cash inflow	104	140
Returns from investments and servicing of finance		
Interest received	5	4
Dividends paid	(17)	(20)
Net cash outflow	(12)	(16)
Taxation paid	(41)	(30)
Investing activities		
Purchase of tangible fixed assets	(60)	(107)
Purchase of goodwill	(1)	(21)
Sale of tangible fixed assets	2	1
Net cash outflow	(59)	(127)
Net cash outflow before financing	(8)	(33)
Financing		
Issue of ordinary share capital	2	2
Decrease in cash and cash equivalents	(6)	(31)

Published notes

Reconciliation of operating profit to net cash inflow from operating activities

	1990	1991
Operating profit	80	99
Depreciation charges	17	21
(Increase) in stocks	(10)	(36)
(Increase)/decrease in debtors	2	(2)
Increase in creditors	15	58
Net cash inflow from operating activities	104	140

ALTERNATIVE CASH FLOW FORMAT

Many analysts are concerned with the longer term ability of companies to generate cash, rather than with the cash movements in a single period. Like them, we prefer to highlight separately the key movements which show management performance, and decisions about working capital and fixed asset investment, and about the financing of the business. We do this in a cash flow statement, which shows 'net funds from operations' before a working capital adjustment which is disclosed separately.

The FRS 1 approach uses working capital movements to convert a funds flow (cash and credit) into a cash flow. But this reflects only one aspect of the change in working capital. The second aspect, which may be more important, is the conscious decision by management to invest more or less in working capital. For example, reductions in total working capital for a company whose ratios used to reflect industry norms may indicate short-term financial pressure. The company may in effect be using working capital to finance fixed asset investment. But the standard cash flow statement does not disclose the change in working capital figure.

Further, in the FRS 1 cash flow statement, it would be possible for 'fixed asset investment' in the year to be very low because outstanding invoices had not been paid, at a time when investment was in fact proceeding at a high level. While the statement correctly reflects *cash* movements, it is of more interest to the analyst looking at longer term trends to know what the commitments are that are being incurred in the year.

In the restated statement the movements in both working capital and fixed assets can be compared with net funds from operations to determine the extent to which the company has been able to finance its investment from internally generated operating funds. The bottom part of the statement shows how any deficit has been financed, or any surplus invested.

Please study the restated version of the Kwik Save cash flow statement for 1990 and 1991, which is set out opposite. Overleaf we go on to discuss the key lines in the restated cash flow statement. We then provide an interpretation of the restated Kwik Save cash flow statement.

KWIK SAVE plc
Restated consolidated cash flow statement, year ended 31 August

	1990 £m	1991 £m
Internal funds/investment		
Operating profit	80	99
Interest received	5	4
	85	103
Items not involving the use of funds: Depreciation	17	21
Gross funds from operations	102	124
Tax	(41)	(30)
Dividends	(17)	(20)
Net funds from operations	44	74
Change in working capital		
Stocks (increase)	(10)	(36)
Debtors (increase)/decrease	2	(2)
Creditors increase	15	58
	7	20
Net cash from operations available for fixed asset investment	51	94
Sale of tangible fixed assets	2	1
Total cash available	53	95
Fixed asset investment		
Fixed assets	(60)	(107)
Purchase of goodwill on acquisitions	(1)	(21)
	(61)	(128)
Financing requirement	(8)	(33)
External financing		
Ordinary share capital	2	2
Investments	6	23
Cash at bank and in hand	(1)	(2)
Bank overdraft	1	10
	8	33

KEY LINES IN THE RESTATED CASH FLOW STATEMENT

The two versions of the Kwik Save cash flow statement contain the same basic information, but they summarize it differently. We would normally want to look at figures showing a five-year trend. In the restated format these are the main lines of interest.

Operating profit

This line links the profit and loss account and funds flow statement. Operating profit includes credit sales and purchases in the period as well as cash sales and purchases. It represents one of the best available measures of a company's operating performance, unaffected by financing or tax. The trend in operating profit signals possible changes in the competitive environment in which the enterprise operates, and changes in management's ability to respond.

Gross funds from operations

The term 'funds' measures cash plus credit; and to arrive at gross funds from operations we have to adjust operating profit by adding back or deducting any 'non-cash' items used to calculate profits. The main adjustments relate to depreciation, gains or losses on fixed asset disposals, and provisions made or released.

Net funds from operations

This is probably the most important line in the statement. It represents the operating 'lifeblood' of the enterprise after paying the necessary outgoings for financing (interest and dividends) and for tax. Although in theory dividend payments can be reduced, in practice dividends are regularly paid, and reduce the funds available for investment in the business.

It is not unusual for companies to make substantial provisions for restructuring their business from time to time. They may show these as extraordinary items below the line in the profit and loss account, or include them in preacquisition charges on an acquisition. Payments under such provisions should be deducted directly from net funds from operations. This reflects their close links with operating expenses.

Change in working capital

The change in working capital shows whether the enterprise is absorbing funds for working capital or releasing them. Certain items of working capital would normally increase with growth in turnover. Allowing for any changes in the ratios relative to industry norms may help analysts to detect signs either of financial stress or of loose control over working capital.

At least part of the cash held at the year-end is 'operating' in nature, and will be absorbed in operations in the next period. There may, however, be surplus cash, either accumulated over the years or as a temporary result of raising equity or debt. Any such surplus cash is not really 'working capital': it is 'negative financing'. It is rarely possible to split cash between the two, so as a rule we exclude cash from working capital, and include it all in the bottom part of the statement.

Net cash from operations available for fixed asset investment

The net cash from operations available for fixed asset investment reflects the position after allowing for a reduction or increase in working capital.

Total cash available

Companies can generate cash from disposals of fixed assets as well as from operations, and the sum of the two sources gives the total cash available for fixed asset investment.

Fixed asset investment

Companies must invest in fixed assets to maintain their productive capacity. In the absence of inflation and technological change, a non-growth company would probably need to invest about as much as historical cost depreciation. To assess whether a company is growing or declining in real terms, though, in comparing fixed asset depreciation and investment, analysts will have to allow for the effects of changes in the economic and technical environment. The trend in capital expenditure over the past five years may signal the required level, assuming that the same policies continue. Where a company is growing, however, it may not be easy to tell how much of the expenditure on tangible fixed assets has been needed to sustain the ongoing business, and how much has expanded it. Analysts can compare fixed capital spending with net funds from operations, adjusted by any working capital change. That will indicate whether or not the company's ongoing operations are generating the cash needed for fixed asset investment.

Another major use of funds may be on acquisitions of other companies, which may be partly financed by disposals. Such items may be large, but hard to predict.

Financing requirement/surplus

If total investment in working capital and fixed assets exceeds total internally generated funds, a deficit will result. In years when significant investment is taking place that is not in itself a cause for concern. But if there are continuous deficits over a five-year period, the conclusion must be that the existing rate of growth depends on regular injections of external finance. This may reflect strong growth which shareholders and lenders are prepared to finance; but it may suggest that past investments are producing an inadequate rate of return. Certainly a succession of negative figures (financing requirements) requires careful analysis.

External financing

The bottom part of the statement shows how a surplus is being invested, or how a financing requirement is being met – from issuing more equity, borrowing, or running down cash balances and short-term marketable investments.

INTERPRETATION OF THE KWIK SAVE RESTATED CASH FLOW STATEMENT

The statement shown on page 157 discloses the flows for 1990 and 1991. For analysis purposes we would normally prefer to use five years' figures.

From the available two years' flows we can see several things:

- operating profit increased significantly from £80 million to £99 million. Clearly 1991 was a good year.
- gross funds from operations rose from £102 million to £124 million, reflecting not only the higher operating profit but also higher depreciation charges.
- net funds from operations rose by two thirds to £74 million. This impressive performance was helped by lower tax payments in 1991. Dividend payments rose from £17 million to £20 million.
- the working capital figures indicate a large increase in stock – up £36 million and an even larger increase in creditors – up £58 million. The stock increase reflects an increase in the number of stores and in the range of products sold. The change in creditors looks high.
- fixed asset investment was very much higher at £107 million. In the year the company made a number of acquisitions. It is clear that the company is going through a period of rapid growth.
- despite increased operating flows and funds provided by creditors, the company still needed an extra £33m of funds in 1991.
- financing was provided in part by running down short-term investments by £23 million, and partly by new overdraft borrowing of £10m.

In future periods analysts will watch carefully the trend in net funds from operations, to ensure that this source is generating sufficient funds to support the substantial investment each year in stock and fixed assets. If creditor financing returns to a lower level, and results in creditor ratios more in line with earlier years, the net source of funds from working capital changes may disappear.

DERIVING A CASH FLOW STATEMENT FROM THE OTHER FINANCIAL STATEMENTS

We can derive a cash flow statement from the opening and closing balance sheets, together with the profit and loss account, and the notes. We saw a simple example in Section 1 (page 11), and we now work through a somewhat more complex case – Harris & Clark plc.

We shall use the simplest system for preparing cash flow statements – the so-called 'indirect' method. It starts with balance sheet differences, analyses retained profit for the period in detail, and then makes certain adjustments for depreciation of fixed assets, for accruals, debtors and creditors, and for taxation and dividends. An alternative approach, using columnar analysis, takes longer, but is more comprehensive: it may be preferred for complex sets of accounts. (Problem 6.4 (page 170) gives a detailed example of columnar analysis.)

The profit and loss account for Harris & Clark plc for 1991 is set out on this page (right); and the balance sheets showing the position as at the end of 1990 and 1991 are set out on the next page (left). Our main task in the analysis is to separate out entries which represent flows of funds from those which are merely book entries, such as depreciation of fixed assets. We shall then convert the funds flows into cash flows by adjusting for changes in debtors and creditors. We thus remove the credit element from the funds flows.

The cash flow statement itself, in the standard format which FRS 1 requires, appears on page 161 (right). We treat cash inflows (receipts or sources) as positive, and cash outflows (payments or uses) as negative.

To prepare the cash flow statement, the main steps are as follows:

1   Enter the profit and loss account figures in the left-hand column of the worksheet; and analyse each amount showing it either as a 'Funds flow' (that is, a flow of either cash or credit), or as a 'Book entry'.
2   Enter the balance sheet differences (1991 figures less those for 1990) in the 'Differences' column of the balance sheet worksheet (sources are positive, uses are negative – in parentheses); and analyse each of them between funds flows and book entries (using details from the notes).
3   Transfer the book entries of the profit and loss account into the balance sheet worksheet.
4   Transfer the final line of the profit and loss account ('retained profit') into the balance sheet worksheet (under 'Share capital and reserves').
5   Total all balance sheet worksheet columns, and make sure they balance.
6   Transfer the detailed amounts from the funds flow columns in both worksheets to the cash flow statement, adjusting the funds flows to cash flows in the process.

HARRIS & CLARK plc

Profit and loss account for the year ended 31 December 1991	Profit & loss account £m	Funds flows £m	Book entries £m
Turnover	510	510	
Depreciation	(28)		(28) (a)
Other costs of sales	(412)	(412)	
Operating profit	70	98	(28)
Interest payable	(15)	(15)	
Profit before tax	55		
Tax	(20)		(20) (b)
Profit after tax	35		
Dividends	(25)		(25) (b)
Retained profit	10	83	(73)

Notes

(a)   the charge for depreciation consists of £32m for ordinary depreciation, less £4m 'gains on disposals of fixed assets'

(b)   the cash flow statement (like the funds flow statement) shows tax and dividends actually *paid* in the year; so we show these as 'book entries', and adjust them later to allow for changes in the end-of-year liability

(c)   Fixed assets

	Cost £m	Depreciation £m
At 1 January 1991	375	160
Additions in year	60	
Charge for year		32
Disposals in year	(10)	(7)
At 31 December 1991	425	185

(d)   during the year the company issued 20 million ordinary £1 shares at 150p each.

HARRIS & CLARK plc
Balance sheet at 31 December 1991

	1991 £m	1990 £m	Difference sources + uses − £m	Funds flows £m	Book entries £m
Fixed assets					
Tangible (net)	240	215	(25) (c)	(60) add. 7 disp.	28 depn.
Investments	40	30	(10)	(10)	
	280	245			
Current assets					
Stocks	100	80	(20)	(20)	
Trade debtors	81	75	(6)	(6)	
Fixed asset debtors	4	−	(4)	(4)	
Cash	45	40	(5)	(5)	
	230	195			
Creditors due within one year					
Trade creditors	65	60	5	5	
Taxation	20	15	5	(15)	20
Dividends	25	20	5	(20)	25
	(110)	(95)			
	400	345			
Creditors due after more than one year					
Loans	(125)	(110)	15	15	
	275	235			
Share capital and reserves					
Called up share capital	120	100	20 (d)	20	
Share premium	10	−	10 (d)	10	
Retained profit	145	135	10	83	(73)
	275	235	−	−	−

HARRIS & CLARK plc
Cash flow statement
Year ended 31 December 1991

	£m	£m
Operating activities		
Operating profit	70	
Depreciation *less* gain on disposal	28	
Stocks	(20)	
Trade debtors	(6)	
Trade creditors	5	
Net cash flow from operating activities		77
Servicing of Finance		
Interest payable	(15)	
Dividends paid	(20)	
		(35)
Taxation paid		(15)
Investing activities		
Tangible fixed assets acquired	(60)	
Proceeds from disposals [7 − 4]	3	
Investments	(10)	
		(67)
Deficit before Financing		(40)
Financing activities		
Issue of share capital	30	
Loans borrowed	15	
		45
Increase in cash balance		5

SUMMARY

In this section we have considered the usefulness of the cash flow statement as an additional source of financial information. We noted that a trend in cash flows over a number of years is likely to be more useful than the figures for only a year or two.

We noted the detailed requirements of FRS 1, the accounting standard on cash flow statements, and its standard format under five headings. The aim is to help users to assess the reporting entity's liquidity, viability, and financial adaptability. We showed two years' published cash flow statements for Kwik Save plc. We also showed the Kwik Save figures in our preferred format, which (among other differences) shows separately the changes in working capital.

In discussing the key items in the restated cash flow statement, we emphasized net funds from operations available for investment. We discussed how the financial surplus (or deficit) for a period revealed the extent to which these covered (or failed to cover) the investment in working capital and in fixed assets.

Finally, we saw how to compile a cash flow statement (by the 'indirect method') from the profit and loss account, the opening and closing balance sheet, and the notes to the accounts. This involves analysing items to distinguish 'book entries' from flows of cash (which really means flows of cash or credit). The standard format shows cash receipts as positive and cash payments as negative.

The main adjustments, under the 'balance sheet difference' method, are to expand on the 'retained profit for the year' figure, and to allow for various fixed asset items such as depreciation and profit or loss on disposal. It is also necessary to adjust tax and dividends, debtors, creditors and accruals in order to determine the actual amounts paid in the year in each case.

6.1 The Burton Group plc: restating funds flow statement

The Burton Group plc's published source and application of funds statement for 1990 is shown opposite (slightly simplified), together with additional information taken from the notes to the accounts.

You are asked to:

(a) restate the figures for both 1990 and 1989 in our suggested format shown on page 157
(b) comment on the salient points.

Please use a separate sheet of paper.
The solution to this problem is shown overleaf.

THE BURTON GROUP plc
Extracts from the notes to the accounts

	1990 £m	1989 £m
Note 3. Interest		
Interest receivable	18	12
Interest payable	(81)	(66)
Interest capitalised	25	23
	(38)	(31)
Note 20. Funds generated from operations		
Profit on ordinary activities before tax	133	217
Depreciation	71	59
Miscellaneous	(22)	(31)
	182	245
Change in working capital		
Stocks	11	19
Debtors	2	15
Creditors	(25)	4
	(12)	38

THE BURTON GROUP plc
Source and application of funds for the financial year ended 1 September

	1990 £m	1989 £m
Sources of funds		
Funds generated from operations	182	245
Net proceeds on sale of investments	176	—
Shares issued for cash less expenses	3	5
Disposals of tangible assets	23	26
Disposals of current asset investments	—	2
Disposals of assets held for sale	28	106
Repayment of loan by a related company	21	—
Decrease in working capital	12	—
	445	384
Application of funds		
Additions to properties and other tangible assets	139	155
Additions to assets held for sale	152	158
Increase in current asset investments	16	–
Taxation paid	49	50
Dividends paid	53	49
Redemption of loan stocks etc.	5	2
Redemption of preference shares in a subsidiary	3	3
Increase in working capital	—	38
	417	455
Increase (decrease) in liquid funds	28	(71)
Represented by:		
Increase (decrease) in bank balances and cash	40	(5)
Increase in bank loans and overdrafts	(12)	(66)
	28	(71)

6.1 The Burton Group plc *Solution*

Restated funds flow statement, year ended 1 September

	1990 £m	1989 £m
Internal funds/investment		
Operating profit	196	271
Interest received	18	12
Items not involving the flow of funds:		
Depreciation	71	59
Miscellaneous	(22)	(31)
Gross funds from operations	263	311
Interest	(81)	(66)
Tax	(49)	(50)
Dividends	(53)	(49)
	(183)	(165)
Net funds from operations	80	146
Change in working capital		
Stocks (increase)	(11)	(19)
Debtors (increase)	(2)	(15)
	(13)	(34)
Creditors increase (decrease)	25	(4)
	12	(38)
Net funds from operations available for fixed asset investment	92	108
Sale of fixed assets		
Disposal of tangible fixed assets	23	26
Disposal of assets held for sale	28	106
Net proceeds on sale of investments	176	—
Total funds available	319	240

Comments

1 Evidently 1990 was not such a profitable year as 1989, with a drop of 28 per cent in operating profit.
2 With outgoings for interest, tax and dividends in total somewhat higher than in 1989, net funds from operations nearly halved, to £80 million.
3 The increase in creditors in 1990 seems quite large, considering that turnover was slightly down in a difficult year for retailing.
4 The Chairman's statement begins with these words:
'The year has been one of major changes for the whole Burton Group. Chief among these was the decision to return to the core retailing business. This resulted in the sale of the Financial Services division and the announcement of our intention to withdraw from property development activities.'
Hence the significant sources of funds from disposals of fixed assets, producing in 1990 funds slightly greater than net funds from operations for the two years 1989 and 1990 together.
5 In each year more than £150 million was spent on property developments – more than the net funds generated from operations. Combined with roughly the same amounts each year being invested in tangible fixed assets, this has led to significant financial pressure.
6 From the relatively small amounts shown under external financing, it is clear that the need for funds over and above the amounts generated from operations was satisfied mainly by the disposals of assets.

Fixed asset investment

	1990	1989
Tangible fixed assets	(139)	(155)
Additions to assets held for sale	(152)	(158)
	(291)	(313)
Financing surplus (requirement)	28	(73)
External financing		
Issue of ordinary shares	3	5
Loans repaid by related company	21	—
Redemption of preference shares and loans	(8)	(5)
Current asset investments decrease (increase)	(16)	2
Cash decrease (increase)	(40)	5
Overdrafts increase	12	66
	(28)	73

6.2 Chapman Piper Limited: Preparing a cash flow statement (balance sheet differences) using the FRS 1 format (page 156)

The 1991 accounts for Chapman Piper Limited are set out here, the profit and loss account on this page, and the balance sheet on the next page.

You are asked to use the worksheets on the next two pages to complete the cash flow statement shown on page 167 (right).

When you have finished check your answer with the solution set out on pages 168 and 169.

CHAPMAN PIPER LIMITED
Profit and loss account for the year ended 31 December 1991

		1991		1990
		£'000		£'000
Turnover		15 000		11 000
Cost of sales		7 500		6 500
		7 500		4 500
Distribution costs	2 000		1 600	
Administrative expenses	900		800	
		2 900		2 400
Trading profit		4 600		2 100
Tax		1 600		700
Profit after tax		3 000		1 400
Dividends		2 000		1 000
Retained profit		1 000		400

Notes

1 Trading profit has been determined after taking into account

	£'000
Depreciation	200
Loss on disposal of fittings	10

2 During the year the freehold shop was revalued and the increase in value of £2 million has been included in a revaluation reserve.

3 Fixed asset movements in the year were

	Cost £'000	Depreciation £'000
Balance 31 December 1990	2 000	(200)
Additions	500	
Disposals	(200)	40
Depreciation for year		(200)
Balance 31 December 1991	2 300	(360)

CHAPMAN PIPER LIMITED

Profit and loss account year ended 31 December 1991 (£'000)	Profit & loss account	Funds flows	Book entries
Turnover			
Cost of sales			
Distribution costs			
Administrative expenses			
Trading profit			
Tax			
Dividends			
Retained profit			

CHAPMAN PIPER LIMITED
Balance sheet at 31 December 1991

	1991 £'000		1990 £'000	
Fixed assets				
Freehold shop		15 000		13 000
Fittings at cost	2 300		2 000	
Less: Depreciation	360		200	
		1 940		1 800
		16 940		14 800
Current assets				
Stock	7 510		5 500	
Debtors	5 025		2 625	
Cash	2 950		1 400	
	15 485		9 525	
Less: **Creditors falling due within one year**				
Tax	1 600		700	
Trade creditors	1 700		500	
Dividends payable	2 000		1 000	
	5 300		2 200	
		10 185		7 325
Total assets less current liabilities		27 125		22 125
Share capital and reserves				
Called up share capital		23 000		21 000
Revaluation reserve		2 000		—
Retained profit		2 125		1 125
		27 125		22 125

CHAPMAN PIPER LIMITED

Balance sheet at 31 December 1991 (£'000)	Balance sheet differences	Funds flows	Book entries
Assets			
Freehold shop			
Fittings			
Stocks			
Debtors			
Cash			
Liabilities			
Share capital			
Revaluation reserve			
Retained profit			
Trade creditors			
Tax			
Dividends			
Retained profit			

CHAPMAN PIPER LIMITED
Cash flow statement for the year ended 31 December 1991

£'000

Operating activities
Trading profit
Depreciation
Loss on disposal of fittings

Dividends paid

Taxation paid

Investment in working capital
Stocks
Debtors
Creditors

Investment in fixed assets
Fittings
Disposal of fittings

Surplus (deficit) before financing

Financing activities
Issue of shares

Increase (decrease) in cash

6.2 Chapman Piper Limited (A): Cash flow statement
Solution

Profit and loss account year ended 31 December 1991 (£'000)

	Profit & loss account	Funds flows	Book entries
Turnover	15 000	15 000	
Cost of sales (Balancing item)	(7 290)	(7 290)	
Distribution costs	(2 000)	(2 000)	
Administrative expenses	(900)	(900)	
Depreciation	(200)		(a) (200)
Loss on disposal FA	(10)		(b) (10)
Trading profit	4 600	4 810	(210)
Tax	(1 600)		(c) (1 600)
Dividends	(2 000)		(d) (2 000)
Retained profit	1 000	4 810	(3 810)

CHAPMAN PIPER LIMITED

Balance sheet at 31 December 1991 (£'000)

	Balance sheet differences	Funds flows	Book entries
Assets			
Freehold shop	2 000		(e) 2 000
Fittings (net)	140		(a) (200)
Additions		500	
Disposals		(160)	
Loss on disposal		10	(b) (10)
Stock	2 010	2 010	
Debtors	2 400	2 400	
Cash	1 550	1 550	
	8 100	6 310	1 790
Liabilities			
Share capital	2 000	2 000	
Revaluation reserve	2 000		(e) 2 000
Retained profit	1 000	4 810	(3 810)
Trade creditors	1 200	1 200	
Tax	900	(700)	(c) 1 600
Dividends	1 000	(1 000)	(d) 2 000
	8 100	6 310	1 790

CHAPMAN PIPER LIMITED

Cash flow statement for the year ended 31 December 1991

	£'000
Operating activities	
Trading profit	4 600
Depreciation	200
Loss on disposal of fittings	10
	4 810
Dividends paid	(1 000)
Taxation paid	(700)
Investment in working capital	
Stocks	(2 010)
Debtors	(2 400)
Creditors	(1 200)
	(3 210)
Investment in fixed assets	
Fittings	(500)
Disposal of fittings	150
	(350)
Surplus (deficit) before financing	(450)
Financing activities	
Issue of shares	2 000
Increase (decrease) in cash	1 550

6.3 Northern Foods plc (B)

Use the information from the Northern Foods accounts (pages 53 to 57) to prepare a funds flow statement, using the balance sheet differences method.

Prepare your own worksheets, for the profit and loss account and for balance sheet differences, on separate sheets of paper. Also prepare your own funds flow statement on a separate sheet of paper.

A solution is shown at the end of the book.

6.4 Harris & Clark plc: Preparing a cash flow statement (columnar analysis)

When we dealt with transaction analysis in Section 3, we found it useful to enter transactions in columnar analysis sheets which permitted us to see easily how the entries were incorporated in the accounting headings. The same approach provides a useful framework for cash flow analysis, and it is illustrated on the opposite page.

The columnar analysis shows clearly the link between the three financial statements; and sets out in a single statement the adjustments which must be made to the actual accounting figures to identify the operating and other flows. The columnar approach is also the best method for complex sets of accounts where adjustments affecting a number of items have to be viewed simultaneously.

The columnar worksheet includes columns for each balance sheet heading with additional columns for 'funds flows' and for 'profit of the year'. The opening and closing balances have been entered from the Harris & Clark balance sheet on page 161. The figures shown in the profit and loss account and notes have also been included in the worksheet.

The detailed steps needed to complete the worksheet are set out below and you are asked to follow each step in turn.

1 Enter the trading profit in the profit of the year column and in funds from operations. (In the worksheet the double-entry principles underlying the balance sheet figures are continued.) The two sides of the worksheets should continue to balance. Thus, it is possible to have a positive entry on both sides, a negative entry on both sides, or positive and negative entries on the same side.
2 The depreciation provision is disclosed in Note (a) to the profit and loss account. This is a 'book entry'. It is deducted in the fixed asset column and added in the cash from operations column. It was deducted in arriving at the trading profit and as a 'non-cash charge' is now added back to give 'funds from operations'.
3 The gain on sale of fixed assets is entered in the 'funds from operations' column and in the 'sale of fixed assets' column. It is part of the flow – 'proceeds from sale of fixed assets'. At a later stage, we expect to pick up the book value of the assets disposed of. This entry eliminates the gain on disposal from funds from operations.
4 The other entries which appear in the profit of the year column are:

- *Interest payable* – on the other side this is a funds flow.
- *Taxation* – this is the tax provision based on the profits of the year. The other side appears in tax payable. The cash outflow for tax in the year is then calculated by taking the opening balance plus the provision, less the closing balance.

- *Dividends* – this is the appropriation of profits for the year. The other side is entered in the dividends payable column. The dividend payment actually made in the year is then calculated, as in the case of taxation, by determining the difference between the total of the opening balance and the appropriation and the closing balance.
- *Retained profit* – the retained profit is deducted and entered in the 'reserve' column (transferred to reserve).

5 Using the information disclosed in the fixed asset note (c).

- the disposals of 10 are deducted from fixed assets. The other side is part of a flow and appears in the 'Sale of FA' column
- additions represent an outflow of funds. They are added in the fixed asset column and deducted in the funds flow column
- depreciation on disposals is entered as a positive figure in the fixed asset column (it eliminates some depreciation) and as a negative figure in the 'Sale of FA' column. We now know that the net book value of the disposal was 10 − 7 = 3.

6 Using the information shown in Note (d) relating to share capital:

- share capital increases by 20 as does the funds flow column
- share premium increases by 10 and so does the funds flow column.

7 We now have taken into account the information contained in the notes. Since there is no further information, the next step is to transfer the balance on the 'sale of FA' column to the funds flow column and the balance on the 'funds from operations' column to the funds flow column.
8 The next step is to total the columns, calculate the differences between the column totals and the closing balance sheet figures and to transfer the differences to the funds flow column. It is assumed that since they have not been identified as book entries they must be funds flows.
9 Finally, transfer the figures to the cash flow statement (page 161).

Assets   **Liabilities**

FA (Net)	Invest-ments	Stocks	Trade drs.	FA drs.	Cash	Sale of FA	Funds from operations	Funds flow	£'000	Share capital and reserves	Profit of year	Loans	Creditors	Tax payable	Dividend payable
215	30	80	75		40				**Opening balances** Trading profit (P&L) Depreciation (Na) Gain on disposal FA (P&L) Interest payable (P&L) Taxation (P&L) Dividends (P&L) Profit retained (P&L) FA–Disposal cost (Nc) –Additions (Nc) –Disposal depreciation (Nc) Share capital (Nd) Share premium (Nd) Proceeds sale FA **Funds from operations**	235		110	60	15	20
									Investments Stocks Debtors Cash Cash from loans Creditors Cash for tax Dividends						
240	40	100	81	4	45			—	**Closing balances**	275		125	65	20	25

Please check your answer against the solution overleaf, and then against the full cash flow statement on page 161.

HARRIS & CLARK – CASH FLOW STATEMENT: YEAR ENDED 31 DECEMBER 1991 – WORKSHEET

Assets / **Liabilities**

FA (Net)	Invest-ments	Stocks	Trade drs.	FA drs.	Cash	Sale of FA	Funds from operations	Funds flow	£'000	Share capital and reserves	Profit of year	Loans	Creditors	Tax payable	Dividend payable
215	30	80	75		40				**Opening balances**	235		110	60	15	20
							70		Trading profit (P&L)		70				
(32)							32		Depreciation (Na)						
						4	(4)		Gain on disposal FA (P&L)						
								(15)	Interest payable (P&L)		(15)				
									Taxation (P&L)		(20)			20	
									Dividends (P&L)		(25)				25
									Profit retained (P&L)	10	(10)				
(10)						10			FA–Disposal cost (Nc)						
60								(60)	–Additions (Nc)						
7						(7)			–Disposal depreciation (Nc)						
								20	Share capital (Nd)	20					
								10	Share premium (Nd)	10					
						(7)		7	Proceeds sale FA						
							(98)	98	**Funds from operations**						
240	30	80	75		40			60		275	—	110	60	35	45
	10							(10)	Investments						
		20						(20)	Stocks						
			6					(6)	Trade debtors						
				4				(4)	FA debtors						
					5			(5)	Cash						
								15	Cash from loans			15			
								5	Creditors				5		
								(15)	Tax paid					(15)	
								(20)	Dividends paid						(20)
240	40	100	81	4	45			—	**Closing balances**	275		125	65	20	25

Section 7

Company taxation

BACKGROUND

UK tax revenue in 1990/91 totalled £203 000 million, just under 50 per cent of national income. The main kinds of tax are shown below:

UK TAX REVENUE 1990/91

			£ billion
Income	Income tax	56 ⎫	
	Employees' national insurance	15 ⎬	93
	Corporation tax	22 ⎭	
Expenditure	Value added tax	31 ⎫	
	Drink and tobacco	10 ⎬	63
	Oil	10 ⎮	
	Miscellaneous	12 ⎭	
Employment	Employers' national insurance		20
Local	Rates and community charge		22
Capital	Gains and transfers		5
			203

The main purpose of taxation is to raise revenue to pay for government spending. This section deals mainly with corporation tax and how it relates to personal income taxes.

The basic 25 per cent* rate of personal income tax applies to income reduced by personal allowances and other deductions. On taxable incomes above £23 700 a year, a 40 per cent higher rate of income tax applies. Inflation-adjusted capital gains exceeding £5 500 a year are subject to income tax rates.

Companies pay corporation tax at a rate of 33 per cent* on taxable profits (25 per cent for smaller companies). Reported company profits before tax in published accounts are adjusted in computing the amount of taxable profits, to substitute tax capital allowances for book depreciation of fixed assets, and for other reasons. Profits earned overseas by UK companies are subject to overseas taxation, and UK corporation tax on those profits is normally reduced by double taxation relief.

Corporation tax is normally payable nine months after the end of a company's financial year; but an advance payment, called advance corporation tax (ACT), is due whenever a company pays dividends to its shareholders. ACT can sometimes complicate the calculation of earnings per share and dividend cover. In this section we discuss all these aspects of company tax; and we conclude by looking at how companies treat corporation tax in their published accounts.

*Unless otherwise stated, all rates of tax are those for 1991/92.

RATES OF TAX

The 'corporation tax year 1991' is the year *beginning* 1 April 1991 (and ending 31 March 1992). This is rather confusing: it would be more usual to call it either the corporation tax (CT) year '1991/92' or '1992', the year in which it *ends*. The rate of corporation tax is 33 per cent for the CT year 1991. (It was 35 per cent for the CT year 1989, and 34 per cent for the CT year 1990.)

When a company's accounting year ends on a date other than 31 March, taxable profits are split on a time basis between CT years in order to determine the *rate* of corporation tax to apply to taxable profits.

Smaller companies

Small companies with taxable profits below £250 000 are liable to a lower rate of corporation tax: 25 per cent. There is marginal relief where taxable profits fall between £250 000 and £1 250 000 a year. Where there are a number of companies within a group, the thresholds are divided between them.

Capital gains

Companies' capital gains are subject to corporation tax. When a company reinvests the proceeds from selling a chargeable asset in another business asset in one of five 'qualifying classes', no chargeable gain arises until the second asset is sold. As a result of this 'rollover' relief, most business fixed asset disposals are tax free as long as replacement continues.

ADJUSTMENTS TO ACCOUNTING PROFITS

The simplest business tax computation begins with reported ('book') profits before tax for a year. Two adjustments are then made to translate accounting profits into taxable profits:

1 Add back any disallowed items of expenditure.
2 Add back the book depreciation charged in the accounts, and deduct instead the statutory tax capital allowances.

Both these adjustments are discussed below. Once computed, the 'taxable profits' for a period are multiplied by the relevant rate(s) of corporation tax to determine the *amount* of tax payable. The format of the tax computation is thus as follows:

SIMPLE CORPORATION TAX COMPUTATION

		£'000
Reported accounting profit before tax		900
Add back: Disallowed expenditure	40	
Book depreciation	260	
		300
		1 200
Less: Tax capital allowances		400
= Taxable profit		800

Corporation tax payable: £800 000 @ relevant tax rate(s)

Losses

Losses are computed in a similar way to profits. For tax purposes, companies may set off losses against current profits; or carry them back to set against taxable profits for the three preceding accounting periods; or carry them forward to set against future profits.

Partnerships

Sole traders and partnerships are liable to income tax on business profits, not to corporation tax (which applies only to limited companies). Taxable profits are computed as for companies, and they are all attributed as personal income (regardless of how much the partners actually withdraw in cash). They are split between the partners in the proportions in which they share profits in the year of assessment. There are special rules concerning tax payable in the opening and closing years of a sole trader or a partnership.

Disallowed expenditure

Sometimes tax officials may regard as 'capital' items which a business has treated as 'revenue' expenditure. The business will then not be allowed to charge the whole of such amounts as expenses against taxable profits in the current year. The amounts charged in the accounts will have to be 'added back' to profits, and written off in stages over a number of years. The difference in treatment here affects the *timing* of the charges against profit, not the total amount of tax (unless the rate of tax changes).

Some expenditure may be completely disallowed as a deduction from profits for tax purposes. This happens either where the law expressly forbids the item as a deduction; or where the tax authorities consider the item not to have been incurred 'wholly and exclusively for the purposes of the trade'. The *intention* to make a profit is what matters, not the actual result.

The Schedule E rules, applying to employees, are stricter than the Schedule D rules, applying to businesses and self-employed people. They require expenses to be 'wholly, exclusively *and necessarily* incurred for the purpose of the office or employment'. In practice, however, expenses are sometimes apportioned for tax purposes between allowable and non-allowable.

Business accounts aim to show a 'true and fair view' of the results, whereas tax officials must enforce legal rules. Since the tax statutes are not always clear (to put it mildly), there is often room for argument and discussion between taxpayers and officials.

Examples of disallowable business expenditure are:

(a) legal expenses in connection with capital transactions (but allowed for revenue purposes, for example protecting a right to an asset)
(b) general reserves for bad debts (but *specific* provisions allowed)
(c) business entertainment expenses (except a reasonable amount for staff).

The Inland Revenue normally accepts consistent business accounting practice as a basis for computing taxable profits. Among the exceptions to this general rule are: the LIFO method of stock valuation (see Section 4), and inflation accounting adjustments to historical cost accounts (see Section 11).

Capital allowances

The UK tax system disallows as a deduction from taxable profits the depreciation of fixed assets charged as an expense in company accounts. Special tax 'capital allowances' (sometimes called 'writing-down allowances') are deducted instead. A company's own depreciation policy, therefore, cannot affect its UK tax charge. (The position is different in some foreign countries.)

All commercial depreciation is automatically disallowed for tax purposes; but tax capital allowances are deductible from taxable profits only where expressly permitted by statute. It follows that certain kinds of capital expenditure attract no tax allowances if there is no statutory provision for it (whether by accident or design).

Plant and equipment and cars are written off by means of a 25 per cent 'annual allowance', computed on the declining balance basis.

On new industrial buildings there is an annual allowance of 4 per cent (straight line) on original cost. There are capital allowances on buildings classified as industrial or agricultural, but not on others (for example not on retail shops, showrooms and offices).

Where it applies, the 25 per cent annual allowance is computed on a 'pool' basis. Any sale proceeds from a fixed asset are deducted from the written-down value (for tax purposes) of the pool of similar assets, and the year's annual allowance (on the declining balance) is reduced accordingly. The result is to delay the tax charge on any 'profit on sale', or the tax allowance on any loss on sale. But over the whole life of the business, the ultimate result is that the total cost of eligible fixed assets, less the total proceeds of sales, is allowed as a deduction from taxable profits.

As well as capital allowances, the government may provide various other financial inducements (outside the tax system) in respect of investments in so-called 'development areas' and 'intermediate areas'. There are also special tax concessions in respect of a small number of 'enterprise zones'.

OVERSEAS TAX

A UK-resident company is liable to corporation tax on its overseas profits, whether remitted to the UK or not. But agreements have been made with most countries for double taxation relief; so overseas profits are usually subject to UK corporation tax only to the extent that the rate of overseas tax is lower.

Company accounts must show separately both the amount of overseas taxation charged and the amount of double taxation relief. Thus a minimum disclosure for a company with overseas profits would be:

	£'000
UK taxation	
Corporation tax	xxx
less: Double taxation relief	(xx)
	xxx
Overseas taxation	xx
	xxx

ADVANCE CORPORATION TAX

Corporation tax is normally payable nine months after the end of a company's financial year. But when a company pays a dividend it must remit advance corporation tax (ACT) to the Inland Revenue sooner than the normal payment date for corporation tax. ACT, amounting to 25/75ths of the net dividend, is payable within fourteen days after the end of a quarter in which a dividend is paid. (From the shareholders' point of view, this counts as 25 per cent basic rate income tax deducted at source from the *gross* dividend.) A company then pays the balance of 'mainstream' corporation tax due on the normal due date, after deducting any ACT already paid in the *basis* accounting period.

Example
Frank Buxton Limited makes taxable profits as follows:

Year to 31 March 1991:   £6 000 000   Tax @ 34% = 2 040 000
Year to 31 March 1992:   £8 000 000   Tax @ 33% = 2 640 000

If a £1 500 000 net final dividend in respect of the year to 31 March 1991 were paid on 1 July 1991, then ACT of £500 000 would be due by 14 October 1991. (25/75 × £1 500 000 = 25% × £2 000 000 gross dividend.)

This ACT payment of £500 000 *paid* in the *basis* period ending 31 March 1992, would be set off against £2 640 000 corporation tax due on taxable profits arising in the financial year 1991/92. So only £2 140 000 mainstream corporation tax would be payable on 31 December 1992. What matters is the accounting year in which the dividend is *paid*, not the one to which the dividend relates.

The ACT set-off is not allowed to reduce the mainstream corporation tax liability below 8 per cent of the taxable income (= 33 per cent − 25 per cent). This restriction operates where a company's dividends (and hence its ACT paid) are high compared with UK taxable profits. Any balance of 'unrelieved' ACT may be carried forward to set off against future corporation tax liabilities. Unrelieved ACT may arise where there are losses, unusually low profits, substantial capital allowances, or substantial overseas profits relative to UK profits. The extent of unrelieved ACT is growing for many large UK multinationals. It is normally written off as part of the tax expense for the year.

Franked investment income

Dividends received by a company from another UK company have been paid out of after-tax income, and are not subject again to corporation tax. The basic rate income tax deducted at source from such 'franked investment income' can be set off against ACT payable by the recipient company when it pays a dividend to its own shareholders. In the accounts, the tax charge includes any such tax, and the franked investment income is shown gross. Special rules apply where a group claims relief in respect of subsidiaries of whose shares the holding company owns at least 75 per cent.

EARNINGS AND DIVIDENDS

Earnings per share

Normal practice is to compute earnings per share by the 'net' method, which divides reported profits after tax by the number of equity shares in issue. This forms the basis for calculating the price/earnings ratio. The 'net' method treats any unrelieved ACT on dividends as part of the tax charge against profit (as do the accounts themselves).

For certain other financial ratios, there are two different methods of calculating earnings per share which ignore the *actual* level of dividends paid. The purpose is to allow comparisons between the earnings of companies which may be following different dividend policies.

For calculating dividend cover (and earnings yield), the 'maximum' ('full') method is used. This method calls 'earnings' the gross equivalent of the maximum amount that a company could have paid as dividends out of the year's profits. This may differ from the 'net' method, if some unrelieved ACT would arise on a 'maximum' dividend payout.

A third method, the 'nil' method, assumes that *no* dividends are paid. It can produce higher earnings per share than the other methods, since in effect it treats any unrelieved ACT as related to dividends rather than to profits. For most companies, earnings on the 'net' basis will be the same as on the 'nil' basis. Where there is a significant difference, the financial press shows the price/earnings ratio (on the net basis) *in parentheses*, to warn of the need for special care.

The example opposite illustrates the net and maximum methods of computing earnings per share, and the various resulting investment measures. To keep it simple, we assume that book profit before tax is the same as taxable profit. The example covers companies (a) with all UK income, and (b) with half UK and half foreign income.

Dividends

For every £100 taxable profit liable to UK corporation tax at 33 per cent, a company is left with £67 available for payment as a *net* dividend. Assuming that taxable profits at £100, are the same as book profits before tax, a company which pays a net dividend of, say, £36 will retain profit for the year of £31.

The £36 net dividend counts as a gross dividend of £48, on which £12 income tax at the basic rate of 25 per cent is imputed to (deemed to have been borne by) the shareholders. £12 is thus available for *repayment* by the Inland Revenue to shareholders whose marginal rate of income tax is less than 25 per cent.

INVESTMENT MEASURES

		(a) All UK income £'000	(b) Half foreign income £'000
Profit before tax (= taxable profit)		1 000	1 000
Tax: UK (33%)		330	165
Foreign (say 50%)		—	250
Profit after tax	A	670	585
Gross dividend	B	500	500
Less: ACT (25% × gross)		125	125
Net dividend paid	C	375	375
Retained profit for year		295	210
Maximum net dividend payable		670	532
Add: ACT 25/75		233	178
Maximum gross dividend payable	D	903	710 (a)
Number of ordinary shares issued	E	10 million	10 million
Share price (assumed)	F	60p	60p
Dividend per share, gross	(B/E) G	5.00p	5.00p
Dividend per share, net	(C/E)	3.75p	3.75p
Dividend yield, gross	(G/F)	8.3%	8.3%
Earnings per share, 'net'	(A/E) H	6.70p	5.85
Price/earnings ratio	(F/H)	9.0	10.3
Earnings per share, 'maximum'	(D/E) I	9.03	7.10
Earnings yield, 'maximum'	(I/F)	15.1	11.8
Dividend cover, 'maximum'	(I/G)	1.81	1.42

(a) Tax 290 = Foreign 250 + minimum UK mainstream CT 40 [= (33% − 25%) × £500]

DEFERRED TAX

Over a fixed asset's whole life, tax capital allowances – where they apply – will equal book depreciation, since both will amount in total to the original cost less ultimate sales proceeds. But the pattern over time may be different. Capital allowances are often higher than straight-line book depreciation in the early years (and therefore lower in the later years).

In theory there are two main ways to *report* the tax expense in accounts; *but the accounting treatment cannot affect the actual tax charge.*

1   Actual tax. Charge as an expense only the actual tax payable on the year's taxable profits. As a proportion of reported pre-tax profits, this may often be *less* than the current rate of corporation tax.
2   Deferred tax. Charge as an expense what the tax charge *would have been* if the company's own book depreciation were deducted for tax purposes. Apart from other timing differences and any disallowed expenditure (which we ignore here), the tax expense will then equal the current rate of corporation tax on reported pre-tax profits. (UK companies use a variant of this.)

Example
George Orwell Limited reported profit before tax of £8 million for the year ended 31 March 1991, after charging book depreciation of £4 million. Capital allowances amounted to £7 million, so the taxable profit was £5 million; and with a tax rate of 34 per cent, the tax actually payable was £1 700 000.

If George Orwell Limited charged as an expense only the actual tax for the year, while another company (Eric Blair Limited) with identical operating results used the deferred tax method, their accounts would show different figures:

	George Orwell (Actual) £'000	Eric Blair (Deferred) £'000
Profit and loss account, 1991		
Profit before tax	8 000	8 000
Corporation tax	1 700	2 720
Profit after tax	6 300	5 280
Balance sheet, end 1991		
Deferred tax liability	—	1 020

As a result of their different methods of accounting for tax, George Orwell would report higher profits after tax (and earnings per share) than Eric Blair in 1991. Eric Blair's tax charge (£2 720 000) would exceed the tax actually payable (£1 700 000) by £1 020 000. This is the 34 per cent tax rate multiplied by the £3 000 000 excess of tax capital allowances (£7 000 000) over book depreciation

(£4 000 000) in 1991. This £1 020 000 difference would increase the 'deferred tax liability' account, which appears on the balance sheet between shareholders' funds and long-term debt.

If in 1992 George Orwell and Eric Blair each had tax capital allowances of £3 000 000, and their financial results were otherwise the same as in 1991, tax in 1992 would be £2 970 000 (£9 000 000 @ 33 per cent). Their 1992 accounts would show the following:

	George Orwell (Actual) £'000	Eric Blair (Deferred) £'000
Profit and loss account, 1992		
Profit before tax	8 000	8 000
Corporation tax	2 970	2 640
Profit after tax	5 030	5 360
Balance sheet, end 1992		
Deferred tax liability		690
		−30*
		660

This time Eric Blair's reported profits after tax are higher than George Orwell's. Eric Blair's deferred tax liability account would fall by £330 000 at the end of 1992 to reflect tax at 33 per cent on the £1 000 000 shortfall of tax capital allowances in 1992 (£3 000 000) below book depreciation (of £4 000 000). In practice the deferred tax account would fall by more than £330 000: not just from £1 020 000 to £690 000, but by a further £30 000 to £660 000 — to reflect the fall of the CT rate from 34 per cent to 33 per cent.

The accumulated balance on a deferred tax liability account represents a *temporary* deferral of tax. In the later years of a fixed asset's life, the actual tax charge will exceed the notional tax charge based on reported profits before tax (since the book depreciation will by then exceed the tax capital allowances). The deferred tax liability account thus continually clears in respect of individual fixed assets. But since most companies go on investing in new replacement fixed assets (which cost more money in time of inflation), the cumulative balance of deferred tax liability may in aggregate continue to grow year after year.

As a matter of fact, UK companies would not exactly follow either George Orwell's or Eric Blair's practice. SSAP 15 requires the use of a deferred tax liability account for short-term temporary timing differences, but not for more permanent aggregate 'deferrals'. Thus UK companies do *not* need to provide for deferred tax in respect of writing-down allowances where the tax benefit is expected to remain in future as a result of recurring timing differences of the same type. Some analysts, however, prefer to make full provision (as is US practice).

ACCOUNTING FOR TAX

Balance sheet

The balance sheet includes corporation tax liabilities on the basis of all the tax due on taxable profits earned up to date. The balance sheet combines overseas tax due with UK corporation tax, including any ACT still outstanding; and shows any dividends payable net.

Thus a company balance sheet normally contains only two items relating to corporation tax:

Current tax liability   (actual and estimated UK and overseas corporation tax due in respect of taxable profits up to the latest balance sheet date, probably payable nine months after the year-end)

Deferred tax liability   (in respect of timing differences expected to result in tax becoming payable fairly soon)

Profit and loss account

The notes analyse the total tax expense for a year between:

1   UK corporation tax (with deferred tax noted separately).
2   Less double tax relief.
3   Overseas tax.
4   Unrecovered ACT.
5   Tax related to income from associated companies.

Any irrecoverable ACT appears as part of the tax charge; it is *not* added to the amount of the net dividends.

Apart from corporation tax on profits, which is shown separately, social security and other taxes are included among operating expenses in the profit and loss account. (If still owing at the balance sheet date, the balance sheet includes them among creditors, but the notes disclose the amount of social security taxes owing separately.) Any reference to 'tax' in company accounts nearly always means 'corporation tax'.

Cash flow statement

Profit before tax is a source of cash, and tax actually paid in the year is a separate use of cash. (Thus changes in 'working capital' in the year *exclude* any change in the current tax outstanding.)

SUMMARY

In this section we first discussed the background to the UK tax system, noting the main sources of £203 billion tax revenue in 1990/91, and some features of personal income tax.

The rate of corporation tax is 33 per cent, but only 25 per cent for smaller companies. Double taxation relief may reduce UK corporation tax on overseas profits.

A simple company tax computation starts with reported profits before tax, adds back disallowed expenditure and book depreciation, and deducts tax capital allowances instead. This gives the amount of taxable profit for the period. On plant and equipment annual allowances are 25 per cent a year on the declining balance basis.

Companies pay corporation tax nine months after the end of their accounting year; but advance corporation tax (ACT) is due sooner, when a company pays a dividend. ACT represents 25/75 of the net dividend (= 25 per cent of the gross dividend), and can be set off later against mainstream corporation tax. From the shareholders' point of view, under the 'imputation system' of corporation tax, ACT counts as the deduction at source of basic rate 25 per cent personal income tax on gross dividends.

Earnings per share is normally calculated on the 'net' basis, by dividing profit after tax by the number of equity shares in issue. The 'maximum' dividend basis is used to calculate dividend yield. For purposes of the higher 40 per cent income tax rate, it is the gross dividend which represents shareholders' income.

A 'deferred tax liability' account is used only for short-term timing differences. The effect is to increase tax expense in the profit and loss account above the actual amount of tax payable. The balance sheet shows any deferred tax liability account between shareholders' funds and long-term debt.

The balance sheet combines actual UK and overseas corporation tax due as a current liability, and the notes to the profit and loss account analyse the net total tax expense.

7.1 Definitions

Please write down below your definition of each of the terms shown. Then compare your answers with the definitions shown overleaf.

(a)   Capital allowances

(b)   Advance corporation tax (ACT)

(c)   The corporation tax year 1991

(d)   Franked investment income

(e)   Deferred tax

(f)   'Mainstream' corporation tax

(g)   Unrecovered ACT

(h)   'Net' earnings per share

(i)   'Maximum' earnings per share

(j)   Dividend cover

7.1 Definitions

(a) *Capital allowances* are statutory 'depreciation' allowances on capital expenditure for tax purposes. They consist of 'annual allowances', normally calculated at 25 per cent on the declining balance of tax written-down value of the 'pool' of assets. Not all capital expenditure qualifies for capital allowances: the criterion is whether or not the statutes allow it, not whether the expenditure is wholly and exclusively for the purpose of the business.

(b) *Advance corporation tax (ACT)* is payable in 1991/92 at a rate of 25/75ths of *net* dividends paid by a company (= 25 per cent of gross dividends). It is due within fourteen days of the end of the quarter in which the dividend is paid, and reduces the 'mainstream' corporation tax liability (payable later by the company). For shareholders, ACT amounts to deduction at source of basic rate income tax from the gross dividends.

(c) *The corporation tax year 1991* is the year *beginning* 1 April 1991 (that is, the year ending 31 March 1992). It determines the *rate* of tax payable on profits, since taxable profits are split on a time basis between corporation tax years. The company's own accounting period determines the *timing* of the payment of mainstream corporation tax (nine months after the year-end).

(d) *Franked investment income* is the gross dividends received from other UK companies. It is not subject to corporation tax, since the profits from which such dividends are paid have already borne corporation tax. The tax deducted at source from franked investment income may be set off against ACT due on dividends paid by a company.

(e) *Deferred tax* is taxation charged in the accounts but not legally payable yet, due to timing differences between the Inland Revenue's treatment of certain items and the accounting treatment in a company's books. Depreciation is usually the most important cause of timing differences. UK companies provide for deferred tax only to the extent that they think it probable that a liability (or asset) will crystallise.

(f) *'Mainstream' corporation tax* is the balance of UK corporation tax due after deducting any ACT already paid in the basis accounting period. It may not be reduced below 8 per cent of taxable profits (= 33 per cent corporation tax less 25 per cent basic rate income tax); hence some ACT may be irrecoverable (for example, where much of a UK company's profits are earned overseas).

(g) *Unrecovered ACT* is advance corporation tax suffered on payment of dividends, but unable to be set off against mainstream corporation tax – at least in the current year. It is likely to arise where there are losses or where most profits are earned overseas.

(h) *'Net' earnings per share* is the usual calculation of earnings per share. It is profit on ordinary activities after taxation for the year divided by the (weighted if necessary) number of ordinary shares outstanding during the year. It is calculated after deducting from profit before tax the full tax charge, including any irrecoverable ACT on dividends paid.

(i) *'Maximum' earnings per share* is a hypothetical calculation of the gross equivalent of the maximum dividend per share that could have been distributed out of the profits for a particular year, taking into account any unrecovered ACT.

(j) *Dividend cover* is 'maximum' earnings per share divided by the actual dividend per share paid (grossed up). In practice it is often simply earnings per share (on the 'net' basis) divided by net dividends per share.

Solutions to the following problems are shown overleaf.

In attempting the following questions, it may help to know recent tax rates:

Basic rate income tax		Corporation tax	
1988/89		CT Year 1988	35%
1989/90	25%	CT Year 1989	35%
1990/91		CT Year 1990	34%
1991/92		CT Year 1991	33%

7.2 Modern Services Limited: Business tax computation

Modern Services Limited reported profits before tax of £8.2 million in the year ended 31 March 1992. Depreciation charged in arriving at this amount totalled £750 000. There were no other disallowable expenses for tax purposes. Tax capital allowances in respect of the year amounted to £450 000.

Prepare the computation of taxable profit for the year; calculate the amount of corporation tax payable; and state when it would be payable if Modern Services Limited declares no dividends.

7.3 Tom, Dick and Harry: Personal tax rates

For 1991/2 personal income tax rates are as follows:

Rate of tax	Taxable income
25%	0–£23 700
40%	over £23 700.

Tom has income of £25 000, Dick of £50 000, and Harry of £75 000, in the year ended 5 April 1992. Assuming that each is entitled to personal allowances and deductions totalling £5 000 in that year, compute their average and marginal rates of income tax (as percentages of total income).

7.4 Richard Steele Limited: Advance corporation tax

In the year ended 30 June 1991, Richard Steele Limited made taxable profits of £6 100 000. A final dividend of 15.0p per share for the year was declared payable on 18 October 1991, in respect of the company's 10 million outstanding 25p ordinary shares.

What are the tax consequences of the dividend payment:

(a) for the shareholders?
(b) for the company?

7.5 Modesty Promotions Limited: Small company rate

In the year ended 31 March 1992, Modesty Promotions Limited had a taxable profit of £180 000. How much corporation tax would be payable? How much tax would have been payable if the company's profits in that year had been £800 000?

7.6 Blue Sky Speculations Limited: Change in tax rate

Blue Sky Speculations Limited made taxable profits of £4 million in the year ended 30 June 1990, and of £3 million in the year ended 30 June 1991.

What would the corporation tax liability amount to in respect of each of these two years?

7.7 Mansell and Horton Limited: Amount and timing of tax

Mansell and Horton Limited ends its accounting year on 30 June. Taxable profits in recent years have been as folllows:

	£ million
Year ended 30 June 1989	3.3
Year ended 30 June 1990	4.1
Year ended 30 June 1991	4.7.

In respect of its 20 million issued ordinary £1 shares, the company paid an interim dividend in March each year, and a final dividend in October. Recent net dividends per share have been paid as follows:

March 1989	1.50p	October 1989	2.50p
March 1990	1.60p	October 1990	2.60p
March 1991	1.68p	October 1991	2.86p.

Calculate the amount and timing of corporation tax paid in respect of the year ended 30 June 1990.

7.2 Modern Services Limited. *Solution*

	£'000
Reported profit before tax	8 200
Add back: Depreciation charged	750
	8 950
Less: Tax capital allowances	450
= Taxable profit	8 500

Corporation tax payable = 33% × £8 500 000 = £2 805 000

This amount of mainstream corporation tax would be payable on 31 December 1992.

7.3 Tom, Dick and Harry. *Solution*

Range of taxable income	Rate of tax	Tom £	Dick £	Harry £
0–£23 700	25%	5 000	5 925	5 925
over £23 700	40%	—	8 520	18 520
Total tax		5 000	14 445	24 445
Average tax rate (as % of total income)		20.0%	28.9%	32.6%
Marginal tax rate		25.0%	40.0%	40.0%

7.4 Richard Steele Limited. *Solution*

(a) the final dividend of £1 500 000 represents a 'gross' dividend of £2 000 000 less basic rate income tax of 25 per cent. The shareholders, where applicable, would be liable to graduated income tax on their share of the gross dividend of 20p per share

(b) the company would have to pay the Inland Revenue ACT of £500 000 on or before 14 January 1992 (that is, 14 days after 31 December 1991, the end of the quarter in which the dividend payable on 18 October 1991 was paid). This would be set off against mainstream corporation tax in respect of the period in which the dividend was paid (that is, in respect of the year ended 30 June 1992). Mainstream corporation tax in respect of that year's taxable profit would be payable on 31 March 1993; so the ACT is payable 14½ months earlier than would otherwise have occurred.

7.5 Modesty Promotions Limited. *Solution*

Since the company's taxable profit is below £250 000, the rate of corporation tax is only 25 per cent. So the corporation tax payable in respect of the year ended 31 March 1992 is: £180 000 × 25 per cent = £45 000.

Had the company's taxable profit been £800 000, then (since this lies between £250 000 and £1 250 000) the marginal system would have operated as follows:

Taxable profit: £250 000 at lower tax rate 25% =	£62 500
Plus: balance of £550 000 at marginal tax rate of 35% =	£192 500
	£255 000

7.6 Blue Sky Speculations Limited. *Solution*

Actual tax liabilities would be as follows (in £'000):

Year ended 30 June 1990:
CT Year 1989: 75% × £4 million = £3 million @ 35% = £1 050 000 ⎫
CT Year 1990: 25% × £4 million = £1 million @ 34% = £ 340 000 ⎬ = £1 390 000

Year ended 30 June 1991:
CT Year 1990: 75% × £3 million = £2.25 million @ 34% = £765 000 ⎫
CT Year 1991: 25% × £3 million = £0.75 million @ 33% = £247 500 ⎬ = £1 012 500

7.7 Mansell and Horton Limited. *Solution*

14 April 1990
ACT on net dividend of £320 000 = £106 667 (= 25/75 × £320 000)
14 January 1991
ACT on net dividend of £520 000 = £173 333 (= 25/75 × £520 000)
31 March 1991

CT 1989: 75% × £4 100 000 = £3 075 000 @ 35%	= £1 076 250
CT 1990: 25% × £4 100 000 = £1 025 000 @ 34%	= £348 500
	£1 424 750
Less: ACT on dividends *paid* in year ended 30 June 1990	£273 334*
	£1,151,416

*£106 667 + £166 667 (= 25/75 × £500 000 net dividend paid in October 1989).

Answers to the following four problems are given at the end of the book.

7.8 Graphic Enterprises Limited: Capital allowances

At 1 January 1991, Graphic Enterprises Limited showed the following amounts for fixed assets in the books (£'000):

Land	£600 (cost)
Factory buildings	£280 (cost) less £105 (accumulated depreciation)
Office buildings	£106 (cost) less £24 (accumulated depreciation)
Plant and machinery	£184 (cost) less £142 (accumulated depreciation)

During the year ended 31 December 1991, there were minor additions to both the factory buildings (costing £20) and the office buildings (costing £14). Depreciation on buildings was charged at 5 per cent each year on cost. New plant costing £22 was acquired during the year, as was second-hand equipment costing £4. Depreciation was charged at 10 per cent (straight line) on all plant (ignoring residual value). No fixed assets were sold during the year, and the company charged a full year's depreciation on all fixed assets acquired during a year.

For tax purposes, written-down values at 1 January 1991 of the various classes of fixed assets were as follows:

Land	£600	Office buildings	£106
Factory buildings	£90	Plant and machinery	£30

You are asked to calculate, in respect of the year 1991:

(a) the depreciation that would be charged in the company's books
(b) the net book value of each fixed asset category at the end of the year
(c) tax capital allowances
(d) the end-of-year tax written-down value for each fixed asset category.

7.9 Archimedes Kaye Limited: Deferred tax

In Archimedes Kaye Limited's year ended 30 June 1990 the company's profits were £2 200 000, after charging depreciation of £400 000 (but before tax). Capital allowances for tax purposes amounted to £1 000 000.

In respect of the year ended 30 June 1990, the company declared a dividend of 2.0p per share (net) on the 10 million ordinary shares outstanding, payable on 1 September 1990.

(a) how much corporation tax is payable in respect of the year? When?
(b) what will the company's reported retained earnings for the year ended 30 June 1990 amount to:
(i)   if the company operates a (full) deferred tax account?
(ii) if it doesn't?

7.10 Regeneration Limited (A): Amount and timing of tax

Regeneration Limited taxable profits in recent years have been as follows (after deducting capital allowances):

Year ended 30 June 1990	£2 000 000
9 months ended 31 March 1991	£1 500 000
Year ended 31 March 1992	£2 400 000

Calculate the corporation tax payable in respect of the above profits. Ignoring dividends, when will it be payable?

7.11 Regeneration Limited (B): Tax on dividend

In respect of the year ended 31 March 1992, Regeneration Limited declared a net dividend of £500 000 payable on 1 June 1992. All the company's shareholders were liable to income tax only at the basic rate of 25 per cent.

If the company's reported profit before tax amounted to £2 400 000:

(a) what extra tax, if any, would be payable as a result of Regeneration Limited's dividend payment; and when would it be paid?
(b) what would the company's retained earnings amount to for the year ended 31 March 1992, assuming that no deferred tax arises?

No answers are given to the following problems:

7.12 Amethyst Limited: Deferred tax

Amethyst Limited, a new company, projects profits of £100 a year (before tax and straight line depreciation) for each of the next 4 years. In year 1 it is planning to spend £160 on some equipment which has a 4 year life (with no residual value). It has no plans for capital spending in years 2, 3, or 4. Taxation in each of the next 4 years is expected to be 40 per cent of taxable profit. A capital allowance of 100 per cent of the cost of fixed assets is available in the year of purchase. Any unused capital allowances can be carried forward to set against taxable profits in future years.

Required:

1 Identify the corporation tax actually payable in each of the next 4 years.
2 Set out the projected profit and loss account for each of the next 4 years, showing profit before and after tax, assuming full deferred taxation.
3 Set out the amount of the deferred taxation balance which would appear in Amethyst Limited's balance sheet at the end of each year, assuming comprehensive deferred tax.

Note: This example using hypothetical rates of tax and allowances identifies the issues involved more simply and clearly than using actual rates.

7.13 Wavendon Limited: Capital allowances

Wavendon Limited is preparing its accounts for the year ended 30 June 1991. In order to estimate its taxation liability, it is about to compute its capital allowances, on the basis of the following data:

	£'000
Purchase of fixed assets in year:	
Plant and equipment	250
Industrial buildings	50
Office building (modification)	60
Tax written down value of fixed assets (at 30 June 1990):	
Plant and equipment	836
Industrial buildings (cost £1 000 000)	280
Disposal of fixed assets in the year:	
Plant and equipment: cost	20
written down value for tax	6
proceeds of sale	9
Depreciation charge in the accounts	225
Credit balance on deferred taxation account at 1 July 1990	300

Required:

1 Compute the capital allowances for the year ended 30 June 1991.
2 Assuming the timing differences between the tax capital allowances and the book depreciation charges are temporary, calculate the charge or credit to the profit and loss account in respect of deferred taxation in 1991. (The company pays corporation tax at the full rate, not at the 'smaller company' rate of 25 per cent.)

7.14 Brotherton's Foods Limited

Brotherton's Foods Limited was established in 1972. Its draft accounts for the year ended 30 June 1991 show a profit on ordinary activities before tax of £1 830 000. In addition there is an extraordinary expense of £170 000 (before tax), being the cost of redundancy payments made to employees.

Among the items charged in arriving at the profit were the following:

		£'000
(a)	Write down of obsolescent stock	104
(b)	Depreciation: plant and equipment	200
	industrial buildings	20
	office premises	5
(c)	Legal expenses in connection with debt collection	25
(d)	Entertaining: overseas customers	6
	staff	8
	other	4
(e)	Provision for bad debts: specific	50
	general	25

Capital allowances for the year amount to £300 000.

The company paid a final dividend of 6p per share (net) for the year ended 30 June 1990 on 10 million shares on 25 October 1990, and is planning to pay a final dividend of 7p per share (net) for the year ended 30 June 1991 on 10 million shares on 23 October 1991. No interim dividend has been paid in either year.

Required:

1 Calculate the corporation tax payable on the results of the year ended 30 June 1991.
2 When will this tax be payable?
3 Prepare as much of Brotherton's Foods Limited profit and loss account as you can for the year ended 30 June 1991.

Section 8
Capital structure

CAPITAL EMPLOYED

In our approach to company accounts we have deducted 'creditors due within one year' from current assets, to give a net figure for 'working capital'. We have thus defined 'capital employed' as total assets less current liabilities (= fixed assets plus working capital). In this section we look more closely at the items comprising capital employed:

1 Ordinary shareholders' funds.
2 Preference share capital.
3 Creditors due after more than one year.
4 Provisions for liabilities and charges.

The table below shows the main distinctions between 'equity' (ordinary share capital and reserves) and 'debt' (creditors due after more than one year). Preference share capital (which, though quite common, is rarely important) falls between the two.

Differences between equity and debt

Capital	Equity	Debt
Period	Permanent	Finite
Amount	Residual: varies	Fixed
Liquidation priority	After all others	Before equity
Income		
Commitment	Discretionary	Legal liability
Amount	Varies	Usually fixed*

*or varies according to an agreed formula

Main differences between equity capital and debt relate to risk and profit. From the investors' point of view, ordinary shares are riskier than loans, but their potential profit – either in dividends or in capital gains through increased market value – may be much higher. To them 'belongs' any residual profit after tax (and after the fixed commitment to pay interest on loans).

From a company's point of view, the reverse is true: debt capital is *cheaper* than equity (partly because interest is tax-deductible); but it is also *riskier*, because of the nature of the legal commitments.

The proportions of equity and debt in the capital structure can vary over time and between companies. An important aspect of corporate financial management is to secure the best possible mix, since it can affect the 'cost of capital' to the company.

ORDINARY SHAREHOLDERS' FUNDS

Ordinary shares are shares in the ownership of a company, and give ultimate rights of control over its affairs. Called up share capital and reserves together ('shareholders' funds') constitute a company's 'equity' capital.

The breakdown of the ordinary shareholders' funds in Finance and General Limited is set out below. We shall follow the balance sheet order in looking first at called up ordinary share capital, and then at the four kinds of reserve.

FINANCE AND GENERAL LIMITED
Called up share capital and reserves

		£'000
Share capital		
Authorized: £5 million		
Called up: 16 million ordinary 25p shares		4 000
Reserves		
Share premium account	2 000	
Other reserves	500	
Profit and loss account	2 500	
Revaluation reserve	1 000	
		6 000
Ordinary shareholders' funds		10 000

Called up share capital

A company's constitution (Memorandum of Association) shows how many shares it is authorized to issue, and also specifies the type and nominal amount of each share; for example, ordinary shares of £1 each, or A ordinary shares of 10p each.

Issued ('called up') ordinary shares represent permanent capital, not normally redeemed during a company's existence. If a shareholder wants to realize his or her investment, he or she must sell the shares to someone else. Such a sale does not directly affect the company, unless it happens to change the controlling interest.

The price the seller can get for his or her shares (the market value) varies as market conditions continually change. Listed companies' shares are owned by the public and traded on a stock exchange. Unlisted companies' shares are privately owned, often by members of one or two families. They can be traded much less freely than listed shares.

When business conditions are difficult, a company's ordinary shareholders may get no dividend at all; but when things improve the level of dividends may be high. Dividends are payable only out of profits (current or past), and there is no guarantee that a company will make a profit. Even if it does, there is no legal commitment to declare any ordinary dividends; the company's directors may choose to retain all the profits within the company. Only *realized* profits are distributable, and then only to the extent that they exceed (cumulative) realized losses.

In a winding up, the legal existence of a company comes to an end. Ordinary shareholders will then receive, not the nominal ('par') amount of their shares, but anything left over after creditors and preference shareholders have been paid in full. The residual amount left per ordinary share has no upper limit, but for an unsuccessful company it could be *nothing*.

Ordinary shareholders cannot be compelled to pay the company more than the nominal amount of each share held: hence the name '(public) limited company'. This contrasts with the position of a partner in a firm, who bears *unlimited* personal liability for the debts of the partnership. If, therefore, a company's assets do not fully cover what is owed to creditors, then *they* will not be paid in full. Creditors cannot look to the ordinary shareholders to make up any shortfall (in the absence of personal guarantees).

Share premium account

The share premium account arises when a company issues ordinary shares at more than the nominal amount per share (see below). Share premiums are not available for distribution as dividends. They may however, be used in 'capitalizing' reserves in connection with 'scrip issues' (see below).

Other reserves

These may include a capital redemption reserve arising on the redemption of redeemable preference shares or cancellation of ordinary shares, amounts resulting from fluctuations in foreign currencies, a consolidation reserve or merger reserve (Section 9).

Profit and loss account

A company retains in the business any profits for a period not paid out in dividends to shareholders. As mentioned earlier (see page 8), this is the link between the profit and loss account and balance sheet. Retained profits increase the accumulated balance on profit and loss account in the balance sheet, which is available for payment of ordinary dividends in future.

It is perhaps worth emphasizing that 'reserves' in a balance sheet do not indicate money available for spending! (Only cash represents that.) Reserves simply help explain how assets have been financed in the past.

Revaluation reserve

When some or all of its fixed assets are revalued, the accounts incorporate any surplus over book value by stating the fixed assets at the new higher amount, and adding the amount of the surplus to revaluation reserve. This is part of the ordinary shareholders' funds; though of course no 'funds' flow into the company merely because the book value of some of its assets has increased. Clearly the resulting changes in equity and net assets may affect return on investment ratios. Revaluing *depreciable* fixed assets (which is less common) may also increase future depreciation charges in the profit and loss account.

A revaluation giving rise to a surplus is illustrated below. The directors of Land Holdings Limited had the company's leasehold property revalued as at 31 December 1991. The market value of the leasehold property was £1.5 million, an increase of £0.5 million over its former book value.

LANDING HOLDINGS LIMITED
Balance sheet at 31 December 1991

	Before revaluation £'000	After revaluation £'000
Leasehold property	1 000[a]	1 500[b]
Net current assets	200	200
Net assets	1 200	1 700
Capital and reserves		
Called up share capital	600	600
Revaluation reserve	—	500
Profit and loss account	200	200
	800	1 300
Loans	400	400
Capital employed	1 200	1 700

a = at cost   b = at valuation

ISSUES OF ORDINARY SHARES

A company can increase its ordinary share capital in a number of ways:

1 Issues on acquisition of another company.
2 Rights issues.
3 Bonus issues.

Issues on acquisition of another company

The accounts of Star Trading Limited are summarized below. There are no long-term creditors. The company's 3.5 million £1 ordinary shares are currently quoted in the market at 300p, and the directors decide to issue a further 1 million shares in order to acquire all the assets of another company, valued at £3 million.

STAR TRADING LIMITED
Balance sheet summary at 30 June 1990

	Before acquisition £'000	After acquisition £'000
Net assets	6 000	9 000
Capital and reserves		
Called up ordinary £1 share capital	3 500	4 500
Share premium account	—	2 000
Profit and loss account	2 500	2 500
Capital employed	6 000	9 000

The £3 million proceeds of the share issue represent:

1 £1 million increase in called up share capital (1 million new ordinary shares with a nominal value of £1 each).
2 £2 million share premium on the issue of 1 million £1 shares at a price of £3 each (that is, 1 million new shares × £2 premium per share).

Rights issues

Star Trading's 4.5 million £1 ordinary shares stand at £3 in the market. What happens if the company, wishing to raise more cash to expand its business, makes a 'rights issue' to existing shareholders? If the company wanted to raise £3.3 million, it could offer £1.5 million new £1 ordinary shares to existing shareholders for 220p cash per share, on the basis of a '1 for 3' rights issue. A holder of 300 £1 ordinary shares would then be entitled to subscribe for 100 new shares at 220p each, involving a cash payment of £220 to the company.

Any shareholders who did *not* wish to invest more cash could sell their rights* in the market.

Because shareholders can always *sell* their rights, in theory it makes no difference to them at what *price* a rights issue is made. If they do nothing, the company would normally sell the rights in the market on their behalf. The buyer of the rights would then subscribe the required 220p per share and obtain the new shares. The result is equivalent to a new issue at the current market price, combined with a bonus issue (see below) whose precise terms depend on the terms of the rights issue. What happens to the market price of the shares after a rights issue depends on how profitably the new capital is invested, as well as on general market conditions.

The balance sheet of Star Trading before and after the 1 for 3 rights issue is summarized below. The total equity capital has increased by £3.3 million, the amount of new cash raised. The 120p premium on the issue of 1.5 million shares has increased the share premium account. (Profit of £0.7 million has been retained since 30 June 1990.)

STAR TRADING LIMITED
Balance sheet summary at 31 March 1991

	Before rights issue £'000	After rights issue £'000
Net assets	9 700	13 000
Capital and reserves		
Called up ordinary £1 share capital	4 500	6 000
Share premium account	2 000	3 800
Profit and loss account	3 200	3 200
Capital employed	9 700	13 000

*Three shares (@ 300p) are worth £9.00 before the issue, so after a 1 for 3 rights issue @ 220p four shares will be worth £11.20 (that is, 280p per share). The rights per share are therefore worth 20p, which also equals the 80p 'discount' (300p–220p) divided by four shares.

Bonus issues and share splits

A 'bonus' (or 'scrip') issue involves capitalizing reserves to issue free shares to existing shareholders. Star Trading has 6 million £1 ordinary shares valued at 280p each. To reduce the share price without impairing the company's financial status, Star Trading could convert some of the £7 million reserves into called up ordinary share capital. If each shareholder were to be issued two bonus shares free for every three shares already held, the balance sheet would then appear as shown below, with 10 million ordinary £1 shares in issue.

After such a 2 for 3 bonus issue, the ordinary share price would fall to three-fifths of its former level – from 280p to 168p. The *total* equity does not change after a bonus issue; but a larger part than before consists of called up share capital, and a smaller part of reserves. The only 'real' change is that the part of the profit and loss account 'capitalized' is no longer legally available to pay dividends. (The share premium never was.)

Share splits aim, like bonus issues, to increase the number of shares in issue, and to reduce the market price per share; but they do *not* involve capitalizing reserves. If Star Trading felt that the share price after the 2 for 3 bonus issue was still too high at 168p, there might be a share split dividing each £1 ordinary share into *four* ordinary shares of 25p each nominal amount. The total called up share capital would remain at its nominal amount of £10 million; but the number of shares in issue would quadruple, from 10 million to 40 million. The share price would fall from 168p to 42p.

STAR TRADING LIMITED
Balance sheet summary

	Before bonus issue £'000	After bonus issue £'000	After share split £'000
Net assets	13 000	13 000	13 000
Capital and reserves			
Called up ordinary share capital	6 000	10 000[a]	10 000[b]
Share premium account	3 800	—	—
Profit and loss account	3 200	3 000	3 000
Capital employed	13 000	13 000	13 000

a = 10 million £1 shares   b = 40 million 25p shares

Notice that a '2 for 3' bonus issue means two new shares *in addition to* every three old shares held, whereas a '4 for 1' share split means four new shares *in place* of every one old share. In neither case is any extra cash raised.

PREFERENCE SHARE CAPITAL

As we noted earlier, in nature preference shares come between ordinary shares and debt. Legally they form part of a company's share capital, but with only limited rights to share in profits. Unlike lenders, who can enforce payment of interest, preference shareholders receive dividends only if the directors propose them. In practice, however, companies usually have little choice but to pay preference dividends, which are normally 'cumulative'. This means that no ordinary dividends are possible until a company has paid all preference dividends due (including any arrears).

The tax rules treat preference dividends like ordinary dividends, as distributions of after-tax profits; whereas debt interest is an *expense* deductible before computing taxable profits. So preference capital tends to be an expensive form of finance. For this reason, a number of companies have redeemed their preference share capital and substituted debt capital instead.

On a winding up, preference shareholders have priority over ordinary shareholders, in the same way that creditors have priority over both preference and ordinary shareholders. Again, however, their rights are limited. No matter how large the remaining surplus a company has after realizing all its assets and paying all its creditors, the preference shareholders will normally receive only the nominal amount of their shares. (The ordinary shareholders will get all the rest.)

Preference shares may seem to provide companies with an attractive, if expensive, form of capital, combining the finite capital liability of debt with the dividend discretion of ordinary shares. But, as we have seen, companies cannot really choose to omit the payment of preference dividends in any period if they want to pay any ordinary dividends.

The 'in between' nature of preference capital can pose problems. It certainly forms part of a company's 'permanent' capital employed. Some analysts treat preference shares as equivalent to debt; but on occasions – for example where a severe cash squeeze exists – the unique nature of preference capital might need explicit recognition.

FINANCE AND GENERAL LIMITED
Balance sheet at 31 December 1992

	£'000
Capital and reserves	
Called up ordinary £1 share capital	4 000
Reserves	6 000
Ordinary shareholders' funds	10 000
7% Preference share capital	2 500
10% Debentures 1998	2 500
Capital employed	15 000

Profit and loss account for the year ended 31 December 1992

	£'000
Profit before interest payable and tax (PBIT)	4 250
Debenture interest payable	250
Profit before tax	4 000
Corporation tax (at 33 per cent)	1 300
Profit after tax	2 700
Preference dividends	175
Profit available for ordinary shareholders	2 525
Ordinary dividends (@ 50p per share)	2 000
Retained profit for the year	525

As shown by the summarized accounts set out above, for Finance and General Limited, the before-tax cost of £2.5 million 10 per cent debentures is £250 000 per year. (After tax, this costs only £167 500.)

Preference dividends are denominated in terms of the 'net-of-tax' dividend payable. On its £2.5 million 7 per cent preference capital, Finance and General Limited actually pays £175 000 net per year. But in order to leave £175 000 available after corporation tax at 33 per cent on profits the company must earn before-tax profits of £261 194 (= £175 000 × 100/67).

The published profit and loss account might show only *aggregate* dividends of £2 175 000; so where a company has preference shares outstanding, analysts may need to refer to the notes to the accounts to find out the split between ordinary and preference dividends.

CREDITORS DUE AFTER MORE THAN ONE YEAR

A company issuing debt capital (borrowing) must pay interest on the amount borrowed, and repay the debt outstanding on the promised date. Failure to do either entitles the lender to take legal action to recover the amount due. If a company goes into liquidation it must pay all debts in full before preference or ordinary shareholders get anything.

Companies may raise long-term debt from banks, insurance companies or other financial institutions, and (for large companies only) from the public via the Stock Exchange. For smaller companies, individual shareholders or directors may sometimes be prepared to advance long-term debt capital on suitable terms.

In its simplest form a loan is merely a contract between lender and borrower, with terms covering the payment of interest and repayment of capital ('principal'). Such a loan could be 'unsecured', with the lender being treated, in the event of winding up, on the same basis as a trade creditor. Often lenders will seek greater protection and 'secure' their rights by a charge or mortgage on some or all of the company's assets. In the event of winding up this will entitle 'secured' lenders to recover their debt in full before trade and other 'unsecured' creditors can receive any proceeds from the charged assets.

The terms of long-term loans can vary. They will often be for a period between five and fifteen years. The rate of interest (which used to be fixed) now tends to vary over time as interest rates in the economy change. Money interest rates will allow for expected future inflation during the loan period. Depending on the financial status of the borrower, the more risk lenders perceive in making a loan, the higher the interest rate they will require, or the more stringent the other conditions they may insist on.

Convertible loans

A special kind of debt capital can be *converted* on pre-arranged terms into ordinary share capital at the holder's option, after which it is the same as other ordinary share capital. If not converted during the option period, the conversion rights lapse, and convertible debt simply becomes straight debt capital.

Companies issuing convertible debt normally *want* it to be converted. In effect they intend to borrow for a few years against the proceeds of a later equity issue. Both for the company and for the holder, the special attraction of convertible debt lies in the period prior to conversion, when it combines the safety of debt with the profit potential of equity. Until it actually is converted, however, convertible debt is debt. It should not be treated as if it was already equity.

Conversion of debt capital will cause interest payable to fall, and profit after tax to increase. But it could sometimes add so many extra ordinary shares to those already outstanding that earnings per share would fall. Where such 'equity dilution' would reduce earnings per share by at least 5 per cent, companies must disclose earnings per share figures computed on *two* bases:

1 Ordinary shares currently in issue.
2 Potential total ordinary shares in issue if all existing conversion rights were exercised.

The example below computes the 'fully diluted' earnings per share of Highways Limited after the assumed conversion of £5 million 8 per cent convertible loan stock into ordinary shares at 250p per share.

HIGHWAYS LIMITED
Balance sheet at 31 March 1992

	Before conversion £ m	After conversion £ m
Capital and reserves		
Called up share capital:		
6 million £1 ordinary shares	6	8
Share premium account	—	3
Profit and loss account	9	9
Shareholders' funds	15	20
Creditors due after more than one year		
8% Convertible loan stock	5	—
Capital employed	20	20

Profit and loss account for the year ended 31 March 1992

	£'000	£'000	
Profit before interest payable and tax	3 400	3 400	
Interest payable	400	—	(a)
Profit before tax	3 000	3 400	
Tax (at 33 per cent)	990	1 122	
	2 010	2 278	
Number of ordinary shares (million)	6	8	(b)
Earnings per share	33.5p	28.5p	

(a) after conversion there is no interest payable

(b) $\dfrac{£5 \text{ million}}{£2.50}$ = 2 million new ordinary £1 shares

GEARING

The proportion of debt and equity within a company's capital structure is decided by its directors. We have already seen in Section 2 the two main ways to measure the burden of debt: (1) debt ratio (debt ÷ capital employed), and (2) interest cover (PBIT ÷ interest payable). A company with a large proportion of debt in its capital structure is said to be highly 'geared' (or 'leveraged'). The higher the financial gearing, the greater the risk for owners of equity capital, but the greater their prospect of profit if all goes well.

Example

Two otherwise identical small companies, Green Limited and Brown Limited, have very different debt ratios. In year 1 the highly geared company Green (debt ratio 50 per cent) has a much higher return on equity than Brown (debt ratio 10 per cent). But in year 2, when profit before interest payable and tax (PBIT) is small, there is nothing left for Green's ordinary shareholders, while Brown's still get a positive return.

	Low gearing BROWN		High gearing GREEN	
	£'000		£'000	
Equity	900		500	
Debt (15% interest)	100		500	
= Capital employed	1 000		1 000	
Debt ratio	10%		50%	

	Year 1 £'000	Year 2 £'000	Year 1 £'000	Year 2 £'000
Return on capital employed	30%	7½%	30%	7½%
PBIT	300	75	300	75
Interest payable	15	15	75	75
Profit before tax	285	60	225	—
Tax (at 25 per cent)	71	15	56	—
Profit after tax	214	45	169	—
Return on equity	23.8%	5.0%	33.8%	0.0%
Interest cover	20.0	5.0	4.0	1.0

The diagram below shows how gearing works. When the return on capital employed exceeds 15 per cent (the rate of interest payable on debt), Green's return on equity is higher than Brown's; but the reverse is true when the return on capital employed is less than 15 per cent.

The effect of gearing is to make return on equity change more sharply than return on total capital employed. Of course this works both ways, when profits are falling as well as when they are rising. As the debt ratio increases, at least beyond a certain level, new capital becomes more expensive as the risk grows, both for lenders of debt capital and for subscribers of equity capital.

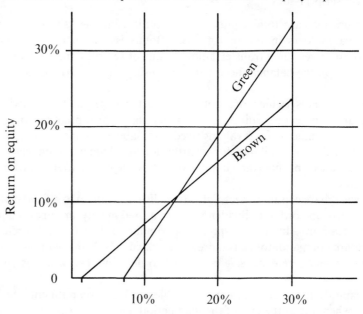

Return on capital employed

As well as this kind of 'financial gearing', most companies also have some degree of 'operational gearing'. This is low if most expenses vary directly with turnover. But when there is a relatively large proportion of fixed expenses, operational gearing is high. The overall riskiness of the ordinary shareholders' investment depends on both sorts of gearing, on business risk as well as on financial risk. The more stable the nature of a particular industry, the higher the debt ratio can safely be.

SUMMARY

The main kinds of 'capital employed' are:

1   Called up ordinary share capital and reserves ('equity').
2   Creditors due after more than one year ('debt').

A company can increase its ordinary share capital in a number of ways:

1   Issues on acquisition of another company.
2   Rights issues.
3   Bonus ('scrip') issues.

Rights issues increase total equity capital, comprising new shares offered to existing shareholders in return for cash. Bonus issues, in contrast, merely 'capitalize' reserves: they transfer amounts out of reserves and into called up share capital on the balance sheet, *without* causing any increase in total equity capital.

'Capital' reserves (which are not available for distribution as dividends) typically arise either on issuing new ordinary shares at a premium over their nominal ('par') value, or on revaluing fixed assets above original cost. 'Revenue' reserves (which *are* available for distribution as dividends) typically arise through 'retained' profits (the cumulative excess of profits after tax over dividends paid).

Preference share capital carries rights (usually cumulative) to a fixed dividend payable before any ordinary dividend, and to a fixed money amount on liquidation or redemption. In these respects it is similar to debt (though preference dividends are not mandatory). But preference dividends, being paid out of after-tax profits, tend to be expensive compared to debt interest, which is charged before tax.

Debt capital carries regular interest payable as a legal commitment, and must be repaid when due at the end of the loan period. Debt has priority over equity share capital in a winding up. From a company's point of view, debt is cheaper than equity capital, but riskier.

Two main ways of measuring a company's debt burden are:

1   Debt ratio (capital).
2   Interest cover (income).

Companies with a high debt ratio (or a low interest cover) are said to be 'highly geared', or to have high 'financial gearing'.

Other categories of capital employed include: minority interests (see Section 9); provisions for liabilities and charges, including deferred taxation (see Section 7); and perhaps interest-bearing short term borrowing (see Section 2).

For the sake of completeness it may be helpful to list (for Randall Limited, below) all the categories of capital employed which are likely to be disclosed, including provisions for liabilities and charges.

RANDALL LIMITED: Capital employed

		£'000
Capital and reserves		
Called up ordinary share capital		xxx
Reserves:		
Share premium account	xxx	
Revaluation reserve	xxx	
Other reserves	xxx	
Profit and loss account	xxx	
	——	
		xxx
		——
		xxx
Preference share capital		xxx
		——
		xxx
Minority interests (see Section 9)		xx
Creditors due after more than one year		
Convertible debentures	xxx	
Long-term loans (secured)	xxx	
Long-term loans (unsecured)	xxx	
Finance lease capitalized (see Section 5)	xxx	
	——	
		xxx
Provisions for liabilities and charges		
Deferred taxation (see Section 7)	xxx	
Provisions for employee benefits	xxx	
Reorganization costs	xxx	
Other provisions	xxx	
	——	
		xxx
Short-term borrowing		xxx

8.1 Definitions

Write down below your definitions of the terms shown. Then compare your answers with those shown on the next page.

(a) Capital employed

(f) Share premium

(b) Ordinary shareholders' funds

(g) A bonus issue

(c) Reserves

(h) Preference share capital

(d) Equity

(i) A highly geared company

(e) Fully diluted earnings per share

(j) A rights issue

8.1 Definitions

(a) *Capital employed* is long-term capital. Its main constituents are equity capital (called up ordinary share capital and reserves) and creditors due after more than one year ('debt' capital). Capital employed also includes other items such as preference share capital, minority interests, and deferred tax and other provisions. Looked at from the asset side, capital employed equals net assets (= fixed assets plus working capital = total assets less current liabilities).

(b) *Ordinary shareholders' funds* consist of called up ordinary share capital plus reserves. Because other items of capital employed are determined independently, ordinary shareholders' funds represents a residual amount, which will be affected by any change in the valuation of net assets.

(c) *Reserves* can be split between 'capital' reserves and 'revenue' reserves. Capital reserves are not available for distribution as dividends to ordinary shareholders. Typically they arise either from share premiums or from revaluation of fixed assets. Revenue reserves are cumulative retained profits, which *are* legally available for distribution as dividends. (But of course, a company also needs *cash*, in order to be able to pay dividends!)

(d) *Equity* is often used as a synonym for 'ordinary shareholders' funds'.

(e) *Fully diluted earnings per share* is what earnings per share would have amounted to if all outstanding convertible loans, convertible preference shares, and all other options outstanding had been converted into ordinary share capital (on the appropriate terms) at the beginning of the period under review. Where this hypothetical earnings per share amount differs materially (that is, by 5 per cent or more) from actual earnings per share for the period, SSAP 3 says it must be disclosed in the accounts too, with 'equal prominence'.

(f) *Share premium* is the excess of the proceeds of an issue of ordinary shares over their nominal ('par') value. It is treated in accounts as a capital reserve, not available for distribution as dividends.

(g) *A bonus issue* (= a 'scrip' issue) is an issue of ordinary shares to existing shareholders pro rata to existing holdings. The company gets no consideration for the new shares: they are free (a 'bonus') to existing shareholders. The shares are not expected to add to the total market value of the shares held, since the value of existing shares will decline in proportion. Bonus shares result from the 'capitalization' of reserves, the process of converting reserves into new issued ordinary share capital. To the extent that revenue reserves are so utilized, a bonus issue may have the effect of reducing the amount available for payment of ordinary dividends in future.

(h) *Preference share capital* is permanent capital carrying priority over ordinary share capital, both as to dividends and as to capital repayment in a winding up. It entitles holders only to a fixed amount of dividends and to a fixed amount in a winding up; but it differs from debt in that payment of preference dividends, unlike debt interest, is not mandatory. But preference dividends are nearly always 'cumulative', which means that if they are 'passed' in respect of a period they have to be made up later before any ordinary dividend may be paid.

(i) *A highly geared company* is one with a high debt ratio (proportion of debt capital to total capital employed), or a low interest cover. This is financial gearing. Operating ('business') gearing means a high proportion of fixed expenses (that is, not varying with sales) to total expenses. It would be normal to have high financial gearing with low operating gearing; and vice versa.

(j) *A rights issue* is an issue of ordinary shares to existing shareholders at a price less than the current market price. 'Rights' to take up such shares are available to shareholders in proportion to their existing holdings. Those shareholders who do not wish to invest more capital in the company by taking up their rights can sell their rights in the market. The value of the rights will vary depending on the difference between the current share price and the issue price. In theory the precise terms of a rights issue should not matter, since it can always be expressed as a combination of a bonus issue and the issue of new shares at the current market price (each of which separately has no value of its own).

8.2 Highsight Properties Limited: Revaluation

The balance sheet of Highsight Properties Limited at 31 July 1992 is shown below. It does not include the results of a professional valuation of land and buildings at £5 000 000 as at 31 July 1992.

Please incorporate the revaluation in the accounts by amending the balance sheet where necessary. The answer is shown overleaf.

HIGHSIGHT PROPERTIES LIMITED
Balance sheet at 31 July 1992

	£'000
Fixed assets	
Land and buildings, at cost less accumulated depreciation	3 400
Net current assets	350
	3 750
Capital and reserves	
Called up share capital	2 000
Profit and loss account	250
	2 250
Creditors due after more than one year	1 500
	3 750

8.3 Whittaker Foods Limited: Bonus issue

The summarized balance sheet of Whittaker Foods Limited at 30 April 1992 is shown below. A bonus issue of ordinary shares on terms of '3 for 4' is proposed.

Please amend the balance sheet to show how it would look after the bonus issue. The answer is shown overleaf.

WHITTAKER FOODS LIMITED
Balance sheet at 30 April 1992

	£'000
Fixed assets	4 700
Net working capital	2 300
	7 000
Capital and reserves	
Called up share capital:	
9.6 million ordinary 25p shares	2 400
Share premium account	600
Profit and loss account	2 200
	5 200
Creditors due after more than one year	1 800
	7 000

8.2 Highsight Properties Limited

Solution

HIGHSIGHT PROPERTIES LIMITED
Balance sheet at 31 July 1992

	£'000
Fixed assets	
Land and buildings, at valuation	5 000
Net current assets	350
	5 350
Capital and reserves	
Called up share capital	2 000
Revaluation reserve	1 600
Profit and loss account	250
	3 850
Creditors due after more than one year	1 500
	5 350

Notes

1 Did you remember to change the description of 'Fixed assets' in the balance sheet from 'at cost less accumulated depreciation' to 'at valuation'? (The date of the valuation should be given in a note to the accounts.)
2 Notice that the debt ratio has fallen 40 per cent to 28 per cent as a result of the revaluation (even though nothing has 'really' changed). What would you expect to happen to: (a) return on net assets? (b) return on equity? (c) interest cover?

8.3 Whittaker Foods Limited

Solution

WHITTAKER FOODS LIMITED
Balance sheet at 30 April 1992

	£'000
Fixed assets	4 700
Net working capital	2 300
	7 000
Capital and reserves	
Called up share capital:	
16.8 million ordinary 25p shares	4 200
Profit and loss account	1 000
	5 200
Creditors due after more than one year	1 800
	7 000

Notes

1 Since there are 9.6 million ordinary shares already in issue, the '3 for 4' bonus issue means issuing a further 7.2 million ordinary 25p shares.
2 Did you remember to change the *number* of ordinary shares in issue, as well as the money amount?
3 Notice that the bonus issue does not affect the total shareholders' funds, which remain at £5.2 million. It merely 'capitalizes' reserves, which already formed part of shareholders' funds.
4 The normal procedure would be to transfer the required amount of £1.8 million (= 7.2 million shares @ 25p each) to issued share capital, first by using capital reserves and then by using the profit and loss account to make up the balance. So here £0.6 million has come from share premium and the balance of £1.2 million from profit and loss account.

8.4 Edwards Limited, Thomas Limited and Charles Limited: Share issues

Each of the above three companies has an issued ordinary share capital of £1 200 000 in £1 shares, an accumulated balance of £700 000 on profit and loss account, and no other reserves. The authorized share capital in each case is £2 000 000.

The companies make the following ordinary share issues:

Edwards Limited issues 200 000 new shares at £1.50 each
Thomas Limited makes a 1 for 3 bonus issue
Charles Limited makes a 1 for 4 rights issue at £2.

Please show below:

(a) the appropriate journal entries in each case (including any cash transactions)
(b) the details of capital and reserves after the various issues.

Answers are shown overleaf.

(a) *Journal entries*

	Dr £'000	Cr £'000
Edwards		
Thomas		
Charles		

(b) *Capital and reserves*

	Edwards £'000	Thomas £'000	Charles £'000
Called up share capital: Ordinary £1 shares			
Reserves:			

8.5 Debt ratios

The accounts of three companies in the same industry are summarized below.

Please calculate and compare their debt ratios and interest covers. The answers are shown overleaf.

	A £'000	B £'000	C £'000
Fixed assets, net	900	1 500	7 000
Current assets	700	900	6 500
	1 600	2 400	13 500
Called up ordinary share capital	300	600	3 000
Reserves	500	800	2 000
7% Preference share capital	—	—	2 000
Long-term 15% loans*	200	300	4 000
Creditors due within one-year	600	700	2 500
	1 600	2 400	13 500
Profit after tax (at 25%)	225	300	1 500

*The loans have all been outstanding throughout the year.

8.4 Edwards Limited, Thomas Limited and Charles Limited

Solution

(a) *Journal entries*

	Dr £'000	Cr £'000
Edwards		
Cash	300	
To ordinary share capital		200
To share premium		100
Being issue of 200 000 new ordinary £1 shares at £1.50 each		
Thomas		
Profit and loss account	400	
To ordinary share capital		400
Being transfer from retained profits to issued ordinary share capital on bonus issue of 400 000 £1 shares		
Charles		
Cash	600	
To ordinary share capital		300
To share premium		300
Being issue of 300 000 new £1 ordinary shares at £2 each		

(b) *Capital and reserves*

	Edwards £000's	Thomas £'000	Charles £'000
Called up share capital:			
Ordinary £1 shares	1 400	1 600	1 500
Reserves:			
Share premium	100	—	300
Profit and loss account	700	300	700
	2 200	1 900	2 500

Notes

1 Details would probably be shown in the notes to the accounts.
2 It may be best to start by considering how much *total* shareholders' funds have been increased by a particular issue.

8.5 Debt ratios

Solution

	A	B	C
Fixed assets, net	900	1 500	7 000
Current assets	700	900	6 500
Less: Creditors due within one year	600	700	2 500
= Net working capital	100	200	4 000
= Net assets	1 000	1 700	11 000
Called up ordinary share capital	300	600	3 000
Reserves	500	800	2 000
= Ordinary shareholders' funds	800	1 400	5 000
7% Preference share capital	–	–	2 000
Long-term 15% loans	200	300	4 000
= Capital employed	1 000	1 700	11 000
Profit before interest and tax	330	445	2 600
Interest	30	45	600
Profit before tax	300	400	2 000
Tax (at 25%)	75	100	500
Profit after tax	225	300	1 500
Preference dividends	—	—	140
Debt ratio =	20%	18%	36%
Interest cover =	11.0	9.9	4.3

Notes

1 The layout has been changed, by subtotalling ordinary shareholders' funds and by deducting creditors due within one year from current assets, so that the balance sheets totals represent capital employed and net assets.
2 Note that the rankings of the debt ratios and the interest covers are not the same.
3 We use debt/capital employed for the debt ratio. The debt/equity ratios would be 25, 21, and 57 per cent respectively.

Answers to the following six problems are shown at the end of the book.

8.6 Kent Traders Limited: Rights issue

The balance sheet of Kent Traders Limited at 30 April 1992 is shown below. You are asked to amend the balance sheet to give effect to a 1 for 4 rights issue on that date at 200p a share.

KENT TRADERS LIMITED
Balance sheet, 30 April 1992

		£'000
Fixed assets, net		750
Current assets		
Stock	260	
Debtors	190	
Cash	70	
	520	
Less: Creditors due within one year	240	
		280
		1 030
Capital and reserves		
Called up share capital:		
1 200 000 ordinary 50p shares		600
Profit and loss account		160
Shareholders' funds		760
Creditors due after more than one year		
Long-term loans		270
		1 030

8.7 Antrobus Lathes Limited: Convertible debt

The 10 per cent convertible loan stock of Antrobus Lathes Limited was all converted in 1992 into ordinary £1 share capital on the basis of 40 ordinary £1 shares for every £100 of 10 per cent loan stock.

You are asked to amend the summarized 1991 accounts shown below to give effect to the conversion of the 10 per cent loan stock at the start of 1992, assuming no other changes to the 1991 figures.

ANTROBUS LATHES LIMITED
Balance sheet at end of 1991

	Actual £'000	With loan converted £'000
Capital and reserves		
Called up ordinary £1 share capital	2 400	
Reserves	1 100	
Shareholders' funds	3 500	
10% Convertible loan stock	1 500	
8% Loan stock	1 000	
Capital employed	6 000	
Debt ratio	$\frac{2\,500}{6\,000} = 42\%$	$\underline{} = \%$
Profit and loss account, 1991		
PBIT	1 430	
Loan interest payable	230	
Profit before tax	1 200	
Tax at 33%	396	
Profit after tax	804	
Earnings per share	$\frac{804}{2\,400} = 33.5\text{p}$	$\underline{} = \text{p}$
Interest cover	$\frac{1\,430}{230} = 6.2$	$\underline{} =$

8.8 Western Enterprises Limited: Share issues

The balance sheet of Western Enterprises Limited at 1 January 1992 is summarized below. Please amend it to record the following events which occurred during the year to 31 December 1992. Assume that retained profit is reflected in increased working capital. Identify your amendments by the letters (a) to (f).

(a) March 1992. 50 000 ordinary £1 shares were issued to employees at £3 each

(b) June 1992. Land and buildings were revalued at £1 500 000

(c) September 1992. There was a 2 for 1 bonus issue

(d) December 1992. Profit for ordinary shareholders for the year was £380 000

(e) a 12p (net) cash dividend is proposed per share

(f) a 1 for 15 bonus issue is also proposed.

WESTERN ENTERPRISES LIMITED
Balance sheet, 1 January 1992

	£'000
Fixed assets	
Land and buildings, at cost	700
Plant, net	1 700
	2 400
Working capital	800
	3 200
Capital and reserves	
Called up ordinary £1 shares	700
Share premium	350
Profit and loss account	950
Ordinary shareholders' funds	2 000
8% £1 Preference shares	200
10% Loan stock	1 000
	3 200

8.9 Sadler Limited (A): Interest cover

Sadler Limited has 200 000 £1 ordinary shares in issue, 60 000 3½% cumulative preference shares of £1 each, and £80 000 10% debentures, repayable in 1998. Reserves amount to £60 000. For the year ended 31 December 1990, the company reported a profit of £40 000 before tax. Tax is to be provided for at 25 per cent. An ordinary dividend of 8p (net) is proposed for the year. Calculate:

(a) the interest cover

(b) the dividend cover for the ordinary dividend.

8.10 Sadler Limited (B): Capital cover

At 31 December 1990, Sadler Limited's profit and loss account balance is £60 000. There are no other reserves. Other accounts are as in the (A) problem. Calculate:

(a) the debt ratio

(b) the amount per share the preference shareholders would receive if the company were liquidated at 31 December 1990, and the net assets – that is, total assets less current liabilities – realized £125 000

(c) the amount per share that ordinary shareholders would receive if the net assets realized £190 000.

8.11 Bell Limited, Book Limited and Candle Limited: Gearing

The net assets of Bell, Book and Candle are identical, but they have different capital structures in 1990 and 1991, as shown below:

	Bell £'000	Book £'000	Candle £'000
Ordinary £1 shares	150	300	400
Reserves	250	500	600
Equity	400	800	1 000
10% Loans	600	200	—
Capital employed (in both 1990 and 1991)	1 000	1 000	1 000

Assume:

(1) Tax rate of 25 per cent.

(2) All 1990 profits after tax are distributed as dividends.

(3) Profit before interest payable and tax is £180 000 in 1990 and £50 000 in 1991.

Please calculate for each company for 1990 and 1991:

(a) return on net assets (= on capital employed) (c) interest cover

(b) return on equity (d) earnings per share

No answers are given for the following problems.

8.12 Grundy International Limited

The balance sheet of Grundy International Limited at 1 January 1992 is summarized below.

GRUNDY INTERNATIONAL LIMITED

Balance sheet at 1 January 1992		£'000
Fixed assets		
Land and buildings, net		1 900
Plant and equipment, net		2 500
Net current assets		1 700
		6 100
Creditors due after more than one year		
10% Debentures 1998	1 500	
8% Convertible loan stock	600	
		2 100
Shareholders' funds		
Ordinary £1 shares	2 300	
Share premium	500	
Profit and loss account	1 200	
		4 000
		6 100

You are asked to show how the balance sheet would need to be amended to record each of the events shown below, which occurred during the year ended 31 December 1992.

(a) January — The 8% convertible loan stock was converted into ordinary shares at 375p each

(b) February — Land and buildings were revalued at £2 700 000

(c) April — There was a 5 for 1 share split

(d) June — The insured value of plant and equipment was increased to £3 000 000

(e) July — There was a 2 for 3 bonus issue

(f) September — There was a fully subscribed rights issue of 1 for 5 at 80p

(g) November — Employees exercised options to buy 400 000 shares at 50p

(h) December — The after-tax return on (beginning-of-year) equity for 1992 was 20 per cent. A cash dividend of 1.8p (net) per share was declared. Assume that any retained profit is reflected in increased net current assets.

8.13 Equivalent rights

Can you prove that a rights issue at a discount from current market price can always be regarded in theory as equivalent to an issue of new shares at the current market price combined with a bonus issue on appropriate terms?

8.14 Scylla Limited and Charybdis Limited

Scylla Limited and Charybdis Limited each reported profit before interest and tax for the calendar year 1991 of £12 million. Each company had issued £20 million 10 per cent debentures on 1 January 1985, which were redeemable in 1995. Each company had 100 million 25p ordinary shares outstanding throughout 1991.

At the start of 1992 each company invested £15 million in a capital project expected to produce an additional £3 million PBIT in 1992. Scylla Limited financed this project by issuing £15 million 12 per cent debentures on 1 January 1992. Charybdis Limited financed the project by issuing 25 million ordinary shares at 60p each on 1 January 1992.

Assuming (i) a tax rate (on reported profits before tax) of 33 per cent; and (ii) that the capital project did produce in each case the expected additional PBIT in 1992, and that the remaining 1992 PBIT for each company was the same as in 1991:

(a) what would each company's 1992 earnings per share amount to?

(b) ignoring assumption (ii) above, at what identical PBIT level in 1992 would the two companies report identical 1992 earnings per share?

8.15 M F Hotskin: Fully diluted earnings per share

Below are shown simplified summarized 1992 consolidated accounts for M F Hotskin plc. You are asked to calculate fully diluted earnings per share for the year ended 30 April 1992, on the basis of the following information:

1 The £10 million 10 per cent convertible unsecured loan stock 1997 is convertible into ordinary 5p shares in January in any of the years 1993 to 1997 on the basis of 11 ordinary 5p shares for every £1 of loan stock.

2 The £60 million 5 per cent cumulative convertible redeemable preference share capital, in shares of £1 each, is convertible into ordinary share capital on 30 September in any of the years 1992 to 2006 on the basis of 1 ordinary share of 5p for every 4 preference shares of £1. The preference shares are redeemable at par on 30 September 2011.

3 Under executive share option schemes, at 30 April 1992 options are outstanding in respect of a total of 4 million ordinary shares, at prices ranging from 45p to 250p per share.

4 Assume a corporation tax rate of 33 per cent.

M F HOTSKIN plc
Consolidated profit and loss account, year ended 30 April 1992

		£ million
Turnover		200
Profit before interest payable and tax		31
Interest payable on convertible loan stock		1
Profit before tax		30
Tax (at 33 per cent)		10
Profit after tax		20
Dividends: Preference	3	
Ordinary	3	
		6
Retained profit for the year		14
Earnings per share		17.0p

M F HOTSKIN plc
Consolidated balance sheet at 30 April 1992

		£ million
Fixed assets		
Tangible		30
Investments		10
		40
Current assets		
Stock	50	
Debtors	45	
Cash	55	
	150	
Less: **Creditors due within one year**	60	
		90
		130
Less: **Provision for liabilities and charges**		10
		120
Capital and reserves		
Called up share capital:		
Ordinary shares of 5p each		5
5% Cumulative convertible redeemable preference £1 shares		60
		65
Reserves		45
		110
Creditors due after more than one year		
10% Convertible unsecured loan stock 1997		10
		120

Section 9
Group accounts

GROUP ACCOUNTS

So far we have been dealing mainly with independent companies and how they report their financial results in accounts. In this section we consider how companies account for holdings of equity shares in other companies. Such shareholdings may be of four kinds:

1 Controlling shareholdings, comprising more than 50 per cent of the voting rights in the company whose shares are held (the 'subsidiary'). Often 100 per cent of the voting rights are held, in which case the subsidiary is 'wholly owned'.
2 Shareholdings between 20 per cent and 50 per cent, where the holding company also participates in the commercial decisions of the 'associated company'.
3 Holdings other than (1) and (2) above, where there is a strong trading link ('trade investments').
4 Other equity holdings. These are simply 'investments', which may be 'listed' on a stock exchange or 'unlisted'.

'Investments' may also include non-equity investments, such as loans or holdings of government securities. These may be either short-term (current) assets, or longer-term (fixed) assets.

Our main concern will be with the first kind of equity investment above, where a 'holding company' controls one or more subsidiaries.

Subsidiaries include partnerships and un-incorporated associations as well as companies. These are collectively known as subsidiary 'undertakings'.

Subsidiaries are defined as including any undertaking which is controlled rather than only those which are controlled by holding more than 50 per cent of the voting rights. This control (or 'dominant influence') may be through an agreement or contract with other parties or with the board of directors.

The 1985 Companies Act requires that where one company controls other companies, the holding company must normally present group ('consolidated') accounts dealing with the state of affairs and profit or loss of 'the company and its subsidiaries'. The holding company must also present its own balance sheet (but not its own profit and loss account).

A holding company may exclude a subsidiary undertaking from consolidation if:

(a) the activities of one or more subsidiaries are so different from other group undertakings that their inclusion would be incompatible with the obligation to give a true and fair view

(b) severe long-term restrictions substantially hinder the exercise of the parent company's rights over the assets or management of a subsidiary undertaking

(c) the interest of the parent is held exclusively with a view to subsequent resale, and the undertaking has not previously been included in the consolidated accounts

(d) it would involve disproportionate expense or undue delay

(e) the subsidiaries are immaterial.

The typical accounts of a holding company with one or more subsidiaries comprise:

1 Directors' report.
2 Group profit and loss account.
3 Group balance sheet.
4 Holding company balance sheet.
5 Group cash flow statement.
6 Notes to the accounts.
7 Auditors' report.
8 Statistical and supplementary statements.

Group accounts for Grand Metropolitan plc for 1990 are set out (slightly simplified) on this page and the next. Please identify all the new accounting headings (marked *) which we have not met before. See how they are presented in the context of the overall format of the profit and loss account and balance sheet with which we are familiar.

The Grand Met financial statements reflect the general nature of the consolidation process. The group profit and loss account:

(a) adds together the earnings of all the group companies, thus combining the profits of the holding ('parent') company with those of its subsidiaries

(b) also includes, but shows separately, the share of trading profits (less losses) of associates before tax

(c) deducts the interest in the group's profit after tax which belongs to the outside shareholders ('minority interests') in subsidiaries which are less than wholly owned. This determines the part of the group profit which is attributable to shareholders in the parent company.

(d) indicates (in the notes to the accounts) the extent to which attributable profits are dealt with in the accounts of the parent company or retained in those of the subsidiaries or associated companies.

(e) shows the dividends paid or proposed to the parent company's shareholders.

GRAND METROPOLITAN plc
Group profit and loss account for the year ended 30 September 1990

	£ million
Turnover	9 394
Operating costs	(8 335)
	1 059
*Income from interests in associates	23*
Trading profit	1 082
Profit on sale of property	79
Net exceptional items	(3)
Interest	(239)
Profit on ordinary activities before tax	919
Tax	(279)
Profit on ordinary activities after tax	640
*Minority interests	(6)*
Profit before extraordinary items	634
Extraordinary items	435
Profit for the financial year	1 069
Ordinary dividends	(198)
Transferred to reserves	871

Note 25 (extract)	Associates' reserves	Profit and loss account†	Total
	£m	£m	£m
Retained profit for year	9	862	871

†Profit and loss account of company and its subsidiaries

In the holding company's balance sheet, the investment in subsidiaries (including any net loans to them) appears as a separate item. The holding company must publish its own balance sheet as well as the group balance sheet.

A group balance sheet:

(a) brings together the assets and liabilities of all group companies, those of the holding company and of its subsidiaries
(b) cancels out inter-company balances
(c) includes in 'investments' the interests in associates (including loans)
(d) shows as 'goodwill' the excess of the purchase price of subsidiary companies over the holding company's share of the called up ordinary share capital and reserves *as at the date of acquisition* (adjusted to fair value). Goodwill in this case has been written off immediately against reserves
(e) shows separately the outside ('minority') shareholders' interests in the equity of subsidiaries.

After studying the Grand Met financial statements, it will be helpful to look a little more closely at how group accounts are prepared, and at the special items which arise only in group accounts. Nearly all medium or large companies have subsidiaries, and therefore have to publish group accounts.

In this section we shall look in turn at: goodwill; brands; pre-acquisition profits; and minority interests.

Then we shall consider: inter-company transactions; non-consolidated subsidiaries; associates; and alternative accounting treatments for mergers and acquisitions.

GRAND METROPOLITAN plc
Balance sheets at 30 September 1990

	Group £ million	Company £ million
Fixed assets		
Intangible assets	2 317	—
Tangible assets	3 756	—
Investments		
*Subsidiaries	—	1 123*
*Associates	151*	—
Other	63	—
	6 287	1 123
Net current assets	584	1 170
Total assets less current liabilities	6 871	2 293
Creditors due after more than one year	(3 116)	(101)
Provisions for liabilities and charges	(328)	—
	3 427	2 192
Capital and reserves		
Called up share capital	508	508
Share premium account	451	451
Revaluation reserve	(940)	—
Special reserve	—	426
*Associates' reserves	17*	—
Profit and loss	3 365	807
	3 401	2 192
*Minority interests	26*	—
	3 427	2 192

Note 24 Called up share capital (extract)	£ m
Ordinary shares of 50p each	496
Cumulative £1 preference shares	12
	508

Note 25 Reserves (extract)	
(write off) Goodwill acquired during the year	(321)*

CONSOLIDATION AND GOODWILL

Let us consider a simple example of consolidation. On 31 December 1991, H purchased all the equity shares in S for £150 000 cash. The separate balance sheets of H Limited (holding company) and S Limited (its wholly-owned subsidiary) are set out opposite (left).

To prepare the group balance sheet (opposite, right), the general approach is to add together ('consolidate') the amounts shown in the separate balance sheets. The consolidation process eliminates H's £150 000 investment in S and S's £90 000 equity capital; and shows as 'goodwill' the £60 000 excess of the purchase price over the fair value of the separable net assets acquired. (In this case we assume that the £90 000 book value of S's equity is the same as the fair value of S's net assets.)

According to SSAP 22, goodwill may be written off immediately against reserves; in which case H's £60 000 goodwill would disappear, and the group reserves would fall by £60 000. Alternatively (as in the example opposite), goodwill may be retained in the balance sheet as an intangible fixed asset costing £60 000; in which case H must amortize (depreciate) it through the profit and loss account over its estimated useful economic life.

Negative goodwill

Goodwill arose because H paid more than £90 000 for S. Had H paid *less* than £90 000 for 100 per cent of S's equity, the difference might have been shown as a reserve on consolidation – 'negative goodwill'.

Consolidation reserves do not occur very often in practice. If the acquisition price is less than the book value of the net assets, the fair value of the separable net assets acquired is also likely to be less than their book value. In that case H, on acquisition, will write them down accordingly.

H LIMITED AND S LIMITED
Balance sheets at 31 December 1991

	Separate £'000		Consolidation adjustments	Consolidated £'000
	H	S		H Group
Fixed assets			(c) + 150)	
Goodwill			(a) − 60) } = 60	
			(b) − 30)	
Plant and machinery	500	70		= 570
Investment in S	150		(c) − 150	
Net current assets	300	60		= 360
	950	130		990
Long-term creditors	250	40		= 290
	700	90	− 90	700
Capital and reserves				
Called up share capital	500	60	(a) − 60	500
Profit and loss account	200	30	(b) − 30	200
	700	90	− 90	700

(a) and (b) are H's interest in S's equity; (c) is H's cost of investment in S. Goodwill of £60 000 is treated as an intangible fixed asset.

BRANDS

As we have seen, SSAP 22 allows companies either to write off the cost of purchased goodwill at once against reserves or else to capitalize it and amortize it against profit over its life. But some companies dislike both these treatments of goodwill. Immediate write-off against reserves reduces the amount of shareholders' funds in the balance sheet; while amortizing the cost over time reduces reported profits. (You can see, on pages 206 and 207, what a difference either treatment of Grand Met's £2 317m brands would make – to £3 401m capital and reserves or to £634m profit after tax in 1990.)

There is currently no accounting standard on how to treat the cost of 'brands'. These are trade names associated with particular consumer products. So some companies have recently begun to distinguish brands from goodwill when they acquire other companies (though valuing brands is difficult). This has the effect of *reducing* the amount of 'goodwill'. These companies capitalize the assumed 'cost' of brands as intangible fixed assets on the balance sheet; but *without* amortizing that cost over time against profit. The effect is to increase shareholders' funds on the balance sheet without reducing reported profit. It thus conveniently overcomes companies' objections to both treatments of goodwill allowed by SSAP 22.

Most marketing expenditure on a brand helps to generate the current period's sales, so it has to be matched against turnover as an expense in the profit and loss account. It is very hard to tell to what extent (if any) it may have increased a brand's 'value'. On grounds of prudence, therefore, companies do not, as a rule, capitalize 'homegrown' brand values. (There is a clear parallel with the treatment of 'revenue investment' spending on research –see page 112.)

Some companies argue, however, that continued spending on purchased brands at least maintains their value. This may often be true: if they spent no money, brand values would probably fall. But the effect (see opposite) is to substitute internally-generated brand value for the depreciating purchase cost. This is an indirect way of capitalizing a highly subjective amount.

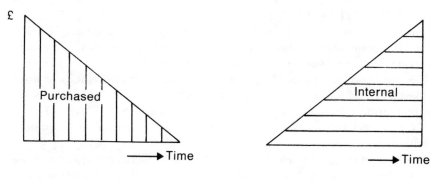

Cost of purchased brand, with notional amortization

Notional build-up of 'internally-generated' brand value

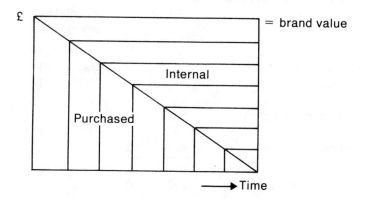

Maintaining a brand's value, by substituting internally-generated brand value for amortization of purchase cost of a brand

PRE-ACQUISITION PROFITS

When H acquired S on 31 December 1991, S had revenue reserves of £30 000. From H's point of view these represent 'pre-acquisition profits' (PAPs). S's £30 000 revenue reserves are not available for *the group* to pay out as dividends.

If S were to distribute its £30 000 reserves as dividends (to H its sole shareholder), H could not, in turn, distribute this amount. Instead H would use the £30 000 dividend from S to write down its investment in S (to £120 000).

S's post-1991 balance sheets will not reveal the extent of pre-acquisition profits.

The balance sheets of H and S one year later, at 31 December 1992 are set out below. The adjustments show the removal of S's £30 000 pre-acquisition profits from group reserves. The 1992 profits (H £100 000, S £42 000) increase net current assets, with other balance sheet items staying the same. The group is assumed to have written off the £60 000 goodwill against reserves at 31 December 1991, (item (d) below) leaving net group reserves then of £140 000. The 1992 profits (H £100 000, S £42 000) have been added to this to give net group reserves at 31 December 1992 of £282 000.

H LIMITED AND S LIMITED
Balance sheets at 31 December 1992

	Separate £'000		Consolidation adjustments	Consolidated £'000
	H	S		H Group
			(c) + 150	
Fixed assets			(a) − 60	
Goodwill			(b) − 30	—
			(d) − 60	
Plant and machinery	500	70		570
Investment in S	150		(c) − 150	
Net current assets	400	102		502
	1 050	172	− 150	1 072
Long-term creditors	250	40		290
	800	132	− 150	782
Capital and reserves				
Called up share capital	500	60	(a) − 60	500
Profit and loss account	300	72	(b) − 30	
			(d) − 60	282
	800	132	− 150	782

(d) Writing off £60 000 goodwill against reserves

210

MINORITY INTERESTS

In the examples so far, H has acquired 100 per cent of S on 31 December 1991. Let us now suppose that H acquired for £100 000 only *two-thirds* of the equity shares in S. The other one-third represents 'minority interests' in S.

Rather than including only two-thirds of each of S's assets and creditors in the group balance sheet, the H group wants to show the total assets it *controls*. So H consolidates 100 per cent of each of S's assets and creditors, but shows as a separate item, 'minority interests', the amount of S's equity which it does not own.

So, too, the group profit and loss account includes 100 per cent of each item in S's profit and loss account; and then deducts separately the share of the group's profit (or loss) after tax which relates to the minority interests.

H LIMITED AND S LIMITED
Balance sheets at 31 December 1991

	Separate £'000		Consolidation adjustments	Consolidated £'000
	H	S	(e) + 100	H Group
Fixed assets			(a) − 40	
Goodwill			(c) − 20	—
			(f) − 40	
Plant and machinery	500	70		570
Investment in S	100		(e) − 100	
Net current assets	350	60		410
	950	130	− 100	980
Long-term creditors	250	40		290
	700	90	− 100	690
Capital and reserves			(a) − 40	
Called up share capital	500	60	(b) − 20	500
			(c) − 20	
Profit and loss account	200	30	(d) − 10	160
			(f) − 40	
	700	90	− 130	660
Minority interests			(b) + 20	30
			(d) + 10	
	700	90	− 100	690

(f) Writing off £40 000 goodwill against reserves

INTER-COMPANY TRANSACTIONS

Certain adjustments are needed in practice to eliminate from group accounts two kinds of inter-company transactions:

(a) inter-company balances
(b) unrealized inter-company profits.

(a) Inter-company balances

It is fairly simple on consolidation to exclude inter-company balances (that is, amounts owing to and by companies in a group). For example, suppose that A owns B and C, and details of net current assets at the balance sheet date include the amounts shown below for debtors and creditors due within one year.

It is easy to see that £92 000 is owed within the group. The group balance sheet eliminates this amount from total debtors and creditors, leaving only *external* debtors (£324 000) and *external* creditors (£235 000). Exactly the same kind of procedure applies to any long-term inter-company loans and advances. The net excess of debtors over creditors remains, of course, at £89 000.

	Separate £'000				Consolidation adjustments	Consolidated £'000
	A	B	C	= Total		A Group
Debtors						
A	*	—	23		a − 23	
B	48	*	—		b − 48	
C	—	21	*		c − 21	
Other (external)	174	87	63			324
	222	108	86	= 416	− 92	324
Creditors due within one year						
A	*	48	—		b − 48	
B	—	*	21		c − 21	
C	23	–	*		a − 23	
Other (external)	140	54	41			235
	163	102	62	= 327	− 92	235

(b) Unrealized inter-company profits

As a single entity for accounting purposes, a group of companies earns no revenue until it sells to the outside world. This is the realization principle applied to a group. Group accounts must therefore eliminate inter-company (intra-group) purchases and sales. More importantly, group accounts must exclude any inter-company profits of subsidiaries until the group has realized them by selling outside. Otherwise the group figures would overstate sales, profits and stock. (It would also be possible to arrange spurious intra-group transactions deliberately to distort the published group accounts.)

The key question is not whether there are inter-company profits; but whether such profits have, at the balance sheet date, been *realized* by the group by sales to outside customers. Group accounts have to exclude only *unrealized* profits. (The eliminations are made on work-sheets outside the books of account. They do not affect the permanent accounting records of the individual companies.)

Suppose S, a subsidiary, has sold goods to H, its holding company, for £48 000, which cost S £30 000. There are three possibilities.

1 Wholly realized by group

Suppose H has sold all the goods costing it £48 000 to outside customers for £60 000. H will show a profit of £12 000, S will show a profit of £18 000, and the group profit is £30 000. That is the £60 000 proceeds from (H's) outside customers, less the £30 000 cost from (S's) outside suppliers. No adjustment is needed, because the group's profits (H £12 000 + S £18 000) have all been realized externally.

2 Wholly unrealized by group

If H has not sold any of the goods purchased from S, H's stock will include them as costing £48 000. But the group accounts must show that stock as costing only £30 000, the cost S paid to outside suppliers. Group profits must be reduced by £18 000 to leave out, for the time being, S's profit on the 'internal' sale to H. The group has not yet realized this profit externally. (Notice how these adjustments preserve double-entry: reduce H's stock value by £18 000, and reduce S's profit by £18 000.)

3 Partly realized by group

If H has sold two-thirds of the goods, and one-third is still in stock, then only one-third of S's £18 000 profit is unrealized by the group; so only £6 000 needs to be subtracted from group stock and from group profit.

THE CONSOLIDATED PROFIT AND LOSS ACCOUNT

The group profit and loss account will contain *all* the income and expenses of subsidiaries down to the profit after tax figure, after eliminating all unrealized inter-company profits.

For example, consider a holding company (H) and its two-thirds owned subsidiary (S), which it has held for a number of years. H controls the activities of S, so the H group accounts show in total the profit or loss resulting from all the activities that the H group controls. However, H *owns* only two-thirds of S's profits, so a deduction is made for the minority shareholders' one-third interest in S's profits after tax.

In the group profit and loss account, only H's dividends are deducted from the figure for profits after tax less minority interests. The dividends which H has received from S are eliminated on consolidation (with a tax adjustment too).

Details of the consolidation of the H group profit and loss account are shown opposite.

If a subsidiary is acquired during the year, only the *post-acquisition* profits of the subsidiary will be included in the group profit and loss account.

Groups provide a ('segmental') breakdown of their turnover, profits and net assets for each class of business and for each geographical area. (Such segmental reporting will be looked at in more detail in Section 12.)

H LIMITED AND S LIMITED

Profit and loss accounts for the year ended 31 December 1991 (extracts)

	Separate		Consolidation adjustments		Group
	£'000		£'000		£'000
	H	S			
Turnover	10 000	5 000	(100)	a	14 900
Operating profit	4 000	2 000	(10)	a	5 990
Dividend from S Ltd.	267		(267)	b	—
Interest payable	(200)	(100)			(300)
Profit before tax	4 067	1 900			5 690
Taxation	1 321	627	(67)	b	1 881
Profit after tax	2 746	1 273			3 809
Minority interests			(424)	c	(424)
Profit available for shareholders in H Ltd.					3 385
Dividends	(1 000)	(300)			(1 000)
Retained profit	1 746	973			2 385

Notes: (all figures in £'000)

a   *Inter-company transactions:* Inter-company sales from H and S amounted to £100, and all the £10 profit thereon is unrealized. Both the sales and the unrealised profits are eliminated on consolidation. (The book value of group stock would also be reduced by £10.)

b   *H's share of S's dividend:* In H Limited's accounts, H's share of S's net dividend is recorded gross of basic rate income tax (as 'franked investment income').

$$\tfrac{2}{3} \times \text{£300 net} = \text{£200 net} \times \frac{100}{75} = \text{£267 gross, less £67 tax.}$$

This is eliminated from the consolidated profit and loss account.

c   *Minority interest:* The one-third minority interest is: $\tfrac{1}{3} \times \text{£1273} = \text{£424}$.

NON-CONSOLIDATED SUBSIDIARIES

Where a holding company (H) does *not* consolidate the accounts of a particular subsidiary (N), for one of the reasons mentioned earlier (page 206), there are two possible accounting treatments: the 'equity' method, which is normal; and the 'cost' method, which is rare.

The 'equity' method

H includes in the group profit and loss account H's entire share of N's profit or loss for the period, regardless of any dividend paid by N. The group balance sheet shows H's investment in N at cost plus H's share of N's post-acquisition retained earnings. Any dividends N pays to H will simply reduce H's investment in N, and increase H's cash balance.

The 'cost' method

H shows the investment in N at cost in the balance sheet, and credits as income in the profit and loss account only dividends received from N. H's accounts ignore any profits of N not paid out in dividends, or any losses (though if the losses were serious enough, H's investment in N might be written down to less than cost).

As a general rule groups should use the 'equity' method. One reason is that a holding company usually *controls* its subsidiary's dividend policy. Using the 'cost' method would enable the holding company to affect reported group profits by changing the subsidiary's dividend, regardless of underlying profits or losses. Thus if the reason for non-consolidation were the *absence* of control, that might justify using the 'cost' method.

Example

The example opposite is based on the following data:

H buys 100 per cent of N at 31 December 1990, for £400 000 cash. In the year ended 31 December, 1991:

1 H makes a profit of £190 000, but pays no dividend.
2 N makes a profit of £70 000, and pays a dividend (to H) of £20 000.

H treats N as a non-consolidated subsidiary.

H LIMITED
Balance sheet at 31 December 1990 (extract)

	£'000
Tangible fixed assets, net	900
Investment in N, at cost	400
Net current assets	500
Net assets	1 800

H LIMITED
Group profit and loss account for the year ended 31 December 1991 (extract)

	'Cost' method £'000	'Equity' method £'000
Profit of H	190	190
Dividend from N	20	—
Share of N's profit	—	70
Total profit	210	260

Group balance sheet at 31 December 1991 (extract)

Tangible fixed assets, net	900	900
Investment in N	400	450(a)
Net current assets	710(b)	710(b)
= Net Assets	2 010	2 060

Notes:
(a) 400 + 50 (N retained earnings = 70 − 20)
(b) 500 + 190 + 20.

ASSOCIATES

Associates are investments which are not controlled (and are therefore not subsidiaries) but the holding company:

(a) holds 20 per cent or more of the equity shares in the associate; and
(b) has a significant influence over the associates' commercial decisions.

SSAP 1 requires companies to use the 'equity' method (rather than the 'cost' method) for associates. The group profit and loss account contains:

Turnover — nothing included from associates

Pre-tax profit — group's share of associates' pre-tax profit, shown separately

Tax — group's share of associates' tax, shown separately

Extraordinary items — group's share of associates' extraordinary items, included in the group figure unless material

Net retained profit — group's share of associates' tax, shown separately.

An example of the layout of a group profit and loss account including associates is shown opposite.

Unrealized inter-company profits resulting from group transactions with associates should be eliminated as for subsidiaries.

The group balance sheet shows the investment in associates at *cost* plus the group's share of associate's *post acquisition earnings*.

The Grand Met balance sheet on page 207 shows this format for including associates.

Accounts must include a list of names of associates and of other companies in which at least a 20 per cent stake is held.

GROUP PROFIT AND LOSS ACCOUNT

Year ended 31 December 1991	£'000	£'000
Turnover		18 000
Trading profit		3 500
Share of associated undertakings' profits before tax		400
Group profit before tax		3 900
Taxation: Group	1 200	
Associated undertakings	140	
		1 340
Group profit after tax		2 560
Dividends		800
Retained profits for the year: Parent company	530	
Subsidiaries	1 170	
Associates	60	
		1 760

Example

On the next page we give an example of the consolidation of a holding company and a subsidiary to work through. The balance sheets at 31 December 1991 and the profit and loss accounts for the year ended on that date, of H Limited and S Limited, are set out. H purchased two-thirds of the equity of S on 31 December 1990, when the balance on S's profit and loss account was £300 000.

Use the worksheet on the next page to prepare the consolidated balance sheet and profit and loss account for the H Group for 1991 under two alternative assumptions: first, that goodwill is being carried forward and written off against profit over ten years (straight line); and, second, that goodwill is written off immediately against reserves.

When you have completed the consolidated accounts for 1991, please compare your work with the solution set out on page 196.

H LIMITED AND S LIMITED
Balance sheets at 31 December 1991

	Separate £'000		Goodwill treated as fixed asset		Goodwill written off against reserves	
			Consolidation adjustments	H Group £'000	Further adjustment	H Group £'000
	H	S				
Fixed assets						
Goodwill						
Plant and machinery	5 000	700				
Investment in S	1 000					
Net current assets	4 500	1 020		———		———
	10 500	1 720				
Creditors due after more than one year	2 500	400		———		———
	8 000	1 320		═══		═══
Capital and reserves						
Called up share capital	5 000	600				
Profit and loss account	3 000	720		———		———
	8 000	1 320				
Minority interests				———		———
	8 000	1 320		═══		═══

Profit and loss accounts for the year ended 31 December 1991

	H	S				
	22 000	5 500		═══		═══
Trading profit	1 740	660				
Interest payable	200	40				
Amortization of goodwill						
Profit before tax	1 540	620		———		———
Taxation	540	200				
Profit after tax	1 000	420		———		———
Minority interests						
	1 000	420		═══		═══

215

H LIMITED AND S LIMITED
Balance sheets at 31 December 1991

	Separate £'000		Goodwill treated as fixed asset		Goodwill written off against reserves	
	H	S	Consolidation adjustments	H Group £'000	Further adjustment	H Group £'000
Fixed assets			+ 1 000(a)		− 400	—
Goodwill			− 400(b) − 200(d) − 40(g)	360	+ 40	
Plant and machinery	5 000	700		5 700		5 700
Investment in S	1 000		− 1 000(a)			
Net current assets	4 500	1 020		5 520		5 520
	10 500	1 720		11 580		11 220
Creditors due after more than one year	2 500	400		(2 900)		(2 900)
	8 000	1 320		8 680		8 320
Capital and reserves						
Called up share capital			− 400(b) − 200(c)	5 000		5 000
	5 000	600	− 200(d) − 100(e) − 140(f) − 40(g)	3 240	− 400 + 40	2 880
Profit and loss account	3 000	720				
	8 000	1 320		8 240		7 880
Minority interests			+ 200(c) + 100(e) + 140(f)	440		440
	8 000	1 320		8 680		8 320

Profit and loss accounts for the year ended 31 December 1991

	H	S		H Group		H Group
Turnover	22 000	5 500		27 500		27 500
Trading profit	1 740	660		2 400		2 400
Interest payable	200	40		240		240
Amortization of goodwill			[(g)]	40	− 40	—
Profit before tax	1 540	620		2 120		2 160
Taxation	540	200		740		740
Profit after tax	1 000	420		1 380		1 420
Minority interests			[(f)]	140		140
	1 000	420		1 240		1 280

ACQUISITIONS AND MERGERS

When one company (H) acquires most of the equity shares in another (S), it is normally accounted for as an 'acquisition'. But where two groups of shareholders continue their shareholdings as before, but on a combined basis, such business combinations may sometimes be treated as 'mergers'.

Under 'acquisition' accounting, as we have seen, any difference between the purchase price and the total fair values of the separate net assets represents 'goodwill'. The group accounts either write off goodwill immediately to reserves or else carry it forward as an asset and amortize it against profit over its useful life. The group includes the results of the acquired business as from the date of acquisition.

'Merger' accounting may be used (but it is not *required*) if:

- the combination results from an offer to holders of all the equity shares
- the offeror obtains at least 90 per cent of each class of equity shares and at least 90 per cent of the votes
- at least 90 per cent of the purchase price consists of equity shares
- the fair value of any consideration other than equity shares does not exceed 10 per cent of the *nominal* value of the equity shares issued.

In a 'merger' the two (or more) companies' assets and creditors are simply combined at their former book values, so no goodwill arises. If the new group's called up share capital exceeds the total of the merging companies' share capitals, the excess is deducted from reserves. If less, the deficit is shown as a reserve.

In a merger the combined retained profits of the merging companies *remain available for distribution as dividends by the new group*. The constituent companies' profits for the *entire* accounting period in which the merger occurred are reported as profits of the combined group for that period; and the profits for earlier periods are also restated on a combined basis. Thus there is no question, under merger accounting, of 'pre-acquisition profits' not being available for dividend, as happens with the acquisition method.

In a merger it is not necessary to follow the Companies Act requirement to include share premium whenever shares are issued for consideration which is greater than their nominal value. In a merger the shares issued are included in the group accounts at their nominal value.

An example showing the differences between the accounting treatment of acquisitions and mergers is set out opposite. It will be clear that under merger accounting a group can show higher profits, lower net assets, lower equity, and make higher distributions from pre-combination reserves.

Example

Company A acquires all company B's 40 000 ordinary £1 shares in exchange for 250 000 ordinary £1 shares in A worth 240p each. The total cost to A is thus £600 000.

BALANCE SHEET SUMMARIES

Before acquisition/merger	A £'000	B £'000
Net assets	1 050	100
Called up share capital	650	40
Reserves	400	60
Capital employed	1 050	100

After acquisition/merger	AB Group 'acquisition' accounting £'000	AB Group 'merger' accounting £'000
Goodwill	500(a)	—
Other net assets	1 150	1 150
	1 650	1 150
Called up share capital	900(b)	900(b)
Share premium account	350(c)	—
Other reserves	400	250(d)
	1 650	1 150

Notes (all amounts in £'000s)

(a) Goodwill is value of A's shares issued £600 less book value of B's net assets (= equity) acquired £100 = £500.
(b) A's original share capital £650 + new shares for acquisition £250 = £900.
(c) Share premium equals issue value 250 000 × 240p = £600 less nominal value of shares issued £250 = £350.
(d) A's reserves of £400 *plus* B's reserves of £60, *less* excess of nominal value of A's shares issued £250 over B's shares acquired £40, that is, £210. £460 – £210 = £250.

SUMMARY

In this section we have seen that a holding company which controls one or more subsidiaries must normally present consolidated group accounts. These involve a number of new accounting headings, in particular goodwill, pre-acquisition profits, and minority interests.

'Goodwill' is the excess of the purchase price of a subsidiary over the fair value of its net separable assets at the date of acquisition. It is normally written off immediately against reserves though it may be carried forward as a fixed asset and amortized against profit over its estimated useful economic life.

Some companies distinguish brands from goodwill when they acquire other companies. They capitalize brands on the balance sheet, but do not amortize them against profit.

A subsidiary's retained profits, earned before the date of acquisition, are 'pre-acquisition profits'. They are not available for the holding company to pay out in dividends. The holding company must use any dividends later received from a subsidiary out of pre-acquisition profits to write down the cost of the investment.

Where a holding company owns less than 100 per cent of a subsidiary's equity shares, the remainder is owned by minority shareholders. Group accounts include 100 per cent of such subsidiaries' net assets and sales and profits, and show separately the amount of 'minority interests in subsidiaries' in the balance sheet, below shareholders' funds; and in the profit and loss account 'minority share of profit' after profit after tax.

On consolidation, inter-company balances between members of a group cancel out; and *unrealized* inter-company profits are eliminated.

Where, for some good reason, a holding company (H) does *not* consolidate the accounts of a subsidiary (N), H should normally use the 'equity' method of accounting. This means taking credit in the group accounts for H's share of N's profit (not just for dividends received); and showing H's investment in N in the group balance sheet at cost plus H's share of N's post-acquisition retained earnings.

The same 'equity' method should be used where a company owns between 20 and 50 per cent of another company's voting shares, and has a significant influence over commercial decisions.

When the businesses of two or more companies are combined, the normal accounting treatment is to use the 'acquisition' method. This gives rise to 'goodwill' in the group accounts (which is normally written off immediately against reserves). Profits and losses are aggregated from the date of the combination.

When, however, the combination is on the basis of a shares-for-shares exchange, and certain other conditions are satisfied, then 'merger' accounting may (not *must*) be used. Under merger accounting no goodwill arises, and results are combined for the *whole* year in which the combination occurs (and for earlier years as well, in group statistics).

9.1 Definitions

Write down below your definitions of the terms shown. Then compare your answers with the definitions overleaf.

(a) Minority interests

(f) Non-consolidated subsidiaries

(b) Pre-acquisition profits

(g) The 'equity' method

(c) Goodwill

(h) The 'cost' method

(d) A subsidiary undertaking

(i) An associated undertaking

(e) 'Merger' accounting

(j) Inter-company profits

9.1 Definitions

(a)   *Minority interests* are the equity interests of shareholders other than the holding company in the net assets (and profits or losses) of subsidiaries which are not wholly owned by the holding company. Group accounts show them separately.

(b)   *Pre-acquisition profits* are the retained profits of subsidiaries at the date of acquisition. They are not available for the holding company to pay out in dividends. The holding company must use any dividends received from subsidiaries out of pre-acquisition profits to write down the cost of the investment in the subsidiary.

(c)   *Goodwill* is the excess of the purchase price paid by a holding company over the fair book value of (its share of) the subsidiary's assets less liabilities at the date of acquisition. It is either written off immediately against reserves; or included in the balance sheet as an intangible fixed asset and amortized against profit over its estimated useful life.

(d)   *A subsidiary undertaking* is a company, partnership or unincorporated association which is controlled by another (the 'holding' company), which either owns (directly or indirectly) more than 50 per cent of its equity capital or controls the composition of its board of directors or controls through an agreement or contract.

(e)   *'Merger' accounting* adds together the book values of the combining companies' assets (so no 'goodwill' arises). It also aggregates profits for periods *before* the date of the merger, as well as after (so no 'pre-acquisition profits' arise). Groups may (not must) use merger accounting only where there is a shares-for-shares exchange, and certain other conditions are satisfied.

(f)   *Non-consolidated subsidiaries* are subsidiaries whose accounts are not consolidated with those of the holding company (for one of the reasons set out on page 206). If material, the accounts of non-consolidated subsidiaries must be presented either separately, or in some suitable combination.

(g)   *The 'equity' method* is normally used (rather than the 'cost' method) to account for non-consolidated subsidiaries and associated companies. The investment is shown in the balance sheet at cost plus the holding company's share of the subsidiaries' retained profits since acquisition. The group profit and loss account includes the holding company's full share of the subsidiaries' profits or losses as they arise (that is, its share of dividends plus its share of retained profits for a period).

(h)   *The 'cost' method* may be used in some circumstances to account for non-consolidated subsidiaries and associated companies. The investment is shown in the balance sheet at cost; and the profit and loss account includes only dividends receivable.

(i)   *An associated undertaking* is a company, partnership or unincorporated association in which another company owns between 20 per cent and 50 per cent of the equity shares, and has a significant influence over its commercial decisions. It is accounted for by the 'equity' method.

(j)   *Inter-company profits* are profits earned by one member company of a group on selling to another member company of the group. An adjustment is necessary in group accounts to eliminate such profits as long as they are *unrealized* from the group's point of view (that is, until the goods concerned have – directly or indirectly – been sold to customers outside the group).

9.2 Whale Limited (A): Simple consolidation

Whale Limited acquired all the equity shares in Minnow Limited for £200 000 in cash on 1 January 1991. At 31 December 1990 (*before* the purchase price had been paid), the two companies' balance sheets were summarized as follows:

	Whale £'000	Minnow £'000
Tangible fixed assets	790	150
Net current assets	230	40
	1 020	190
Less: Long-term debt	70	60
	950	130
Called up share capital	500	80
Reserves	450	50
Shareholders' funds	950	130

Please draw up Whale Limited's consolidated balance sheet immediately after the acquisition, on the assumptions (1) that Minnow Limited is its only subsidiary, and (2) that goodwill is carried forward in the balance sheet as an intangible fixed asset, to be amortized against profit over its useful life.

The answer is shown overleaf.

9.3 Dexter Limited (A): Minority interests

On 1 April 1990 Dexter Limited (which previously had no subsidiaries) acquired 75 per cent of the equity share capital of Close Limited for 50 000 £1 ordinary shares. At 31 March 1990 Dexter Limited's ordinary shares were valued at 180p each. The two companies' summarized balance sheets at 31 March 1990 had been as follows:

	Dexter £'000	Close £'000
Tangible fixed assets	251	72
Net current assets	64	12
	315	84
Less: Long-term debt	78	20
	237	64
Capital and reserves		
Called up share capital (£1 shares)	150	40
Reserves	87	24
Shareholders' funds	237	64

Please draw up Dexter Limited's group balance sheet immediately after the acquisition, assuming that goodwill is written off immediately to reserves.

The answer is shown overleaf.

9.2 Whale Limited (A) *Solution*

WHALE LIMITED
Group* balance sheet at 1 January 1991

	Whale £'000	Minnow £'000	Consolidation adjustments £'000	Whale Group £'000
Tangible fixed assets	790	150		= 940
Goodwill			(a) + 200 (b) − 130	70(c)
Net current assets	230	40	(a) − 200	70(d)
	1 020	190	− 130	1 080
Less: Long-term debt	70	60		= 130
	950	130		950
Called up share capital	500	80	(b) − 80	500
Reserves	450	50	(b) − 50	450
Shareholders' funds	950	130	− 130	950

Notes (£'000)

(a) £200 purchase price
(b) £130 Minnow equity
(c) Goodwill £70 = £200 purchase price − £130 Minnow equity
(d) Whale £230 less £200 purchase price paid (to Minnow's *shareholders*, not to Minnow Limited) = £30 + Minnow £40 = £70.

*There is no significant difference between the headings 'Group accounts' and 'Consolidated accounts'.

9.3 Dexter Limited (A) *Solution*

DEXTER LIMITED
Group balance sheet at 1 April 1990

	Dexter £'000	Close £'000	Consolidation adjustments £'000	Dexter Group £'000
Tangible fixed assets	251	72		= 323
Goodwill			(b) + 90 (c) − 30 (e) − 18 (g) − 42	—
Investment in Close			(a) + 90 (b) − 90	—
Net current assets	64	12		= 76
	315	84	—	399
Less: Long-term debt	78	20		= 98
	237	64	—	301
Called up share capital	150	40	(a) + 50 (c) − 30 (d) − 10	200
Share premium			(a) + 40	40
Reserves	87	24	(e) − 18 (f) − 6 (g) − 42	45
Shareholders' funds	237	64	− 16	285
Minority interests			(d) + 10 (f) + 6	16
	237	64	—	301

Notes (£'000): (a) 50 000 new £1 shares issued at 180p = £90 proceeds. £50 is nominal share capital, so the £40 'excess' is share premium; (b) £90 cost of investment in Close; (c) and (e) 75% of Close's equity = (75% × £40) + (75% × £24) = £30 + £18 = £48; (d) and (f) 25% of Close's equity = (25% × £40) + (25% × £24) = £10 + £6 = £16; (g) Cost of investment £90 less 75% of Close's equity £48 = £42 goodwill, written off against reserves.

9.4 Whale Limited (B): Consolidating profits

Whale Limited's consolidated ('group') balance sheet at 1 January 1991 is shown on the previous page (left) (see the solution to Whale Limited (A)).

In the year ended 31 December 1991, Whale Limited made a profit after tax of £150 000, and Minnow Limited made a profit after tax of £40 000. No dividends were paid or proposed by either company.

You are asked to draw up Whale Limited's consolidated balance sheet at 31 December 1991. Please make the following assumptions:

1 The 1991 profits for each company were reflected entirely in net current assets.
2 Long-term debt and the net book value of tangible fixed assets for each company remained unchanged during 1991.
3 Goodwill is being amortized against profit over ten years.

The answer is given overleaf.

9.5 Dexter Limited (B): Pre-acquisition profits

At 31 March 1991 the balance sheets of Dexter Limited and Close Limited were as summarized below. In the year ended 31 March 1991 Dexter made a profit after tax of £40 000, and Close made a profit after tax of £12 000. Neither company paid a dividend in respect of the year.

Dexter Limited had acquired 75 per cent of the equity share capital of Close Limited on 1 April 1990, when Close's reserves amounted to £24 000.

You are asked to draw up Dexter's group balance sheet at 31 March 1991 in the right hand column below.

The answer is given overleaf.

Balance sheets at 31 March 1991

	Dexter	Close	Consolidation adjustments	Dexter Group
	£'000	£'000	£'000	£'000
Tangible fixed assets	280	85		
Investment in Close	48*			
Net current assets	87	17		
	415	102		
Less: Long-term debt	90	26		
	325	76		
Called up share capital	200	40		
Share premium	40	—		
Profit and loss account	85	36		
Shareholders' funds	325	76		

*The 75 per cent investment in Close represents purchase price £90 less £42 goodwill written off to reserves (which is £90 less 75 per cent × £64 Close equity at date of acquisition).

9.4 Whale Limited (B)

Solution

WHALE LIMITED
Group balance sheet at 31 December 1991

	Whale £'000	Minnow £'000	Consolidation adjustments £'000	Whale Group £'000
Tangible fixed assets	790	150		= 940
Goodwill			(c) + 200 (d) − 80 (e) − 50 (f) − 7	63
Investment in subsidiary	200		(c) − 200	—
Net current assets	180(a)	80		= 260
	1 170	230	− 137	1 263
Less: Long-term debt	70	60	—	130
	1100	170	− 137	1 133
Called up share capital	500	80	(d) − 80	500
Reserves	600(b)	90(b)	(c) − 50 (f) − 7	633
Shareholders' funds	1 100	170	− 137	1 133

Notes (£'000)
(a) Whale's £230 net current assets at 31 December 1990 was reduced by the £200 cost of the shares in Minnow Limited, making £30 at 1 January 1991. The retained profits for 1991, £150, are added, to make £180 at 31 December 1991.
(b) Reserves have gone up by £150 and £40 respectively, the (retained) profits for the year.
(c) The £200 cost to Whale of the shares in Minnow goes to goodwill, as before.
(d) The £80 called up share capital in Minnow Limited (entirely owned by Whale) goes to goodwill, as before.
(e) Minnow's pre-acquisition profits (£50) also go to goodwill; but the post-acquisition profits (£40) remain, to be added in as part of the group's distributable reserves.
(f) Goodwill is being written off (amortized) in the group profit and loss account over ten years: 70/10 = 7.

9.5 Dexter Limited (B)

Solution

DEXTER LIMITED
Group balance sheet at 31 December 1991

	Dexter £'000	Close £'000	Consolidation adjustments £'000	Dexter Group £'000
Tangible fixed assets	280	85		= 365
Goodwill			(a) − 30 (c) − 18 (e) + 48	—
Investment in Close	48		(e) − 48	—
Net current assets	87	17		= 104
	415	102	− 48	469
Less: Long-term debt	90	26	—	116
	325	76	− 48	353
Called up share capital	200	40	(a) − 30 (b) − 10	200
Share premium	40	—		= 40
Profit and loss account	85	36	(c) − 18 (d) − 9	94
Shareholders' funds	325	76	− 67	334
Minority interests			(b) + 10 (d) + 9	19
	325	76	− 48	= 353

Notes (£'000)
(a) 75 per cent of Close's share capital, owned by Dexter, goes to goodwill.
(b) The other 25 per cent of Close's share capital goes to minority interests.
(c) Dexter's 75 per cent share of Close's pre-acquisition profits (£24) goes to goodwill. In future years the adjustment will be the same.
(d) 25 per cent of the *whole* of Close's profit and loss account balance at 31 March 1991 (£36) goes to minority interests.
(e) The £48 balance of the original £90 investment (after writing off £42 goodwill against reserves) cancels out against the net tangible assets of £48.

Answers to the following five problems are given at the end of the book.

9.6 Barber Limited and Jenkins Limited: Non-consolidated subsidiaries

Barber Limited and Jenkins Limited are identical companies. At 31 December 1990 they each purchased all the share capital of identical subsidiaries. The 1991 trading results were identical for the two holding companies and for the two subsidiaries.

Summarized 1991 accounts for holding company and subsidiary are shown below, showing the £400 000 cash payment the holding company made in each case at 31 December 1990 for its investment in the subsidiary. Neither holding company proposes to consolidate the accounts of its subsidiary (because the nature of the businesses is too different). Barber proposes to use the 'cost' method, and Jenkins the 'equity' method.

You are asked to summarize the relevant parts of the final 1991 accounts of Barber Limited and Jenkins Limited respectively.

	Holding company £'000	Subsidiary £'000
Net assets	3 600	280
Investment in subsidiary	400	
Profit after tax, 1991	500	100
Dividend paid	300	—
Retained profits, 1991	200	100

What difference would it make to your results if the subsidiary paid a dividend of £75 000 in respect of 1991?

9.7 Leach Limited and Dixon Limited: Mergers

Leach Limited and Dixon Limited agreed to combine their businesses at 1 April 1991. Their summarized balance sheets at 31 March 1991 are shown below. Neither company had any long-term debt. The arrangement was that Leach Limited would issue 20 million £1 ordinary shares (valued at 200p each) in exchange for all Dixon Limited's share capital.

How would Leach Limited's consolidated balance sheet appear at 1 April 1991.

(a) if the combination were treated as an 'acquisition' by Leach Limited?
(b) if the combination were treated as a 'merger'?

Summarized balance sheets at 31 March 1991

	Leach £ million	Dixon £ million
Called up share capital	40	20
Profit and loss account	20	15
Shareholders' funds/net assets	60	35

9.8 Triple Enterprises Limited: Multiple consolidation

At 31 March 1991 three companies in the same industrial sector agreed to merge their businesses into a new single company, to be called Triple Enterprises Limited.

Their balance sheets at 31 March 1991 before the merger are summarized below:

	Brighton Brands £'000	Corbett Chemicals £'000	Duckham Drugs £'000
Fixed assets, net	260	330	210
Net working capital	280	410	110
	540	740	320
Less: Long-term debt	150	200	60
	390	540	260
Capital and reserves			
Called up share capital	120	200	80
Profit and loss account	270	340	180
Shareholders' funds	390	540	260

For the purposes of the merger, the values of the shares in the three companies were agreed as follows:

Brighton Brands   £500 000
Corbett Chemicals £600 000
Duckham Drugs   £400 000.

Certain fixed assets were revalued upwards accordingly in all three companies; and in addition Corbett's stocks were written down by £30 000. After these adjustments, shareholders' funds in each of the three companies' balance sheets were shown at the agreed valuation figure.

You are asked to prepare the initial consolidated balance sheet of Triple Enterprises Limited on 1 April 1991, assuming that each of the three constituent predecessor companies became wholly owned subsidiaries, and that shareholders in each of the companies received £1 ordinary shares in Triple Enterprises Limited in exchange for their existing shares, in accordance with the agreed valuations at 31 March 1991. If you need any extra information, make (and state) some suitable assumption, and work with that to complete your answer.

9.9 Chain Industries Limited: Indirect interests

Chain Industries Limited, an industrial holding company, owns 60 per cent of A Limited's share capital. A owns 60 per cent of B's share capital; B owns 60 per cent of C's; C owns 60 per cent of D's; and D owns 60 per cent of E's share capital. How much of E's share capital does Chain Industries Limited (indirectly) own, if in each case the 40 per cent minority interest is owned by shareholders unconnected with Chain Industries? Would you expect Chain Industries Limited to consolidate E's accounts? Why or why not?

If shareholders' funds in the balance sheets of the various companies at 31 December 1990 are as shown below, and if Chain Industries Limited has no other subsidiaries which are not wholly owned, at what figure would you expect minority interests to stand in the consolidated balance sheet at 31 December 1990?

Shareholders' funds

	£'000
Chain Industries Limited	999
A Limited	420
B Limited	300
C Limited	180
D Limited	240
E Limited	100

9.10 Philip Limited: Inter-company trading

Philip Limited traded with its wholly owned subsidiary Sidney Limited. In the year ended 31 March 1991, Sidney had sold Philip for £80 000 goods which had cost £50 000. At 31 March 1991 Philip still held in stock goods which had been invoiced from Sidney at £20 000.

What, if any, consolidation adjustments are needed? Why?

No answer is given to the following problem.

9.11 Portswood plc

On 1 October 1990, Portswood plc acquired 60 per cent of the share capital of William Kelsey plc, by paying £4.5 million cash. On that date the share capital and reserves of Kelsey amounted to £5.0 million, and the fair value of Kelsey's net assets was equal to their book value. Extracts from the accounts of the two companies for the year ended 30 September 1991 appear below:

	Portswood £ m	William Kelsey £ m
Tangible fixed assets, net	9.0	5.0
Investment in William Kelsey plc	4.5	—
Net current assets	4.5	1.4
	18.0	6.4
Less: Loans over one year	(3.2)	(1.0)
	14.8	5.4
Ordinary £1 share capital	10.0	4.0
Revenue reserves	4.8	1.4
	14.8	5.4
Profit after taxation	1.5	1.0
Dividends payable	1.0	0.6
Retained profit for the year	0.5	0.4

The Kelsey dividend has *not* been included in Portswood's profit above. Goodwill is to be written off over 10 years on the straight-line basis.

Questions

1 Prepare a consolidated balance sheet for the Portswood plc Group as at 30 September 1991.
2 Complete the *pro forma* consolidated profit and loss account for the Portswood plc Group for the year ended 30 September 1991. (Hint: As a first step you should incorporate Portswood's share of the Kelsey dividend in Portswood's balance sheet.)

Consolidated profit and loss account
Year ended 30 September 1991

	£ m
Profit after taxation	
Less: Minority interests	———
Available for ordinary shareholders (in Portswood)	
Dividends payable	———
Retained	

Section 10
International accounting

BACKGROUND

International trade and multinational business have expanded vastly during the second half of the twentieth century. As a result, many business people have found it necessary to understand the systems of reporting business performance and financial position that are used in other countries.

Probably the most important countries for international accounting are: United States, United Kingdom, Japan, France, Germany, and the Netherlands. All have large gross domestic products and shares of world trade, have most of the world's largest companies and the most important stock exchanges, and all are founder members of the International Accounting Standards Committee (IASC).

There are serious obstacles to understanding accounts across national borders: different languages and cultures; different legal systems and tax rules; and different currencies and accounting practices. In this section we concentrate mainly on contrasts between UK and US accounting. We shall look first at accounting terminology, then at different balance sheet formats, then at certain key differences between UK and US accounting practices. We shall also consider briefly some contrasts between the UK/US approach on the one hand and those of the other four countries. Finally we review the difficult but essential problem of translating foreign currencies into the reporting currency for accounting purposes.

As well as obstacles to understanding foreign accounts, there are also factors leading towards harmonization. The IASC has published thirty-one International Accounting Standards (see page 313) and works closely with the various national professional accounting bodies. The International Organisation of Securities Commissions (IOSCO) co-ordinates the approach of various stock exchanges and capital market agencies around the world. The European Economic Community (EEC) aims to harmonize accounting practices among its twelve member countries (including four of the most important). It also has the power to enforce its views.

TERMINOLOGY: UK AND US

On this page we show examples of different accounting terms used in the UK and the US. The list is not exhaustive; but we have tried to show the items most likely to occur in practice.

UK	US
PROFIT AND LOSS ACCOUNT	**INCOME STATEMENT**
Turnover	Net sales
Profit after tax	Net income
Company	Corporation
plc (public limited company)	Inc (Incorporated)
Gearing	Leverage
Merger	Pooling of interests
Acquisition	Purchase
Bonus issue	Stock dividend

UK	US
BALANCE SHEET	**STATEMENT OF FINANCIAL POSITION**
Fixed assets	
Tangible: land and buildings	Property (real estate)
plant and machinery	plant and equipment
Investments – in associates	Investments – in affiliates
Current assets	
Stocks	Inventories
Debtors	Accounts receivable
Cash	Cash and cash equivalents
Creditors: amounts falling due within one year	**Current liabilities**
Bank loans and overdrafts	Short-term borrowings (notes payable)
Creditors	Accounts payable
Corporation tax	Income taxes
Dividends	n/a
Net current assets	n/a
Creditors: amounts falling due after more than one year	**Long-term debt**
Capital and reserves	**Shareholders' equity (Net worth)**
Called up share capital – ordinary	Capital stock – common
– preference	– preferred
Share premium	Paid-up surplus
Revaluation reserve	n/a
Profit and loss account	Retained earnings

BALANCE SHEET FORMATS

UK law enacts EEC directives aiming to standardize the formats of company accounts throughout Western Europe. Schedule 4 of the Companies Act 1985 (as amended by the Companies Act 1989) contains the provisions relating to the form and content of accounts. Section A sets out general rules relating to disclosure; and Section B (see Appendix 5) contains the two permitted balance sheet formats and the four profit and loss account formats.

In this book we began by using the 'net asset' format. First, this format lists fixed assets and working capital (= net assets), and then shows the main sources of long-term funds, namely long-term borrowing and shareholders' funds (= capital employed). This is a useful format while learning about accounts; but in practice many UK companies deduct 'creditors: amounts due after more than one year' from 'total assets less current liabilities'. This gives a figure which balances with 'capital and reserves' (including minority interests). An example of this layout is shown opposite (top) for General Trading Limited.

Instead of the British 'vertical' layout, American balance sheets often use the 'horizontal' layout, which shows assets on the left and liabilities on the right. An example is set out opposite (below) for General Trading Inc. This also shows that the American balance sheet has a different order: it shows the most liquid assets at the top, and the least liquid assets at the bottom. The liabilities and equities side follows a similar pattern.

In the American version of General Trading's 1992 balance sheet we have used US terminology. The only item with exactly the same name is 'cash'! American practice would leave dividends payable as part of retained earnings until actually declared, so we have included that item in retained earnings.

The American balance sheet may look strange at first sight; but in practice it is not too difficult to cope with these differences in format and terminology. An example of an actual American horizontal balance sheet is shown in problem 10.1 H. J. Heinz Company (page 235). A number of large American companies now use a vertical balance sheet format, though with the items in a different order from UK balance sheets.

British format (vertical)

GENERAL TRADING LIMITED
Balance sheet at 31 March 1992 £'000

Tangible fixed assets	800
Current assets	900
Less: **Creditors due within one year** (current liabilities)	300
Net current assets (working capital)	600
Total assets less current liabilities	1 400
Less: **Creditors due after more than one year**	200
	1 200
Capital and reserves	
Called up share capital	1 000
Profit and loss account	200
	1 200

American format (horizontal)

GENERAL TRADING INC
Balance sheet at March 31 1992

Current assets		$	Current liabilities		$
Cash		150 000	Income taxes		50 000
Accounts receivable		350 000	Accounts payable		190 000
Inventories		400 000			240 000
		900 000			
			Long-term debt		200 000
Property					
Real estate	300 000		**Stockholders' equity**		
Plant and equipment	500 000		Common stock	1 000 000	
			Retained earnings	260 000	
		800 000			1 260 000
		1 700 000			1 700 000

UK/US DIFFERENCES IN ACCOUNTING PRACTICES

We intend here to review only the main differences in accounting practices between the UK and the US. We have already mentioned most of them earlier. In several areas UK accounting standards allow alternatives, whereas US standards usually require all companies to follow the same practice.

UK companies often revalue land and buildings upwards (see Section 5), while US accounts adhere firmly to historical cost. This affects return on equity, return on net assets, debt ratio, fixed asset turnover. The impact on profit is usually small.

US accounting standards require companies to capitalize purchased goodwill and amortize it against profit. The UK standard SSAP 22 permits the US practice, but allows companies to write off goodwill immediately against reserves (see Section 9). Most UK companies prefer to follow the alternative practice. The impact can be very large, both on assets and on reported profits.

US standards require comprehensive ('full') deferral of tax; while the UK standard SSAP 15 calls for partial deferral only, to the extent that a liability (or asset) is thought 'likely' to crystallize (see Section 7). In UK accounts this tends to increase after-tax profit and reduce the amount of the deferred tax liability. It can also make comparing different UK companies' results less reliable.

As we saw in Section 4, many US companies use the LIFO method (Last In First Out) of valuing stock (inventory), which is rare (though not forbidden) in the UK. The effect is to reduce US profits (and assets).

The UK standard SSAP 23 defines a 'merger' less precisely than the US definition. Companies which meet UK conditions for a merger can choose whether to use merger accounting or acquisition accounting for business combinations (see Section 9). US companies which meet the more detailed US conditions for a 'pooling of interests' (= merger), however, are obliged to use 'pooling of interests' rather than 'purchase' (= acquisition) accounting.

UK companies are allowed by SSAP 13 to capitalize development spending which meets certain conditions (see Section 4); but US companies have to expense all research and development expenditure (other than on fixed assets). In practice, nearly all UK companies follow US practice.

All the above differences can affect reported profits as well as the balance sheet. Finally we should mention two differences in practice which affect only one of these two statements: the first affecting reported profits but not the balance sheet, and the second vice versa.

The UK Standard SSAP 6 defines 'extraordinary items' more broadly than the US (see Section 4); and practice varies in the UK, especially with respect to closing-down costs and profits or losses on disposal of businesses. Whether items are reported 'below the line' as 'extraordinary' or above the line can make a big difference to reported earnings per share.

US companies deduct dividends from shareholders' funds when they are actually declared payable. UK companies, however, deduct *proposed* final dividends relating to a financial year from the profit and loss account balance for that year; and then show it as a current liability in the balance sheet. Not perhaps a very important difference, but quite a noticeable one.

Very few topics are covered by one country's accounting standards but not by the other's. It seems that US standards on interim accounts, capitalizing interest, and off-balance sheet risk are not yet covered by UK standards. Similarly there appear to be no US standards yet on post-balance sheet events and value added tax. There are many more US standards than UK ones, because UK practice is to amend earlier standards, whereas US practice is to issue an additional amending standard where necessary.

We have listed some of the main differences between UK and US accounting practices; but the overall aims of accounting in the two countries, and the detailed rules laid down by accounting standards, are mostly very similar.

UK/US ACCOUNTING VERSUS OTHER COUNTRIES

At the start of this section we mentioned six obstacles to understanding accounts across national borders. Only one, currency, is a major problem in comparing UK and US accounts. Language, culture, legal systems, tax rules, and accounting practices are all similar (though clearly not identical, as we have just seen).

When we come to compare 'Anglo-American' accounting with other countries, however, the obstacles multiply. Probably the Netherlands is closest in philosophy to the UK/US approach: it has a well-developed capital market, with three very large multinational companies in Philips Lamps, Royal Dutch-Shell, and Unilever. In all three countries the notion of 'general acceptance' of accounting rules by the business community is very important. But differences in language and in legal systems present formidable hurdles to mutual understanding.

For the remaining three countries, Japan, France and Germany, problems of comparison with Anglo-American accounting are even greater, because the underlying philosophy has developed in a quite different way. In particular, government influence on accounting has been far more evident in these three countries than in the UK and the US.

One important example of this concerns depreciation of fixed assets. In the UK and the US, companies make commercial estimates of a 'true and fair' amount of depreciation to charge each year. These will normally be quite different from the 'capital allowances' permitted under the tax rules. In countries where government influence on accounting is much greater, however, it is normal for the depreciation charged in the accounts to be exactly the same as that allowed for tax purposes. One consequence is that there may be no need for deferred tax accounts, since there may be no timing differences between book depreciation and tax depreciation. More important, however, is that the depreciation charged in the accounts may not represent a realistic commercial estimate. By following tax rules often designed to 'encourage' investment in fixed assets, accounts may charge 'too much' depreciation (from a strictly commercial point of view), and hence understate profits.

Since capital markets and outside shareholders have had less influence in France and Germany, accounting has tended to be conservative. The emphasis has been on financial soundness in balance sheets, with hidden reserves by no means unknown. In contrast, in the UK and the US the need to report to more 'mobile' public owners has led accounts to focus more on reported annual earnings.

The EEC now holds that the aim of accounts is to present a 'true and fair view' of a company's performance and financial position. In this respect the Continental Europeans have accepted the long-standing Anglo-American approach. Achieving this result after entering the Community seventeen years 'late' may be regarded as a genuine triumph of British diplomacy. But not all member states will understand exactly the same thing by that phrase. (Nor, indeed, do all UK accountants!)

In trying to summarize the different accounting practices in the six countries discussed in this section, it may be helpful to employ the hierarchy developed by Nobes. This picture inevitably over-simplifies, but it suggests some of the key differences between the countries. Of the eight EEC countries not named below, all but Ireland belong in the right-hand part of the diagram.

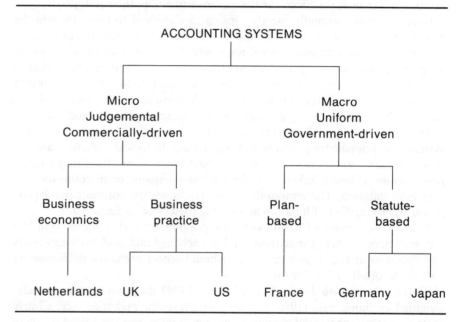

231

FOREIGN CURRENCY TRANSLATION

In recent years many companies have acquired foreign businesses, and many others have built up their foreign interests from retained profits and local borrowings. As a result numerous multinational companies have emerged, each controlling many foreign enterprises.

Accounting for such groups poses problems, especially when foreign exchange rates fluctuate. Groups must translate foreign subsidiaries' accounts into the holding company's domestic currency. There are two ways to do this: the 'closing rate' method and the 'temporal' method.

SSAP 20 on 'Foreign Currency Translation' regards a holding company's investment as being in a subsidiary's whole business rather than in individual assets and liabilities. So it uses the same rate of exchange (the closing rate) for all assets and liabilities (in effect, for the 'net investment' in the equity).

Groups should normally use the closing rate method to translate into the reporting currency all assets and liabilities of foreign subsidiaries, associates or branches. They should translate a foreign subsidiary's profits or losses either at an average rate for the period or at the closing rate; and record exchange differences as a movement on reserves. The effect is to treat the 'foreign exchange' part of reserves as a 'currency equalization account'; which implicitly assumes that over the years, gains and losses on exchange will cancel out.

The temporal method regards transactions as part of a single worldwide system (the rationale for group accounts), and uses historical exchange rates for non-monetary assets. Group accounts should use it where the foreign enterprise's trade is closely linked with the holding company, or in countries with very high inflation. The temporal method resembles the constant purchasing power (CPP) method of inflation accounting (described in Section 11).

Individual companies should use the temporal method: they should translate non-monetary assets at the acquisition date exchange rate, and monetary assets and liabilities at the closing rate. They should report exchange differences as part of the profit or loss for the year.

The charts opposite show between 1980 and 1991 the pound sterling's trade-weighted exchange rate (1985 = 100) and US dollar exchange rate. Clearly there have been substantial changes in exchange rates over the period (as there were in the 1970s too). They make it difficult for multinational companies to make sensible long-term economic decisions (for example, about where to locate factories). They also make accounting (and understanding accounts) much harder.

232

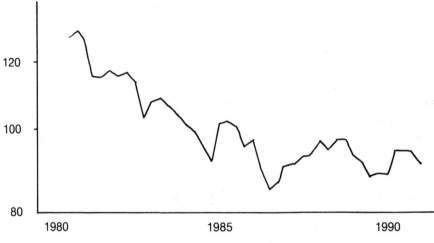

**THE POUND STERLING
TRADE-WEIGHTED EXCHANGE RATE
1985 = 100**

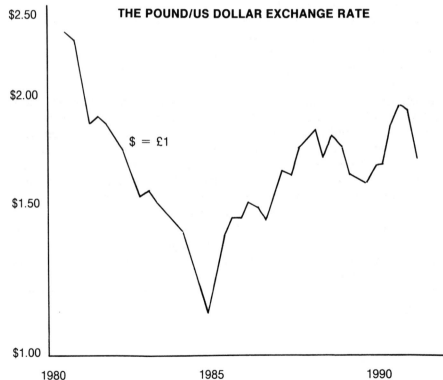

THE POUND/US DOLLAR EXCHANGE RATE

$ = £1

Example

The accounts on the right show the balance sheet at 31 December 1991, and the profit and loss account for the year ended on that date, for Overseas Trading Limited. When the company started trading at the end of 1990 its balance sheet showed (in $'000): plant and equipment $900, net current assets $600, less loan $300 = called up share capital $1 200.

The company trades in stock which turns over very quickly, and is therefore treated in the example in the same way as liquid assets. During the year there was no change in the fixed assets, or in the loan. At the start of the year the exchange rate was $3 = £1, but this had become $2 = £1 by the end of the year. The average rate during the year was $2.5 = £1. (This has been used to translate the profit and loss account.)

The accounts opposite have been prepared on two bases, using the closing rate method and the temporal method respectively. According to the closing rate method, the profit for the year – $600 – amounted to £240; and return on equity was 27 per cent (it was 33 per cent in dollar terms). Under the temporal method, profit for the year was £367; and return on equity was 48 per cent.

The closing rate method credits the gain on exchange (£60) to reserves; while the temporal method credits the gain on exchange (£120) to the profit and loss account. These amounts are calculated as follows:

Closing rate method

Profit for year $600: at average rate ($2.5) = £240
at closing rate ($2.0) = £300

Gain on exchange £60

Temporal method

Opening net monetary assets $300: at opening rate ($3.0) = £100
at closing rate ($2.0) = £150

£50

Cash generated in year $700*: at average rate ($2.5) = £280
at closing rate ($2.0) = £350

£70

Gain on exchange £120

*$700 = $600 profit after tax plus $100 depreciation.

OVERSEAS TRADING LIMITED
Balance sheet at 31 December 1991

	Currency $'000		Closing rate method £'000		Temporal method £'000
Plant and equipment	900	2.0	450	3.0	300
Less: Depreciation	100	2.0	50	3.0	33
	800		400		267
Net current assets	1 300	2.0	650	2.0	650
Less: Loan	(300)	2.0	(150)	2.0	(150)
	1 800		900		767
Called up share capital	1 200	2.0	600	3.0	400
Reserve: Gain on exchange	—	*	60		—
Profit and loss account	600	2.5	240	*	367
	1 800		900		767

Profit and loss account
Year ended 31 December 1991

Turnover	1 500	2.5	600	2.5	600
Cost of sales	(470)	2.5	(188)	2.5	(188)
Depreciation	(100)	2.5	(40)	3.0	(33)
Gain on exchange	—		—	*	120
	930		372		499
Interest payable	30	2.5	12	2.5	12
Profit before tax	900		360		487
Tax	300	2.5	120	2.5	120
Profit after tax	600	2.5	240		367

*no single exchange rate applies

SUMMARY

In this section we have noted the rapid development in the last forty years of world trade and the spread of multinational companies. This has led to a need for accounting across national borders.

We have tried to identify the major obstacles to international comparisons of accounts: language and culture, legal systems and tax rules, currencies and accounting practices. We also noted some of the bodies working to harmonize global accounting, the IASC, IOSCO, and the EEC.

We have focused on contrasts between UK and US accounting, even though their accounting philosophies and practices are similar. We looked at differences in terminology and in balance sheet formats; and (more importantly) at major accounting differences in practice. These were in respect of: revaluation of fixed assets, treatment of goodwill, deferred tax, stock valuation, business combinations, research and development, and extraordinary items and dividends payable.

We also briefly compared Anglo-American accounting with that of other countries – the Netherlands, and France, Germany, and Japan. Countries like the UK and the US, where stock market influence is important, emphasize annual earnings per share figures. In other countries, where many banks and other shareholders regard themselves as long-term investors, balance sheet soundness has been more important.

Finally we examined the question of foreign currency translation, identifying the two main methods (the closing rate method and the temporal method), and showing in outline how each works. Large currency fluctuations over the past twenty years have caused serious problems for the managements of multinational companies. One of these problems concerns measuring and reporting the results of their world-wide operations. It is by no means clear that the next twenty years will be less tempestuous in this respect.

10.1 H. J. Heinz Company: Restating a US balance sheet

Restate this US company's group balance sheet as at 1 May 1991 in the normal vertical UK format, using UK terminology. You may prefer to group certain items which UK companies would normally show in detail in the Notes. When you have completed your restated balance sheet, check it against our proposed solution overleaf.

H. J. Heinz Company: Consolidated Balance Sheet at 1 May 1991

Assets (dollars in thousands)

Current Assets:	
Cash and cash equivalents	$ 150 979
Short-term investments, at cost which approximates market	162 985
Receivables (net of allowances: $11 563)	678 109
Inventories:	
Finished goods and work-in-process	677 599
Packaging material and ingredients	290 260
	967 859
Prepaid expenses and other current assets	159 853
Total current assets	2 119 785
Property, Plant and Equipment:	
Land	39 918
Buildings and leasehold improvements	529 041
Equipment, furniture and other	2 195 511
	2 764 470
Less accumulated depreciation	1 041 729
Total property, plant and equipment, net	1 722 741
Other Noncurrent Assets:	
Investments, advances and other assets	343 526
Goodwill (net of amortization: $67 553)	498 029
Other intangibles (net of amortization: $44 285)	251 301
Total other noncurrent assets	1 092 856
Total assets	$4 935 382

Liabilities and shareholders' equity (dollars in thousands)

Current Liabilities:	
Short-term debt	$ 381 164
Portion of long-term debt due within one year	128 593
Accounts payable	515 459
Salaries and wages	86 660
Accrued marketing	74 403
Other accrued liabilities	177 993
Income taxes	65 437
Total current liabilities	1 429 709
Long-Term Debt and Other Liabilities:	
Long-term debt	716 937
Deferred income taxes	344 834
Other	169 039
Total long-term debt and other liabilities	1 230 810
Shareholders' Equity:	
Capital stock:	
Third cumulative preferred, $1.70 first series, $10 par value	538
Common stock, 287 401 000 shares issued, $.25 par value	71 850
	72 388
Additional capital	149 526
Retained earnings	2 889 476
Cumulative translation adjustments	(99 750)
	3 011 640
Less:	
Treasury shares, at cost (27 966 044 shares)	692 547
Unearned compensation relating to the ESOP	44 230
Total shareholders' equity	2 274 863
Total liabilities and shareholders' equity	$4 935 382

10.1 H. J. Heinz Company

Solution

H. J. HEINZ COMPANY
Consolidated Balance Sheet at 1 May 1991

		$ million
Fixed assets		
Tangible fixed assets	Note 1	1 723
Intangibles	Note 2	749
Investments		344
		2 816
Current assets		
Stocks	Note 3	968
Debtors	Note 4	838
Investments		163
Cash etc.		151
		2 120
Less: **Creditors falling due within one year**		
Short-term borrowings	Note 5	(510)
Other creditors	Note 6	(920)
		(1 430)
Net working capital		690
Total assets less current liabilities		3 506
Creditors falling due after more than one year		
Long-term borrowings		(717)
Provisions for liabilities and charges	Note 7	(514)
Capital and reserves		
Called-up share capital		72
Share premium account		150
Retained profits		2 889
Other reserves		(836)
		2 275

Note 1. Tangible fixed assets

	$ million
Land and buildings, at cost	569
Equipment and furniture, etc., at cost	2 196
	2 765
Less: accumulated depreciation	1 042
Net book value	1 723

Note 2. Intangibles

Goodwill, at cost	566	
Less: accumulated amortization	68	
		498
Other intangibles, at cost	295	
Less: accumulated amortization	44	
		251
		749

Note 3. Stocks

Packaging material and ingredients	290
Finished goods and work-in-progress	678
	968

Note 4. Debtors

Trade debtors (net of provisions 12)	678
Prepayments, etc.	160
	838

Note 5. Short-term borrowings

Short-term borrowings	381
Long-term borrowings, due within one year	129
	510

Note 6. Other creditors (current)

Trade creditors	516
Accrued liabilities	339
Taxation	65
	920

Note 7. Provisions for liabilities and charges

Deferred taxation	345
Other	169
	514

10.2 A common language?

Can you identify the UK equivalents for each of the following US accounting terms? Answers are shown overleaf.

a   Accounts receivable
b   Common stock
c   Inventories
d   Income statement
e   Inc.
f   Current liabilities
g   Long-term debt
h   Accounts payable.

10.3 Northern Foods plc (C): restating a UK balance sheet

You will find the 1991 group balance sheet of Northern Foods plc set out in Problem 2.4 (on page 53). Please attempt, on a separate sheet of paper, to restate this UK company's balance sheet in the horizontal US format, using US terminology.

When you have completed your attempt (make sure the balance sheet balances!), check with our proposed solution overleaf.

10.4 Hanson plc: UK/US accounting differences

Hanson plc has extensive interests in the United States. The company reports to its shareholders on how various items have been treated in its (UK) accounts, and how they would appear under US GAAP (Generally Accepted Accounting Principles).

Write down, in two or three sentences each, what you would expect Hanson to say about each of the following five items. When you have done so, check overleaf against what Hanson actually did say on each item in its 1991 Annual Report.

a   Goodwill

b   Taxation

c   Revaluation of land and buildings

d   Discontinued operations

e   Ordinary dividends

10.2 A common language?

Solution

a   Trade debtors
b   Ordinary shares
c   Stocks
d   Profit and loss account
e   Ltd.
f   Creditors: amounts falling due within one year
g   Creditors: amounts falling due after one year
h   Trade creditors.

10.4 Hanson plc

a   **Goodwill.** Arising on the acquisition of a subsidiary [goodwill is] written off in the year in which that subsidiary is acquired. Under US GAAP such goodwill is capitalized and is amortized through the profit and loss account over its estimated useful life, not exceeding 40 years.

b   **Taxation.** Deferred taxation is not provided where, in the opinion of the directors, no liability is likely to arise in the foreseeable future. However, under US GAAP, deferred taxation would be provided on a full deferral basis.

c   **Revaluation of land and buildings.** Periodically land and buildings are revalued on an existing use basis by professionally qualified external valuers and such assets are written up to the appraised value. Depreciation is, where applicable, calculated on these revalued amounts . . . The amount of additional depreciation charged in respect of the revalued properties is not material.

d   **Discontinued operations.** When operations, which are regarded as separate business segments, are sold their results and the profit or loss on disposal are reported as extraordinary items. Under US GAAP they are reported as arising from discontinued operations with the prior year being adjusted accordingly. Any remaining goodwill relating to such business is written off in determining the profit or loss on disposal.

e   **Ordinary dividends.** Final ordinary dividends are provided in the year in respect of which they are proposed on the basis of the recommendations by the directors which requires subsequent approval by the shareholders. Under US GAAP dividends are not provided until formally declared.

The above answers are taken from page 45 of Hanson plc's 1991 Annual Report.

10.3 Northern Foods plc (C)

Solution

NORTHERN FOODS PLC
Statement of Financial Position, March 31 1991

	£ m		£ m
ASSETS		**LIABILITIES AND EQUITY**	
Current assets		**Current liabilities**	
Cash	20.1	Accounts payable	134.8
Accounts receivable	136.2	Loans payable	68.2
Prepaid expenses	6.7	Taxation	53.3
Inventories	54.2	Accrued liabilities	36.2
	217.2		292.5
Property plant and equipment		**Long-term loans**	5.3
At cost [or valuation]	592.1		
Less: Accum. depreciation	191.9	**Other liabilities**	14.2
	400.2	**Stockholders' Equity**	
		Common shares of 25p each	55.6
		Capital surplus	61.3
		Other reserves	16.4
		Net income retained	172.1
			305.4
	617.4		617.4

Answers to the following two problems are given at the end of the book.

10.5 Parkside Limited (A): The closing rate method

Parkside Limited, a UK company, established a wholly-owned Ruritanian subsidiary, Blue Moon, in 1989 when the exchange rate was £1 = R$4.00. Parkside uses the closing rate method for incorporating Blue Moon's accounts in the group accounts for the year ended 31 December 1991. At 31 December 1990, the exchange rate was £1 = R$3.00. The average rate for the year 1991 was £1 = R$2.50; and the closing rate at 31 December 1991 was £1 = R$2.00.

The summarized profit and loss account and balance sheet for Blue Moon for 1991 are shown below in terms of Ruritanian dollars. You are asked:

a   to show how Blue Moon's Ruritanian dollar accounts should be translated into pounds for inclusion in the Parkside group accounts. In particular, calculate 'exchange differences' for the year 1991, and show where this item would appear in the group accounts.

b   how would the amounts to include in the 1991 Parkside group accounts be different using the average rate for the year instead of the closing rate to translate the profit and loss account?

Blue Moon: Profit and loss account, Year ended 31 December 1991

	R$'000
Sales	7 000
Depreciation (1/6 × 1 800)	300
Other expenses	6 560
Profit	140

Blue Moon: Balance sheet as at 31 December 1991

	1991	1990
	R$'000	R$'000
Fixed assets	1 200	1 500
Working capital	560	360
	1 760	1 860
(Long-term debt)	(720)	(960)
	1 040	900
Capital and reserves:		
Called up share capital	200	200
Retained profits	840	700
	1 040	900

10.6 Parkside Limited (B): The temporal method

Refer to the information in 10.5 Parkside Limited (A).

Fixed assets, all acquired in 1989 for R$1 800, when the exchange rate was £1 = R$4.00, are being written off on the straight-line method over 6 years (zero residual value). You are asked to show how Blue Moon's Ruritanian dollar accounts should be translated into pounds for inclusion in the Parkside group accounts for 1991 if the temporal method were used. Assume that the average rate for the year (£1 = R$2.50) is used for the profit and loss account.

No answers are shown to the following problems.

10.7 Grand Imperial plc (A): Closing rate method

Grand Imperial plc, a UK Company, established a wholly-owned Bolonian subsidiary, Ananam, in 1985, when the exchange rate was £1 = 12 Bolonian pesos (Bp).

Recent exchange rates have been as follows:

£1 = Bp	1990	1991	1992
Average rate for the year	6.00	4.50	3.50
Closing rate	5.00	4.00	3.00

Ananam's summarized accounts for 1991 and 1992, in terms of Bolonian pesos, are shown opposite. Grand Imperial uses the average rate for the year to translate profits and losses.

You are asked to show, on a separate sheet of paper, what amounts for Ananam would be included in Grand Imperial plc's group accounts for 1991 and 1992; and to explain how exchange differences for each year have been calculated.

10.8 Grand Imperial plc (B): Temporal method

You are asked to show what amounts for Ananam would be included in Grand Imperial plc's group accounts for 1991 and 1992 assuming the temporal method is used.

Details of purchases of plant and equipment have been as follows:

Date	Exchange rate £1 =	Cost Bp'000
1985	12 Bp	3,600
1986	10	3,000
1987	9	1,800
1988	8	800
1989	7.50	1,500
1990	6	1,200
		11,900
1991	4.50	1,350
		13,250
1992	3.50	1,400
		14,650

The freehold land was acquired for 4.8 million Bp in 1985.

Ananam: Profit and loss account	1991 Bp'000	1992 Bp'000
Sales	26,480	30,240
Depreciation	1,325	1,465
Other operating expenses	23,265	27,045
Profit before interest and tax	1,890	1,730
Interest	630	770
Profit before tax	1,260	960
Tax	495	385
Profit after tax	765	575

No dividends were paid in respect of either year.

Ananam: Balance sheet at 31 December	1990 Bp'000	1991 Bp'000	1992 Bp'000
Fixed assets			
Freehold land	4,800	4,800	4,800
Plant and equipment: Cost	11,900	13,250	14,650
(Accum. depn.)	(5,040)	(6,365)	(7,830)
Net	6,860	6,885	6,820
	11,660	11,685	11,620
Working capital	6,420	8,160	9,800
(Long-term debt)	(4,000)	(5,000)	(6,000)
	14,080	14,845	15,420
Capital and reserves			
Share capital	6,000	6,000	6,000
Retained profits	8,080	8,845	9,420
	14,080	14,845	15,420

Section 11

Inflation accounting

BACKGROUND

Since 1970 inflation rates in most countries have been high and fluctuating. This has led to an intense review of the usefulness of historical cost (HC) accounting in times of inflation. The worldwide debate has involved business people and politicians, as well as accountants and academics.

After years of discussion and consultation, in January 1973 the UK Accounting Standards Committee (as it then was) proposed a system called 'Current Purchasing Power' (CPP) accounting. In fact a more accurate and less confusing name is Constant Purchasing Power accounting, and we use this description from now on in this section. (In the United States the same CPP system is called either 'General Price Level Accounting' or 'Constant Dollar Accounting'.)

Any proposed system of inflation accounting was bound to raise important economic and political issues, and in July 1973 the British government set up the Sandilands Committee to look into the question. Its report in September 1975 rejected CPP accounting, and proposed instead a system of current value accounting, to be known as Current Cost Accounting (CCA).

After a great deal of public discussion and debate, and two CCA Exposure Drafts, in March 1980 the Accounting Standards Committee finally published SSAP 16 on Current Cost Accounting. It required larger UK companies to publish at least supplementary CCA accounts in addition to HC accounts. A similar process of discussion in the United States resulted in large American companies being required to publish, in addition to HC accounts, summary figures under both CCA and CPP conventions.

Both CPP and CCA were criticized on a number of grounds. Neither commanded anything like unanimous support. The CPP accounting standard (SSAP 7) was withdrawn when the government committee proposed CCA; and the CCA standard itself (SSAP 16) was dropped in 1985, when it became clear that CCA had failed to establish itself. Another reason why the 'inflation accounting' debate has faded in the early 1990s is the relative decline in the rate of inflation. It is not clear whether this is temporary.

In this section we consider how to measure inflation, and the ways in which it can seriously affect unadjusted historical cost accounts. We outline some of the *ad hoc* steps which companies have taken to adjust their HC accounts; and we review the basic principles, first of Constant Purchasing Power accounting (CPP); and then of Current Cost Accounting (CCA).

MEASURING THE RATE OF INFLATION

Inflation, in simple terms, is 'too much money chasing too few goods'. If the money supply increases faster than the supply of goods and services, then (subject to certain qualifications) prices expressed in money terms tend to rise, and there is 'inflation'.

For most people in the United Kingdom, the 'rate of inflation' means the rate of increase in the monthly Retail Prices Index (RPI). This index measures changes over time in the money cost of a representative sample of goods – an average family's 'household shopping basket'. The rate of inflation which the RPI signals is only approximate. The buying pattern of many families may not correspond exactly to that of the 'average' family; and patterns of spending, and the technical qualities of goods, change over time, which can be hard to allow for accurately. Appendix 4 (on page 316) gives details of the RPI in recent years.

The chart below shows annual rates of increase in the RPI from 1971 to 1990. They average just over 10 per cent a year. Over the twenty-year period the average level of retail prices rose nearly seven times. (This compares with the preceding twenty years between 1951 and 1970, during which period prices doubled.) No wonder that accountants and others have spent so much effort trying to solve the accounting problems posed by inflation.

ANNUAL INCREASES IN RETAIL PRICES INDEX
1971—1990
with 15-year average annual rates of increase*

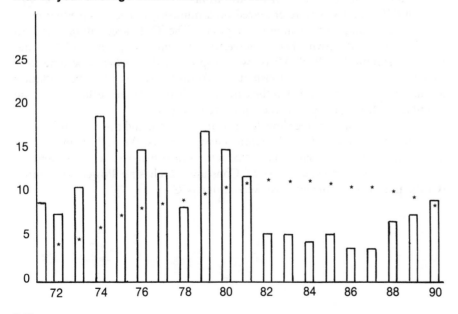

Currency debasement

So far we have been talking about money prices rising, with the RPI reflecting the 'average' rate of increase. But another approach is to measure the *fall* in the 'purchasing power' of the pound. This is what the CPP approach does. From this point of view, 'inflation' of money prices reflects 'debasement' of the currency unit. The percentages are not the same: when the RPI doubles (increases by 100 per cent), the purchasing power of the pound halves (falls by 50 per cent).

The pound's purchasing power halved between 1945 and 1965; it halved again between 1965 and 1975; and it halved *again* between 1975 and 1980. Thus between 1945 and 1980, the pound lost more than 7/8ths of its value – nearly 90 per cent in just over a single generation! This has had a devastating effect on historical cost accounts. The chart below pictures (on a log scale) the fall in the purchasing power of the pound between 1970 and 1990.

PURCHASING POWER OF THE POUND
1970 – 1990

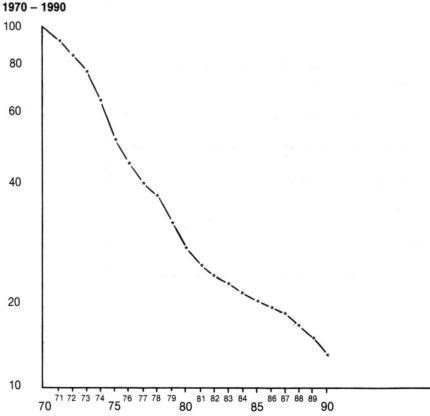

TWO CONTRASTING METHODS OF 'INFLATION ACCOUNTING'

The two main methods of 'inflation accounting' take different views of 'capital'; hence arrive at different measurements of 'profit'.

Constant purchasing power (CPP) accounting seeks to maintain the *purchasing power of the equity interest*; and uses changes in the Retail Prices Index (RPI) as the basis for adjusting historical cost (HC) accounts. In effect CPP proposes to continue using HC accounting, but to change the *unit of measurement* from money to a 'unit of constant purchasing power'.

Current cost accounting (CCA), on the other hand, aims to maintain the *productive capacity of a company's assets*; and reflects the specific price changes experienced by a going concern. CCA continues to use money as the unit of measurement in accounts, but proposes to switch from *past costs* to *'current costs'*.

CPP allows for 'general inflation' but not for 'relative price changes'. If a product's money price increases by 12 per cent in a period in which the RPI increases by 7 per cent, CPP attributes 7 percentage points of the price rise to 'general inflation' (which CPP allows for), and 5 percentage points to 'relative price changes' (which CPP ignores).

But CCA advocates argue that to measure the impact of inflation on (say) a textiles company, the price changes which are relevant are those relating to a sample of textile products, and not a household shopping basket. This implies a difference between CCA and HC accounting even when 'prices in general' are stable (as measured by the RPI). For, in a dynamic economy, the money prices of specific goods and services will fluctuate, whether there is 'general inflation' or not.

The table opposite summarizes the contrast between CPP and CCA. Because CPP tries to allow for general inflation and CCA for specific price changes (up or down), they are not strictly alternatives to each other. Hence there is no logical inconsistency in *combining* CPP with CCA in the bottom right quadrant.

		DEFINITION OF 'COST'	
		Past cost	Current value
UNIT OF ACCOUNT	Monetary unit	Historical cost (HC)	Current cost accounting (CCA)
	Unit of constant purchasing power	Constant purchasing power (CPP)	Combination of CPP and CCA

PROBLEMS IN USING UNADJUSTED HISTORICAL COST ACCOUNTS IN TIMES OF INFLATION

The extent to which historical cost accounts are misleading in times of inflation can vary. When inflation exceeds (say) 5 per cent a year, accounts may greatly understate long-life assets in the balance sheet, and greatly overstate profit.

The Companies Act 1985 permits (but does not require) companies to *revalue* fixed assets in their balance sheet (see Section 5); and most large companies have revalued some or all of their interests in land and buildings (the longest-life assets) at least once in the past twenty years. However, infrequent revaluations scarcely affecting *depreciable* fixed assets have done little to overcome performance measurement problems due to inflation.

Directors have sometimes regarded much of the HC reported profit as simply not available for dividends. Such retention of reported 'profit' may have helped to prevent paying out capital by mistake; but the profit and loss account has still overstated profit. The misleading impression has sometimes been accentuated by fanciful charts showing apparent 'growth' in sales or earnings over time, much of which has been due solely to inflation.

Some companies in the past used 'depreciation lives' for fixed assets which were shorter than 'useful lives', but this is no longer allowed. It helped to correct the profit reported, but led to even greater understatement of net book values of assets. So return on investment ratios often continued to be highly inaccurate.

Thus actual responses to the problems caused by inflation in measuring financial performance have included *ad hoc* adjustments to the values of fixed assets, or to their estimated lives, and attempts to downgrade the meaning of reported results. But these are inadequate. High rates of inflation cause historical cost accounts to give misleading impressions, because:

- they understate asset values, showing fixed assets at purchase costs of many years earlier
- they overstate profit which cannot be paid out in dividends without impairing 'real' capital
- they understate expenses:
  - basing depreciation on out-of-date fixed asset costs
  - using cost of sales figures which are too low
- ratios often exaggerate the level of performance:
  - profit margins compare overstated profits with current turnover
  - returns on investment relate overstated profits to understated investment
- trends in sales, profits, dividends and equity capital may reflect growth in money terms while 'real' growth rates are much lower, or even negative.

Errors caused within companies

Managers using unadjusted historical cost accounts in times of inflation may:

- overlook the need to improve low profit levels if depreciation and cost of sales reflect out-of-date costs
- fix prices too low if they understate costs and overstate profit
- pay excessive dividends, if they overstate the amounts available
- allocate resources wrongly, on the basis of the results of different business segments. (Past performance, as well as forecast future results, often influences investment decisions.)

In each of these areas where management exercises judgement, many factors contribute to decisions. But in times of inflation historical cost figures may easily mislead decision-makers.

Errors caused outside companies

Many different kinds of outsiders use companies' accounting information. In particular, decisions by the following groups may have damaging consequences if based on historical cost data in times of inflation:

- government – in relation to taxes, purchase contracts, price controls (if any)
- employees – in wage bargaining
- investors – in allocating resources between different sectors of the economy, and between different companies within a sector.

Thus the results of using unadjusted historical cost figures in times of inflation may be serious. A better system of accounting which properly allows for the impact of inflation on financial statements is urgently needed. In recent years, as we have seen, two different systems have emerged as alternatives to historical cost accounting: constant purchasing power (CPP) accounting and current cost accounting (CCA). But for the time being neither seems to command general acceptance. Their different approaches were contrasted on page 243, and we now discuss their basic principles and working in more detail. To do this we shall examine the accounts of a small company – Paint Making Limited – first on a historical cost (HC) accounting basis, then using CPP accounting, and finally using CCA.

HISTORICAL COST ACCOUNTING

Accountants have used historical cost (HC) accounting for many years to measure companies' financial performance and position. As we have seen in earlier sections, there are problems in measuring and recording certain kinds of assets, and in matching costs against revenues to determine profit or loss. Even so, on the whole, HC accounting has been a satisfactory system for practical purposes, in the absence of prolonged rapid inflation.

The HC balance sheet shows the way in which a business has invested shareholders' funds and other capital in assets of different kinds; and the HC profit and loss account discloses the profit or loss earned in the accounting period.

The concept of 'capital' in HC accounts is 'the money amount of the shareholders' equity interest'. When there is no general inflation (when the 'purchasing power of money' is stable), then 'money capital' is the same thing as 'purchasing power capital'. As we saw in Section 4 (page 103), the increase in shareholders' funds between one balance sheet date and the next – after allowing for capital changes, such as new issues of shares and for dividends – represents the profit or loss for the period.

Example

In the example opposite, Paint Making Limited was formed at the end of 1991, and started trading at the beginning of 1992. Straight-line depreciation on equipment was based on an 8-year life. Profit for 1992 was £30 000, of which £24 000 was paid out in dividends. Thus the company could legally have paid out an extra £6 000 in dividends. That would have left the shareholders' funds at £200 000, exactly the same money amount as at the beginning of 1992.

PAINT MAKING LIMITED

HC balance sheet at 31 December

	1992 £'000	1991 £'000
Fixed assets		
Land and buildings at cost	40	40
Equipment: Cost	120	120
Depreciation	15	—
	105	120
Net current assets	61	40
	206	200
Capital and reserves		
Called up share capital	200	200
Profit and loss account	6	0
	206	200

HC Profit and loss account
Year ended 31 December 1992

		£'000
Turnover		480
Cost of goods sold	360	
Depreciation	15	
Distribution and administration expenses	60	
		435
Profit before tax		45
Tax		15
Profit after tax		30
Dividends		24
Retained profit for the year		6

CONSTANT PURCHASING POWER ACCOUNTING

In the early 1970s the UK accounting profession supported the Constant Purchasing Power (CPP) method of inflation accounting; and in 1974 issued SSAP 7 as the accounting standard on 'Accounting for changes in the purchasing power of money'. The title made it clear that the 'problem' which inflation causes is changes in the accounting unit of measurement (money).

CPP aims to adjust HC accounts solely for changes in the *general* purchasing power of money. It is, in fact, strictly still a form of 'historical cost' accounting; but it uses as the unit of account not the monetary unit (as in HC), but a 'unit of constant purchasing power'. According to this approach, if there were no general inflation, CPP would be identical with HC, and there would be no need for 'inflation accounting', since there would be no inflation. In measuring profit or loss, CPP aims to maintain the purchasing power of the shareholders' equity interest.

CPP accounting requires accounts to express all financial amounts in units of the same 'purchasing power' – normally (but not necessarily) that of the monetary unit at the closing balance sheet date. CPP argues that HC accounts add together amounts stated in *different* units of measurement (even though in the UK money amounts of different years are all called 'pounds'). So CPP indexes all money amounts in HC accounts by reference to the change in the RPI between the date when each item occurred and the base date, normally the closing balance sheet date.

CPP regards money of different dates as being, in effect, 'foreign currencies'; it uses an index system to translate money amounts into terms of the same 'currency', much the same as the 'temporal system' (see Section 10). CPP 'dates' purchasing power amounts by means of a subscript before the £ symbol: thus, $_{92}$£150. CPP determines profit or loss for a period by measuring the change in the *purchasing power* of the shareholders' equity interest (after excluding new capital issues, dividends paid, and so on). The basic question which CPP raises is whether in times of inflation it is more *useful* to account in terms of money or in terms of (constant) purchasing power.

The CPP approach was never widely adopted in practice because, as a result of the Sandilands Committee's report in September 1975, the government instructed the Accounting Standards Committee to implement a form of current cost accounting (CCA). So the CPP accounting standard SSAP 7 was withdrawn.

Paint Making Limited – Example

CPP accounts for Paint Making Limited for the year 1992 are set out on the next page. They allow for inflation of 15 per cent in 1992. The RPI is assumed to stand at 100.0 in December 1991 and at 115.0 in December 1992, with the rate of inflation steady throughout the year.

Balance sheet

The figures need explaining. The money cost of fixed assets purchased at the end of 1991 must be multiplied by 1.15 to express their cost in end-of-1992 pounds. Thus the CPP accounts show land and buildings at £46 000 (£40 000 × 115/100) and restate plant and equipment figures in a similar way. This is not to 'revalue' fixed assets, certainly not at 'current values'; but to *restate* their original cost in terms of up-to-date purchasing power. Thus constant purchasing power accounting is really a form of historical cost accounting; but it indexes original money costs to allow for subsequent general inflation. CPP restates share capital in the same way as the cost of fixed assets.

The HC balance sheet already expresses closing net current assets in end-of-year pounds, so CPP accounts do not need to restate the amount.

Profit and loss account

The profit and loss account items (apart from depreciation) require adjustment too, but of a different magnitude. We assume that the figures in the HC profit and loss account represent 'average-for-the-year' pounds; and we further assume that inflation occurred at a steady rate all through the year. Hence we multiply the 1992 profit and loss account items by 1.07 (that is, 115.0/107.5) to translate from mid-1992 pounds to end-1992 pounds.

Depreciation is different. Here we simply take one-eighth of the adjusted (CPP) cost figure. This results in a CPP charge of £17 000 in end-1992 pounds, instead of the £15 000 charged in the HC accounts. The difference between HC and CPP depreciation could be much larger with older fixed assets, or with a higher rate of inflation, as the table below shows. For example, with average inflation of 10% a year and a 15-year asset life, the understatement is 97%.

HC depreciation understatement

CPP – HC
HC

Life in years	Inflation rate per year		
	5%	10%	15%
10	30	63	99
15	45	97	157
20	60	135	220

PAINT MAKING LIMITED
CPP balance sheet at 31 December 1992

		$_{92}$£'000
Fixed assets		
Land and buildings at cost	(40 × 1.15)	46
Equipment: Cost	(120 × 1.15)	138
Depreciation		17
		121
Net current assets		61
		228
		═══
Capital and reserves		
Called up share capital	(200 × 1.15)	230
Profit and loss account	(see details)	(2)
		228
		═══

CPP profit and loss account
for year ended 31 December 1992

			$_{92}$£'000
Turnover	(480 × 1.07)		513
Cost of goods sold	(360 × 1.07)	385	
Depreciation		17	
Distribution and administration expenses	(60 × 1.07)	64	
			466
			47
Loss on monetary assets	(see details)		7
Profit before tax			40
Tax	(15 × 1.07)		16
Profit after tax			24
Dividends	(24 × 1.07)		26
Retained for the year			(2)

Loss on monetary assets

In CPP accounts there is an *extra* profit and loss account item which does not appear at all in HC accounts. This is the item: 'loss on monetary assets' (or 'gain on monetary liabilities'). It arises in CPP accounts because the measuring unit is a unit of constant purchasing power. (It does not arise in HC accounts, of course, where the measuring unit *is* money.)

In Paint Making's case, we shall assume that all net current assets are 'monetary' in nature. (Treating stocks in this way normally makes little difference in practice.) We then calculate the amount of the (purchasing power) loss on monetary assets as follows:

		$_{92}$£'000
Opening working capital*	(40 × 1.15)	46*
Closing working capital		61
Average working capital		53½*
Loss of purchasing power in year:		
Percentage**		13%**
In CPP terms* (53½ × 0.13)		7

* in end-of-period pounds
** increase in RPI was 15.0%, hence loss of purchasing power in year was 100 − (100/115) = 13.0%

We see on a CPP basis, in 1992 Paint Making Limited distributed some of its dividends out of (purchasing power) 'capital' – in contrast with what the HC accounts showed. We can also see that while HC return on equity in 1992 was 14.6%, the CPP figure was only 10.5%.

In this example we are using only the figures for 1992. If we had figures for earlier years, we would have made a further adjustment to restate the earlier years' figures in terms of end-1992 purchasing power. (Problems 11.2 and 11.13 at the end of this section deal with such adjustments.)

CURRENT COST ACCOUNTING

SSAP 16, the accounting standard on Current Cost Accounting (CCA), was issued in 1980 (and withdrawn in 1985). It required annual financial statements for all but small companies to include current cost accounts as well as historical cost (HC) figures. Companies could publish either CCA or HC accounts as the 'main' accounts, with extra information either in the notes or in the form of supplementary accounts.

CCA regards as the main problem changes in the prices of fixed assets and stocks. Hence CCA adjustments to HC accounts aim to show such 'real' assets at their *current* costs (not their actual historical costs), both in the balance sheet and in the profit and loss account.

CCA extends to all real assets on a regular and systematic basis the *ad hoc* revaluations that some HC accounts apply to some fixed assets from time to time (see Section 5). Changes in asset 'costs' appear in a revaluation reserve in the CCA balance sheet (as part of shareholders' funds).

CCA, in contrast to CPP, is not a system of accounting for general inflation. The case for using current costs rather than historical costs is (in theory) just as strong when there is no general inflation. CCA takes the view that companies are concerned, not so much with 'general' inflation, but with the specific price changes of the goods they themselves buy and sell. Therefore CCA includes current costs (rather than historical costs) of the specific assets a business uses. This aims to ensure the business maintains its operating capability, as represented by its fixed assets, stocks, and monetary working capital.

'Current cost operating profit' (before interest and tax) matches current costs against sales turnover to determine the current cost profit or loss from operations. It makes three adjustments to HC operating profits:

1 a *depreciation adjustment*, being the difference between depreciation based on current costs of fixed assets, and that based on historical costs;
2 a *cost of sales adjustment* (COSA), being the difference between the current costs of stocks consumed in the period and their historical costs;
3 a *monetary working capital adjustment* (MWCA), being the amount needed to maintain the real volume of 'monetary working capital' (which is roughly working capital less stocks).

Balance sheet valuations

SSAP 16 required CCA balance sheets to show assets at their 'value to the business', defined as 'the lower of net current replacement cost and recoverable amount'. Recoverable amount is the higher of an asset's net realizable value (on disposal) and, where applicable, the amount recoverable from its further use. The diagram below illustrates.

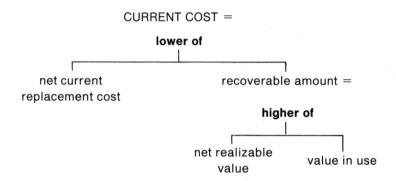

Because the CCA balance sheet includes only those same assets which appear in an HC balance sheet (though some at different values), it does *not* attempt to disclose the 'total value' of the business. Thus our comments in Section 1 (page 5) about the misleading nature of the American expression 'net worth' *apply with equal force to CCA balance sheets.*

SSAP 16 required offices, factories and shops to be valued by professional valuers at least once every five years, at their net current replacement cost. Specialized buildings, such as chemical plants or breweries, were to be valued in the same way as plant and machinery.

For plant and machinery, CCA accounts use the current replacement cost net of depreciation. Companies must obtain current costs for each distinct kind of asset, such as production machinery, vehicles, office equipment, and so on. They normally do so by applying to the historical cost the change in a relevant asset index since the date of acquisition. In rare cases companies might use 'economic value', that is, the net present value of the expected remaining cash flows from using an asset.

The current cost of stock will normally be obtained by adjusting historical costs by the use of suitable specific price indices (or possibly from current price lists). If the difference between HC and CCA stocks at the balance sheet date is small, CCA balance sheets may use the same figure as for HC. But the current cost profit and loss account will still need to make a cost of sales adjustment (COSA). Thus CCA aims to get the profit and loss account advantages of the LIFO method of valuing stock (see Section 4) without its balance sheet disadvantages.

Paint Making Limited – Example

We assumed that the RPI in Paint Making Limited's case stood at 100.0 in December 1991 and at 115.0 in December 1992. These were the index numbers we used in preparing CPP accounts. For CCA accounts, however, we need different specific price indices for each of the main types of asset. Let us assume that professional valuers revalued Paint Making's land and buildings at £50 000 at December 1992, and that the relevant specific price indices changed as follows:

	end 1991	end 1992
Equipment	100.0	110.0
Monetary working capital	100.0	120.0

Balance sheet

The CCA balance sheet adjusts the equipment's historical cost by reference to the change in its specific price index (£120 000 × 110/100 = £132 000); and the one-eighth straight-line depreciation is then calculated on the gross *current* cost.

The HC balance sheet already shows the net current assets at 'current cost' levels, so no adjustment is needed; but we shall have to use the change in the monetary working capital index to calculate the necessary profit and loss account charge.

PAINT MAKING LIMITED

CCA balance sheet at 31 December

	1992 £'000	1991 £'000
Fixed assets		
Land and buildings	50	40
Equipment: Current cost	132	120
Depreciation	16	—
	116	120
Net current assets	61	40
	227	200
Capital and reserves		
Called up share capital	200	200
Revaluation reserve	31	—
Profit and loss account	(4)	—
	227	200

CCA profit and loss account
Year ended 31 December 1992

		£'000
Turnover		480
Cost of goods sold	360	
Depreciation	15	
Distribution and administration expenses	60	
		435
HC profit before tax		45
Current cost adjustments:		
Depreciation adjustment	1	
Monetary working capital adjustment	9	
		10
Current cost profit before tax		35
Tax		15
Current cost profit after tax		20
Dividends		24
Current cost balance retained		(4)

Profit and loss account

The current cost profit and loss account for Paint Making Limited shows three 'current cost adjustments' to the HC trading profit before tax:

1 The depreciation adjustment in 1992 is simply the excess of CCA depreciation (£16 000) over HC depreciation (£15 000).

2 The monetary working capital adjustment (MWCA) here covers the whole of the net current assets (that is, including stocks). To calculate the MWCA the 'averaging' method uses opening (100), closing (120), and average (assumed 110) index numbers for 1992, as shown below:

	£'000	£'000
Closing net current assets	61 × 110/120 =	56
Opening net current assets	40 × 110/100 =	44
Increase in year 1992	21	(12)
of which *volume* change = at average prices	12	
leaving as due to *price*.		9 (MWCA)

That part of the change in net current assets due to *price* changes, rather than to volume changes, is the monetary working capital adjustment (MWCA); it appears in the profit and loss account as a current cost adjustment to the HC trading profit; and increases the current cost revaluation reserve in the balance sheet.

3 The cost of sales adjustment (COSA) in Paint Making Limited's case is included in the MWCA which we have just calculated. Often the price index for stocks also applies to monetary working capital and the two adjustments can be combined; but where different indices are appropriate, then two separate calculations must be made.

The current cost operating profit in 1992 now becomes £35 000 and the profit after tax £20 000. As a result, in the current cost accounts it appears that dividends paid in 1992 have exceeded available current cost profits after tax by £4 000; and this deficit is deducted from capital and reserves in the balance sheet.

The current cost revaluation reserve of £31 000 consists of the increased valuation of land and buildings (+ 10) and of gross equipment (+ 12), together with the MWCA (+ 9).

The CCA return on equity is 8.8 per cent in 1992. Like the CPP figure, this percentage is lower than that derived from the HC accounts.

Gearing adjustment

In the Paint Making example, we have so far considered the three current cost adjustments to HC operating profit:

1 Depreciation adjustment.
2 Cost of sales adjustment (COSA).
3 Monetary working capital adjustment (MWCA).

In addition, when a proportion of the net operating assets is financed by net borrowing, SSAP 16 required a further adjustment – the 'gearing adjustment'. This would normally *reduce* the effect of the above three current cost operating adjustments. The gearing adjustment reflects the extent to which current cost operating adjustments do not have to be financed from equity funds because of the existence of debt capital.

SSAP 16 required two steps to calculate the gearing adjustment:

(a) express 'net borrowing' (that is, borrowing less cash) as a proportion of net operating assets (in current cost terms)
(b) multiply the total of the three current cost operating adjustments by the 'borrowing proportion' so determined.

When SSAP 16 was being introduced there was much debate about the gearing adjustment, and how to calculate it. Not everyone agreed with it (the Sandilands Committee did not recommend it); and in practice the calculations could be complex. Paint Making's accounts contain no debt, so require no gearing adjustment. If, however, you would like to work through an example of the gearing adjustment, Problem 11.10 contains one.

CCA: the overall system

The outline CCA balance sheet on the right presents an overview of the current cost accounting system (with hypothetical numbers). The following points may be noted:

1 The current cost reserve (detailed below) includes unrealized as well as realized gains. The 'realized' element represents the net cumulative total of the current cost adjustments which have passed through the CCA profit and loss account.

CURRENT COST RESERVE (Paint Making)

Unrealized gains		
+ Fixed asset revaluations	22	
− CCA extra depreciation	(1)	
+ Stock revaluation	—	
		21
Realized gains		
+ CCA extra depreciation	1	
+ COSA ⎫		
+ MWCA ⎬	9	
− Gearing adjustment	—	
		10
		31

CCA BALANCE SHEET

Equity 45 (including current cost reserve)		Fixed assets 50 (including unrealized gains)	
Debt 25		Stock 30 (including unrealized gains)	
Overdraft 15			
Creditors 15		Debtors 20	
	100		100

(40 bracket spans Debt and Overdraft)

CCA OPERATING ADJUSTMENTS

Extra depreciation	X
COSA	X
MWCA	X
	—
CCA Operating adjustments	= X

2 The revaluation surplus on depreciable fixed assets becomes 'realized' through the depreciation adjustment.

3 There are two separate calculations with respect to stocks, to determine:

a the 'unrealized' revaluation gain on end-of-year stock held (often not calculated because of the very small difference between the HC and CCA value); and

b the 'realized' cost of sales adjustment (COSA).

4 The monetary working capital adjustment (MWCA) allows for a company's net exposure to price changes in respect of the excess of debtors over trade creditors. Where appropriate, the COSA and MWCA may be combined.

5 The gearing adjustment transfers from current cost reserve to CCA profit and loss account the debt-financed proportion of the *realized* holding gains deriving from current cost operating adjustments.

It should also be appreciated that the precise detailed CCA system required by SSAP 16 is not the only possible CCA system; though many of the principles would presumably remain.

SUMMARY

In this section we have tried to cover the problem of 'inflation accounting' reasonably fully, yet as simply as possible. We noted the existence of fluctuating rates of inflation averaging 10 per cent a year over the past twenty years.

We considered the serious effects of inflation on historical cost (HC) accounts; and noted how in times of inflation HC accounts overstate profits and understate assets. We saw how some companies have tried on an *ad hoc* basis partially to adjust HC accounts to allow for some of the effects of price changes.

It is important to recognize that constant purchasing power (CPP) accounting and current cost accounting (CCA) are trying to achieve different things. Hence it is quite feasible to *combine* the two systems.

CPP

Constant purchasing power (CPP) accounting regards the accounting problem of inflation as being the fall in the value ('purchasing power') of the monetary unit. It seeks to maintain the *purchasing power* of shareholders' equity. Hence CPP adjusts all items in HC accounts according to the date on which they arose, by applying a single index of 'general inflation'. CPP uses the RPI as a measure of the extent of general inflation from month to month.

The main CPP adjustments within a period are:

1 to fixed assets and depreciation;
2 to stocks and cost of sales;
3 in respect of gains (or losses) on net monetary liabilities (or assets). Adjustments 2 and 3 are sometimes combined.

There is also an important CPP adjustment to prior years' results in order to restate all figures in accounts and in summary statistics into terms of the same ('constant') purchasing power, and thus to permit sensible comparisons over periods of five to ten years.

CCA

CCA regards as the main problem of inflation, changes in prices of fixed assets and stocks. It seeks to maintain the operating capacity of the business. We noted the different CCA adjustments to HC accounts:

1 Revalue fixed assets and stocks.
2 Calculate the three CCA operating adjustments:
   a depreciation adjustment
   b cost of sales adjustment (COSA)
   c monetary working capital adjustment (MWCA).
   (Note: b and c are sometimes combined.)
3 Calculate the gearing adjustment.

The current cost (revaluation) reserve consists of unrealized gains as well as realized gains which have passed through the CCA profit and loss account. The three current cost adjustments are applied to the HC operating profit before interest payable and tax, to arrive at current cost operating profit. After charging interest payable and tax, the gearing adjustment reduces the CCA operating adjustments by the extent of the gearing proportion. This avoids double counting in respect of price changes effectively financed by debt capital.

252

11.1 Definitions

Please write out below your understanding of what the following terms mean. If you need to, use extra paper. When you have completed writing out your answers, compare them carefully with those shown overleaf.

(a) Current cost operating profit

(b) Operating capability

(c) The CCA depreciation adjustment

(d) The CCA cost of sales adjustment

(e) The CCA monetary working capital adjustment

(f) The CCA gearing adjustment

(g) General inflation

(h) Current cost 'value to the business'

(i) The current cost reserve

(j) A unit of constant purchasing power

11.1 Definitions

(a) *Current cost operating profit* is the surplus arising from the ordinary activities of the business after allowing for the impact of price changes on the funds needed to maintain its operating capability. There are three main adjustments to historical cost profit: the depreciation adjustment, the cost of sales adjustment (COSA), and the monetary working capital adjustment (MWCA).

(b) *Operating capability* is the volume of goods and services which the business can produce with its existing resources. It is represented in accounting terms by the net operating assets (fixed assets, stocks and monetary working capital) at current cost. This concept of 'capital' underpins current cost accounting: it distinguishes CCA from historical cost (HC) accounting, which aims to maintain the money amount of shareholders' funds (share capital and reserves), and from constant purchasing power (CPP) accounting, which aims to maintain the purchasing power of shareholders' funds.

(c) *The CCA depreciation adjustment* allows for the impact of price changes in determining the total charge against revenue for depreciation of fixed assets. It is the difference between current cost depreciation for a period and historical cost depreciation.

(d) *The CCA cost of sales adjustment* (COSA) allows for the impact of price changes in determining the total charge against revenue for stock consumed. It is the difference between the current cost of stock consumed during the period and the historical cost of stock charged. COSA can be calculated either item by item or by the 'averaging method', using an index of relevant price changes.

(e) *The CCA monetary working capital adjustment* (MWCA) represents the change in the amount of finance needed for MWC as a result of changes in the input prices of goods and services used by the business. A business's MWC is the total of trade debtors and prepayments (plus any stocks not subject to a COSA) less trade creditors and accruals: it is an integral part of the net operating assets. Where stock is mostly financed by net creditors (after deducting debtors from creditors), the credit for MWCA will largely offset the debit for COSA. The averaging method is used to calculate MWCA, which may be combined with COSA.

(f) *The CCA gearing adjustment* reduces the adjustments made for depreciation, cost of sales and monetary working capital in arriving at current cost operating profit, to the extent that net operating assets are financed by net borrowing and thus do not need to be maintained from equity funds. The gearing adjustment reduces the current cost operating adjustments by the proportion of net borrowing to net borrowing plus equity. 'Net borrowing' is the excess of all liabilities fixed in monetary terms other than those included within MWC over the aggregate of all current assets not subject to a COSA or included within MWC. The gearing adjustment does not depend on the company's ability or intention to maintain the same gearing in future.

(g) *General inflation* is measured in the UK by increases in the monthly RPI which records changes in the money cost over time of a representative sample of retail goods – loosely an average family's 'household shopping basket'.

(h) *Current cost 'value to the business'* is normally net current replacement cost, unless a permanent diminution to below that amount has been recognized. If so, then 'value to the business' is the higher of (a) the asset's net realizable value and (b) the amount recoverable from its further use.

(i) *The current cost reserve* in the current cost balance sheet includes:

    (a) unrealized revaluation surpluses on fixed assets, stocks and investments, and

    (b) realized amounts equal to the cumulative net total of the depreciation adjustment, COSA and MWCA, and the gearing adjustment.

(j) *A unit of constant purchasing power* is used in CPP accounting as a unit of account (instead of money, as in HC accounting). It is derived from an index measuring general inflation, such as the RPI. CPP accounts normally use 'end-of-most-recent-period' purchasing power units as a matter of practical convenience. Use of CPP units is helpful, in times of inflation, in comparing financial amounts over time.

11.2 Paint Making Limited (A): CPP accounts for 1993

Refer back to the Paint Making Limited example on pages 245 to 247. Assume the rate of RPI inflation in 1993 was 10 per cent. Thus the RPI, which stood at 100.00 in December 1991, and at 115.0 in December 1992, stood at 126.5 in December 1993. As before assume the rate of inflation was steady throughout the year (so that the mid-1993 RPI may be taken as 120.6).

Required:

(a) Prepare CPP accounts for 1993
(b) To provide comparative figures for the above, *restate* the 1992 CPP figures (shown in end-1992 pounds on page 247) in terms of end-1993 pounds.

The 1993 HC balance sheet and profit and loss account for Paint Making Limited are shown opposite.

11.3 Paint Making Limited (B): CCA accounts for 1993

Refer back to the Paint Making Limited example on pages 245 to 250.

Assume the relevant specific price index levels (December 1991 = 100.0) were as follows:

	end 1992	end 1993
Plant and equipment	110.0	118.0
Monetary working capital	120.0	135.0

Assume also that the value of the land and buildings has risen to £60 000 by December 1993.

Required:

(a) Prepare CCA accounts for 1993
(b) Explain your calculation of:
   (i) MWCA
   (ii) Current cost revaluation reserve at December 1993.

The 1993 HC balance sheet and profit and loss account for Paint Making Limited are shown opposite.

You may prefer to answer this question after you have answered questions 11.4 to 11.11 relating to Thames Manufacturing Limited.

PAINT MAKING LIMITED
HC balance sheet at 31 December

	1993 £'000
Fixed assets	
Land and buildings at cost	40
Equipment: Cost	120
Depreciation	30
Net	90
Net current assets	84
	214
Capital and reserves	
Called up share capital	200
Profit and loss account	14
	214

HC Profit and loss account
Year ended 31 December 1993

		£'000
Turnover		600
Cost of goods sold	450	
Depreciation	15	
Distribution and administration expenses	75	
		540
Profit before tax		60
Tax		20
Profit after tax		40
Dividends		32
Retained profit for the year		8

11.2 Paint Making Limited (A)

Solution

PAINT MAKING LIMITED
CPP balance sheet at 31 December

		(a) 93 £'000	(b) 93 £'000	92 £'000
Fixed assets				
Land and buildings at cost	(40 × 1.265)	51	51	46
Equipment: Cost	(120 × 1.265)	152	152	138
Depreciation		38	19	17
Net		114	133	121
Net current assets		84	67	61
		249	251	228
Capital and reserves				
Called up share capital	(200 × 1.265)	253	253	230
Profit and loss account	(see details)	(4)	(2)	(2)
		249	251	228

CPP Profit and loss account year ended 31 December

		93 £'000	93 £'000	92 £'000
Turnover	(600 × 1.05)	630	567	515
Cost of goods sold	(450 × 1.05)	472	425	386
Depreciation		19	19	17
Distribution and administration expenses	(75 × 1.05)	79	71	65
		570	515	468
		60	52	47
Loss on monetary assets		7	8	7
Profit before tax		53	44	40
Tax	(20 × 1.05)	21	18	16
Profit after tax		32	26	24
Dividends	(32 × 1.05)	34	28	26
Retained for the year		(2)	(2)	(2)

11.3 Paint Making Limited (B)

Solution

(a) PAINT MAKING LIMITED
CCA balance sheet at 31 December

	1993 £'000	1992 £'000
Fixed assets		
Land and buildings	60	50
Equipment: Current cost	142	132
Depreciation	36	16
	106	116
Net current assets	84	61
	250	227
Capital and reserves		
Called up share capital	200	200
Revaluation reserve	58	31
Profit and loss account	(8)	(4)
	250	227

CCA profit and loss account Year ended 31 December

	£'000	£'000
Turnover	600	480
Cost of goods sold	450	360
Depreciation	15	15
Distribution and administration expenses	75	60
	540	435
HC Profit before tax	60	45
Current cost adjustments:		
Depreciation adjustment	3	1
Monetary working capital adjustment	9	9
Current cost profit before tax	48	35
Tax	20	15
Current cost profit after tax	28	20
Dividends	32	24
Retained for the year	(4)	(4)

11.3 Paint Making Limited (B):

Solution (continued)

(b)(i)	**MWCA**	£'000			£'000
	Closing net current assets	84	× 127½/135	=	79
	Opening net current assets	61	× 127½/120	=	65
	Increase in year 1993	23			14
	of which *volume* change	14			
	leaving as due to price:	9			

(ii)	**Current cost revaluation reserve**	£'000
	At 31 December 1992	31
	Plus: Land and buildings	10
	Equipment	10
	Monetary working capital	9
		60
	Less: Backlog depreciation (36-16-18)	−2
	At 31 December 1993	58

11.4 to 11.11 Thames Manufacturing Limited (A): Preparing current cost accounts

The historical cost accounts for Thames Manufacturing Limited for the year ended 31 December 1992 are set out on page 258. The solutions to the next eight problems in this section will constitute the company's 1992 current cost accounts and supporting schedules.

In summary, the problems are as follows:

11.4 Determine the current cost of fixed assets at 31 December 1991, and the entry in the current cost reserve.

11.5 Determine the current cost of stock at 31 December 1991, and the entry in the current cost reserve.

11.6 Determine the current cost of fixed assets at 31 December 1992, the current cost depreciation charge and the transfer to current cost reserve.

11.7 Calculate the cost of sales adjustment for 1992.

11.8 Determine the current cost of stock at 31 December 1992.

11.9 Calculate the monetary working capital adjustment for 1992.

11.10 Calculate the gearing adjustment for 1992.

11.11 Draw up the current cost financial statements for 1992.

For each problem, blank worksheets are included to assist you in calculating the current cost figures. It is suggested that, as you complete each problem, you transfer the appropriate figures to the pro forma current cost balance sheet, profit and loss account, and statement of current cost reserve set out on pages 265 and 263. The solution to each step is shown on the page immediately following the worksheet.

THAMES MANUFACTURING LIMITED
HC profit and loss account
Year ended 31 December 1992

		£
Turnover		200 000
Cost of sales	86 000	
Depreciation	24 000	
		110 000
		90 000
Interest payable		5 000
Profit before taxation		85 000
Taxation		30 000
Profit after taxation		55 000
Dividend		15 000
Retained profit for the year		40 000

Further information needed to prepare the CCA accounts is set out below.

1 The value of the land at the end of 1991 was £100 000, its historical cost. At the end of 1992 the value was stated by a professional valuer to be £120 000.

2 *Production machinery*

	Historical cost at 31.12.91	
	Cost	Depreciation
Purchased 1.1.90 (5-year life)	£40 000	£16 000
Purchased 1.1.91 (5-year life)	£80 000	£16 000
	£120 000	£32 000

3 Stock held at the end of 1991 and 1992 had been purchased during the final four months of the year.

4 The average age of debtors and creditors was one month.

5 Relevant indices for production machinery and stock were as follows:

	Production machinery			Stock		
	1990	1991	1992	1990	1991	1992
January	100	110	121	185	203	243
September				198	238	258
October				200	240	260
November				201	241	261
December	110	121	132	202	242	262

THAMES MANUFACTURING LIMITED
HC balance sheet at 31 December 1992

		1992		1991
		£		£
Fixed assets				
Land, at cost		100 000		100 000
Production machinery				
Cost	120 000			120 000
Less: Depreciation	56 000			32 000
		64 000		88 000
		164 000		188 000
Current assets				
Stock	100 000			32 000
Debtors	70 000			30 000
Cash	23 000			12 000
	193 000			74 000
Less: **Creditors due within one year**				
Trade creditors	20 000			20 000
Dividends	15 000			—
Taxation	30 000			—
	65 000			20 000
		128 000		54 000
		292 000 .		242 000
Less: Long-term debt		30 000		20 000
		262 000		222 000
Shareholders' fund				
Called up share capital		150 000		£50 000
Retained profits		112 000		72 000
		262 000		222 000

11.4 Determine the current cost of fixed assets at 31 December 1991, and the entry in the current cost reserve

Land

Production machinery
The current cost at 31 December was:

Date purchased	Historical Cost		× Index =	Current Cost	
	Cost £	Dep'n £		Cost £	Dep'n £
1 January 1990	40 000	16 000	$\times \dfrac{121}{100} =$		
1 January 1991	80 000	16 000			
	120 000	32 000			
	32 000				
Net book value	88 000				

Enter current cost reserve £ _____

Enter current cost figures in opening balance sheet (on page 265).

11.5 Determine the current cost of stock at 31 December 1991, and the entry in the current cost reserve

Relevant index numbers are:	31 October 1991	240
	31 December 1991	242
	CCA stock	Unrealized revaluation surplus

Stock at 31 December 1991:
Historical cost × Index

£ _____ × _____ = £ _____ £ _____
CCA BS CC reserve

At this stage enter the total of the current cost reserve in the opening current cost balance sheet (on page 265).

11.6 Determine the current cost of fixed assets at 31 December 1992, the current cost depreciation charge and the transfer to current cost reserve

	1.1.92 £	× Index =	Revalued £	Surplus £	Dep'n charge £	31.12.92 £
Land						
				CC Reserve		CCA BS

	1.1.92 £	× Index =	Revalued £	Surplus £	Dep'n charge £	31.12.92 £
Production machinery						
Cost	136 400					
Depreciation	(36 960)					
				CC Reserve		CCA BS

HC depreciation charge _____

CCA depreciation adjustment _____
CCA P&L

259

11.4 Determine the current cost of fixed assets at 31 December 1991, and the entry in the current cost reserve *Solution*

Land
The current cost and historical cost are the same.

Production machinery
The current cost at 31 December was:

Date purchased	Historical Cost Cost £	Dep'n £	× Index =	Current Cost Cost £	Dep'n £
1 January 1990	40 000	16 000	$\times \dfrac{121}{100} =$	48 400	19 360
1 January 1991	80 000	16 000	$\dfrac{121}{110}$	88 000	17 600
	120 000	32 000		136 400	36 960
	32 000			36 960	
Net book value (a)	88 000		(b)	99 440	

Enter current cost reserve (b) − (a)   £11 440

Enter current cost figures in opening balance sheet (on page 265).

11.5 Determine the current cost of stock at 31 December 1991, and the entry in the current cost reserve *Solution*

Relevant index numbers are: 31 October 1991   240
                            31 December 1991   242

                            CCA stock   Unrealized
                                               revaluation
                                               surplus

Stock at 31 December 1991:
Historical cost × Index

£32 000	$\times \dfrac{242}{240^*} =$	£32 267	£267
		CCA BS	CC reserve

At this stage enter the total of the current cost reserve in the opening current cost balance sheet (on page 265).

* Index up to year-end from mid-point of stockholding period.

11.6 Determine the current cost of fixed assets at 31 December 1992, the current cost depreciation charge and the transfer to current cost reserve *Solution*

	1.1.92 £	× Index =	Revalued £	Surplus £	Dep'n charge £	31.12.92 £
Land	100 000		120 000	20 000	—	120 000
				CC Reserve		CCA BS

	1.1.92 £	× Index =	Revalued £	Surplus £	Dep'n charge £	31.12.92 £
Production machinery						
Cost	136 400	$\times \dfrac{132}{121} =$	148 800	12 400		148 800
Depreciation	(36 960)	$\times \dfrac{132}{121} =$	(40 320)	(3 360)	(29 760)*	(70 080)
	99 440		108 480	9 040	(29 760)	78 720
				CC Reserve		CCA BS

HC depreciation charge		(24 000)
CCA depreciation adjustment		(5 760)
		CCA P&L

* 1/5 × £148 800 = £29 760.

260

11.7 Calculate the cost of sales adjustment for 1992

The relevant index numbers are:
  Opening stock
  Closing stock
  Average for the year 1992

The HC stock increase of £   combines a volume and a price change:

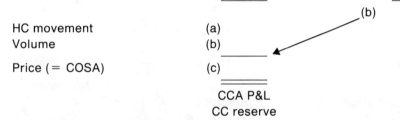

	HC £	× Index =	Average prices £
HC closing stock		× ⸺ =	
HC opening stock			
	_____		_____ (b)
HC movement	(a)		
Volume	(b)		
Price (= COSA)	(c)		

CCA P&L
CC reserve

Enter COSA in CAA profit and loss account and in current cost reserve.

11.8 Determine the current cost of stock at 31 December 1992

Relevant index numbers are:

	CCA stock £	Unrealized revaluation surplus £
Opening stock (31.12.91)	32 267	267
Closing stock (31.12.92)	*	____
*(HC) × ⸺ =		
	CCA BS	CC reserve

11.9 Calculate the monetary working capital adjustment for 1992

The relevant index numbers (using the same index as for COSA) are:
  Opening MWC
  Closing MWC
  Average for the year 1992

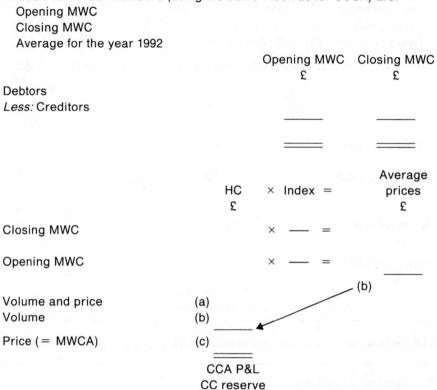

	Opening MWC £	Closing MWC £
Debtors		
Less: Creditors	_____	_____
	=====	=====

	HC £	× Index =	Average prices £
Closing MWC		× ⸺ =	
Opening MWC		× ⸺ =	
			_____ (b)
Volume and price	(a)		
Volume	(b)		
Price (= MWCA)	(c)		

CCA P&L
CC reserve

11.7 Calculate the cost of sales adjustment for 1992 *Solution*

The relevant index numbers are:

Opening stock	(31.10.91)	240
Closing stock	(31.10.92)	260
Average for the year 1992 (estimated)		252

The HC stock increase of £68 000 combines a volume and a price change:

	HC £	× Index =	Average prices £
HC closing stock	100 000	× $\frac{252}{260}$ =	96 923
HC opening stock	32 000	× $\frac{252}{240}$ =	33 600
		(b)	63 323

HC movement	(a)	68 000
Volume	(b)	63 323
Price (= COSA)	(c)	4 677

CCA P&L
CC reserve

11.8 Determine the current cost of stock at 31 December 1992 *Solution*

Relevant index numbers are:

31.10.91	240
31.12.91	242
31.10.92	260
31.12.92	262

	CCA stock £	Unrealized revaluation surplus £
Opening stock (31.12.91)	32 267	267
Closing stock (31.12.92)	100 769*	769
		502

*$100\,000 \times \frac{262}{260} = 100\,769$

CCA BS   CC reserve

11.9 Calculate the monetary working capital adjustment for 1992 *Solution*

The relevant index numbers (using the same index as for COSA) are:

Opening MWC	(30.11.91)	241
Closing MWC	(30.11.92)	261
Average for the year 1992 (estimated)		252

	Opening MWC £	Closing MWC £
Debtors	30 000	70 000
Less: Creditors	20 000	20 000
	10 000	50 000

	HC £	× Index =	Average prices £
Closing MWC	50 000	× $\frac{252}{261}$ =	48 276
Opening MWC	10 000	× $\frac{252}{241}$ =	10 456
		(b)	37 820

Volume and price	(a)	40 000
Volume	(b)	37 820
Price (= MWCA)	(c)	2 180

CCA P&L
CC reserve

11.10 Calculate the gearing adjustment for 1992

$$\frac{Gearing}{adjustment} = \frac{Average\ net\ borrowing}{Average\ net\ CCA\ operating\ assets} \times \frac{CC\ operating}{adjustments}$$

Average net borrowing

	Opening £	Closing £
	___	___
	===	===

Average = £ ===

Average net CCA operating assets

	Opening £	Closing £
	___	___
	===	===

Average = £ ===

Gearing proportion = ——— = %

Gearing adjustment = % × £ = £ ===

CCA P&L
CC reserve

11.11 Current cost reserve

At 31 December 1991

	Total = £	Unrealized + £	Realized £
Adjustment to HC balance sheet:			
Production machinery (4)			
Stock (5)			
	___		___
	=	+	
	===	===	===

At 31 December 1992

	Total = £	Unrealized + £	Realized £
Balance at 31 December 1991			
Movements in 1992:			
Revaluation of assets			
Land (6)			
Production machinery (6)			
Stock (8)			
CC operating adjustments			
Extra depreciation (6)			
COSA (7)			
MWCA (9)			
Gearing adjustment (10)			
	___	___	___
	=	+	
	===	===	===

11.10 Calculate the gearing adjustment for 1992 *Solution*

$$\text{Gearing adjustment} = \frac{\text{Average net borrowing}}{\text{Average net CCA operating assets}} \times \text{CC operating adjustments}$$

Average net borrowing

	Opening £	Closing £
Debt	20 000	30 000
Taxation	—	30 000
Cash	(12 000)	(23 000)
	8 000	37 000
Average =		£22 500

Average net CCA operating assets

	Opening £	Closing £
Fixed assets	199 440	198 720
Stock	32 267	100 769
Monetary working capital	10 000	50 000
	241 707	349 489
= Net borrowing + Equity:		
Net borrowing	8 000	37 000
Equity (per CCA BS)	233 707	297 489
+ Proposed dividend	—	15 000
	241 707	349 489
Average =		£295 598

$$\text{Gearing proportion} = \frac{22\,500}{295\,598} = 7.61\%$$

Gearing adjustment = 7.61% × £12 617* = £960

*CC operating adjustments:

	£
Depreciation	5 760
COSA	4 677
MWCA	2 180
	12 617

CCA P&L
CC reserve

11.11 Current cost reserve *Solution*

At 31 December 1991

		Total £	=	Unrealized £	+	Realized £
Adjustment to HC balance sheet:						
Production machinery	(4)	11 440		11 440		
Stock	(5)	267		267		
Balance at 31 December 1991 as shown in CCA BS		11 707	=	11 707	+	—

At 31 December 1992

		Total £	=	Unrealized £	+	Realized £
Balance at 31 December 1991		11 707		11 707		—
Movements in 1992:						
Revaluation of assets						
Land	(6)	20 000		20 000		
Production machinery	(6)	9 040		9 040		
Stock	(8)	502		502		
CC operating adjustments						
Extra depreciation	(6)	—		(5 760)		5 760
COSA	(7)	4 677				4 677
MWCA	(9)	2 180				2 180
Gearing adjustment	(10)	(960)				(960)
Balance at 31 December 1992 as shown in CCA BS		47 146	=	35 489	+	11 657

THAMES MANUFACTURING LIMITED
CCA balance sheet
31 December 1992

		1992		1991	
		£		£	
Land			(6)	100 000	
Production machinery					
Cost	(6)				(4)
Less: Depreciation	(6)				(4)
			(6)		(4)
Current assets					
Stock	(8)				(5)
Debtors	70 000			30 000	
Cash				12 000	
Less: Creditors due within one year					
Trade Creditors	20 000			20 000	
Dividends	15 000			—	
Taxation	30 000			—	
	(65 000)			(20 000)	
Less: Long-term debt		(30 000)		(20 000)	
Called up share capital		150 000		150 000	
Current cost reserve			(11)		(11)
Retained profits				72 000	
Shareholders' funds					

THAMES MANUFACTURING LIMITED
CCA profit and loss account
Year ended 31 December 1992

			£
Historical cost profit before interest			90 000
Less: Current cost operating adjustments			
Depreciation		(6)	
COSA		(7)	
MWCA		(9)	
Current cost operating profit			
Less: Interest payable	5 000		
Deduct: Gearing adjustment		(10)	
Taxation			30 000
Current cost profit attributable to ordinary shareholders			
Dividends			15 000
Retained profit for the year			
Balance brought forward			72 000
Retained profits carried forward			

Solution

THAMES MANUFACTURING LIMITED
CCA balance sheet
31 December 1992

			1992 £		1991 £	
Land			120 000	(6)	100 000	
Production machinery						
Cost	148 800	(6)			136 400	(4)
Less: Depreciation	(70 080)	(6)			36 960	(4)
			78 720	(6)	99 440	(4)
			198 720		199 440	
Current assets						
Stock	100 769	(8)			32 267	(5)
Debtors	70 000				30 000	
Cash	23 000				12 000	
			193 769		74 267	
Less: Creditors due within one year						
Trade Creditors	20 000				20 000	
Dividends	15 000				—	
Taxation	30 000				—	
			65 000		20 000	
			128 769		54 267	
			327 489		253 707	
Less: Long-term debt			(30 000)		(20 000)	
			297 489		233 707	
Called up share capital			150 000		150 000	
Current cost reserve			47 146	(11)	11 707	(11)
Retained profits			100 343		72 000	
Shareholders' funds			297 489		233 707	

THAMES MANUFACTURING LIMITED
CCA profit and loss account
Year ended 31 December 1992

			£
Historical cost profit before interest			90 000
Less: Current cost operating adjustments			
Depreciation	5 760	(6)	
COSA	4 677	(7)	
MWCA	2 180	(9)	
			12 617
Current cost operating profit			77 383
Less: Interest payable	5 000		
Deduct: Gearing adjustment	960	(10)	
			4 040
			73 343
Taxation			30 000
Current cost profit attributable to ordinary shareholders			43 343
Dividends			15 000
Retained profit for the year			28 343
Balance brought forward			72 000
Retained profits carried forward			100 343

Answers to the next two problems are shown at the end of the book.

11.12 Thames Manufacturing Limited (B): Restating 1991 CCA balance sheet

When you have completed the CCA accounts for 1992 (11.4 to 11.11), and compared your answers with those shown, please look again at the CCA balance sheet at 31 December 1992 (on page 266). This also contains comparative figures as at 31 December 1991.

You are now asked to restate these 1991 CCA balance sheet figures for Thames Manufacturing Limited in figures more directly comparable with those at 31 December 1992. Use the RPI, assuming it stood at 100.0 in December 1991, and at 105.0 in December 1992.

11.13 Thames Manufacturing Limited (C): Preparing CPP accounts

HC accounts for Thames Manufacturing Limited for 1992 are set out on page 258. You are asked to use those HC accounts, together with the following information, to produce CPP accounts for 1992, together with comparative balance sheet figures for 1991.

Additional information is as follows:

1 The RPI stood at 100.0 in December 1991, and at 105.0 in December 1992. The 'average' RPI for calendar 1992 was 102.5.
2 The CPP cost of land in end-1991 pounds, was £105 000 at December 1991; and the CPP cost of production machinery at December 1991, on the same basis, was £127 000.
3 Please treat stock as a monetary asset (so that net monetary assets at December 1991 amounted to £34 000 – that is, £54 000 net working capital less £20 000 long-term debt).
4 Remember you will need to translate the CPP profit and loss account from 'average' 1992 pounds into terms of end-of-1992 pounds.
5 Remember you will need to restate the comparative 1991 CPP balance sheet into terms of end-1992 pounds for the 1992 accounts.
6 Assume that called up share capital was £150 000 on 1 January 1990; and that the RPI was 91.2 then.

No answers are given for the following problems:

11.14 Forty-four years on

In April 1947 (RPI = 7.4), the 40 per cent rate of inheritance tax started at a level of £150 000. At what level would the 40 per cent rate need to have started in April 1991 (RPI = 133.1) in order to be starting at the same purchasing power level as in 1947? (The actual starting point in April 1991 for the inheritance tax rate of 40 per cent was £140 000.)

11.15 Capital gain?

The FT-Actuaries 500-Share Index was started at 100 in April 1962 (with the RPI then standing at 13.5). The record level for the 500-Share Index was reached in September 1991 (RPI = 134.6), when it touched 1425. In August 1972, the date of a previous peak (RPI = 21.9), the Index had reached 228; though by December 1974 (RPI = 29.6) it had fallen to 64.

(a) What proportion of its August 1972 value had the Index lost by September 1991, (i) in money terms? (ii) in 'real' terms?
(b) Approximately what proportion of the August 1972 level did the 500-Share Index reach in September 1991, in terms of constant purchasing power?
(c) How much 'real' value had the 500-Share Index, gained or lost by early December 1991 (RPI = 136.0), when it stood at 1291, (i) compared with its starting point in April 1962? (ii) compared with August 1972?

11.16 Reed International plc

Overleaf are shown five-year (HC) statistics for Reed International plc, showing financial highlights up to 31 March 1987. Also shown are current cost results (unaudited), together with some five-year CCA statistics indexed to 1987 prices.

(a) Calculate (where necessary) and compare HC and CCA/CPP profit margins and return on capital employed over the five years.
(b) Comment on the differences in the earnings per share figures, and in the trends.
(c) What other features of the indexed CCA statistics strike you as worthy of comment, and why?

£ million	1987	1986	1985	1984	1983
Turnover	1,950	1,931	2,115	2,043	1,809
Trading Profit	201	150	127	113	77
Profit before Tax	188	137	108	96	61
Attributable to Shareholders	127	95	64	68	40
Shareholders' Funds	695	630	649	597	553
Outside Shareholders' Interests	3	4	4	4	4
Net Indebtedness	188	79	171	189	189
Funds Employed	886	713	824	790	746
Trading Profit % Turnover	10·3	7·8	6·0	5·5	4·3
Trading Profit % Funds Employed	22·6	21·0	15·4	14·3	10·3
Net Indebtedness % Funds Employed	21·3	11·1	20·8	23·9	25·3
Net Assets per Ordinary Share	145p	132p	136p	126p	117p
Ordinary Share Prices – High	447p	221p	150p	113p	82p
– Low	203p	137p	97p	66p	58p
Earnings per Ordinary Share	26·6p	19·9p	13·4p	14·4p	8·4p
Net Dividend per Ordinary Share	8·0p	5·6p	4·6p	4·1p	3·5p
Dividend Cover	3·3	3·5	2·9	3·5	2·4
Interest Cover	14·8	9·8	6·1	6·1	4·5

CURRENT COST RESULTS

Current Cost Results (unaudited)

The provision of current cost accounts is no longer a mandatory requirement of UK Accounting Standards. The data given below is based on guidance given in the Accounting Standards Committee's Handbook, *Accounting for the effects of changing prices.*

£ million	1987	1986
Adjustments made to Historical Cost Results		
Additional depreciation of tangible fixed assets.	(23·6)	(22·4)
Other amounts written off tangible fixed assets.	(1·6)	(1·3)
Cost of sales	(4·9)	1·3
Monetary working capital	(3·2)	(2·0)
Exceptional items	(5·7)	(11·2)
Related companies	(0·1)	(0·7)
Adjustment to Operating Profit.	(39·1)	(36·3)
Gearing adjustment.	5·7	3·6
Adjustment to Attributable Earnings	(33·4)	(32·7)
Adjustment attributable to Capital Employed	125·5	123·2

Analysis of CCA Trading Profit

£ million	1987	1986		1987	1986
Class of business			Country of origin		
Reed Publishing UK.	39·3	20·8	UK	83·3	55·7
Reed Publishing USA	41·4	36·5	Europe	13·4	11·1
Consumer Publishing	18·8	2·4	USA	44·0	32·9
Packaging	17·9	19·1	Canada	17·7	11·0
European Paper	19·8	17·6	Rest of World	3·1	3·9
North American Paper	14·0	8·1			
Reed Trading	4·8	6·4			
Paint and DIY.	20·3	15·9			
Central Items	(11·5)	(7·6)			
Continuing activities	164·8	119·2			
Discontinued activities	(3·3)	(4·6)			
Total	161·5	114·6	Total	161·5	114·6

£ million	1987	1986	1985	1984	1983
Statistics for five years indexed to 1987 prices					
Turnover	1,950	2,013	2,318	2,367	2,199
CCA Trading Profit.	162	120	76	77	46
CCA Capital Employed.	1,119	1,028	1,176	1,108	1,143
CCA Earnings per Ordinary Share	19·6p	13·6p	3·4p	7·3p	1·6p
Net Dividend per Ordinary Share.	8·0p	5·9p	5·1p	4·8p	4·3p

Section 12

Interpreting company accounts

We have now completed Sections 3 to 11, which were introduced at the end of Section 2 (page 40) with the comment:

'It is important for people who use accounting figures to understand what accounts really mean. They should know how companies record transactions and summarize them in financial statements; and they should appreciate the various possible ways to value assets and to measure profit or loss.'

Now we know what is involved, it is evident that external analysts must exercise caution in drawing conclusions from accounts. This applies whether they are shareholders (actual or potential), employees, creditors, professional financial analysts, or government officials. Analysts must be aware of the normal margins of error which are inevitable in compiling accounts for large and complex organizations. They must also recognize the degree to which subjective judgements necessarily affect critical areas of asset valuation and hence determination of profit or loss.

We have looked at accounting statements from various angles, and in this final section we shall consider:

1   Disclosure and accounting conventions.
2   Comparisons over time and between companies.
3   Accounting matters requiring special attention.
4   Financial analysis and economic reality.

We shall then examine ICI's 1990 accounts in detail, drawing on the knowledge we have been accumulating throughout the book concerning company financial statements. We shall review the four main steps in the analysis of company accounts:

1   Overview analysis.
2   Financial ratio analysis.
3   Segment analysis.
4   Funds flow analysis.

Finally, we shall interpret the results of our analysis.

DISCLOSURE AND ACCOUNTING CONVENTIONS

Except where the results of a completed transaction are being measured, accounting profit or loss is not a matter of certainty, but involves subjective judgement. The more transactions are incomplete, the longer the timespan between their beginning and end, and the larger their size, the greater will be the possible range of profit or loss figures.

The requirement for accounting treatment to be 'consistent' from year to year aims to minimize distortions due to changes in opinion. In a changing business environment, however, accounting treatment can properly change from time to time (subject to adequate disclosure).

Accounting conventions owe much to their historical roots, and conservatism is a fundamental feature. This often leads to a tendency to understate the position. Intangible assets such as goodwill, trade marks, and the results of research and development, of marketing promotion, or even of staff training may be extremely valuable. Yet they provide little or no immediate security for creditors, so balance sheets often include them at very small amounts, or omit them completely. Hence in the accounts of firms providing services rather than making products, 'return on capital' ratios may seem unrealistically high.

In periods of inflation, as we saw in Section 11, the accounting convention of using historical cost fails to reflect the real position. Inflation can affect the level of profit or loss as well as many of the balance sheet figures. Companies must retain sufficient reported 'profits' in the business and at least appear to increase their permanent capital (in money terms); otherwise there is a serious danger of distributing real capital in the mistaken belief that it is 'profit'.

Company chairmen often say that their company's most important asset is its employees. But company balance sheets do not show this asset; nor is any capital sum usually payable directly in 'acquiring' employees. (Football clubs are a well-known exception, but they treat the cost as 'revenue' expenditure.) In trying to match spending better against future benefits, it would be hard to tell how much of someone's pay to capitalize under 'human resource accounting', and how to amortize the asset.

COMPARISONS OVER TIME AND BETWEEN COMPANIES

The trend in a company's results over a number of years, prepared on a consistent basis, is likely to provide a more useful means of appraising its performance and financial status than the results for a single year. Consistency is important, and the analyst using published figures may require adjustments in order to disclose a realistic trend. Certainly the effects of inflation are likely to be important in looking at trends over longer periods of time.

Comparisons between the published results of different companies are much less trustworthy than comparisons over time for a single company. Companies, even in the same 'industry', may engage in different activities, they may be of unequal size, and may have started at different points in time. Thus in a stores analysis one company may be a supermarket, another a department store and a third a small specialist grocer. All are in the 'retail trade', but what does comparing their results show?

At a more technical accounting level, companies may not have adopted the same approach in compiling their accounts. We have seen earlier the differences in profits and assets which can stem from alternative approaches to valuing stock, depreciation of fixed assets, expenditure allocation, deferred taxation, and so on. We shall adjust our financial ratios for the alternative treatments of goodwill later.

Financial information about leading companies appears daily in the financial press. Various investment services, and publications such as *The Times 1000*, provide longer-term data about the financial results of a whole range of companies. The figures for each company, over the previous five or ten years, use information from published accounts, often adjusted to try to make them comparable with other companies' figures. Adjustments may include standardizing the tax charge, excluding 'non-recurring' profits or losses, and adjusting earnings per share to allow for scrip issues during the period.

Detailed comparisons between the results of different companies within an industry are also made, for example by trade federations. Naturally the compilers of such statistics are well aware of the problems inherent in comparisons based on published accounts. The Centre of Interfirm Comparison, for example, makes extensive amendments to published data by using a great deal of additional information supplied in confidence by subscribers to its service. Such adjustments are essential to obtain meaningful detailed comparisons, as we saw in Section 2 with the example of Brown and Green (page 40). To the extent that the analyst is denied access to the required level of detail, he or she must move with considerable caution.

ACCOUNTING MATTERS REQUIRING SPECIAL ATTENTION

It may be useful to summarize here those items in accounts where the analyst may need to exercise special care. These are items where the required detail may not be readily available in the accounts and supporting notes and reports, or where alternative accounting treatments are permissible and adjustments may be necessary to allow reasonable comparability either over time or between companies. Where adequate detail is not available, particular care will be needed in drawing conclusions from figures.

The items are classified under four headings:

1 Capital employed.
2 Fixed assets.
3 Working capital.
4 Profit and loss account.

Capital employed

Has called up ordinary share capital increased during the period?
    If so, why? Rights issue? Bonus (scrip) issue? Acquisition?
    Are 'per share' figures calculated using appropriately weighted number of shares? Are prior years' figures comparable?

What individual items have caused significant movements on reserves?
    Do any of them really belong in the profit and loss account?
Is there any preference capital?

Is any long-term debt convertible into ordinary shares?
    On what terms?
    Have appropriate measures been calculated on a 'fully diluted' basis?

Is any long-term debt repayable within the near future?
    If so, will it be refinanced with more debt?

Has all lease financing been correctly identified?
    Have any prior year adjustments been made?
    Are any long-term operating leases really finance leases?

Are there significant borrowings in foreign currencies?
    Are they matched by foreign assets?
    How are exchange losses and gains treated?

Should short-term borrowing be included in capital employed?
Should any cash balances be offset against short-term borrowing?

Is the treatment of pensions appropriate? Is information revealed?

Fixed assets

Where fixed assets are shown 'at historical cost':
    How old are they? What is their estimated current value?
    How would revaluation affect the depreciation charge?

Where fixed assets are shown 'at valuation':
    When was the valuation made, and on what basis?
    How have values changed since that date?
    Might the assets be more valuable if used for other purposes?

What method of depreciation is used?
    What asset lives are used?
    Has adequate provision been made for technological obsolescence?

Are any assets leased? What is their value?
    How much are the annual rentals? How long is the commitment?

Have any substantial acquisitions or disposals been made in the year?
    At what point in the year were the acquired assets brought into the accounts or the disposed assets taken out?

Is goodwill:
    Written off against reserves?
    Being amortized by charges against profit?

What treatment has been adopted for other intangible assets?

Are acquisitions being accounted for (a) using acquisition accounting with fair values attached to assets or (b) using merger accounting with historical book values being shown?

Has the status of any investments changed during the period?
    Subsidiaries? Associates? Trade investments?
    Non-consolidated subsidiaries?

What is the difference between cost and market value of listed investments?
    Is market value used if lower than cost?

Working capital

On what basis has stock and work-in-progress been valued?
　What provision has been made for slow-moving stock and losses?

How are contracts in progress valued?
　How much profit has been taken so far?
　Are provisions for contingencies adequate?

Are sufficient details of debtors given?
　What amount is owed in foreign currencies?
　How much has been provided for bad debts?
　Can the total be split between domestic and foreign debtors?
　Have any debtors been discounted? (See contingent liabilities.)
　Are there any long-term debtors?

How much 'revenue' expenditure is being carried forward to future periods?
　What does it represent? Development? Advertising?
　Is the amount deferred increasing from period to period?

Is any tax recoverable shown as an asset?
　How certain of recovery is it?

Is cash distinguished from interest-bearing short-term investments?
　How does the total of liquid resources compare with short-term borrowing?
　Do net liquid resources look either excessive or inadequate?

Have any bank overdrafts been outstanding for more than twelve months?
　If so, should they be regarded as medium-term liabilities?

Are any 'provisions' included in current liabilities?
　What is their nature? Are the amounts adequate?

Profit and loss account

Most balance sheet items above will also affect the profit and loss account. Consideration must be given to the impact of inflation which is not reflected in the historical cost expense figures. Special effort may be needed to obtain ten-year statistics in sufficient detail for both profit and loss account and balance sheet items.

How are sales and trading profit split among the main activities?
　To what extent are changes due to price changes?
　To what extent to volume changes?
　Does inter-company transfer pricing policy distort the analysis?
　What is the impact of foreign exchange differences?
　How much interest payable, if any, has been capitalized?

Has the apparent proportion of profit taken in tax changed?
　What deferred taxation policy is being followed?

Has the share of profit (or loss) attributable to minority interests in subsidiaries changed? If so, is it clear why?

Were any mergers, acquisitions or disposals made in the year?
　For what fraction of the year were sales and profits included?

Are profits and losses on sales of fixed assets:
　Treated as adjustments of depreciation charges?
　Disclosed separately 'above the line' in the profit and loss account?
　Treated as 'below the line' items in the profit and loss account?
　Transferred directly to reserves?

What has been included in extraordinary items?
　Should any of these items be regarded as part of the ordinary activities of the company?
　Do any items tend to recur year after year?
　Are any provisions being made for future reorganization costs?

Is is clear which items have been transferred directly to reserves without going through the profit and loss account?
　Is such treatment appropriate in each case?

FINANCIAL ANALYSIS AND ECONOMIC REALITY

Financial analysis is a means of finding out about a company's performance over time in the markets in which it operates. We also want to know about its financial status (level of debt and short-term liquidity). The diagram overleaf shows a framework which we can use for these purposes. We can relate some items to others (for example profit to sales and profit to investment). But to understand the economic realities of the business in its market environment, we need to identify *changes* taking place through time.

To achieve success a company must simultaneously perform well in three competitive markets – the financial markets, the product/customer markets and the markets for labour and other supplies. There is increasing pressure for companies to report on such matters as staff recruitment, training and turnover, but accounts do not directly reflect success in the labour markets. In the longer term, poor performance in relation to employees and suppliers is likely to show in low profit, and some financial measures show more directly a company's degree of success in the financial and product/customer markets.

The diagram overleaf represents the financial and accounting links between these markets. On the left-hand side, success is reflected in financial markets in the value of the company, its share price. On the right-hand side, success in product/customer markets can be measured in terms of sales and profit growth and in the level of utilization of assets. Here detailed accounting numbers directly indicate levels of performance, and changes in them over time reflect both internal changes within the company and external changes in the business environment.

Between share price, which looks forward, and return on equity, which (as reported in accounts) looks backward, the link is only tenuous, at least in the short term. The bigger the changes affecting a company, the less will past results be a good guide to likely future achievement. General conditions in the financial markets affect share prices, which also reflect the market's view of uncertainty – both the risk inherent in the business, and that related to the methods of financing. Accounting measures cannot completely reflect whether returns have been adequate in relation to risk; but volatility of past earnings trends and comparisons with returns of other companies in the same industry will give some indication.

The remaining boxes in the diagram represent a comprehensive accounting model with parts directly linked to each other. It is thus possible to identify, for example, whether a falling return on equity is caused by increasing charges for interest or for tax. Similarly, changes in return on net assets may be due to changes in margins or asset utilization, which in turn may be caused by changes in volume, prices, costs, and the level of use of fixed assets and working capital.

Financial analysis directs attention to where change is taking place. Rarely will the accounting numbers *explain* the reasons for a change; but an analyst with clearly defined questions is more likely to obtain relevant answers. He or she may see declining margins; may discover that the problem lies in two out of several product lines; but he or she then needs to find out from management *why* profit is declining – is it increased costs or lower prices, and what is causing them? We saw in Section 2 how to extend the accounting model in detail by using the pyramid of ratios and breaking down profit/sales and sales/net assets into their constituent parts.

The framework of the pyramid can apply in two directions – either breaking down aggregate figures into more detail, or building them up from below. Similarly, financial analysis using the framework overleaf moves from left to right within the diagram: changes in return on equity are 'explained' by changes in one or more elements to its right. In planning, management can use the same model, starting at the right and moving to the left: to find out, for example, what will happen to return on equity if sales volume increases by 20 per cent, or if productivity or asset utilization increases by 10 per cent.

Such a framework, although crude, can help both to diagnose factors contributing to success or failure, and to assess the impact of management decisions on a company's financial performance. But this accrual accounting framework does not show cash flows; and profit-making companies can still experience liquidity problems. The solvency and liquidity ratios will reflect this, but it is wise to use the ratio framework in conjunction with cash flow statements compiled to show details of flows over a number of years.

FRAMEWORK FOR LINKING FINANCIAL AND BUSINESS OBJECTIVES

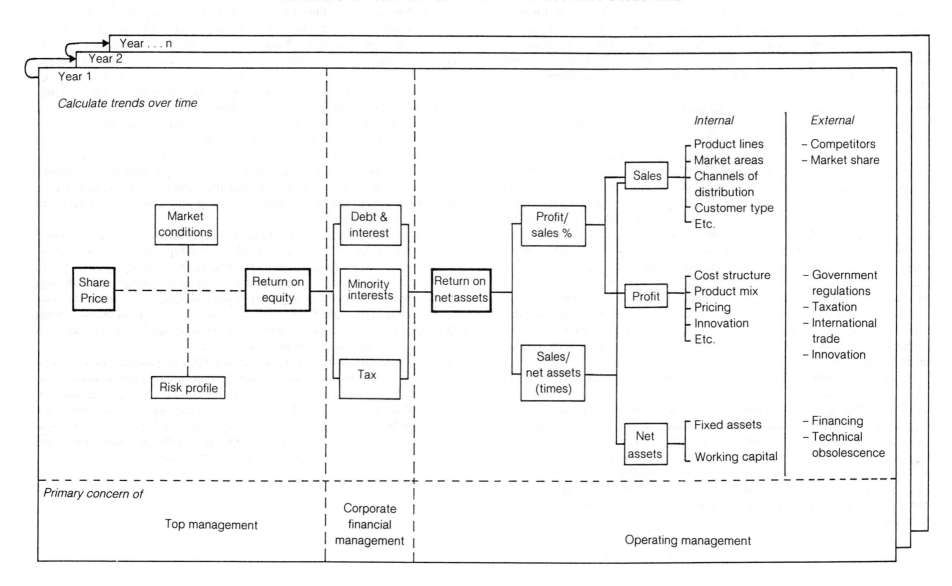

ANALYSIS OF ICI's 1990 ACCOUNTS

Substantial extracts from the 1990 accounts of Imperial Chemical Industries plc are set out on the next few pages. Please study them and prepare a financial analysis. To complete the analysis, the steps needed are:

- *prepare an overview analysis* (see below)

- *prepare financial ratio analysis for 1989 and 1990* (worksheets are on pages 283 and 285 and our worked solutions appear on pages 284 and 286

- *examine a segment analysis* (detailed statements are on page 278

- *study a five-year funds flow statement* (the statement on page 287 has been prepared from the published funds flow statements from 1986 to 1990)

- *prepare an amended financial ratio analysis* for 1989 and 1990 after adding back (capitalizing) goodwill written off to reserves. The worksheet is on page 289, with an explanation. Our worked solutions appear on page 290

- prepare an interpretation of the figures shown in the accounts, in the summary of ratios (page 291), in the segment analysis (pages 292 and 293) and in the funds flow statement (page 294). Please use a separate sheet for this. Our own comments appear on pages 295 and 296.

You may wish to use the analysis forms in Appendix 6 (pages 326 to 335).

OVERVIEW ANALYSIS

The first step is to prepare an overview analysis using the figures shown in the ICI five-year record (on page 287). The purpose is to obtain a first impression of the group's recent history. The data we use for the overview is that disclosed by the company itself. The key figures we want to use are for turnover, net assets, operating profit, profit after tax and earnings per share. Frequently the five-year record does not provide exactly the figures we want. We must then use the closest available approximations. The resulting overview statement is shown opposite. The share price data come from the *Financial Times*.

After studying the statement opposite, please turn to the detailed figures shown in the accounts and notes to find the information needed for the financial ratio analysis for 1989 and 1990 (to be completed on pages 283 and 285).

(To fit suitably on our pages, notes 12 and 21 are slightly out of number order.)

ICI – OVERVIEW ANALYSIS 1986 – 1990

Year ended 31 December	1986	1987	1988	1989	1990
Key figures £ million					
Turnover	10 136	11 123	11 699	13 171	12 906
Total assets less current liabilities	6 149	5 817	6 390	7 653	7 393
Trading profit	1 049	1 297	1 470	1 467	1 029
Profit attributable to ordinary shareholders	600	760	881	930	617
Earnings per share (pence)	92.0	113.6	129.7	135.0	87.9
Growth %					
Turnover		9.7	5.2	12.6	(2.0)
Total assets less current liabilities		(5.4)	9.9	19.8	(3.4)
Trading profit		23.6	13.3	(0.2)	(29.9)
Profit attributable to ordinary shareholders		26.7	15.9	5.6	(33.7)
Earnings per share (pence)		23.5	14.2	4.1	(34.9)
Retail Prices Index		3.7	6.8	7.7	9.3
Stock market information					
Company share price (end March)	1 313	980	1 181	1 082	1 052
Annual % change					
Company share price		(25.4)	20.5	(8.4)	(2.8)
FT All-Share Index		(8.6)	18.8	3.6	6.5
FT Industry Index		(17.9)	23.1	(1.3)	3.2

GROUP PROFIT AND LOSS ACCOUNT
For the year ended 31 December 1990

	Notes	1990 £ m	1989 £ m
Turnover		12,906	13,171
Operating costs	2	(12,057)	(11,884)
Other operating costs	2	180	180
Trading profit	2	1,029	1,467
Share of profits less losses of associated undertakings	3	154	279
Net interest payable	4	(206)	(219)
Profit on ordinary activities before taxation		977	1,527
Tax on profit on ordinary activities	5	(338)	(531)
Profit on ordinary activities after taxation		639	996
Attributable to minorities		(22)	(66)
Net profit attributable to parent company		617	930
Extraordinary items	7	53	127
Net profit for the financial year		670	1,057
Dividends	8	(389)	(381)
Profit retained for year		281	676
Earnings before extraordinary items per £1 Ordinary Share	9	87.9p	135.0p

GROUP RESERVES ATTRIBUTABLE TO PARENT COMPANY

	Note	1990 £ m	1989 £ m
At beginning of year		4,320	3,242
Profit retained for year			
Company		381	25
Subsidiary undertakings		(53)	621
Associated undertakings		(47)	30
		281	676
Amounts taken direct to reserves		(638)	402
At end of year	21	3,963	4,320

BALANCE SHEETS
At 31 December 1990

		Group		Company	
	Notes	1990 £ m	1989 £ m	1990 £ m	1989 £ m
ASSETS EMPLOYED					
Fixed assets					
Tangible assets	10	4,947	4,856	1,074	999
Investments:					
Subsidiary undertakings	11			4,189	4,375
Participating interests	12	483	767	220	223
		5,430	5,623	5,483	5,597
Current assets					
Stocks	13	2,214	2,380	395	421
Debtors	14	2,590	2,885	1221	702
Investments and short-term deposits	15	388	250	–	18
Cash	15	177	133	7	20
		5,369	5,648	1,623	1,161
Total assets		10,799	11,271	7,106	6,758
Creditors due within one year					
Short-term borrowings	16	(447)	(771)	(5)	(48)
Current instalments of loans	20	(78)	(109)		
Other creditors	17	(2,881)	(2,738)	(814)	(1,855)
		(3,406)	(3,618)	(819)	(1,903)
Net current assets (liabilities)		1,963	2,030	804	(742)
Total assets less current liabilities		7,393	7,653	6,287	4,855
FINANCED BY					
Creditors due after more than one year					
Loans	20	1,670	1,627	555	574
Other creditors	17	154	86	1,698	540
		1,824	1,713	2,253	1,114
Provisions for liabilities and charges	18	549	497	39	(38)
Deferred income: Grants not yet credited to profit		63	94	6	8
Minority interests		286	335		
Capital and reserves attributable to parent company					
Called-up share capital	19	708	694	708	694
Reserves					
Share premium account		446	384	446	384
Revaluation reserve		50	56		
Other reserves		381	486	533	768
Profit and loss account		3,014	3,096	2,302	1,925
Associated undertakings' reserves		72	298		
Total reserves	21	3,963	4,320	3,281	3,077
Total capital and reserves attributable to parent company		4,671	5,014	3,989	3,771
		7,393	7,653	6,287	4,855

The accounts on pages 32 to 57 were approved by the Board of Directors on 11 March 1991 and were signed on its behalf by:

Sir Denys Henderson *Director*
C. M. Short *Director*
P.G. Rogerson *General Manager – Finance*

STATEMENT OF SOURCES AND APPLICATIONS OF GROUP FUNDS
For the year ended 31 December 1990

	Notes	1990 £ m	1989 £ m
SOURCES			
Funds generated from operations			
Trading profit		1,029	1,467
Depreciation		525	536
Dividends from associated undertakings		69	135
Extraordinary charges	‡	(7)	–
Miscellaneous items, including exchange		77	(165)
		1,693	1,973
Less: interest and taxation paid during year			
Interest (net)		(205)	(221)
Taxation		(424)	(593)
Sources net of interest and taxation		1,064	1,159
APPLICATIONS			
Dividends paid during year			
Parent company		384	364
Subsidiary undertakings to minority shareholders		37	42
		421	406
Fixed assets			
Tangible assets		1,013	1,080
Disposals of tangible assets		(160)	(61)
Acquisitions and new investments	22	497	373
Disposals of business and undertakings	22	(747)	(579)
		603	813
Working capital changes			
Stocks decrease (1989 increase)		(74)	219
Debtors decrease (1989 increase)		(186)	450†
Creditors increase (excluding dividends, interest and taxation)		(107)	(131)
		(367)	538
Total applications		657	1,757
Surplus (1989 Deficit)		407	(598)
FINANCED BY			
Issues of ICI Ordinary Shares		141	101
Movement in other external finance		94	(5)
Increase in loans (1989 decrease)		17	(53)
Decrease in short-term borrowings (1989 increase)		(477)	482
Increase in cash, current asset investments and short-term deposits (1989 decrease)	*	(182)	73
		(407)	598

† Includes an amount of £239m received on 2 January 1990 in respect of the disposal of ICI's over-the-counter pharmaceuticals business in the USA.

‡ Represents the cash effect of extraordinary items (note 7) other than those relating to disposals.

* Represents the difference between amounts shown in the opening and closing balance sheets. Other items do not correspond to the change in balance sheet amounts, due to effects of acquisitions and disposals of subsidiary undertakings and effects of retranslating opening currency balances of overseas subsidiary undertakings at closing exchange rates.

NOTES RELATING TO THE ACCOUNTS

1 COMPOSITION OF THE GROUP

The Group accounts consolidate the accounts of Imperial Chemical Industries PLC (the Company) and its subsidiary undertakings, of which there were 628 at 31 December 1990. Owing to local conditions and to avoid undue delay in the presentation of the Group accounts, 105 subsidiaries, representing 10 per cent of Group total assets, made up their accounts to dates earlier than 31 December, but not earlier than 30 September.

2 TRADING PROFIT

	1990 £ m	1989 £ m
Turnover	12,906	13,171
Operating costs		
Cost of sales	(7,885)	(7,901)
Distribution costs	(883)	(881)
Research and development (£591m (1989 £559m)) and technical service (£88m (1989 £80m))	(679)	(639)
Administrative and other expenses	(2,571)	(2,401)
Employees' profit-sharing bonus	(39)	(62)
	(12,057)	(11,884)
Other operating income		
Government grants	30	27
Royalties	32	31
Other income	118	122
	180	180
Trading profit	1,029	1,467
Total charge for depreciation included above	525	536
Gross profit, as defined by the Companies Act 1985	5,021	5,270

3 SHARE OF PROFITS LESS LOSSES OF ASSOCIATED UNDERTAKINGS

	1990 £ m	1989 £ m
Share of profits less losses		
Dividend income	69	135
Share of undistributed profits less losses	66	88
Share of profits less losses before tax	135	223
Gains less losses on disposals of investments	22	51
Amounts written off investments (including provisions raised £3m (1989 £5m) and released £nil (£10m))	(3)	5
	154	279

4 NET INTEREST PAYABLE

	1990 £ m	1989 £ m
Interest payable and similar charges		
Loan interest	155	175
Interest on short-term borrowings and other financing costs	125	112
	280	287
Interest receivable and similar income from current asset investments		
Listed redeemable securities	(9)	(8)
Short-term deposits	(64)	(57)
	(73)	(65)
Exchange gains on short-term currency borrowing and deposits	(1)	(3)
	206	219

5 TAX ON PROFIT ON ORDINARY ACTIVITIES

	1990 £m	1989 £m
ICI and subsidiary undertakings		
United Kingdom taxation: Corporation tax	109	206
Double taxation relief	(43)	(43)
Deferred taxation	2	19
	68	182
Overseas taxation: Overseas taxes	186	250
Deferred taxation	39	22
	225	272
	293	454
Associated undertakings	45	77
Tax on profit on ordinary activities	338	531

Deferred taxation

The amounts of deferred taxation accounted for at the balance sheet date and the potential amounts of deferred taxation are disclosed below.

	Group 1990 £m	Group 1989 £m	Company 1990 £m	Company 1989 £m
Accounted for at balance sheet date (see note 18)				
Timing differences on UK capital allowances and depreciation	63	53		
Miscellaneous timing differences	10	125	10	17
Advance corporation tax recoverable	(80)	(79)	(80)	(79)
	(7)	99	(70)	(62)
Not accounted for at balance sheet date				
UK capital allowances utilized in excess of depreciation charged	330	324	151	157
Miscellaneous timing differences	(65)	16	11	1
	265	340	162	158
Full potential deferred taxation	258	439	92	96

6 SEGMENT INFORMATION

Geographic areas

The information opposite is re-analysed in the table below by geographic area. The figures for each geographic area show the net operating assets owned by and the turnover and profits made by companies located in that area; export sales and related profits are included in the areas from which those sales were made.

	Net operating assets 1990 £m	Net operating assets 1989 £m	Turnover 1990 £m	Turnover 1989 £m	Profit 1990 £m	Profit 1989 £m
United Kingdom						
Sales in the UK			2,966	2,872		
Sales overseas			3,160	3,359		
	2,801	2,580	6,126	6,231	295	612
Continental Europe	1,061	1,026	3,152	2,928	157	225
The Americas	1,494	1,839	3,651	3,876	382	382
Asia Pacific	863	1,058	2,047	2,100	136	236
Other countries	155	175	403	451	29	45
	6,374	6,678	15,379	15,586	999	1,500
Inter-area eliminations			(2,473)	(2,415)	30	(33)
			12,906	13,171		
Trading profit					1,029	1,467

Industry segments

The table below sets out information, on a worldwide basis, for each of the Group's industry segments. The Group's policy is to transfer products internally at external market prices.

	Total assets less current liabilities 1990 £m	1989 £m	Turnover 1990 £m	1989 £m	Profit 1990 £m	1989 £m
Consumer and Specialty Products	2,534	2,756	5,351	5,297	600	568
Industrial Products	2,703	2,614	5,640	5,722	324	789
Agriculture	1,137	1,308	2,190	2,257	122	141
Miscellaneous			199	242	(20)	(33)
			13,380	13,518	1,026	1,465
Net operating assets	6,374	6,678				
Inter-segment eliminations			(474)	(347)	3	2
Non-operating and miscellaneous assets	1,019	975				
	7,393	7,653	12,906	13,171		
Trading profit					1,029	1,467
Share of profits less losses of associated undertakings					154	279
Net interest payable					(206)	(219)
Profit on ordinary activities before taxation					977	1,527

Non-operating and miscellaneous assets include assets in course of construction, investments in associated undertakings and other participating interests, current asset investments, short-term deposits and cash, less short-term borrowings.

	Capital expenditure 1990 £m	1989 £m	Depreciation 1990 £m	1989 £m
Consumer and Specialty Products	405	517	198	177
Industrial Products	475	388	196	230
Agriculture	109	154	92	103
Other	24	21	39	26
	1,013	1,080	525	536

7 EXTRAORDINARY ITEMS

	Group 1990 £m	1989 £m
Gain on disposal of the investment in Enterprise Oil plc (net of charge for taxation of £9m)	520	
Charge for reshaping the ICI Group business portfolio, comprising withdrawals through business divestments, closures and other restructuring measures. The charge is net of estimated disposal proceeds and includes the expense of obtaining substantial cost reductions which are a significant part of the objective (net of tax relief of £50m of which £46m is deferred)	(300)	
Charge for the withdrawal from UK compound fertilizer manufacture and restructuring, with a view to ultimate divestment, of the ammonium nitrate business (net of tax relief of £12m of which £9m is deferred)	(128)	
ICI's share of an extraordinary item in Tioxide Group PLC, whilst an associated undertaking, relating to its fundamental restructuring (net of tax relief of £2m)	(39)	
Disposal of over-the-counter pharmaceuticals business in the USA (net of deferred tax of £83m)		127
	53	127

The gain on disposal of the investment in Enterprise Oil plc is the difference between the proceeds on disposal and the holding value of the investment. The holding value of the investment and associated undertakings' reserves had been reduced by £134m in the Group accounts reflecting ICI's share of goodwill adjustments to reserves made in the accounts of Enterprise Oil plc.

8 DIVIDENDS

	1990	1989	1990	1989
	pence per £1 Share		£ m	£ m
Interim, paid 1 October 1990	21p	21p	148	145
Second interim, to be confirmed as final, payable 25 April 1991	34p	34p	241	236
	55p	55p	389	381

9 EARNINGS BEFORE EXTRAORDINARY ITEMS PER £1 ORDINARY SHARE

	1990	1989
Earnings for Ordinary Shareholders, before extraordinary items (£m)	617	930
Average Ordinary Shares in issue during year, weighted on a time basis (millions)	702	689
Earnings per £1 Ordinary Share	87.9p	135.0p

10 TANGIBLE FIXED ASSETS

	Land and buildings £ m	Plant and equipment £ m	Payments on account and assets in course of construction £ m	Total £ m
GROUP				
Cost or as revalued				
At beginning of year	1,744	6,983	919	9,646
Exchange adjustments	(168)	(472)	(86)	(726)
Revaluations and adjustments	2	8		10
New subsidiary undertakings	68	244	69	381
Capital expenditure			1,013	1,013
Transfers	162	834	(996)	—
Disposals and other movements	(61)	(676)		(737)
At end of year	1,747	6,921	919	9,587
Depreciation				
At beginning of year	628	4,162		4,790
Exchange adjustments	(48)	(232)		(280)
Revaluations and adjustments	1	4		5
Disposals and other movements	(34)	(531)		(565)
Charge for year	67	623		690
At end of year	614	4,026		4,640
Net book value at end 1990	1,133	2,895	919	4,947
Net book value at end 1989	1,116	2,821	919	4,856

The Group depreciation charge of £690m shown above comprises £525m charged in arriving at trading profit and £165m charged under extraordinary items.

The net book value of the tangible fixed assets of the Group includes capitalized finance leases of £56m comprising cost of £123m and depreciation thereon of £67m. The depreciation charge for the year in respect of capitalized leases was £6m and finance charges £12m.

	Group 1990 £ m	1989 £ m	Company 1990 £ m	1989 £ m
The net book value of land and buildings comprised:				
Freeholds	1,077	1,063	263	235
Long leases (over 50 years unexpired)	40	39	5	5
Short leases	16	14		
	1,133	1,116	268	240

	Group				Plant and	
	Land and buildings			Plant and equipment		
	1990	1989		1990	1989	
Revalued assets included in tangible fixed assets	£ m	£ m		£ m	£ m	
At revalued amount	128	159		175	240	
Depreciation	51	65		140	185	
Net book value	77	94		35	55	
At historical cost	67	83		149	211	
Depreciation	33	42		127	178	
Net book value	34	41		22	33	

11 INVESTMENTS IN SUBSIDIARY UNDERTAKINGS

	Shares £ m	Loans £ m	Total £ m
Cost			
At beginning of year	2,632	1,866	4,498
Exchange adjustments	(199)	(212)	(411)
Additions	549	615	1,164
Disposals	(4)		(4)
Transfers to subsidiary undertakings	(667)		(667)
Repayments		(222)	(222)
At end of year	2,311	2,047	4,358
Provisions			
At beginning of year	(111)	(12)	(123)
Exchange adjustments	5		5
Additions	(66)	(3)	(69)
Releases	12	6	18
At end of year	(160)	(9)	(169)
Balance sheet value at end 1990	2,151	2,038	4,189
Balance sheet value at end 1989	2,521	1,854	4,375

Cost includes scrip issues capitalized £38m (1989 £38m).

	1990 £ m	1989 £ m
Shares in subsidiary undertakings which are listed investments:		
Balance sheet value	63	77
Market value	341	610

13 STOCKS

	Group 1990 £ m	1989 £ m	Company 1990 £ m	1989 £ m
Raw materials and consumables	652	669	106	110
Stocks in process	237	277	78	86
Finished goods and goods for resale	1,325	1,434	211	225
	2,214	2,380	395	421

14 DEBTORS

	Group 1990 £ m	1989 £ m	Company 1990 £ m	1989 £ m
Amounts due within one year				
Trade debtors	1,922	2,071	—	3
Amounts owed by subsidiary undertakings			1,102	620
Amounts owed by associated undertakings	33	21	1	1
Other debtors*	373	572	79	63
Prepayments and accrued income	151	126	36	14
	2,479	2,790	1,218	701
Amounts due after more than one year*	111	95	3	1
	2,590	2,885	1,221	702

12 INVESTMENTS IN PARTICIPATING INTERESTS

	Associated undertakings Shares £m	Associated undertakings Loans £m	Other participating interests £m	Total £m
GROUP				
Cost				
At beginning of year	475	5	15	495
Exchange adjustments	(25)	(1)		(26)
Additions	214	8	3	225
Reclassified as subsidiary undertakings	(29)			(29)
Disposals and repayments	(236)	(2)	(1)	(239)
At end of year	399	10	17	426
Share of post-acquisition reserves less losses				
At beginning of year	300			300
Exchange adjustments	(33)			(33)
Retained profits less losses	(47)			(47)
Reclassified as subsidiary undertakings	(86)			(86)
Disposals	(53)			(53)
Other movements	(7)			(7)
At end of year	74			74
Provisions				
At beginning of year	(24)	(3)	(1)	(28)
Exchange adjustments	2			2
Other movements	10	(1)		9
At end of year	(12)	(4)	(1)	(17)
Balance sheet value at end 1990	461	6	16	483
Balance sheet value at end 1989	751	2	14	767

Cost includes scrip issues capitalized £5m (1989 £9m).

The above investments included:
1990

Investments listed on The International Stock Exchange, London	21		2	23
Other listed investments	111			111
Balance sheet value	132		2	134
Market value	192		10	202
1989				
Investments listed on The International Stock Exchange, London	295		2	297
Other listed investments	120			120
Balance sheet value	415		2	417
Market value	1,020		16	1,036

16 SHORT-TERM BORROWINGS

Bank borrowings				
Secured by – fixed charge	3	1		
– floating charge	14	25		
Unsecured	353	648	4	48
	370	674	4	48
Other borrowings (unsecured)	77	97	1	
	447	771	5	48

17 OTHER CREDITORS

Amounts due within one year				
Trade creditors	1,083	1,108	143	132
Amounts owed to subsidiary undertakings			145	1,271
Amounts owed to associated undertakings	9	25	–	4
Corporate taxation	284	333	118	74
Value added and payroll taxes and social security	101	93	–	7
Other creditors*	797	660	107	70
Accruals	366	283	60	61
Dividends to Ordinary Shareholders	241	236	241	236
	2,881	2,738	814	1,855
Amounts due after more than one year				
Amounts owed to subsidiary undertakings			1,686	534
Other creditors*	154	86	12	6
	154	86	1,698	540

* Includes costs charged as extraordinary in 1990, obligations under finance leases (note 23) and accrued pension costs (note 28).

18 PROVISIONS FOR LIABILITIES AND CHARGES

	At beginning of year £m	Profit and loss account £m	Amounts paid or becoming current £m	Acquisition and other movements £m	At end of year £m
GROUP					
Deferred taxation:					
Advance corporation tax recoverable	(79)		(1)		(80)
Other tax†	178	(14)	(67)	(24)	73
	99	(14)	(68)	(24)	(7)
Employee benefits*	178	40	(10)	4	212
Reshaping, environmental and other provisions	220	185	(76)	15	344
	497	211	(154)	(5)	549

†The movement in the year includes taxation arising on the extraordinary items.
*Includes provisions for unfunded pension costs (note 28).

19 CALLED-UP SHARE CAPITAL OF PARENT COMPANY

	Authorized £m	Allotted, called-up and fully paid 1990 £m	1989 £m
Ordinary Shares (£1 each)	708	708	694
Unclassified shares (£1 each)	142		
	850	708	694

The number of Ordinary Shares issued during the year totalled 13.7m comprising issues in respect of the acquisition of Tyler Corporation 6.7m, the Employees' Profit-Sharing Scheme 4.0m, and conversions of loan stock and exercise of warrants and options 3.0m.

At 31 December 1990 there were options outstanding in respect of 14,886,235 Ordinary Shares of £1 under the Company's share option schemes for staff (1989 12,531,895) normally exercisable in the period 1991 to 2000 (1990 to 1999) at subscription prices of £5.95 to £15.12 (£5.33 to £15.12). The weighted average subscription price of options outstanding at 31 December 1990 was £10.03.

20 LOANS

	Repayment dates	Group 1990 £ m	Group 1989 £ m	Company 1990 £ m	Company 1989 £ m
Secured loans					
US dollars (5½ to 10⅞%)	1991/2012	38	51		
Australian dollars (10.3 to 17.1%)	1991/97	39	56		
Other currencies	1991/99	71	49		
Total secured		148	156		
Secured by fixed charge		142	146		
Secured by floating charge		6	10		
Unsecured loans					
Sterling:					
9¾ to 11¼% bonds	1992/2005	400	400	400	400
9¾% Notes	1993	75	75	75	75
8½% convertible bonds	1999		13		
Others	1991/96	128	41		
		603	529	475	475
US dollars:					
9¾% bonds	1990		28		
7½% to 8% Eurodollar bonds	1991/96	54	66		
8⅛ to 9.05% bonds	1991/2006	268	333		
8.85 to 8.9% medium-term notes	1994/2002	26	31		
9½% Notes	2000	156			
Others	1991/2013	73	51		
		577	509		
Australian dollars (9.6 to 15½%)	1991/93	86	106	80	99
Canadian dollars (10⅝ to 14½%)	1991/96	68	87		
Swiss francs (3½ to 4½%)	1991/99	175	180		
Other currencies	1991/2002	91	94		
Multi-currency credit facility†			75		
Total unsecured		1,600	1,580	555	574
Total loans		1,748	1,736	555	574

† Variable interest; repayable and redrawable at borrower's option.

	Group 1990 £ m	Group 1989 £ m	Company 1990 £ m	Company 1989 £ m
Loans or instalments thereof are repayable:				
After 5 years from balance sheet date:				
Lump sums	617	608	200	200
Instalments	222	219	–	62
	839	827	200	262
From 2 to 5 years	603	643	200	312
From 1 to 2 years	228	157	155	–
Total due after more than one year	1,670	1,627	555	574
Total due within one year	78	109		
	1,748	1,736	555	574
Aggregate amount of loans repayable by instalments any of which fall due after 5 years	489	462	–	125

22 ACQUISITIONS, NEW INVESTMENTS AND DISPOSALS

During the year the Group acquired interests in the following undertakings all of which have been accounted for by the acquisition method of accounting. The effect of these acquisitions on the Group results was not material.

Tioxide Group PLC – remaining 50% ordinary shareholding not already owned
Tyler Corporation (parent company of Atlas Powder Company and its subsidiary undertakings)
Edward J. Funk & Sons, Inc
CXA Ltd – remaining 30% shareholding not already owned
'Novacote' Division of Weserland-Farbenfabrik von Höveling GmbH

Net assets acquired:
The fair value adjustments made to the net assets and liabilities acquired are set out in the table below:

	Book value at acquisition £ m	Re-valuations £ m	Provisions £ m	Accounting policy alignments £ m	Fair value to the Group £ m
Fixed assets	404	13		(15)	402
Current assets	336	(3)		6	339
Total assets	740	10		(9)	741
Deferred income	5				5
Provisions for liabilities and charges	8		38	(3)	43
Creditors					
Loans	172				172
Short-term borrowings	152				152
Other	158		18	1	177
Total liabilities	495		56	(2)	549
Minorities	5				5
Net assets	240	10	(56)	(7)	187

Attributable to the Group's 50% shareholding in Tioxide Group PLC prior to acquisition of remaining shareholding	101
Net assets of subsidiary undertakings acquired	86
Goodwill	210
Fair value of consideration for subsidiary undertakings	296
Investment in participating interests	201
Acquisitions and new investments	497

Consideration for acquisitions and new investments:

Shares allotted and to be allotted, including share premium	79
Cash	418
	497

Statutory share premium relief under Section 131 of the Companies Act 1985 has been taken in respect of the acquisition of Tyler Corporation; goodwill written off to reserves has been reduced by £65m being the premium on the shares issued in 1990 (see note 21).

Fixed and current assets are adjusted to fair value based on external valuations and internal reviews; provisions for closure are made where appropriate. Other acquisition provisions reflect the projected costs of reorganisation, integration of the businesses acquired and provisions for environmental improvements.

Disposals
Proceeds from disposals of businesses and subsidiary undertakings in 1990 amounted to £47m (1989 £458m) and of participating interests amounted to £700m (£121m) of which £679m related to the disposal of Enterprise Oil plc.

23 LEASES

The total rentals under operating leases, charged as an expense in the profit and loss account, are disclosed below.

	Group 1990 £ m	1989 £ m
Hire of plant and machinery	87	116
Other	52	38
	139	154

Commitments under operating leases to pay rentals during the year following the year of these accounts are given in the table below, analysed according to the period in which each lease expires.

	Group 1990 £ m	1989 £ m	Company 1990 £ m	1989 £ m
Land and buildings:				
Expiring within 1 year	9	4		
Expiring in years 2 to 5	10	18		
Expiring thereafter	14	15	4	2
	33	37	4	2
Other assets:				
Expiring within 1 year	24	17	3	2
Expiring in years 2 to 5	46	61	12	3
Expiring thereafter	5	8	1	1
	75	86	16	6

Obligations under finance leases comprise:

	Group 1990 £ m	1989 £ m	Company 1990 £ m	1989 £ m
Rentals due within 1 year	24	6	1	1
Rentals due in years 2 to 5	100	17	4	4
Rentals due thereafter	38	48	2	3
Less: interest element	(64)	(39)	(2)	(3)
	98	32	5	5

Obligations under finance leases are included in other creditors (note 17).

24 EMPLOYEE COSTS

The average number of people employed by the Group in 1990 was 132,100 (1989 133,800) and the staff costs incurred during the year in respect of those employees were:

	1990 £ m	1989 £ m
Salaries	2,270	2,094
Social security costs	216	189
Pension costs	151	143
Severance costs	69	46
Other employment costs	73	68
Employees' profit-sharing bonus	39	62
	2,818	2,602
Less: amounts allocated to capital expenditure, etc.	(50)	(44)
Charged in arriving at trading profit	2,768	2,558
Severance payments made during the year relating to extra-ordinary items*	6	–
Total employee costs in respect of people employed by the Group	2,774	2,558

* Included in this item is an amount to bring severance costs shown above, which include accrued costs, to payments made in year.

21 RESERVES

	Share premium account £ m	Revaluation £ m	Other £ m	Profit and loss account £ m	Associated undertakings £ m	1990 Total £ m	1989 Total £ m
GROUP							
Reserves attributable to parent company							
At beginning of year	384	56	486	3,096	298	4,320	3,242
Profit retained for year				328	(47)	281	676
Amounts taken direct to reserves							
Share premiums	62	65†				127	90
Goodwill		(65)†	(145)		(145)*	(355)	(41)
Exchange adjustments		(8)	(138)	(231)	(33)	(410)	367
Other movements			3		(3)	–	(14)
	62	(8)	(135)	(376)	(181)	(638)	402
Other movements between reserves		2	30	(34)	2		
At end of year	446	50	381	3,014	72	3,963	4,320

* Includes ICI's share of goodwill adjustments to reserves made in the accounts of Enterprise Oil plc.

In the Group accounts, £116m of net exchange gains on foreign currency loans (1989 losses £69m) have been offset in reserves against exchange losses on the net investment in overseas subsidiary and associated undertakings.

The cumulative amount of goodwill resulting from acquisitions during 1990 and prior years, net of goodwill attributable to subsidiary undertakings or businesses disposed of prior to 31 December 1990, amounted to £1,708m (1989 £1,504m).

For the purpose of calculating the basis of the borrowing limits in accordance with the Articles of Association, the total of the sums standing to the credit of capital and revenue reserves of the Company and its subsidiary undertakings, to be added to the nominal amount of the share capital of the Company, was £5,082m at 31 December 1990.

27 COMMITMENTS AND CONTINGENT LIABILITIES

	Group 1990 £ m	1989 £ m	Company 1990 £ m	1989 £ m
Commitments for capital expenditure not provided for in these accounts (including acquisitions):				
Contracts placed for future expenditure	357	261	37	60
Expenditure authorized but not yet contracted	569	910	126	174
	926	1,171	163	234

AUDITORS' REPORT

To the Members of Imperial Chemical Industries PLC.

We have audited the financial statements on pages 32 to 57 in accordance with Auditing Standards.

In our opinion these financial statements give a true and fair view of the state of affairs of the Company and the Group at 31 December 1990 and of the profit and sources and applications of funds of the Group for the year ended and have been properly prepared in accordance with the Companies Act 1985.

London
11 March 1991

KPMG Peat Marwick McLintock
Chartered Accountants

FINANCIAL RATIO ANALYSIS

Performance ratios

	1990	1989
Return on equity		
Tax ratio		
Return on net assets		
Return on fixed asset investments		
Return on net operating assets		
Operating profit margin		
Net operating asset turnover		
Tangible fixed asset turnover		
Stock days (sales basis)		
Trade debtors days (sales basis)		
Trade creditors days (COGS basis)		

When you have calculated all the ratios, compare your figures with those shown overleaf.

283

		1990			**1989**	
Return on equity %	(1)	$\dfrac{617}{4671}$	= 13.2		$\dfrac{930}{5014}$	= 18.5
Tax ratio %		$\dfrac{338}{977}$	= 34.6		$\dfrac{531}{1527}$	= 34.8
Return on net assets	(2)	$\dfrac{977 + 280}{7393 + 447 + 78 + 24}$ $\dfrac{1257^*}{7942}$	= 15.8		$\dfrac{1527 + 287}{7653 + 771 + 109 + 6}$ $\dfrac{1814}{8539}$	= 21.2
Return on fixed asset investments %	(3)	$\dfrac{135}{483}$	= 28.0		$\dfrac{223}{767}$	= 29.1
Return on net operating assets %		$\dfrac{977 + 280 - 135}{7393 + 447 + 78 + 24 - 483} = \dfrac{1122}{7459}$	= 15.0		$\dfrac{1527 + 287 - 223}{7653 + 771 + 109 + 6 - 767} = \dfrac{1591}{7772}$	= 20.5
Operating profit margin %		$\dfrac{1122}{12906}$	= 8.7		$\dfrac{1591}{13171}$	= 12.1
Net operating asset turnover		$\dfrac{12906}{7459}$	= 1.73		$\dfrac{13171}{7772}$	= 1.69
Tangible fixed asset turnover	(4)	$\dfrac{12906}{4947 - 919} = \dfrac{12906}{4028}$	= 3.20		$\dfrac{13171}{4856 - 919} = \dfrac{13171}{3937}$	= 3.35
Stock (days) (sales basis)	(5)	$\dfrac{12906}{2214}$	= 5.83 62.6 days		$\dfrac{13171}{2380}$	= 5.53 66.0 days
Trade debtors (days) (sales basis)		$\dfrac{12906}{1922}$	= 6.71 54.4 days		$\dfrac{13171}{2071}$	= 6.36 57.4 days
Trade creditors (days) (COGS basis)		$\dfrac{7885}{1083}$	= 7.28 50.1 days		$\dfrac{7901}{1108}$	= 7.13 51.2 days

Notes

1 This ratio measures return on ordinary shareholders' funds.
2 In this ratio we compare PBIT with net assets. We add interest paid (Note 4) to profit before tax. We add to total assets less current liabilities the short-term borrowings, current instalments of loans (balance sheet) and obligations under finance leases <1 yr (note 23).
3 Fixed asset investment income is shown in Note 3. The investments (Note 12) include associated undertakings and other participating interests.
4 In calculating tangible fixed asset turnover, we exclude assets in course of construction £919 million (Note 10).
5 An alternative ratio is stock days on cost of sales basis.

Financial status ratios*		1990	1989
Solvency			
Debt/capital employed	(1)		
	(2)		
Interest cover			
Liquidity			
Current ratio	(1)		
	(2)		
Acid test	(1)		
	(2)		

Stock market ratios

Share price 1989 1082 p.
           1990 1052 p.

Earnings per share

Price/earnings ratio

Dividend yield %

Dividend cover (times)

*Treat current instalment of bank loans, overdrafts and current lease finance as (1) Capital employed, (2) Current liabilities.

Note

When you have calculated the ratios, compare your figures with those shown overleaf. If your figures are different, find out why. You may have made different assumptions which may be quite valid, in which case your figures would not be 'wrong'.

		1990		**1989**	
Solvency					
Total debt/Capital employed %	(1)	$\dfrac{1670 + 447 + 78 + 98}{7393 + 447 + 78 + 24} = \dfrac{2293}{7942}$	= 28.9	$\dfrac{1627 + 771 + 109 + 32}{7653 + 771 + 109 + 6} = \dfrac{2539}{8539}$	= 29.7
Long-term debt/Capital employed	(2)	$\dfrac{1670 + 74}{7393} = \dfrac{1744}{7393}$	= 23.6	$\dfrac{1627 + 26}{7653} = \dfrac{1653}{7653}$	= 21.6
Interest cover		$\dfrac{1257}{280}$	= 4.49	$\dfrac{1814}{287}$	= 6.32
Liquidity					
Current ratio	(1)	$\dfrac{5369}{3406 - 447 - 78 - 24} = \dfrac{5369}{2857}$	= 1.88	$\dfrac{5648}{3618 - 771 - 109 - 6} = \dfrac{5648}{2732}$	= 2.07
	(2)	$\dfrac{5369}{3406}$	= 1.58	$\dfrac{5648}{3618}$	= 1.56
Acid test	(1)	$\dfrac{5369 - 2214}{2857} = \dfrac{3155}{2857}$	= 1.10	$\dfrac{5648 - 2380}{2732} = \dfrac{3268}{2732}$	= 1.20
	(2)	$\dfrac{3155}{3406}$	= 0.93	$\dfrac{3268}{3618}$	= 0.90
Stock market ratios					
Earnings per share (Note 9)		$\dfrac{617}{702}$	= 87.9p	$\dfrac{930}{689}$	= 135.0p
Price earnings ratio (March price)		$\dfrac{1052}{87.9}$	= 12.0	$\dfrac{1082}{135.0}$	= 8.0
Dividend yield (%)	(3)	$\dfrac{55.0 \times 100/75}{1052} = \dfrac{73.3}{1052}$	= 6.97	$\dfrac{55.0 \times 100/75}{1082} = \dfrac{73.3}{1082}$	= 6.78
Dividend cover (times)		$\dfrac{87.9}{55.0}$	= 1.60	$\dfrac{135.0}{55.0}$	= 2.45

Notes

1   Debt includes longer-term borrowing, finance leases and short-term borrowings (Notes 17, 20 and 23).

2   Short-term borrowings, current loan instalments and current finance leases are treated as current liabilities (Notes 16, 17 and 23).

3   Yields are normally stated gross of taxation. The basic income tax rate was 25 per cent in 1989 and 1990.

GROUP FINANCIAL RECORD

For the years ended 31 December

	1986 £ m	1987 £ m	1988 £ m	1989 £ m	1990 £ m
Balance sheet					
Tangible fixed assets	3,912	3,750	4,092	4,856	4,947
Investments	333	417	524	767	483
Current assets					
Stocks	1,734	1,812	2,004	2,380	2,214
Debtors	2,015	2,162	2,324	2,885	2,590
Cash and short-term investments	692	646	456	383	565
	4,441	4,620	4,784	5,648	5,369
Total assets	8,686	8,787	9,400	11,271	10.799
Creditors due within one year:					
Short-term borrowings	(441)	(559)	(289)	(771)	(447)
Current instalments of loans	(74)	(46)	(50)	(109)	(78)
Other creditors	(2,022)	(2,365)	(2,671)	(2,738)	(2,881)
Total assets less current liabilities	6,149	5,817	6,390	7,653	7,393
Creditors due after more than one year:					
Loans	1,538	1,511	1,627	1,627	1,670
Other creditors	83	70	137	86	154
Provisions and deferred income	459	434	397	591	612
Minority interests	404	357	304	335	286
Capital and reserves attributable to parent company	3,665	3,445	3,925	5,014	4,671
	6,149	5,817	6,390	7,653	7,393
Turnover and profits					
Turnover	10,136	11,123	11,699	13,171	12,906
Trading profit (after depreciation)	1,049	1,297	1,470	1,467	1,029
Depreciation	491	464	484	536	525
Share of profits less losses of associated undertakings	95	157	162	279	154
Interest other than loan interest (net)	7	8	(2)	(44)	(51)
Profit before loan interest	1,151	1,462	1,630	1,702	1,132
Loan interest	(135)	(150)	(160)	(175)	(155)
Profit before taxation	1,016	1,312	1,470	1,527	977
Taxation	(382)	(504)	(540)	(531)	(338)
Attributable to minorities	(34)	(48)	(49)	(66)	(22)
Net profit attributable to parent company, before extraordinary items	600	760	881	930	617
Extraordinary items	(43)	–	(44)	127	53
Dividends	(238)	(277)	(341)	(381)	(389)
Profit retained, transferred to reserves	319	483	496	676	281
Sources and applications of funds					
Sources net of interest and taxation	1,062	1,308	1,235	1,159	1,064
Dividends	(249)	(283)	(317)	(406)	(421)
Fixed asset expenditure:					
Tangible assets	(608)	(682)	(766)	(1,019)	(853)
Investments less disposals	(548)	(430)	(116)	206	250
Working capital changes	94	(187)	(77)	(538)	367
Surplus/(Deficit)	(249)	(274)	(41)	(598)	407
Return on assets					
Profit before loan interest as a percentage of assets employed (average total assets less current liabilities)	19.4	24.4	26.7	24.2	15.0

ICI ORDINARY SHARE COMPARISONS

	1986	1987	1988	1989	1990
Millions					
Shares in issue					
At year-end	657	676	683	694	708
Weighted average for year	652	669	679	689	702
£ per £1 Ordinary Share					
Stock Market price					
Highest	11.16	16.45	11.84	13.35	12.51
Lowest	7.27	9.65	9.50	10.13	8.08
Year-end	10.68	10.82	10.13	11.34	8.66
Earnings per £1 Ordinary Share	92p	114p	130p	135p	88p
Dividends					
Dividends (net)	36p	41p	50p	55p	55p
Dividends grossed up for imputed tax credit	51p	56p	67p	73p	73p*
Dividends (net) in 1990 money (adjusted by RPI)	46p	51p	59p	60p	55p
Balance sheet value of Ordinary shareholders' equity at end of year – £ per £1 Ordinary Share	5.58	5.10	5.75	7.22	6.60
Indexed value of the £, expressed in average 1990 £s, based on RPI	1.29	1.24	1.18	1.09	1.00

*Assumes a basic rate of income tax of 25 per cent.

Adjusting key ratios for capitalizing goodwill

The performance and financial status ratios we calculated on pages 284 and 286 were based on the figures provided by the company without adjustment. As we discussed in the section on 'Accounting matters requiring special attention', adjustments often need to be made to the ratios for items which would improve the comparison between companies or between years.

One of the major adjustments to aid analysis is capitalizing any goodwill which has been written off to reserves. This restores the accumulated reserves and increases the assets, significantly affecting not only the return on equity and return on assets ratios, but also the gearing and asset turnover ratios.

Companies from 1990 onwards disclose the accumulated goodwill written off to reserves. In ICI's accounts, note 21 states that £1 708 million of accumulated goodwill has been written off, compared to £1 504 million in 1989. The acquisitions note 22 shows £210 million of goodwill purchased and written off, which agrees with the reserves note 21 after adjusting for the £145 million related to an associate which was disposed of during the year. The difference between the £210 million and the £204 million increase in accumulated goodwill written off (£1 708 million – £1 504 million) is probably due to disposals during the year.

In the table opposite the accumulated goodwill written off each year has been deduced by working back from the 1990 figure and subtracting the yearly movements.

These figures for goodwill should be used to adjust any ratios which include reserves or assets. Amortizing the capitalized goodwill as required for US companies reporting under US GAAP, would also affect the profit ratios.

Using the figures for goodwill and the worksheet provided on the next page, adjust the ratios for the effects of capitalizing goodwill.

Goodwill at cost

		£ m
1986	Opening balance	574
	Goodwill acquired	
	– Glidden companies	222
	– Other, including adjustment in 1987	25
		821
1987	Goodwill acquired	
	– Stauffer companies	456
	– Société Européene de Semences SA	83
	– Other, including adjustments in 1988	19
		1379
1988	Goodwill acquired	
	– Berger (Australasia) + Selley's Chemicals	25
	– BAPCO	21
	– Other, including adjustment in 1989	38
		1463
1989	Goodwill acquired	41
		1504
1990	Goodwill acquired	210
	– Goodwill adjustment	(6)
		1708

FINANCIAL RATIOS ADJUSTED FOR CAPITALIZED GOODWILL

Performance ratios

	1990	1989
Return on equity		
Return on net assets		
Return on net operating assets		
Operating net asset turnover		
Fixed asset turnover		

Financial status ratios

| Debt/capital employed* | (1) | | |
| | (2) | | |

*Treat current instalments of bank loans, overdrafts and current lease finance as (1) Capital employed, (2) Current liabilities.

FINANCIAL RATIOS ADJUSTED FOR CAPITALIZED GOODWILL

Performance ratios		**1990**		**1989**	
Return on equity	$\dfrac{617}{4671 + 1708} = \dfrac{617}{6379}$	= 9.7	$\dfrac{930}{5014 + 1504} = \dfrac{930}{6518}$	= 14.3
Return on net assets	$\dfrac{1257}{7942 + 1708} = \dfrac{1257}{9650}$	= 13.0	$\dfrac{1814}{8539 + 1504} = \dfrac{1814}{10043}$	= 18.1
Return on net operating assets	$\dfrac{1122}{7459 + 1708} = \dfrac{1122}{9167}$	= 12.2	$\dfrac{1591}{7772 + 1504} = \dfrac{1591}{9276}$	= 17.2
Net operating asset turnover	$\dfrac{12906}{7459 + 1708} = \dfrac{12906}{9167}$	= 1.41	$\dfrac{13171}{7772 + 1504} = \dfrac{13171}{9276}$	= 1.42
Fixed asset turnover	$\dfrac{12906}{4028 + 1708} = \dfrac{12906}{5736}$	= 2.25	$\dfrac{13171}{3937 + 1504} = \dfrac{13171}{5441}$	= 2.42

Fixed status ratios

		1990		**1989**	
Debt/Capital employed (1)	$\dfrac{2293}{7942 + 1708} = \dfrac{2293}{9650}$	= 23.8	$\dfrac{2539}{8539 + 1504} = \dfrac{2539}{10043}$	= 25.3
(2)	$\dfrac{1744}{7393 + 1708} = \dfrac{1744}{9101}$	= 19.2	$\dfrac{1653}{7653 + 1504} = \dfrac{1653}{9157}$	= 18.1

ICI
Summary of key figures and ratios
Year ended 31 December

	1986	1987	1988	1989	1990
Performance ratios					
Return on equity (%) (a)	16.4	22.1	22.4	18.5	13.2
(b)	13.4	15.8	16.4	14.3	9.7
Tax ratio (%)	37.6	38.4	36.7	34.8	34.6
Return on net assets % (a)	18.3	23.7	25.2	21.2	15.8
(b)	15.1	19.5	20.7	18.1	13.0
Return on fixed asset investments (%)	26.7	37.4	28.4	29.1	28.0
Return on net op. assets (%)					
(a)	17.8	22.7	24.9	20.5	15.0
(b)	15.8	18.5	20.2	17.2	12.2
Operating profit margin (%)	11.1	12.3	13.2	12.1	8.7
Net operating asset T/O					
(times) (a)	1.60	1.85	1.89	1.69	1.73
(b)	1.42	1.51	1.53	1.42	1.41
Fixed asset turnover					
(times) (a)	2.98	3.55	3.47	3.35	3.20
(b)	2.40	2.46	2.42	2.42	2.25
Stock (days) (sales basis)	62.4	59.5	62.5	66.0	62.6
Trade debtors (days)	58.6	53.2	55.3	57.4	54.4
Trade creditors (days) (COGS basis)	43.7	44.5	50.6	51.2	50.1

(a)   Ratios with goodwill written off to reserves (per the accounts)
(b)   Ratios including capitalized goodwill

ICI
Summary of key figures and ratios (continued)
Year ended 31 December 1990

	1986	1987	1988	1989	1990
Financial status ratios					
Total debt/Capital employed					
% (a)	30.8	32.9	29.2	29.7	28.9
(b)	27.4	27.1	24.0	25.3	23.8
Interest cover (times)	6.0	7.2	7.5	6.3	4.5
Current ratio	2.2	2.0	1.8	2.1	1.9
Acid test	1.3	1.2	1.0	1.2	1.1
Stock market ratios					
Earnings per share	92.0	113.6	129.7	135.0	87.9
Price/earnings ratio	14.3	8.6	9.1	8.0	12.0
Dividend yield %	3.9	5.7	5.6	6.8	7.0
Dividend cover (times)	2.6	2.8	2.6	2.5	1.6
Stock market indicators					
Share price (end March)	1313	980	1181	1082	1052
Annual % change					
Share price	38.0	(25.4)	20.5	(8.4)	(2.8)
All-share index	22.2	(8.6)	18.8	3.6	6.5
Industry index	35.0	(17.9)	23.1	(1.3)	3.2

SEGMENT ANALYSIS

ICI – PRODUCT ACTIVITY – 1990

Product	Turnover £m					% of turnover					Annual growth %				Profit £m					Profit/turnover %				
	1986*	1987*	1988	1989	1990	1986*	1987*	1988	1989	1990	1987*	1988	1989	1990	1986*	1987*	1988	1989	1990	1986*	1987*	1988	1989	1990
CONSUMER & SPECIALTY PRODUCTS																								
Pharmaceuticals	1 047	1 105	1 172	1 334	1 415	10.0	9.7	9.7	9.9	10.6	5.5	6.1	13.8	6.1	311	322	321	399	489	29.7	29.1	27.4	29.9	34.6
Paints	780	1 293	1 363	1 628	1 639	7.5	11.3	11.3	12.0	12.2	65.8	5.4	19.4	0.7	50	96	101	100	108	6.4	7.4	7.4	6.1	6.6
Other effect products	1 849	1 944	2 058	2 354	2 321	17.7	17.0	17.1	17.4	17.3	5.1	5.9	14.4	(1.4)	182	184	150	69	3	9.8	9.5	7.3	2.9	0.1
Internal sales	(8)	(10)	(25)	(19)	(24)	(0.1)	(0.1)	(0.2)	(0.1)	(0.2)	–	–	–	–	–	–	(1)	–	–	–	–	–	–	–
	3 668	4 332	4 568	5 297	5 351	35.2	37.9	38.0	39.2	40.0	18.1	5.4	16.0	1.0	543	602	571	568	600	14.8	13.9	12.5	10.7	11.2
INDUSTRIAL PRODUCTS																								
General chemicals	1 742	1 884	1 995	2 064	2 000	16.7	16.5	16.6	15.3	14.9	8.2	5.9	3.5	(3.1)	178	220	274	293	153	10.2	11.7	13.7	14.2	7.7
Petrochemicals and plastics	2 809	2 763	2 702	3 001	2 891	26.9	24.1	22.5	22.2	21.6	(1.6)	(2.2)	11.1	(3.7)	230	320	416	417	103	8.2	11.6	15.4	13.9	3.6
Fibres	624	668	626	704	700	6.0	5.8	5.2	5.2	5.2	7.1	(6.3)	12.5	(0.6)	58	45	53	27	18	9.3	6.7	8.5	3.8	2.6
Industrial explosives	329	339	364	414	510	3.2	3.0	3.0	3.1	3.8	3.0	7.4	13.7	23.2	27	39	48	48	50	8.2	11.5	13.2	11.6	9.8
Internal sales	(562)	(484)	(431)	(461)	(461)	(5.4)	(4.2)	(3.6)	(3.4)	(3.4)	–	–	–	–	–	–	(1)	4	–	–	–	–	–	–
	4 942	5 170	5 256	5 722	5 640	47.4	45.2	43.7	42.3	42.1	4.6	1.7	8.9	(1.4)	493	624	790	789	324	10.0	12.1	15.0	13.8	5.7
AGRICULTURE																								
Agrochemicals and plants	756	901	1 179	1 338	1 362	7.2	7.8	9.8	9.9	10.2	19.2	30.9	13.5	1.8	29	53	120	152	110	3.8	5.9	10.2	11.4	8.1
Fertilizers, etc.	915	858	814	938	856	8.8	7.5	6.8	6.9	6.4	(6.2)	(5.1)	15.2	(8.7)	(17)	–	(11)	(11)	12	(1.9)	–	(1.4)	(1.2)	1.4
Internal sales	(14)	(15)	(18)	(19)	(28)	(0.1)	(0.1)	(0.2)	(0.1)	(0.2)	–	–	–	–	–	–	–	–	–	–	–	–	–	–
	1 657	1 744	1 975	2 257	2 190	15.9	15.2	16.4	16.7	16.4	5.3	13.2	14.3	(3.0)	12	53	109	141	122	0.7	3.0	5.5	6.2	5.6
Miscellaneous	166	199	224	242	199	1.6	1.7	1.9	1.8	1.5	19.9	12.6	8.0	(17.8)	5	20	7	(33)	(20)	3.0	10.1	3.1	(13.6)	(10.0)
	10 433	11 445	12 023	13 518	13 380	100.0	100.0	100.0	100.0	100.0	9.7	5.1	12.4	(1.0)	1 053	1 299	1 477	1 465	1 026	10.1	11.4	12.3	10.8	7.7
Inter-Segment eliminations	(297)	(322)	(324)	(347)	(474)							SEE NOTE			(4)	(2)	(7)	2	3					
	10 136	11 123	11 699	13 171	12 906						9.7	5.2	12.6	(2.0)	1 049	1 297	1 470	1 467	1 029	10.3	11.7	12.6	11.1	8.0

	Net assets £m					Profit/Net assets %				
Consumer and Specialty Products	2 062	1 955	2 268	2 756	2 534	26.3	30.8	25.2	20.6	23.7
Industrial Products	2 547	2 207	2 235	2 614	2 703	19.4	28.3	35.3	30.2	12.0
Agriculture	1 084	1 217	1 237	1 308	1 137	1.1	4.4	8.8	10.8	10.7
	5 693	5 379	5 740	6 678	6 374	18.5	24.1	27.0	21.9	16.1
Non-operating and miscellaneous assets	456	438	650	975	1 019					
	6 149	5 817	6 390	7 653	7 393	17.1	22.3	23.0	19.2	13.9

NOTE
* In 1987, Oil and Gas business was disposed and remaining oil activities included in Industrial Products (1986 restated).

Market	Turnover £ m					% of turnover					Annual growth %			
	1986	1987	1988	1989	1990	1986	1987	1988	1989	1990	1987	1988	1989	1990
United Kingdom														
Home	2 530	2 703	2 663	2 872	2 966	21.2	20.5	19.2	18.4	19.3	6.8	(1.5)	7.8	3.3
Exports	2 771	2 927	3 031	3 359	3 160	23.2	22.2	21.9	21.6	20.5	5.6	3.6	10.8	(5.9)
Total	5 301	5 630	5 694	6 231	6 126	44.4	42.7	41.1	40.0	39.8	6.2	1.1	9.4	(1.7)
Continental West Europe	2 238	2 539	2 718	2 928	3 152	18.7	19.3	19.6	18.8	20.5	13.4	7.1	7.7	7.7
The Americas	2 455	2 934	3 196	3 876	3 651	20.5	22.3	23.1	24.8	23.8	19.5	8.9	21.3	(5.8)
Australasia & Far East	1 554	1 668	1 861	2 100	2 047	13.0	12.7	13.4	13.5	13.3	7.3	11.6	12.8	(2.5)
Other countries inc. India														
Sub-continent	406	393	389	451	403	3.4	3.0	2.8	2.9	2.6	(3.2)	(1.0)	15.9	(10.6)
	11 954	13 164	13 858	15 586	15 379	100.0	100.0	100.0	100.0	100.0	10.1	5.3	12.5	(1.3)
Inter-territory eliminations	(1 818)	(2 041)	(2 159)	(2 415)	(2 473)						–	–	–	–
Totals as per P&L Account	10 136	11 123	11 699	13 171	12 906						9.7	5.2	12.6	(2.0)

Market	Profit £ m					Trading profit/sales %					Net operating assets £ m					Trading profit/Net op. assets %				
	1986	1987	1988	1989	1990	1986	1987	1988	1989	1990	1986	1987	1988	1989	1990	1986	1987	1988	1989	1990
United Kingdom –																				
Home & Export	487	617	664	612	295	9.2	11.0	11.7	9.8	4.8	2 575	2 539	2 513	2 580	2 801	18.9	24.3	26.4	23.7	10.5
Continental																				
West Europe	134	184	276	225	157	6.0	7.2	10.2	7.7	5.0	810	713	735	1 026	1 061	16.5	25.8	37.6	21.9	14.8
The Americas	224	271	320	382	382	9.1	9.2	10.0	9.9	10.5	1 402	1 219	1 399	1 839	1 494	16.0	22.2	22.9	20.8	25.6
Asia Pacific	119	156	184	236	136	7.7	9.4	9.9	11.2	6.6	760	712	905	1 058	863	15.7	21.9	20.3	22.3	15.8
Other countries	40	35	35	45	29	9.9	8.9	9.0	10.0	7.2	146	196	188	175	155	27.4	17.9	18.6	25.7	18.7
	1 004	1 263	1 479	1 500	999	8.4	9.6	10.7	9.6	6.5	5 693	5 379	5 740	6 678	6 374	17.6	23.5	25.8	22.5	15.7
Adjustments	45	34	(9)	(33)	30															
Totals as per P&L Account	1 049	1 297	1 470	1 467	1 029	10.3	11.7	12.6	11.1	8.0	5 693	5 379	5 740	6 678	6 374	18.4	24.1	25.6	22.0	16.1

ICI
Published group funds flows statements 1986 – 1990
Year ended 31 December

	Notes	1986 £ m	1987 £ m	1988 £ m	1989 £ m	1990 £ m
SOURCES						
Funds generated from operations						
Trading profit	1	1 049	1 297	1 470	1467	1 029
Depreciation	2	491	464	484	536	525
Petroleum revenue tax paid, less provided	3	(42)	–	–	–	–
Government grants credited to profit, less received	4	(9)	(19)	(20)	(22)	–
Dividends from associated undertakings	5	56	65	77	135	69
Extraordinary items	6	–	–	(52)	–	(7)
Miscellaneous items, including exchange	7	(60)	(9)	(99)	(143)	77
		1 485	1 798	1 860	1 973	1 693
Less: Interest and tax paid during year						
Received	8a	69	59	58	65	73
Paid	8b	(202)	(210)	(225)	(287)	(280)
Balance (Ex gains, etc.)	8c	8	10	1	1	2
Interest (net)	8	(125)	(141)	(166)	(221)	(205)
Taxation	9	(298)	(349)	(459)	(593)	(424)
Sources net of interest and taxation		1062	1308	1235	1159	1064
APPLICATIONS						
Dividends paid during year						
Parent company	10	222	254	291	364	384
Subsidiaries to minority shareholders	11	27	29	26	42	37
		249	283	317	406	421
Fixed assets						
Tangible assets	12	643	708	811	1 080	1 013
Disposals of tangible assets	13	(35)	(26)	(45)	(61)	(160)
Acquisitions and new investments	14	578	544	265	373	497
Disposals of businesses and undertakings	15	(30)	(114)	(149)	(579)	(747)
		1156	1112	882	813	603
Working capital changes						
Stocks increase/(decrease)	16	(115)	169	136	219	(74)
Debtors increase/(decrease)	17	(45)	68	108	450	(186)
Creditors increase (excluding dividends, interest and taxation)	18	66	(50)	(167)	(131)	(107)
		(94)	187	77	538	(367)
Total applications		1311	1582	1276	1757	657
(Deficit)/Surplus		(249)	(274)	(41)	(598)	407
Financed by						
Issues of ICI Ordinary Shares	19	50	140	65	101	141
Repayment of ICI Preference Stock	20	(7)	–	–	–	–
Movement in other external finance	21	(7)	(6)	(36)	(5)	94
Increase/(decrease) in loans	22	178	(24)	92	(53)	17
Increase/(decrease) in s.t. borrowings	23	(70)	118	(270)	482	(477)
Increase/(decrease) in cash, current asset investments and s.t. deposits	24	105	46	190	73	(182)
		249	274	41	598	(407)

ICI
Restated group funds flow statements 1986 – 1990
Year ended 31 December

		1986 £ m	1987 £ m	1988 £ m	1989 £ m	1990 £ m
Internal funds/investment						
Trading profit	1	1 049	1 297	1 470	1 467	1 029
Investment Income	5 + 8a	125	124	135	200	142
		1 174	1 421	1 605	1 667	1 171
Add/(deduct) items not involving a flow of funds and adjustments						
Depreciation	2	491	464	484	536	525
Provn. for def. liabs., other	3 + 4	(51)	(19)	(20)	(22)	–
Extraordinary item	6	–	–	(52)	–	(7)
Resvs. & govt. grts. credited	7 + 8c*	(52)	1	(98)	(142)	79
Gross funds from operations		1 562	1 867	1 919	2 039	1 768
Interest	8b	(202)	(210)	(225)	(287)	(280)
Tax	9	(298)	(349)	(459)	(593)	(424)
Dividend to shareholders	10	(222)	(254)	(291)	(364)	(384)
Dividend to minorities	11	(27)	(29)	(26)	(42)	(37)
		(749)	(842)	(1 001)	(1 286)	(1 125)
Net funds available from Operations		813	1 025	918	753	643
Sales of fixed assets	13	35	26	45	61	160
Disposals of businesses and undertakings	15	30	114	149	579	747
Totally internally generated funds		878	1 165	1 112	1 393	1 550
Working capital (increase)/decrease						
Stock (increase)/decrease	16	115	(169)	(136)	(219)	74
Debtors (increase)/decrease	17	45	(68)	(108)	(450)	186
		160	(237)	(244)	(669)	260
Creditors increase/(decrease)	18	(66)	50	167	131	107
		94	(187)	(77)	(538)	367
		972	978	1 035	855	1 917
Fixed asset investment etc.						
Purchase of fixed assets	12	(643)	(708)	(811)	(1 080)	(1 013)
Purchase of subsidiaries + investments	14	(578)	(544)	(265)	(373)	(497)
		(1 221)	(1 252)	(1 076)	(1 453)	(1 510)
(Financing requirement)/surplus	£m	(249)	(274)	(41)	(598)	407
External financing						
Ordinary share capital	19	50	140	65	101	141
Minorities/Preference shares	20 + 21	(14)	(6)	(36)	(5)	94
Loans	22	178	(24)	92	(53)	17
Short term borrowings	23	(70)	118	(270)	482	(477)
Liquid resources	24	105	46	190	73	(182)
Financing/(investment)		249	274	41	598	(407)

INTERPRETATION

ICI Group: year ended 31 December 1990

1 a The results achieved in 1990 were considerably below the 1989 figures:

Group sales £12.9 billion (− 2%)
Profit on ordinary activities before tax £977 million (− 36%)
Profit on ordinary activities after tax and minorities
£617 million (− 34%)

The decline reflects the downturn in the level of world trade. In his statement the chairman said: 'When I suggested [a year ago] that I saw no return to the dark days of recession, I was clearly wrong.'

b Profit for the year was determined before extraordinary items (net of tax) as follows:

	£ m
Gain on disposal of investment in Enterprise Oil	520
Net charge for reshaping ICI's business portfolio	(300)
Charge for withdrawal from UK compound fertilizer manufacture, and restructuring the ammonium nitrate business (with a view to ultimate divestment)	(128)
ICI's share of an extraordinary item in Tioxide Group plc relating to its fundamental restructuring	(39)
	53

Some of the above charges seem to be very closely associated with normal business activities, and some analysts might feel they should be deducted in arriving at profit for the year.

2 a The reported return on net assets, after writing off against reserves goodwill arising on acquisitions, declined sharply in the year:

	1990 %	1989 %
Return on equity	13.2	18.5
Return on net operating assets	15.0	20.5

b If goodwill is capitalized (but not amortized against profits) the returns are lower:

Return on equity	9.7	14.3
Return on net operating assets	12.2	17.2

The return would be even lower if goodwill were written off against profits over, say, ten or twenty years. (It is, of course, difficult to know what the appropriate life for goodwill is.)

c The results would be considerably worse still if inflation accounting adjustments were made (see Section 11). For example, the table on page 246 suggests that for assets with a 15-year life (which is what ICI estimates on average for its plant and equipment) historical cost depreciation would need to be nearly doubled to provide for depreciation in 'real' (CPP) terms. Clearly an extra (after-tax) expense of some £500 million a year would make a huge difference to ICI's results. (It would, for example, probably leave the ordinary dividend uncovered by 'real' (CPP) earnings in several of the last ten years.)

3 a Turnover declined in the year by 2 per cent in a tough economic environment. The performance of the three main industry segments showed:

	1990 Sales		Profit/Sales		Profit/Net Assets	
			1990	1989	1990	1989
	£ m	Growth	%	%	%	%
Consumer and speciality products	5 351	+ 1%	11	11	24	21
Industrial products	5 640	− 1%	6	14	12	30
Agriculture	2 190	− 3%	6	6	11	11

b From this and the detail from the Operational Review in the Annual Report (not reproduced here) relating to individual businesses, it can be seen that:

- in consumer and specialty products, pharmaceuticals did relatively well, achieving 6 per cent sales growth and profits 23 per cent higher
- industrial products had much lower profits, especially in petrochemicals and plastics (down over £300 million)
- Agriculture, representing 16 per cent of sales, experienced a decline in sales of 3 per cent, and continuing low profit margins.

c Overall a major problem facing ICI centres on greatly reduced margins. Apart from pharmaceuticals and industrial explosives, the remaining £11 billion ICI sales in 1990 generated average profit margins of only 4 ½ per cent (down from 9 per cent in 1989).

4   The working capital ratios changed little.

Stock (on a sales basis) fell from 66 to 63 days (from a high 110 days to 103 days on a cost of sales basis).
Trade debtors fell from 57 days to 54 days.
Trade creditors fell from 51 days to 50 days.
The current ratio and acid test ratio are in line with industry norms.

5   If goodwill is capitalized, gearing (total debt/net assets) fell from 25.3 per cent to 23.8 per cent. With lower profits, interest cover fell from 6.3 times to 4.5 times; and would be even lower if some of the large negative 'extra-ordinary' items [see 1b above] were taken into account.

6   Net funds from operations fell from £753 million to £643 million, the third reduction in successive years. This compares with £1 025 million at the peak of the cycle in 1987 (equivalent to about £1 275 million in 1990 pounds).

Dividend payments to shareholders have risen from £222 million in 1986 to £384 million in 1990, while trading profit fell from £1 049 million in 1986 to £1 029 million in 1990. Reported dividend cover fell sharply in 1990.

ICI spent just over £1 billion on the purchase of fixed assets, and nearly £500 million on acquisitions. Without a reduction in working capital of £367 million and disposals of businesses of £747 million, there would have been a significant financing requirement in 1990 (as there was in 1989).

Surplus funds in 1990 were used to repay short-term borrowings of £477 million, and to increase cash and short-term investment balances by £182 million.

In future ICI will need to generate more net operating funds, otherwise the group may have to reduce its capital expenditure programme.

7   ICI's share price fell in the year to March 1991 by 2.8 per cent. ICI's share price has now underperformed the industry index in each of the last four years.

SUMMARY

In this final section we have reviewed some of the problems of accrual accounting. We looked again at aspects of disclosure and accounting conventions; at incomplete transactions, consistency, conservatism, inflation accounting and the accounting treatment of the costs of employees. We noted that trends over a number of years are likely to be more useful to the analyst than numbers and ratios for a single year; and we discussed some of the problems in trying to compare the financial results of different companies. We summarized a number of accounting matters requiring special attention when accounts are analysed. Then we outlined a framework for relating financial analysis to economic reality in the context of a number of specific competitive market environments over time.

The rest of the section contained a detailed analysis of the 1990 accounts of the ICI group, in four main stages: overview analysis; financial ratio analysis; segment analysis; and funds flow analysis.

In each area we looked at results over five years. The overview analysis and financial ratio analysis were similar to that carried out in Section 2. The adjustment of the ratios for goodwill was an illustration of the importance of amending ratios for accounting matters which require special attention. The segment analysis was new: it contained an analysis of sales, profits and capital employed, between classes of business and between geographical areas. The analysis included profit margin trends over five years, together with returns on capital employed in each sector of the business. We then looked at the funds flow statement published by the company over a five-year period, with the figures restated in a format similar to that in Section 6.

Finally we listed some comments by way of *interpretation* of all the analysis.

From this section it should be evident that a great deal of information can be obtained about a company's affairs and financial position from a well-presented set of accounts. Analysts need an understanding of the structure of company accounts and of the way they are prepared. Most important, they also need the patience and determination to pursue the analysis as far as possible.

12.1 Whitbread plc 1991 accounts

On the next few pages extensive extracts from Whitbread's 1991 accounts are set out. You are asked to use all the available information and produce an analysis of the 1991 results. Working on separate worksheets draw up:

- an overview statement
- financial ratio analysis, including adjusting for goodwill written off to reserves
- segment analysis.

When you have completed your analysis write down the main conclusions which you think can be drawn. You can then compare your answers with those set out on pages 306 to 312.

The stock market prices to use in your analyses are

1987	363p
1988	307p
1989	338p
1990	455p
1991	448p

These are the share prices at the end of June following the publication of the accounts.

WHITBREAD PLC
Review of Operations
Year ended 2nd March 1991

Group operating structure

The Group is organised into six operating divisions.

Whitbread Beer Company

Portfolio of ales, stouts and lagers includes Stella Artois, Heineken, Trophy bitter, Fremlins bitter, Wethereds, Boddingtons, Murphys Irish Stout, Flowers.

Whitbread Pub Partnership

Formed in 1990 to manage the transition required by the Supply of Beer Orders. Wide variety of pubs – large city centre houses, smart city bars, community locals, country pubs. Total of 4 291 properties.

Whitbread Inns

Controls some 1 600 managed pubs.
Brewers Fayre, Roast Inn, Mulligans, Wayside Inns, Henry's.

Whitbread Restaurants

Has more than 500 outlets. Beefeater, Berni, TGI Fridays, Churrasco (Germany), The Keg (Canada, USA, Australia).

Pizza Hut (UK, France, Belgium, Holland), Pizza Hut Express.

Whitbread Leisure

Covers Hotels (Country Club Hotels, Lansbury Hotels, Travel Inn) and Thresher and Wine Rack with some 1 000 outlets.

GROUP PROFIT AND LOSS ACCOUNT
Year ended 2 March 1991

	Notes	52 weeks 1991 £ m	53 weeks 1990 £ m
Turnover including share of associated undertakings		2 248.2	2 491.2
Share of associated undertakings		(188.4)	(440.1)
Turnover excluding share of associated undertakings	2	2 059.8	2 051.1
Operating costs less other income	3	(1 749.4)	(1 731.1)
Interest	4	(18.9)	(54.3)
Profit on ordinary activities before taxation		291.5	265.7
Taxation	5	(71.1)	(65.8)
Profit on ordinary activities after taxation		220.4	199.9
Allocation to Share Ownership Scheme (after taxation)	6	(4.6)	(3.8)
Minority interests		(5.6)	(6.4)
Preference dividends		(0.4)	(0.4)
Profit before extraordinary items		209.8	189.3
Extraordinary items (after taxation)	7	(58.3)	338.1
Profit earned for ordinary shareholders	8	151.5	527.4
Ordinary dividends	9	(72.7)	(65.3)
Retained profit for the year	19	78.8	462.1
Earnings per share (pence)	10		
Basic		47.29	43.18
Fully diluted		46.72	42.51

REPORT OF THE AUDITORS

Report of the Auditors to the Members of Whitbread PLC

We have audited the accounts on pages 00 to 00 in accordance with Auditing Standards.

In our opinion the accounts give a true and fair view of the state of affairs of the Company and of the Group at 2 March 1991 and of the profit and source and application of funds of the Group for the year then ended and have been properly prepared in accordance with the Companies Act 1985.

Ernst & Young
Chartered Accountants
London
22 May 1991

WHITBREAD PLC – BALANCE SHEETS
2 March 1991

	Notes	Group 1991 £ m	Group 1990 £ m	Company 1991 £ m	Company 1990 £ m
Fixed assets					
Tangible assets	11	2 929.2	2 703.6	2 326.1	2 502.7
Investments	12	294.4	307.0	798.8	439.3
		3 223.6	3 010.6	3 124.9	2 942.0
Current assets and liabilities					
Stocks	13	118.4	113.6	104.9	95.7
Debtors	14	265.9	193.6	228.5	154.8
Cash at bank and in hand		127.9	126.1	103.8	92.6
		512.2	433.3	437.2	343.1
Creditors – amounts falling due within one year	15	(577.8)	(482.6)	(525.5)	(418.7)
Net current liabilities		(65.6)	(49.3)	(88.3)	(75.6)
Total assets less current liabilities		3 158.0	2 961.3	3 036.6	2 866.4
Creditors – amounts falling due after more than one year					
Loan capital	16	(390.9)	(261.0)	(326.5)	(200.1)
Provisions for liabilities and charges	17	(106.8)	(81.8)	(81.2)	(63.8)
		2 660.3	2 618.5	2 628.9	2 602.5
Capital and reserves					
Called up share capital	18	121.2	120.2	121.2	120.2
Share premium account	18	86.3	76.0	86.3	76.0
Other reserves – non distributable	19	1 103.3	1 109.0	928.0	1 149.7
Profit and loss account	19	1 286.4	1 253.0	1 493.4	1 256.6
		2 597.2	2 558.2	2 628.9	2 602.5
Minority interests		63.1	60.3	—	
		2 660.3	2 618.5	2 628.9	2 602.5

S. C. Whitbread ⎫
⎬ Directors
P. J. Jarvis ⎭

22 May 1991

SOURCE AND APPLICATION OF FUNDS
Year ended 2 March 1991

	1991 £ m	1991 £ m	1990 £ m	1990 £ m
Source of funds				
Profit on ordinary activities before taxation		**291.5**		265.7
Items not involving the movement of funds:				
Depreciation		**71.7**		66.1
Retained profits of associated undertakings		**(6.8)**		(6.3)
Profit on disposal of fixed assets and other movements		**(15.3)**		(20.2)
Funds generated by operations		**341.1**		305.3
Sale of property and plant		**52.6**		54.9
Realisation of fixed asset investments		**66.2**		57.1
Sale of businesses		**—**		556.9
Total source of funds		**459.9**		974.2
Applications of funds				
Investment in:				
New businesses (note 20)	**131.0**		121.7	
Property and plant	**270.0**		308.7	
Fixed asset investments	**73.9**		72.7	
		474.9		503.1
Working capital requirements:				
Increase in stocks	**3.9**		2.2	
Increase in debtors	**27.1**		27.1	
(Increase) in creditors	**(70.2)**		(37.5)	
		(39.2)		(8.2)
Reorganisation costs		**43.2**		13.8
Total operational application of funds		**478.9**		508.7
Dividends		**72.9**		62.2
Taxation		**59.0**		48.3
Total application of funds		**610.8**		619.2
Cash flow prior to funding changes		**(150.9)**		355.0
Issue of shares and minority contributions received		**11.6**		10.9
Loan capital received		**164.7**		14.3
Loan capital repaid		**(32.6)**		(275.9)
Cash and overdrafts of undertakings acquired and disposed of during the year		**1.2**		(9.5)
Balance sheet movement of cash at bank and in hand less bank overdrafts		**(6.0)**		94.8

WHITBREAD PLC
Five year summary

Profit and loss account	1987	1988	1989	1990**	1991
Turnover including associated undertakings (£m)	n/a	2 059.9	2 259.8	2 491.2	2 248.2
Turnover excluding associated undertakings (£m)	1 533.9	1 688.7	1 845.3	2 051.1	2 059.8
Profit before tax (£m)	158.9	187.2	223.2	265.7	291.5
Profit before interest and tax as % of turnover	n/a	10.6%	11.7%	12.8%	13.8%
Tax charge as % of profit before tax	30.6%	29.5%	26.0%	24.8%	24.4%
Basic earnings per share (pence)*	26.98	30.73	36.17	43.18	47.29
Ordinary dividends per share (pence)	8.9	10.6	12.6	14.8	16.3
Interest cover (times covered)	5.8	7.0	6.4	5.9	16.4
Dividend cover (times covered)	3.0	2.8	2.9	2.9	2.9
Average number of employees – full time	21 671	22 791	26 954	31 033	32 168
– part time	26 052	26 383	27 238	31 571	33 480

NOTES:
* The basis for calculating earnings per share for 1987 to 1990 has been changed to the weighted average number of shares in issue.
** 1990 figures have been adjusted to reflect the change in accounting policy whereby results of overseas business are translated at average exchange rates and to reflect the inclusion of WIC as a subsidiary undertaking.

Balance sheets (£m)	1987	1988	1989	1990	1991
Tangible fixed assets	1 269.7	1 401.9	2 537.2*	2 703.6	2 929.2
Investments	177.5	189.8	215.5	307.0	294.4
Total fixed assets	1 447.2	1 591.7	2 752.7	3 010.6	3 223.6
Current assets	415.7	434.9	417.6	433.3	512.2
Creditors – amounts falling due within one year	(371.7)	(436.1)	(437.3)	(482.6)	(577.8)
Net current assets/(liabilities)	44.0	(1.2)	(19.7)	(49.3)	(65.6)
Total assets less current liabilities	1 491.2	1 590.5	2 733.0	2 961.3	3 158.0
Creditors – amounts due after more than one year	(352.9)	(423.9)	(517.8)	(261.0)	(390.9)
Provisions for liabilities and charges	(6.9)	(22.1)	(10.7)	(81.8)	(106.8)
	1 131.4	1 144.5	2 204.5	2 618.5	2 660.3
Called up share capital	109.7	117.8	118.7	120.2	121.2
Share premium account	50.6	55.0	63.4	76.0	86.3
Reserves	956.2**	950.2	1 994.8*	2 362.0	2 389.7
	1 116.5	1 123.0	2 176.9	2 558.2	2 597.2
Minority interests	14.9	21.5	27.6	60.3	63.1
	1 131.4	1 144.5	2 204.5	2 618.5	2 660.3
Gearing percentage***	32.3%	36.3%	23.4%*	7.1%	12.4%
Net asset value per ordinary share (pence)	277.1	257.8	497.4	577.5	580.9

NOTES:
* U.K. Properties were revalued in 1989.
** 1987 figures have been adjusted to reflect the change in accounting policy in 1988 for intangible assets.
*** Gearing represents loan capital and bank overdrafts less cash at bank and in hand expressed as a percentage of capital, reserves and minority interests.

Cash flow (£ m)	1987	1988	1989	1990	1991
Sources					
Profit before tax	158.9	187.2	223.2	265.7	291.5
Depreciation and other non-cash items	44.3	56.1	31.0	30.1	50.8
Funds generated by operations	203.2	243.3	254.2	295.8	342.3
Sales of business	0.1	21.6	60.6	556.9	—
Sales of fixed assets	84.2	45.6	71.7	112.0	118.8
	287.5	310.5	386.5	964.7	461.1
Uses					
Expansion of the business	(226.3)	(436.2)	(341.1)	(503.1)	(474.9)
Working capital	6.5	49.9	(48.6)	8.2	39.2
Dividends	(32.1)	(37.2)	(49.5)	(62.2)	(72.9)
Taxation	(23.4)	(34.6)	(51.8)	(48.3)	(59.0)
Other uses	(9.5)	(10.7)	(3.7)	(13.8)	(43.2)
Cash flow prior to funding changes	2.7	(158.3)	(108.2)	345.5	(149.7)
Funding					
Shares issued and minority contributions	3.6	104.0	7.3	10.9	11.6
Loans received less repaid	55.4	52.4	102.6	(261.6)	132.1
Improvement/(reduction) in cash resources	61.7	(1.9)	1.7	94.8	(6.0)

NOTES TO THE ACCOUNTS

1 CHANGES TO COMPARATIVE AMOUNTS

As stated in the Directors' Report, Whitbread Investment Company, PLC (WIC) is now categorised as a subsidiary undertaking rather than an associated undertaking. Comparative amounts have been restated to reflect this change, which results in an increase in profit before tax of £5.8m (1990 – £5.2m). There is no effect on turnover, because Whitbread Investment Company, PLC is an investment company, or on earnings. Changes to opening balances of investments and reserves are shown in notes 12b, 12c, 12d and 19.

The effect of the holding of Whitbread Investment Company, PLC's investment in Whitbread PLC has not been accounted for as it is not material in the context of the Group accounts.

Other changes are referred to in note A of Accounting Policies.

2 ANALYSIS OF TURNOVER AND PROFIT

	1991 £ m	1990 £ m
Geographical analysis of turnover		
United Kingdom	1 897.8	1 716.4
Rest of the World	162.0	121.1
Discontinued businesses	—	213.6
	2 059.8	2 051.1

Operational analysis of turnover and profits	Turnover 1991 £ m	Profit 1991 £ m	Turnover 1990 £ m	Profit 1990 £ m
Beer and other drinks	897.2	71.1	747.6	61.8
Pub partnerships	273.6	65.7	251.9	63.2
Managed retail estate	1 260.5	128.7	1 145.9	120.6
Discontinued businesses	—	—	226.1	34.5
Divisional turnover and operating profit	2 431.3	265.5	2 371.5	280.1
Profit on retail property disposals		36.3		33.4
Income from property development and investments		14.1		16.3
		315.9		329.8
Deduct: Central services		(21.4)		(21.5)
Interest		(3.0)		(42.6)
Inter-operational sales	(371.5)		(320.4)	
	2 059.8	291.5	2 051.1	265.7

A charge for interest has been made to "Beer and other drinks" to reflect the net cost of financing trade loans made to customers. Interest stated above has therefore been adjusted by a charge to Beer and other drinks of £15.9m (1990 – £11.7m). The above figures exclude turnover of associated undertakings.

3 PROFIT AND LOSS ACCOUNT DETAILS

	1991 £ m	1990 £ m
Turnover (excluding associated undertakings)	2 059.8	2 051.1
Cost of sales	(1 515.3)	(1 476.3)
Gross profit	544.5	574.8
Distribution to customers	(39.7)	(41.7)
Administration and other costs	(256.1)	(273.0)
Amounts written off investments	(3.2)	(2.5)
	245.5	257.6
Profit on retail property disposals	36.3	33.4
Income from associated undertakings	9.0	10.2
Investment income (note 3a)	19.6	18.8
	310.4	320.0
Interest (note 4)	(18.9)	(54.3)
Profit on ordinary activities before taxation	291.5	265.7

3 PROFIT AND LOSS ACCOUNT DETAILS (continued)

	1991 £ m	1990 £ m
Included above are:		
Depreciation (note 11)	71.7	66.1
Operating lease rentals		
– hire of plant and machinery	1.7	3.8
– property	19.3	14.0
Research and development expenditure	5.3	5.1
Auditors' remuneration	0.7	0.6
Directors' emoluments (note 3b)	1.7	1.4
Staff costs (note 3c)	404.8	370.3
Property rents received, less outgoings	38.7	30.7

3a INVESTMENT INCOME

	1991 £ m	1990 £ m
Dividends and interest receivable from:		
Listed participating interests	4.5	3.7
Other listed investments	9.4	9.1
Unlisted investments	0.3	0.3
Trade loans	5.4	5.7
	19.6	18.8

4 INTEREST

	1991 £ m	1990 £ m
Interest payable and similar charges		
Debenture stocks and loans repayable within five years, and bank overdrafts	43.3	70.3
Debenture stocks and loans repayable after five years	15.9	9.9
	59.2	80.2
Deduct:		
Interest receivable on short term deposits	(31.3)	(16.9)
Interest capitalised	(7.7)	(9.0)
Interest relating to properties acquired from Grand Metropolitan PLC which are to be sold	(1.3)	—
	18.9	54.3

5 TAXATION

	1991 £ m	1990 £ m
Current taxation on profits for the year		
U.K. Corporation Tax at 34.085% (1990 – 35%)	63.4	58.0
Tax on franked investment income	3.2	2.6
Overseas tax	1.8	2.2
	68.4	62.8
Adjustments to earlier periods	(0.2)	0.2
	68.2	63.0
Associated undertakings	2.9	2.8
	71.1	65.8

The charge for U.K. Corporation Tax has been relieved by £17.0m (1990 – £15.1m) in respect of accelerated capital allowances.

Deferred taxation

The potential amount of deferred taxation not provided for in these accounts is £130.5m (1990 – £118.4m) mainly in respect of accelerated capital allowances.

No provision has been made for any chargeable gains which might arise in the event of properties being sold at their revalued amounts, as in the ordinary course of business the majority of properties would be retained indefinitely. No provision has been made for any additional liability to U.K. or overseas taxation on the distribution of unappropriated profits or reserves of certain overseas subsidiary and associated undertakings.

7 EXTRAORDINARY ITEMS

	1991 £ m	1990 £ m
The following amounts derive from events outside the ordinary activities of the business:		
Extraordinary charges:		
Net profit/(loss) on disposal of industrial properties, investments and businesses, including £0.1m (1990 – £1.3m) attributable to associated undertakings	(16.4)	404.1
Costs arising from the Government Orders following the Monopolies and Mergers Commission inquiry – see footnote	(55.0)	(64.0)
Extraordinary items before tax	(71.4)	340.1
Tax on extraordinary items	13.1	(2.0)
	(58.3)	338.1

The costs arising from the Government Orders consist of those inherent in implementing the requirements of the Orders plus those necessary to make the changes in the strategy and structure of the Group which will be essential in the changed market. The costs include: redundancy, relocation, recruitment, legal and systems costs related to the formation of the Whitbread Beer Company and Whitbread Pub Partnerships; the rationalisation of beer production facilities; and preparing the Group's tenanted pubs for the new arrangements.

9 ORDINARY DIVIDENDS

	1991 £ m	1990 £ m
Interim 4.30 pence per share (1990 – 3.80 pence)	19.1	16.7
Proposed final 12.00 pence per share (1990 – 11.00 pence)	53.6	48.6
16.30 pence per share (1990 – 14.80 pence)	72.7	65.3

10 EARNINGS PER SHARE

Basic earnings per share is calculated by dividing earnings for ordinary shareholders, before extraordinary items, of £209.8m (1990 – £189.3m) by the weighted average number of ordinary shares in issue during the year, 443.6m (1990 – 438.4m). Fully diluted earnings per share is the basic earnings per share adjusted for the notional effect of the conversion into fully paid shares of options on share capital, fully diluted earnings being £211.7m (1990 – £191.2m), and the number of shares being 453.1m (1990 – 449.8m).

11 TANGIBLE FIXED ASSETS

	Industrial property £ m	Retail property £ m	Plant & machinery £ m	Total £ m
Whitbread Group				
Gross amounts 3 March 1990	147.6	2 266.2	598.4	3 012.2
Foreign exchange movements	(0.1)	(6.1)	(0.4)	(6.6)
Businesses acquired	0.2	87.8	3.0	91.0
Additions	2.5	147.7	112.1	262.3
Interest capitalised	—	4.9	0.9	5.8
Disposals	(2.3)	(47.9)	(42.0)	(92.2)
Revaluation	—	11.3	—	11.3
Reclassifications	0.3	3.8	(4.1)	—
Gross amounts 2 March 1991	148.2	2 467.7	667.9	3 283.8
Depreciation 3 March 1990	(3.6)	(26.3)	(278.7)	(308.6)
Foreign exchange movements	—	1.7	0.1	1.8
Businesses acquired	—	(0.7)	(0.8)	(1.5)
Depreciation for the year	(3.1)	(6.7)	(61.9)	(71.7)
Disposals	0.5	1.7	23.1	25.3
Revaluation	—	0.1	—	0.1
Reclassifications	(0.1)	—	0.1	—
Depreciation 2 March 1991	(6.3)	(30.2)	(318.1)	(354.6)
Net book amounts 2 March 1991	141.9	2 437.5	349.8	2 929.2
Net book amounts 3 March 1990	144.0	2 239.9	319.7	2 703.6

Whitbread Group

Chartered Surveyors in the employment of the Group carried out a professional valuation of the Group's properties in the United Kingdom at 25 February 1989 and properties of certain subsidiaries were revalued on 2 March 1991. Containers have been revalued to deposit price. If these and previous revaluations had not taken place, the values of fixed assets would have been:

	Industrial property £ m	Retail property £ m	Plant & machinery £ m	Total £ m
Gross amounts	90.2	1 118.8	667.9	1 876.9
Depreciation	(25.1)	(29.9)	(318.1)	(373.1)
Net book amounts 2 March 1991	65.1	1 088.9	349.8	1 503.8
Net book amounts 3 March 1990	72.1	859.0	319.6	1 250.7

Net book amounts of properties	Freehold	Long leasehold	Short leasehold	Total
2 March 1991	2 210.0	234.2	135.2	2 579.4
3 March 1990	2 109.3	180.5	94.1	2 383.9

	1991 £ m	1990 £ m
Gross amounts of properties		
As valued 1990/91	131.0	
As valued 1988/89	2 013.3	2 173.5
As valued 1984/85	10.3	10.9
As valued 1980/81	—	0.3
At cost	461.3	229.1
	2 615.9	2 413.8

Capital expenditure for which no provision has been made		
Commitments	54.6	32.1
Authorised, not committed	45.0	56.7
	99.6	88.8

12 INVESTMENTS

	Group 1991 £ m	Group 1990 £ m	Company 1991 £ m	Company 1990 £ m
Subsidiary undertakings (note 12a)	—	—	614.9	231.0
Associated undertakings (note 12b)	81.4	118.3	57.8	107.3
Participating interests (note 12c)	25.2	25.2	—	—
Other (note 12d)	187.8	163.5	126.1	101.0
	294.4	307.0	798.8	439.3

12b INVESTMENT IN ASSOCIATED UNDERTAKINGS

	Listed £ m	Unlisted £ m	Loans £ m	Total £ m
Whitbread Group				
Investment 3 March 1990 as published	31.8	65.5	52.8	150.1
Adjustment for WIC	(31.8)	—	—	(31.8)
Investment 3 March 1990 revised	—	65.5	52.8	118.3
Additions	—	0.9	1.2	2.1
Disposals	—	(26.1)	(1.2)	(27.3)
Transfers (to)/from subsidiary undertakings	—	0.8	(13.9)	(13.1)
Share of retained profits less losses	—	4.0	—	4.0
Other movements	—	(2.6)	—	(2.6)
Investment 2 March 1991	—	42.5	38.9	81.4
Market value or Directors' valuation				
2 March 1991	—	88.0	38.9	126.9
3 March 1990	—	128.4	52.8	181.2

Principal associated undertakings

	Country of incorporation or registration	Total equity par value (a)	Whitbread holding of (a)	Total loan capital (£m) (b)	Whitbread holding of (b)
W. H. Brakspear & Sons PLC	England	£0.4m	27%	0.1	—
Britannia Soft Drinks Ltd.	England	£21.8m	25%	80.3	23%
William Grant & Sons (UK Sales) Ltd.	England	£0.1m	30%	0.5	—
Marchesi L e P Antinori Spa*	Italy	Lire 5bn	48%	—	—
Pizza Hut (UK) Ltd.	England	£0.8m	50%	39.2	50%

The country of incorporation is also the main area of operations. The activities of the above companies are similar to certain activities of the Whitbread Group. The investments are held directly by Whitbread PLC except where marked with an asterisk.

12c. PARTICIPATING INTERESTS

In accordance with the Companies Act 1985, as amended by the Companies Act 1989, the investments below, which comprise more than 20% of the equity capital of the undertakings, are described as "Participating Interests". These investments are mainly held through the Whitbread Investment Company, PLC, which is an investment company and has no board representation and does not participate in commercial or financial policy decisions of the undertakings. They are not therefore regarded as associated undertakings and are included at cost not equity value.

	Listed £m
Cost 3 March 1990	25.2
Adjustment for WIC	
Cost 3 March 1990 revised and 2 March 1991	25.2
Market value 2 March 1991	127.0
3 March 1990	131.7

	Country of incorporation or registration	Total equity par value (a)	Whitbread holding of (a)	Total loan capital (£m) (b)	Whitbread holding of (b)	Latest reported pre-tax profit
The Boddington Group plc	England	£24.8m ord	27%	17.0	—	£20.1m
Marston, Thompson & Evershed plc	England	£22.0m ord	38%	0.6	—	£17.4m
Morland & Co. plc	England	£4.2m ord	44%	—	—	£6.2m
		£0.1 pref	—			

12d OTHER INVESTMENTS

	Listed £m	Unlisted £m	Trade loans £m	Total £m
Whitbread Group				
Cost 3 March 1990 as published	15.3	2.8	93.4	111.5
Adjustment for WIC	52.2	2.7	—	54.9
Cost 3 March 1990 revised	67.5	5.5	93.4	166.4
Additions	9.9	0.1	61.3	71.3
Disposals	(7.9)	(3.1)	(33.5)	(44.5)
Cost 2 March 1991	69.5	2.5	121.2	193.2
Provisions 3 March 1990	—	—	(2.9)	(2.9)
Movements	—	—	(2.5)	(2.5)
Provisions 2 March 1991	—	—	(5.4)	(5.4)
Net book amounts 2 March 1991	69.5	2.5	115.8	187.8
Net book amounts 3 March 1990	67.5	5.5	90.5	163.5
Market value or Directors' valuation				
2 March 1991	316.9	11.9	115.8	444.6
3 March 1990	296.8	14.1	90.5	401.4

Included in listed investments at 2 March 1991 is Whitbread Investment Company, PLC's investment in Whitbread PLC, consisting of cost £19.7m and market value of £237.7m.

13 STOCKS

	Group 1991 £m	Group 1990 £m	Company 1991 £m	Company 1990 £m
Raw materials and consumables	15.7	18.9	12.3	13.0
Work in progress	21.5	20.8	20.5	20.2
Development properties under construction	3.9	3.7	—	—
Finished goods	77.3	70.2	72.1	62.5
	118.4	113.6	104.9	95.7

The estimated replacement cost of stocks is not materially different from the above carrying value.

14 DEBTORS

Trade debtors	91.2	88.1	71.2	67.8
Associated undertakings	1.6	2.8	1.5	2.8
Properties acquired from Grand Metropolitan PLC which are to be sold	34.6	—	34.6	—
Other debtors	55.8	53.9	51.5	42.8
Prepayments and accrued income	36.5	17.8	30.3	13.9
Tax recoverable	—	3.5	—	0.2
Deferred taxation – Advance Corporation Tax	17.8	16.2	17.8	16.2
– Corporation Tax on provisions	28.4	11.3	21.6	11.1
	265.9	193.6	228.5	154.8

16 LOAN CAPITAL

	Repayment dates	Interest rates	1991 £m	1990 £m
Whitbread PLC				
Secured:				
Debenture stocks, redeemable by instalments at par by operation of annual sinking funds	1991 to 2004	4.5–9.75%	18.1	18.5
Other redeemable debenture stocks	2011	11.625%*	135.0	—
Unsecured:				
Loan stocks	1991 to 2005	7.25–10.5%	44.0	44.0
Loan notes	1991 to 1999	7.5–8.5%	4.1	5.0
Irredeemable loan stock		5.75%	1.3	1.3
Multi currency facility	1994	Variable	127.3	110.3
U.S. dollar loans	1991 to 1994	Variable	—	2.5
U.S. dollar loans	1991 to 1992	7.7–8.875%	18.7	36.3
Belgian franc loans	1991 to 1992	7.9%	3.3	3.4
Total – Whitbread plc			351.8	221.3
Subsidiary undertakings				
Secured:				
Debenture	Not fixed	Nil	1.4	1.7
Debenture	1991 to 1992	6.5%	1.5	1.5
Stepped interest debenture	2010	7–12%	15.0	15.0
Other loans	1991 to 1992	Variable	2.8	0.2
Unsecured:				
Medium term loans	1997	Variable	40.0	37.0
Other loans	1993 to 2008	Variable	6.4	5.5
Total – Group			418.9	282.2

* The Company has entered into agreements which swap the fixed interest rate of the 11.625% debenture stock for variable rates until 2011.

16 LOAN CAPITAL (continued)

	Group 1991 £ m	Group 1990 £ m	Company 1991 £ m	Company 1990 £ m
Summarized as follows:				
Bank loans repayable:				
Within one year or on demand	21.4	20.7	18.7	20.7
Between one and two years	1.5	18.1	–	18.1
Between two and five years	130.6	113.8	130.6	113.7
Over five years – repayable by instalments	1.1	0.1	–	–
– other	40.0	37.0	–	–
Other loans repayable:				
Within one year or on demand	6.6	0.5	6.6	0.5
Between one and two years	4.2	6.7	4.2	6.7
Between two and five years	8.7	15.1	8.7	13.6
Over five years – repayable by instalments	2.4	2.5	2.4	2.4
– other	202.4	67.7	180.6	45.6
	418.9	282.2	351.8	221.3
Deduct loan capital falling due within one year (note 15)	(28.0)	(21.2)	(25.3)	(21.2)
Falling due after more than one year	390.9	261.0	326.5	200.1

The total of instalment loans, any part of which falls due after more than five years, amounts to £3.5m (1990 – £2.5m). Debenture stocks and secured loans are secured by a fixed and floating charge on certain Group tangible fixed assets.

15 CREDITORS – AMOUNTS FALLING DUE WITHIN ONE YEAR

	Group 1991 £ m	Group 1990 £ m	Company 1991 £ m	Company 1990 £ m
Loan capital (note 16)	28.0	21.2	25.3	21.2
Bank overdrafts	38.9	31.1	35.6	15.4
Trade creditors	141.6	127.2	127.6	113.2
Associated undertakings	7.9	17.0	1.5	13.3
Corporation Tax	59.7	59.3	65.9	56.5
Other taxes and social security	38.3	36.7	36.6	35.6
Accruals and deferred income	63.3	54.8	51.2	43.1
Other creditors	146.5	86.7	128.2	71.8
Proposed final dividend on ordinary shares	53.6	48.6	53.6	48.6
	577.8	482.6	525.5	418.7

17 PROVISIONS FOR LIABILITIES AND CHARGES

	Group Rationalisation/ reorganisation provisions £ m	Group Acquisition provisions £ m	Group Total £ m	Company Rationalisation/ reorganisation provisions £ m	Company Acquisition provisions £ m	Company Total £ m
3 March 1990	63.8	18.0	81.8	63.8	–	63.8
Foreign exchange	–	(0.8)	(0.8)	–	–	–
Provided	55.0	21.2	76.2	55.0	–	55.0
Used	(37.6)	(12.8)	(50.4)	(37.6)	–	(37.6)
2 March 1991	81.2	25.6	106.8	81.2	–	81.2

18 SHARE CAPITAL

	Authorised 1991 £ m	Authorised 1990 £ m	Allotted, called-up and fully paid 1991 £ m	Allotted, called-up and fully paid 1990 £ m
Preference stocks				
3.15% (issued as 4.5%) 1st cumulative	0.6	0.6	0.6	0.6
3.15% (issued as 4.5%) 2nd cumulative	0.4	0.4	0.4	0.4
3.85% (issued as 5.5%) 3rd cumulative	2.1	2.1	2.1	2.1
4.20% (issued as 6%) 3rd cumulative	3.7	3.7	3.7	3.7
4.90% (issued as 7%) 3rd cumulative	3.0	3.0	3.0	3.0
	9.8	9.8	9.8	9.8
'A' limited voting ordinary shares of 25p each	119.5	119.5	107.3	106.3
'B' ordinary shares of 25p each	4.1	4.1	4.1	4.1
Unclassified shares of 25p each	16.6	16.6	–	–
	150.0	150.0	121.2	120.2

19 RESERVES

	Acquisition and other non-distributable reserves £ m	Revaluation reserve £ m	Profit & loss account £ m	Associated undertakings £ m	Total £ m
Whitbread Group					
3 March 1990 as published	–	1 083.2	1 249.9	28.9	2 362.0
Adjustment for WIC	22.8	–	3.1	(25.9)	–
3 March 1990 revised	22.8	1 083.2	1 253.0	3.0	2 362.0
Foreign exchange relating to:					
Overseas investments			(3.0)	0.1	(2.9)
Overseas investment financing			4.3		4.3
Profit retained			74.8	4.0	78.8
Realised revaluation surplus transferred to current year profit and loss account		(23.6)	(10.0)	0.1	(33.5)
Revaluation of fixed assets		7.5	(0.1)	(2.5)	4.9
Goodwill			(25.3)	(0.1)	(25.4)
Other movements	1.5		(7.3)	7.3	1.5
2 March 1991	24.3	1 067.1	1 286.4	11.9	2 389.7

Profit and loss account balances are fully distributable.

The cumulative amount of goodwill written off to date, net of disposals, amounts to £219.9m (1990 – £212.7m).

20 ACQUISITION OF BUSINESSES

	1991 Book value of assets acquired £ m	Fair value adjustments £ m	Assets acquired at fair value £ m
Fixed assets	90.7	(1.2)	89.5
Working capital, excluding cash	37.4	(0.1)	37.3
Cash and overdrafts	1.2	–	1.2
Loan capital	(2.0)	–	(2.0)
Net assets acquired	127.3	(1.3)	126.0
Transferred from investments	(14.3)	0.7	(13.6)
Provisions for future trading losses	–	(3.4)	(3.4)
Other provisions	–	(17.8)	(17.8)
Tax on provisions	–	6.5	6.5
Minority interests	8.0	–	8.0
Goodwill, including acquisition costs	10.0	15.3	25.3
Cash paid for acquisitions	131.0	–	131.0

Included above are figures relating to the acquisition of properties and other business assets from Grand Metropolitan PLC as follows:

Fixed assets	75.6	0.6	76.2
Working capital, excluding cash	0.8	–	0.8
Properties which are to be sold	38.2	(3.6)	34.6
Cash and overdrafts	0.1	–	0.1
Net assets acquired	114.7	(3.0)	111.7
Provisions for future trading losses	–	(2.3)	(2.3)
Other provisions	–	(16.4)	(16.4)
Tax on provisions	–	5.2	5.2
Goodwill, including acquisition costs	1.4	16.5	17.9
Cash paid for acquisition	116.1	–	116.1

Properties which the Group does not intend to retain are included in debtors at their estimated realisable value – see note 14. Provision has been made as above for the forecast net losses after interest of operating these outlets until their disposal. The interest attributable to these has been deducted from the Group interest charge – see note 4.

21 CONTINGENT LIABILITIES

	Group 1991 £ m	Group 1990 £ m	Company 1991 £ m	Company 1990 £ m
Guarantees of banking facilities	65.2	59.7	124.2	100.8
Other	1.1	1.8	1.1	1.8
	66.3	61.5	125.3	102.6

22 LEASE COMMITMENTS

	Property £ m	Plant and machinery £ m	1991 Total £ m	Property £ m	Plant and machinery £ m	1990 Total £ m
Whitbread Group						
Annual payments under operating leases which expire:						
Within one year	0.5	0.3	0.8	0.3	0.1	0.4
Between one and five years	5.9	1.2	7.1	3.4	1.1	4.5
After five years	17.7	–	17.7	12.5	–	12.5
	24.1	1.5	25.6	16.2	1.2	17.4

Having completed our extracts from the notes to the accounts, we now go on to show our analysis. Please prepare your own analysis before reading on.

WHITBREAD PLC – Year ended 2 March 1991
OVERVIEW STATEMENT

	1987	1988	1988(1)	1989	1990(2) restated	1991
Key figures (£m)						
Turnover	1 554	1 689	1 689	1 845	2 051	2 060
Net assets	1 491	1 590	2 566	2 733	2 961	3 158
Profit before tax and EI	158.9	187.2	187.2	223.2	265.7	291.5
Growth annual %						
Turnover	1.4	8.7	8.7	9.2	11.2	0.4
Net assets	8.0	6.6	6.6	6.5	8.3	6.7
Profit before tax and EI	16.2	17.8	17.8	19.2	19.0	9.7
Economic indicators – annual % change (1st quarter)						
World trade	1.9	6.0	6.0	5.1	2.2	0.3
UK trade	2.7	5.1	5.1	1.7	0.3	(3.5)
Retail price index	3.8	17.8	3.3	8.0	7.5	8.7
Stock market indicators						
Share price (end June) 'A' Ord.	363	307	307	338	455	448
Annual % change						
Share price	18.2	(15.4)	(15.4)	10.1	34.6	(1.5)
All share index	40.6	(17.1)	(17.1)	(2.6)	6.3	(0.9)
Industry index (brewers & distillers)	22.5	(6.5)	(6.5)	18.7	21.4	7.0

Notes

(1) The 1988 figures have been restated to include the 1989 Property Revaluation of £976m, in order that the trend from 1988 to 1989 onwards can be established. The restatement is made by adding £976m to the 1988 figure for Fixed Assets.

(2) Restated 1990 figures reflect changes in accounting policy to include overseas results at average rates of exchange. WIC is included as a subsidiary not as an associated company. 1988 and 1989 figures have not been adjusted since changes are not material.

WHITBREAD PLC – PRODUCT ANALYSIS 1987 – 1990
(prior to restatement of figures in 1991)

Product group	Sales £ m				% of sales				% growth			
	1987	1988	1989	1990	1987	1988	1989	1990	1987	1988	1989	1990
BEER – Brewing and wholesaling	622.8	644.5	692.0	757.8	40.1	38.2	37.5	37.0	6.2	3.5	7.4	9.5
RETAILING – Managed outlets, restaurants, etc.	732.5	859.6	990.5	1 154.3	47.1	50.9	53.7	56.4	15.7	17.3	15.2	16.5
WINE & SPIRITS – Distilling	337.5	333.0	315.5	299.8	21.7	19.7	17.1	14.6	(32.4)	(11.8)	(5.3)	(5.0)
	1 692.8	1 837.1	1 998.0	2 211.9	108.9	108.8	108.3	108.0	(1.5)	8.5	8.8	10.7
Inter-operational sales	(138.9)	(148.4)	(152.7)	(163.7)	(8.9)	(8.8)	(8.3)	(8.0)	(25.2)	6.8	2.9	7.2
TOTAL	1 553.9	1 688.7	1 845.3	2 048.2	100.0	100.0	100.0	100.0	1.4	8.7	9.3	11.0

Product group	Profit £ m				Profit/Sales %			
	1987	1988	1989	1990	1987	1988	1989	1990
BEER – Brewing and wholesaling	92.4	100.4	108.7	124.1	14.8	15.6	15.7	16.4
RETAILING – Managed outlets, restaurants, etc.	69.4	83.1	100.1	117.9	9.5	9.7	10.1	10.2
WINES & SPIRITS – Distilling	26.5	31.7	35.4	44.0	7.9	9.5	11.2	14.7
	188.3	215.2	244.2	286.0	11.1	11.7	12.2	12.9
Profit on retail disposals	8.0	10.3	24.8	33.4	–	–	–	–
Income from related cos. investments, etc.	9.7	8.5	18.1	14.4	–	–	–	–
Deduct: Central services	(13.8)	(15.7)	(22.9)	(21.3)	–	–	–	–
Interest	(33.3)	(31.1)	(41.0)	(52.3)	–	–	–	–
TOTAL	158.9	187.2	223.2	260.2	10.2	11.1	12.1	12.7

WHITBREAD PLC – PRODUCT ANALYSIS 1990 – 1991 (restated)

Product group	Sales £ m 1990	1991	% sales 1990	1991	% growth 1990	1991
Beer and other drinks	747.6	897.2	36.4	43.5	–	20.0
Pub partnerships	251.9	273.6	12.3	13.3	–	8.6
Managed retail estates	1 145.9	1 260.5	55.9	61.2	–	10.0
Discontinued businesses	226.1	–	11.0	–	–	–
	2 371.5	2 431.3	115.6	118.0	18.7	2.5
Inter-operational sales	(320.4)	(371.5)	(15.6)	(18.0)	109.8	15.9
TOTAL	2 051.1	2 059.8	100.0	100.0	11.2	0.4

Product group	Profit £m 1990	1991	Profit/Sales % 1990	1991
Beer and other drinks**	61.8	71.1	8.3	7.9
Pub partnerships	63.2	65.7	25.1	24.0
Managed retail estates	120.6	128.7	10.5	10.2
Discontinued businesses	34.5	–	15.3	–
	280.1	265.5	11.8	10.9
Profit on retail disposals	33.4	36.3	–	–
Income from property development, investments, etc.	14.4	14.1	–	–
Deduct:				
Central services	(21.5)	(21.4)	–	–
Interest	(42.6)	(3.0)	–	–
TOTAL	265.7	291.5	13.0	14.2

* Product groups have been revised in 1991 annual report
** Includes profit contributions from Whitbread's 22.5% shareholding in Britvic

GEOGRAPHICAL ANALYSIS 1990 – 1991 (restated)

Geographical area	Sales £ m 1990	1991	% of sales 1990	1991	% growth 1991
United Kingdom	1 716.4	1 897.8	83.7	92.1	10.6
Rest of the world	121.1	162.0	5.9	7.9	33.8
Discontinued businesses	213.6	–	10.4	–	–
TOTAL	2 051.1	2 059.8	100.0	100.0	0.4

WHITBREAD PLC
Year ended 2 March 1991
Summary of key figures and ratios (including capitalized goodwill)

	1987	1988	1988**	1989	1990* restated	1991
Performance ratios						
Return on equity (%)	9.2	11.4	6.1	7.2	7.4	8.1
(b)	9.2	11.4	5.3	6.3	6.9	7.5
Tax ratio (%)	30.6	29.5	29.5	26.0	24.8	24.4
Return on investments (%)	14.2	13.3	13.3	12.4	10.8	13.0
Return on net operating assets (%) (a)	12.2	13.5	8.2	9.5	11.2	10.5
(b)	12.2	13.5	7.3	8.4	10.4	9.8
Operating profit margin (%)	11.5	12.1	12.1	13.6	15.3	15.5
Net operating asset turnover (times) (a)	1.07	1.10	0.68	0.70	0.73	0.68
(b)	1.1	1.1	0.60	0.62	0.68	0.63
Tangible fixed asset turnover (times) (a)	1.22	1.19	0.71	0.73	0.76	0.70
(b)	1.22	1.19	0.63	0.64	0.70	0.65
Stock (days) (sales basis)	41.0	40.3	40.3	32.6	19.6	20.3
Trade debtors (days)	31.6	28.7	28.7	23.6	15.7	16.2
Trade creditors (days) (COS basis)	37.7	39.3	39.3	35.0	31.4	34.1
Financial status ratios						
Total debt/capital employed % (a)	26.5	28.3	17.8	20.5	10.4	14.2
(b)	26.5	28.3	15.9	18.2	9.7	13.3
Interest cover (times)	5.3	5.9	5.9	4.8	4.2	5.8
Current ratio	1.41	1.14	1.14	1.08	1.01	1.00
Acid test	0.80	0.65	0.65	0.65	0.74	0.77
Stock market ratios						
Earnings per share	26.6	29.3	29.3	36.0	43.2	47.3
Price/earnings ratio	13.6	10.3	10.3	9.4	10.5	9.5
Dividend yield %	3.4	4.8	4.8	4.9	4.3	4.8
Dividend cover (times)	3.0	2.8	2.8	2.9	2.9	2.9
Stock market indicators						
Share price (end June) 'A' ord.	363	307	307	338	455	448
Annual % change						
Share price	18.2	(15.4)	(15.4)	10.1	34.6	(1.5)
All share index	40.6	(17.1)	(17.1)	(2.6)	6.3	(0.9)
Industry index (brewers & distillers)	22.5	(6.5)	(6.5)	18.7	21.4	7.0

Notes
 * Restated 1990 figures reflect changes in accounting policy
** The 1988 figures have been restated to include the 1989 Property Revaluation of £976m.
(a) Ratios with goodwill written off to reserves (per the accounts)
(b) Ratios including capitalized goodwill

PERFORMANCE RATIOS

	1991		1990 Restated	
Return on equity %	$\dfrac{209.8}{2597.2 - 9.8} = \dfrac{209.8}{2587.4}$	= 8.1	$\dfrac{189.3}{2558.2 - 9.8} = \dfrac{189.3}{2548.4}$	= 7.4
Tax ratio %	$\dfrac{71.1}{291.5}$	= 24.4	$\dfrac{65.8}{265.7}$	= 24.8
Return on fixed asset investments	$\dfrac{9.0 + 14.2}{81.4 + 25.2 + 69.5 + 2.5} = \dfrac{23.2}{178.6}$	= 13.0	$\dfrac{10.2 + 13.1}{118.3 + 25.2 + 67.5 + 5.5} = \dfrac{23.3}{216.5}$	= 10.8
Return on operating net assets	$\dfrac{291.5 + 59.2 - 7.7 - 1.3 - 23.2}{3158.0 + 28.0 + 38.9 - 178.6} = \dfrac{318.5}{3046.3}$	= 10.5	$\dfrac{265.7 + 80.2 - 9.0 - 23.3}{2961.3 + 21.2 + 31.1 - 216.5} = \dfrac{313.6}{2797.1}$	= 11.2
Profit margin	$\dfrac{318.5}{2059.8}$	= 15.5	$\dfrac{313.6}{2051.1}$	= 15.3
Net operating asset turnover	$\dfrac{2059.8}{3046.3}$	= 0.68	$\dfrac{2051.1}{2797.1}$	= 0.73
Fixed asset turnover	$\dfrac{2059.8}{2929.2}$	= 0.70	$\dfrac{2051.1}{2703.6}$	= 0.76
Stock turnover (days) (sales/stock)	$\dfrac{2059.8}{118.4 - 3.9} = \dfrac{2059.8}{114.5}$	= 17.99 (20.3 days)	$\dfrac{2051.1}{113.6 - 3.7} = \dfrac{2051.1}{109.9}$	= 18.66 (19.6 days)
Trade debtors (days) (sales/trade debtors)	$\dfrac{2059.8}{91.2}$	= 22.59 (16.2 days)	$\dfrac{2051.1}{88.1}$	= 23.28 (15.7 days)
Trade creditors (days) (COS/trade creditors)	$\dfrac{1515.3}{141.6}$	= 10.70 (34.1 days)	$\dfrac{1476.3}{127.2}$	= 11.61 (31.4 days)

		1991		1990 Restated	
Solvency					
Total debt/Capital employed	(a)	$\dfrac{390.9 + 28.0 + 38.9}{3158.0 + 28.0 + 38.9} = \dfrac{457.8}{3224.9}$	= 14.2	$\dfrac{261.0 + 21.2 + 31.1}{2961.3 + 21.2 + 31.1} = \dfrac{313.3}{3013.6}$	= 10.4
Long-term debt/capital employed	(b)	$\dfrac{390.9}{3158.0}$	= 12.4	$\dfrac{261.0}{2961.3}$	= 8.8
Interest cover		$\dfrac{291.5 + 59.2 - 7.7 - 1.3}{59.2} = \dfrac{341.7}{59.2}$	= 5.8	$\dfrac{265.7 + 80.2 - 9.0}{80.2} = \dfrac{336.9}{80.2}$	= 4.2
Liquidity					
Current ratio	(a)	$\dfrac{512.2}{577.8 - 28.0 - 38.9} = \dfrac{512.2}{510.9}$	= 1.00	$\dfrac{433.3}{482.6 - 21.2 - 31.1} = \dfrac{433.3}{430.3}$	= 1.01
	(b)	$\dfrac{512.2}{577.8}$	= 0.89	$\dfrac{433.3}{482.6}$	= 0.90
Acid test	(a)	$\dfrac{512.2 - 118.4}{510.9} = \dfrac{393.8}{510.9}$	= 0.77	$\dfrac{433.3 - 113.6}{430.3} = \dfrac{319.7}{430.3}$	= 0.74
	(b)	$\dfrac{393.8}{577.8}$	= 0.68	$\dfrac{319.7}{482.6}$	= 0.66
Stock market ratios					
Earnings per share		$\dfrac{209.8}{443.6}$	= 47.3p	$\dfrac{189.3}{438.4}$	= 43.2p
Price earnings ratio		$\dfrac{448}{47.3}$	= 9.5	$\dfrac{455}{43.2}$	= 10.5
Dividend yield (%)		$\dfrac{16.30 \times 100/75}{448} = \dfrac{21.73}{448}$	= 4.8	$\dfrac{14.80 \times 100/75}{455} = \dfrac{19.73}{455}$	= 4.3
Dividend cover (times)		$\dfrac{47.3}{16.30}$	= 2.90	$\dfrac{43.2}{14.8}$	= 2.92

Notes

(a)   including interest bearing current liabilities as debt
(b)   excluding interest bearing current liabilities

ADJUSTED RATIOS TO CAPITALIZE GOODWILL WRITTEN OFF TO RESERVES

	Acquisitions and goodwill	Goodwill written off
	Written off prior to 1988	103.3
1988	James Burrough plc (dispose of Aureon discotheques)	206.3
		309.6
1989	Small acquisitions	30.4
		340.0
1990	Boddington Group plc Restaurant chains	86.1
		426.1
	Less Goodwill previously written off on the Spirits businesses which have now been sold	213.4
		212.7
1991	Berni Inn and outlets from Grand Metropolitan	25.4
		238.1
	Less goodwill previously written off on businesses now sold	18.2
		219.9

Revised ratios capitalizing the goodwill which have been written off in the published accounts

	Original		Revised

Return on equity

$$1990 \quad \frac{189.3}{2548.4} = 7.4 \qquad \frac{189.3}{2548.4 + 212.7} = \frac{189.3}{2761.1} = 6.9$$

$$1991 \quad \frac{209.8}{2587.4} = 8.1 \qquad \frac{209.8}{2587.4 + 219.9} = \frac{209.8}{2807.3} = 7.5$$

Return on net operating assets

$$1990 \quad \frac{313.6}{2797.1} = 11.2 \qquad \frac{313.6}{2797.1 + 212.7} = \frac{313.4}{3009.8} = 10.4$$

$$1991 \quad \frac{318.5}{3046.3} = 10.5 \qquad \frac{318.5}{3046.3 + 219.9} = \frac{318.5}{3266.2} = 9.8$$

Net operating asset turnover

$$1990 \quad \frac{2051.1}{2797.1} = 0.73 \qquad \frac{2048.2}{2797.1 + 212.7} = \frac{2048.2}{3009.8} = 0.68$$

$$1991 \quad \frac{2059.8}{3046.3} = 0.68 \qquad \frac{2059.8}{3046.3 + 219.9} = \frac{2059.8}{3266.2} = 0.63$$

Tangible fixed asset turnover   **Fixed asset turnover (including intangibles) (times)**

$$1990 \quad \frac{2051.1}{2703.6} = 0.76 \qquad \frac{2051.1}{2703.6 + 212.7} = \frac{2051.1}{2916.3} = 0.70$$

$$1991 \quad \frac{2059.8}{2929.2} = 0.70 \qquad \frac{2059.8}{2929.2 + 219.9} = \frac{2059.8}{3149.1} = 0.65$$

Total debt/capital employed

$$1990 \quad \frac{313.3}{3013.6} = 10.4 \qquad \frac{313.3}{3013.6 + 212.7} = \frac{313.3}{3226.3} = 9.7$$

$$1991 \quad \frac{457.8}{3224.9} = 14.2 \qquad \frac{457.8}{3224.9 + 219.9} = \frac{457.8}{3444.8} = 13.3$$

WHITBREAD PLC
Restated funds flow statements 1987 – 1991

	Notes	1987	1988	1989	1990 restated	1991
Internal funds/investment						
Group operating profit	1(h)	173.7	198.4	242.4	291.0	281.8
Add Interest + investment income	1(c+d+f+g)	6.4	8.8	14.7	44.7	59.9
Dividends – related cos.	1(b)–3	5.8	5.9	6.3	3.9	2.2
Profit on disposal FA	4	(5.4)	(8.6)	(22.2)	(20.2)	(15.3)
Depreciation	2	44.5	51.0	57.9	66.1	71.7
Other	5	(0.6)	4.9	–	–	–
		224.4	260.4	299.1	385.5	400.3
Gross funds from operations						
Interest	1(e)	(36.4)	(35.8)	(50.6)	(80.2)	(59.2)
Tax	20	(23.4)	(34.6)	(51.8)	(48.3)	(59.0)
Dividends	19	(32.1)	(37.2)	(49.5)	(62.2)	(72.9)
		(91.9)	(107.6)	(151.9)	(190.7)	(191.1)
Net funds from operations		132.5	152.8	147.2	194.8	209.2
Extraordinary items and provisions	17	(9.5)	(10.7)	(3.7)	(13.8)	(43.2)
		123.0	142.1	143.5	181.0	166.0
Sale of fixed assets	6	37.9	45.8	103.1	611.8	52.6
Sales of fixed asset investments	7	46.4	21.4	29.2	57.1	66.2
Total internally generated funds		207.3	209.3	275.8	849.9	284.8
Working capital (inc.)/dec.						
Stocks inc/(dec)	14	(1.0)	(4.7)	(12.0)	(2.2)	(3.9)
Debtors inc/(dec)	15	(14.0)	(2.5)	(6.6)	(27.1)	(27.1)
		(15.0)	(7.2)	(18.6)	(29.3)	(31.0)
Creditors (inc)/dec	16	21.5	57.1	(30.0)	37.5	70.2
		6.5	49.9	(48.6)	8.2	39.2
		213.8	259.2	227.2	858.1	324.0
Fixed asset investment etc.						
Purchase of fixed assets	12	(152.0)	(176.2)	(258.7)	(308.7)	(270.0)
Subsidiaries and intangible assets	11–22	(4.1)	(201.6)	(26.8)	(131.2)	(129.8)
Investment in associated companies + other inv.	13	(57.7)	(39.7)	(49.9)	(72.7)	(73.9)
		(213.8)	(417.5)	(335.4)	(512.6)	(473.7)
(Financial requirement)/ surplus	£m	0.0	(158.3)	(108.2)	345.5	(149.7)
External financing						
Issue of shares (incl. minorities 1990 + 1991)	9 + 23	2.6	102.9	5.0	10.9	11.6
Minorities	10	1.0	1.1	2.3	–	–
Loans	8–18 + 24–25	55.4	52.4	102.6	(261.6)	132.1
Overdrafts and cash	26	(59.0)	1.9	(1.7)	(94.8)	6.0
Financing/(investment)	£ m	0.0	158.3	108.2	(345.5)	149.7

WHITBREAD PLC
Published funds flow statements 1987 – 1991

	1987	1988	1989	1990 restated	1991
Source of funds					
1 Profit on ordinary activities before tax	158.9	187.2	223.2	265.7	291.5
Items not involving movement of funds:					
2 Depreciation	44.5	51.0	57.9	66.1	71.7
3 Retained profits of related companies	(9.4)	(9.9)	(10.4)	(6.3)	(6.8)
4 Profit on disposal of fixed assets	(5.4)	(8.6)	(22.2)	(20.2)	(15.3)
5 Other	(0.6)	4.9	–	–	–
Funds generated by operations	188.0	224.6	248.5	305.3	341.1
6 Sale of property and plant, and subsidiary	37.9	45.8	103.1	611.8	52.6
7 Realization of FA investments	46.4	21.4	29.2	57.1	66.2
8 Additional loan capital	69.4	229.0	292.0	–	–
9 Issue of shares	2.6	102.9	5.0	–	–
10 Minority contribution to new subsidiary	1.0	1.1	2.3	–	–
Total source of funds	345.3	624.8	680.1	974.2	459.9
Application of funds					
Investment in:					
11 Subsidiaries	16.6	220.3	32.5	121.7	131.0
12 Property and plant	152.0	176.2	258.7	308.7	270.0
13 FA investment	57.7	39.7	49.9	72.7	73.9
	226.3	436.2	341.1	503.1	474.9
Working capital requirements					
14 Increase in stocks	1.0	4.7	12.0	2.2	3.9
15 Increase in debtors	14.0	2.5	6.6	27.1	27.1
16 (Increase) in creditors	(21.5)	(57.1)	30.0	(37.5)	(70.2)
	(6.5)	(49.9)	48.6	(8.2)	(39.2)
17 Rationalization charges	9.5	10.7	3.7	13.8	43.2
Total commercial use of funds	229.3	397.0	393.4	508.7	478.9
18 Repayment of loan capital	14.0	176.6	189.4	–	–
19 Dividends	32.1	37.2	49.5	62.2	72.9
20 Taxation	23.4	34.6	51.8	48.3	59.0
£m	298.8	645.4	684.1	619.2	610.8
Cash flow prior to funding changes					
21 Net increase/(decrease)	46.5	(20.6)	(4.0)	355.0	(150.9)
22 Funds movement resulting from acquisition/disposal of subsidiaries	12.5	18.7	5.7	(9.5)	1.2
23 Issue of shares and minority contributions received				10.9	11.6
24 Loan capital received				14.3	164.7
25 Loan capital repaid				(275.9)	(32.6)
Balance sheet movement of cash at bank and in hand less overdrafts	59.0	(1.9)	1.7	94.8	(6.0)

WHITBREAD PLC
Adjustments to published funds flow statements 1987 – 1991

		1987	1988	1989	1990 restated	1991
1 Group operating profit						
(a) Profit on ordinary activities before tax		158.9	187.2	223.2	265.7	291.5
(b) Income of related companies		(15.2)	(15.8)	(16.7)	(10.2)	(9.0)
(c) Interest received (N4)		(1.7)	(2.8)	(4.6)	(16.9)	(31.3)
(d) Interest capitalized (N4)		(1.4)	(1.9)	(5.0)	(9.0)	(7.7)
(e) Interest paid (N4)		36.4	35.8	50.6	80.2	59.2
(f) Interest re Grand Met properties (N4)		–	–	–	–	(1.3)
(g) Investment income (N3)		(3.3)	(4.1)	(5.1)	(18.8)	(19.6)
(h) Operating profit	£m	173.7	198.4	242.4	291.0	281.8
Earnings-related companies						
1 (b) Income (from P&L notes)		15.2	15.8	16.7	10.2	9.0
3 Retained profits		9.4	9.9	10.4	6.3	6.8
1 (b)-3 Dividends declared	£m	5.8	5.9	6.3	3.9	2.2
Loan capital						
8 or 24 Loan capital increase		69.4	229.0	292.0	14.3	164.7
18 or 25 Loan capital repaid		14.0	176.6	189.4	275.9	32.6
8–18 or 24–25	£m	55.4	52.4	102.6	(261.6)	132.1

WHITBREAD PLC
Summary and interpretation of the 1991 accounts analysis

1 In markets which became more difficult as the year progressed, Whitbread's profit before tax rose 10 per cent to £292 million, helped by a £35 million fall in net interest paid. Sales at £2 060 million were virtually static, less than 8 per cent being outside the UK.

2 The overall margin rose from 15.3 per cent to 15.5 per cent, including profits of £36 million (£33 million in 1990) on disposals of properties. At a trading level, however, pressure on profit margins led to a slight decline in margins in each business sector:

	Sales 1991 £ m	Profit 1991 £ m	Profit/Sales 1991 %	Profit/Sales 1990 %
Beer and other drinks	897	71	7.9	8.3
Pub partnerships	274	66	24.0	25.1
Managed retail outlets	1 260	129	10.2	10.5
	2 431	266	10.9	11.8
Miscellaneous		26		
(Inter-operational sales)	(371)			
	2 060	292		

Overall cost of sales were 73.5 per cent (up from 72.0 per cent in 1990), while administration and other costs declined to 12.4 per cent (from 13.3 per cent). The apparent profitability of individual businesses obviously depends to some extent on transfer prices.

3 Return on equity rose from 7.4 per cent to 8.1 per cent, while return on net operating assets fell from 11.2 per cent to 10.5 per cent. These returns, which look low, take into account the property revaluation of £976 million in 1989. (They do not, however, add back the goodwill written off to reserves.)

4 Asset turnover looks low. On revalued assets it fell from 0.73 to 0.68. This reflects tangible fixed asset additions of £262 million and static sales.

5   Results for 1991 were determined before taking into account extra-ordinary items and other write-offs, as follows:

Extraordinary items	1991 £ m	1990 £ m
Net loss on disposal of industrial properties, investments and businesses	(16)	404 profit
Costs arising from MMC inquiry	(55)	(64)
	(71)	340
Tax thereon	13	(2)
	(58)	338

Other write-offs	
Provisions on acquisitions (mainly Berni Inns)	
for future trading losses	3
other	18
Goodwill on Berni acquisition	
written off to reserves	25
	46

These amounts, especially the MMC inquiry costs, seem significant compared to profit after tax on ordinary activities of £210m.

6   Working capital ratios were virtually unchanged in the year:

	1991	1990
Stock days (sales basis)	20.3	19.6
Trade debtor days	16.2	15.7
Trade creditor days (cost of sales basis)	34.1	31.4

Total debtor days and total creditor days rose, reflecting outstanding year-end balances relating to the Berni acquisition.

Current ratio and acid test ratio show little change, and both look reasonable.

7   Gearing rose from 10.4 per cent to 14.2 per cent. Interest cover rose from 4.2 times to 5.8 times. The ratios reflect high asset values, and debt repayment in 1990 following disposal of the wines and spirits business for £542 million.

8   Net funds from operations rose from £195 million to £209 million; but after allowing for payments under extraordinary items and provisions, there was a fall from £181 million to £166 million.

Capital expenditure continued at a high level (£474 million) in the year.

During the year Whitbread acquired 150 outlets and the Berni brand name from Grand Metropolitan for £115 million. With £60 million outstanding on the Berni acquisition at the year-end, working capital provided a net £39 million.

Over the last 5 years Whitbread's total fixed capital spending has averaged about £400 million a year, compared with net funds from operations of £150 million. The gap of some £250 million a year has been financed by various disposals averaging £100 million a year, plus the 1990 proceeds of £542 million from selling the wines and spirits business to Allied-Lyons.

In 1991 the financing requirement of £150 million was financed by borrowing.

9   During the 4 years 1987 to 1991, the company's share price dropped by 6 per cent in real terms. In 1991 the share price declined by 1.5 per cent, while the brewing industry index rose by 7 per cent.

10 Whitbread is investing heavily in a range of related brewing, retailing, and hotel activities. It needs to show higher returns from the investments made.

Appendix 1

ACCOUNTING STANDARDS
as at 31 December 1991

SSAP	Topic	Issued	Revised
1	Associated Companies	January 1971	April 1982
2	Accounting Policies	November 1971	
3	Earnings Per Share	February 1972	August 1984
4	Government Grants	April 1974	July 1990
5	Value Added Tax	April 1974	
6	Extraordinary Items	April 1974	August 1986
7*	*Current Purchasing Power*	*May 1974*	
8	Taxation (imputation system)	August 1974	December 1977
9	Stocks and Work in Progress	May 1975	September 1988
10*	*Source and Application of Funds*	July 1975	
11*	*Deferred Tax*	*August 1975*	
12	Depreciation	December 1977	January 1987
13	Research and Development	December 1977	January 1989
14	Group Accounts	September 1978	
15	Deferred Tax	October 1978	May 1985
16*	*Current Cost Accounting*	*March 1980*	
17	Post Balance Sheet Events	August 1980	
18	Contingencies	August 1980	
19	Investment Properties	November 1981	
20	Foreign Currency Translation	April 1983	
21	Leases and Hire Purchase Contracts	August 1984	
22	Goodwill	December 1984	
23	Acquisitions and Mergers	April 1985	
24	Pension Costs	May 1988	
25	Segmental Reporting	June 1990	

FRS

1	Cash Flow Statements	September 1991	

*Subsequently withdrawn or lapsed.

INTERNATIONAL ACCOUNTING STANDARDS
as at 31 December 1991

IAS	Topic
1	Accounting Policies
2	Inventories
3	Consolidated Financial Statements
4	Depreciation
5	Information to be Disclosed in Financial Statements
6*	*Accounting Treatment of Changing Prices*
7	Statement of Changes in Financial Position
8	Unusual and Prior Period Items
9	Research and Development Activities
10	Contingencies and Post-Balance Sheet Events
11	Construction Contracts
12	Taxes on Income
13	Presentation of Current Assets and Current Liabilities
14	Reporting Financial Information by Segment
15	Information Reflecting the Effects of Changing Prices
16	Property, Plant and Equipment
17	Leases
18	Revenue Recognition
19	Retirement Benefits, in Employers' Accounts
20	Government Grants
21	Changes in Foreign Currency Exchange Rates
22	Business Combinations
23	Capitalization of Borrowing Costs
24	Related Party Disclosures
25	Investments
26	Reporting by Retirement Benefit Plans
27	Consolidated Financial Statements
28	Investments in Associates
29	Financial Reporting in Hyper-inflationary Economies
30	Disclosure in the account of Banks and Financial Institutions
31	Investments in Joint Ventures

*Subsequently lapsed.

Appendix 2

ACRONYMS

ACT	Advance Corporation Tax
ASB	Accounting Standards Board
BS	Balance Sheet
BV	Book Value
CA	Current Assets
CCA	Current Cost Accounting
COGS	Cost Of Goods Sold
COSA	Cost Of Sales Adjustment
CPP	Constant Purchasing Power
DPR	Dividend Payout Ratio
DPS	Dividend Per Share
DY	Dividend Yield
ED	Exposure Draft
EPS	Earnings Per Share
EY	Earnings Yield
FA	Fixed Assets
FASB	Financial Accounting Standards Board (USA)
FG	Finished Goods
FIFO	First In First Out
FRS	Financial Reporting Standard
GAAP	Generally Accepted Accounting Principles (USA)
GPLA	General Price Level Adjustments (USA)
HC	Historical Cost
IAS	International Accounting Standard
ICAEW	Institute of Chartered Accountants in England and Wales
IOSCO	International Organization of Securities Commissions
LIFO	Last In First Out
Ltd	Limited
MI	Minority Interest
MV	Market Value
MWCA	Monetary Working Capital Adjustment
NBV	Net Book Value
NRV	Net Realizable Value
P & L	Profit and Loss
PAP	Pre-Acquisition Profit
PAT	Profit After Tax
PBIT	Profit Before Interest payable and Tax
PBT	Profit Before Tax
P/E	Price/Earnings (ratio)
plc	Public Limited Company
RC	Replacement Cost
RE	Retained Earnings
RM	Raw Materials (stock)
RI	Residual Income
ROI	Return On Investment
RPI	Retail Prices Index
SL	Straight Line (depreciation)
SSAP	Statement of Standard Accounting Practice
TB	Trial Balance
VAT	Value Added Tax
WC	Working Capital
WIP	Work-In-Progress

Appendix 3

BIBLIOGRAPHY

The Background and structure of company accounts

ICAEW: *Survey of Published Accounts*, annually.
Sir Ronald Leach and Edward Stamp (eds): *British Accounting Standards: The First 10 Years*, Woodhead-Faulkner, 1981.
Peter Taylor and Stuart Turley: *The Regulation of Accounting*, Blackwell, 1986.
Companies Act, 1985, Fourth Schedule (as amended by *Companies Act, 1989*).

Analysing company accounts

George Foster: *Financial Statement Analysis*, Prentice-Hall, 2nd edn, 1986.
C. A. Westwick: *How to Use Management Ratios*, Gower, 2nd edn, 1987.

Recording business transactions

Paul Gee: *Spicer and Pegler's Book-keeping and Accounts*, Butterworths/HFL, 20th edn, 1988.

Measuring profit or loss

T. A. Lee: *Income and Value Measurement*, Nelson, 3rd edn, 1986.
R. H. Parker, G. C. Harcourt, and G. Whittington (eds): *Readings in the Concept and Measurement of Business Income*, Philip Allan, 2nd edn, 1986.

Fixed assets and depreciation

W. T. Baxter: *Depreciation*.

Cash flow statements

R. K. Jaedicke and R. T. Sprouse: Accounting Flows: *Income, Funds and Cash*, Prentice-Hall, 2nd edn, 1983.

Taxation

J. A. Kay and M. A. King: *The British Tax System*, Oxford, 5th edn, 1990.
Allied Dunbar Tax Guide, annually.
Tolley's Corporation Tax, annually.

Capital structure

Richard Brealey and Stewart Myers: *Principles of Corporate Finance*, McGraw-Hill, 4th edn, 1991.
J. M. Samuels and F. M. Wilkes: *Management of Company Finance*, Van Nostrand Reinhold, 5th edn, 1990.

Group accounts

H. K. Jaeger: *The Structure of Consolidated Accounting*, Macmillan, 2nd edn, 1984.

International accounting

David Alexander and Simon Archer: *The European Accounting Guide*, Academic Press, 1992.
S. J. Gray, L. G. Campbell, and J. C. Shaw: *International Financial Accounting*, Macmillan, 1984.
Christopher Nobes and Robert Parker (eds): *Comparative International Accounting*, Prentice-Hall, 3rd edn, 1991.

Inflation accounting

W. T. Baxter: *Inflation Accounting*, Philip Allan, 1984.
David Tweedie and Geoffrey Whittington: *The Debate on Inflation Accounting*, Cambridge, 1984.

Interpreting company accounts

Ernst & Young: *UK GAAP*, Longman, 2nd edn, 1991.
I. Griffiths: *Creative Accounting*, Sidgwick and Jackson, 1986.
Geoffrey Holmes and Alan Sugden: *Interpreting Company Reports and Accounts*, Woodhead-Faulkner, 4th edn, 1990.
Michael Jameson: *A Practical Guide to Creative Accounting*, Kogan Page, 1988.

Appendix 4

RETAIL PRICES INDEX

A Post-war series

June	1947	100.0 to January 1956	153.4
January 1956		100.0 to January 1962	117.5
January 1962		100.0 to January 1974	191.8
January 1974		100.0 to January 1987	395.5
January 1987		100.0	

Published monthly in the *Employment Gazette*.

B Annual averages (January 1987 = 100.0)

1960	12.5	1970	18.5	1980	66.9
1961	12.9	1971	20.3	1981	74.8
1962	13.4	1972	21.7	1982	81.2
1963	13.7	1973	23.7	1983	85.0
1964	14.2	1974	27.5	1984	89.2
1965	14.8	1975	34.2	1985	94.6
1966	15.4	1976	39.8	1986	97.8
1967	15.8	1977	46.2	1987	101.9
1968	16.5	1978	49.9	1988	106.9
1969	17.4	1979	56.7	1989	115.2
				1990	126.1
				1991	133.5

C Annual rates of increase (calendar year)

1960	2%	1970	8%	1980	15%
1961	4%	1971	9%	1981	12%
1962	3%	1972	8%	1982	5%
1963	2%	1973	11%	1983	5%
1964	5%	1974	19%	1984	5%
1965	4%	1975	25%	1985	6%
1966	4%	1976	15%	1986	4%
1967	2%	1977	12%	1987	4%
1968	6%	1978	8%	1988	7%
1969	5%	1979	17%	1989	8%
				1990	9%
				1991	5%

Appendix 5

Companies Act 1985, Schedule 4: Form and content of company accounts (as amended by Schedules 1 and 2 of the Companies Act 1989)

PART I: GENERAL RULES AND FORMATS

Section A: General rules

1 (1) Subject to the following provisions of this Schedule –
(a) every balance sheet of a company shall show the items listed in either of the balance sheet formats set out below in section B of this Part; and
(b) every profit and loss account of a company shall show the items listed in any one of the profit and loss account formats so set out;
in either case in the order and under the headings and subheadings given in the format adopted.

(2) Subparagraph (1) above is not to be read as requiring the heading or subheading for any item to be distinguished by any letter or number assigned to that item in the format adopted.

2 (1) Where in accordance with paragraph 1 a company's balance sheet or profit and loss account for any financial year has been prepared by reference to one of the formats set out in section B below, the directors of the company shall adopt the same format in preparing the accounts for subsequent financial years of the company unless in their opinion there are special reasons for a change.

(2) Particulars of any change in the format adopted in preparing a company's balance sheet or profit and loss account in accordance with paragraph 1 shall be disclosed, and the reasons for the change shall be explained, in a note to the accounts in which the new format is first adopted.

3 (1) Any item required in accordance with paragraph 1 to be shown in a company's balance sheet or profit and loss account may be shown in greater detail than required by the format adopted.

(2) A company's balance sheet or profit and loss account may include an item representing or covering the amount of any asset or liability, income or expenditure not otherwise covered by any of the items listed in the format adopted, but the following shall not be treated as assets in any company's balance sheet –

(a) preliminary expenses;
(b) expenses of and commission on any issue of shares or debentures; and
(c) costs of research.

(3) In preparing a company's balance sheet or profit and loss account the directors of the company shall adapt the arrangement and headings and sub-headings otherwise required by paragraph 1 in respect of items to which an Arabic number is assigned in the format adopted, in any case where the special nature of the company's business requires such adaptation.

(4) Items to which Arabic numbers are assigned in any of the formats set out in section B below may be combined in a company's accounts for any financial year if either –

(a) their individual amounts are not material to assessing the state of affairs or profit or loss of the company for that year; or
(b) the combination facilitates that assessment;

but in a case within paragraph (b) the individual amounts of any items so combined shall be disclosed in a note to the accounts.

(5) Subject to paragraph 4(3) below, a heading or subheading corresponding to an item listed in the format adopted in preparing a company's balance sheet or profit and loss account shall not be included if there is no amount to be shown for that item in respect of the financial year to which the balance sheet or profit and loss account relates.

(6) Every profit and loss account of a company shall show the amount of the company's profit or loss on ordinary activities before taxation.

(7) Every profit and loss account of a company shall show separately as additional items –

(a) any amount set aside or proposed to be set aside to, or withdrawn or proposed to be withdrawn from, reserves; and
(b) the aggregate amount of any dividends paid and proposed.

4 (1) In respect of every item shown in a company's balance sheet or profit and loss account the corresponding amount for the financial year immediately preceding that to which the balance sheet or profit and loss account relates shall also be shown.

(2) Where that corresponding amount is not comparable with the amount to be shown for the item in question in respect of the financial year to which the balance sheet or profit and loss account relates, the former amount shall be adjusted and particulars of the adjustment and the reasons for it shall be disclosed in a note to the accounts.

(3) Paragraph 3(5) does not apply in any case where an amount can be shown for the item in question in respect of the financial year immediately preceding that to which the balance sheet or profit and loss account relates, and that amount shall be shown under the heading or subheading required by paragraph 1 for that item.

5 Amounts in respect of items representing assets or income may not be set off against amounts in respect of items representing liabilities or expenditure (as the case may be), or vice versa.

Section B: The required formats for accounts

Preliminary

6 References in this Part of this Schedule to the items listed in any of the formats set out below are to those items read together with any of the notes following the formats which apply to any of those items, and the requirement imposed by paragraph 1 to show the items listed in any such format in the order adopted in the format is subject to any provision in those notes for alternative positions for any particular items.

7 A number in brackets following any item in any of the formats set out below is a reference to the note of that number in the notes following the formats.

8 In the notes following the formats –

(a) the heading of each note gives the required heading or subheading for the item to which it applies and a reference to any letters and numbers assigned to that item in the formats set out below (taking a reference in the case of Format 2 of the balance sheet formats to the item listed under 'Assets' or under 'Liabilities' as the case may require); and

(b) references to a numbered format are to the balance sheet format or (as the case may require) to the profit and loss account format of that number set out below.

Balance sheet formats

Format 1

A   Called up share capital not paid (*1*)

B   Fixed assets

   I   Intangible assets

      1   Development costs

      2   Concessions, patents, licences, trade marks and similar rights and assets (*2*)

      3   Goodwill (*3*)

      4   Payments on account

   II   Tangible assets

      1   Land and buildings

      2   Plant and machinery

      3   Fixtures, fittings, tools and equipment

      4   Payments on account and assets in course of construction

   III   Investments

      1   Shares in group undertakings

      2   Loans to group undertakings

      3   Interests in associated undertakings
Other participating interests

      4   Loans to undertakings in which the company has a participating interest

      5   Other investments other than loans

      6   Other loans

      7   Own shares (*4*)

C   Current assets

   I   Stocks

      1   Raw materials and consumables

      2   Work-in-progress

      3   Finished goods and goods for resale

      4   Payments on account

   II   Debtors (*5*)

      1   Trade debtors

      2   Amounts owed by group undertakings

      3   Amounts owed by undertakings in which the company has a participating interest

      4   Other debtors

      5   Called up share capital not paid (*1*)

      6   Prepayments and accrued income (*6*)

   III   Investments

      1   Shares in group undertakings

      2   Own shares (*4*)

      3   Other investments

   IV   Cash at bank and in hand

D   Prepayments and accrued income (*6*)

E   Creditors: amounts falling due within one year

      1   Debenture loans (*7*)

      2   Bank loans and overdrafts

      3   Payments received on account (*8*)

      4   Trade creditors

      5   Bills of exchange payable

      6   Amounts owed to group undertakings

      7   Amounts owed to undertakings in which the company has a participating interest

      8   Other creditors including taxation and social security (*9*)

      9   Accruals and deferred income (*10*)

F   Net current assets (liabilities) (*11*)

G   Total assets less current liabilities

H   Creditors: amounts falling due after more than one year

      1   Debenture loans (*7*)

      2   Bank loans and overdrafts

      3   Payments received on account (*8*)

      4   Trade creditors

      5   Bills of exchange payable

      6   Amounts owed to group undertakings

      7   Amounts owed to undertakings in which the company has a participating interest

      8   Other creditors including taxation and social security (*9*)

      9   Accruals and deferred income (*10*)

I   Provisions for liabilities and charges

      1   Pensions and similar obligations

      2   Taxation, including deferred taxation

      3   Other provisions

J   Accruals and deferred income (*10*)

K   Capital and reserves

   I   Called up share capital (*12*)

   II   Share premium account

   III   Revaluation reserve

   IV   Other reserves

      1   Capital redemption reserve

      2   Reserve for own shares

      3   Reserves provided for by the articles of association

      4   Other reserves

   V   Profit and loss account

Minority interests

Balance sheet formats

Format 2

ASSETS

A   Called up share capital not paid (*1*)

B   Fixed assets
   I   Intangible assets
      1   Development costs
      2   Concessions, patents, licences, trade marks and similar rights and assets (*2*)
      3   Goodwill (*3*)
      4   Payments on account
   II   Tangible assets
      1   Land and buildings
      2   Plant and machinery
      3   Fixtures, fittings, tools and equipment
      4   Payments on account and assets in course of construction
   III   Investments
      1   Shares in group undertakings
      2   Loans to group undertakings
      3   Interests in associated undertakings
        Other participating interests
      4   Loans to undertakings in which the company has a participating interest
      5   Other investments other than loans
      6   Other loans
      7   Own shares (*4*)

C   Current assets
   I   Stocks
      1   Raw materials and consumables
      2   Work-in-progress
      3   Finished goods and goods for resale
      4   Payments on account
   II   Debtors (*5*)
      1   Trade debtors
      2   Amounts owed by group undertakings
      3   Amounts owed by undertakings in which the company has a participating interest
      4   Other debtors
      5   Called up share capital not paid (*1*)
      6   Prepayments and accrued income (*6*)

   III   Investments
      1   Shares in group undertakings
      2   Own shares (*4*)
      3   Other investments
   IV   Cash at bank and in hand

D   Prepayments and accrued income (*6*)

LIABILITIES

A   Capital and reserves
   I   Called up share capital (*12*)
   II   Share premium account
   III   Revaluation reserve
   IV   Other reserves
      1   Capital redemption reserve
      2   Reserve for own shares
      3   Reserves provided for by the articles of association
      4   Other reserves
   V   Profit and loss account
   Minority interests

B   Provisions for liabilities and charges
      1   Pensions and similar obligations
      2   Taxation including deferred taxation
      3   Other provisions

C   Creditors (*13*)
      1   Debenture loans (*7*)
      2   Bank loans and overdrafts
      3   Payments received on account (*8*)
      4   Trade creditors
      5   Bills of exchange payable
      6   Amounts owed to group undertakings
      7   Amounts owed to undertakings in which the company has a participating interest
      8   Other creditors including taxation and social security (*9*)
      9   Accruals and deferred income (*10*)

D   Accruals and deferred income (*10*)

Notes on the balance sheet formats

(1)   Called up share capital not paid
(Formats 1 and 2, items A and C.II5.)
This item may be shown in either of the two positions given in Formats 1 and 2.

(2)   Concessions, patents, licences, trade marks and similar rights and assets
(Formats 1 and 2, item B.I.2.)
Amounts in respect of assets shall only be included in a company's balance sheet under this item if either –

(a)   the assets were acquired for valuable consideration and are not required to be shown under goodwill; or

(b)   the assets in question were created by the company itself.

(3)   Goodwill
(Formats 1 and 2, item B.I.3.)
Amounts representing goodwill shall only be included to the extent that the goodwill was acquired for valuable consideration.

(4)   Own shares
(Formats 1 and 2, items B.III.7 and C.III.2.)
The nominal value of the shares held shall be shown separately.

(5)   Debtors
(Formats 1 and 2, items C.II.1 to 6.)
The amount falling due after more than one year shall be shown separately for each item included under debtors.

(6)   Prepayments and accrued income
(Formats 1 and 2, items C.II.6 and D.)
This item may be shown in either of the two positions given in Formats 1 and 2.

(7)   Debenture loans
(Format 1, items E.1 and H.1 and Format 2, item C.1.)
The amount of any convertible loans shall be shown separately.

(8)   Payments received on account
(Format 1, items E.3 and H.3 and Format 2, item C.3.)
Payments received on account of orders shall be shown for each of these items in so far as they are not shown as deductions from stocks.

(9)   Other creditors including taxation and social security
(Format 1, items E.8 and H.8 and Format 2, item C.8)
The amount for creditors in respect of taxation and social security shall be shown separately from the amount for other creditors.

(10)   Accruals and deferred income
(Format I, items E.9, H.9 and J and Format 2, items C.9 and D.)
The two positions given for this item in Format 1 at E.9 and H.9 are an alternative to the position at J, but if the item is not shown in a position corresponding to that at J it may be shown in either or both of the other two positions (as the case may require).

The two positions given for this item in Format 2 are alternatives.

(11)   Net current assets (liabilities)
(Format 1, item F.)
In determining the amount to be shown for this item any amounts shown under 'prepayments and accrued income' shall be taken into account wherever shown.

(12)   Called up share capital
(Format 1, item K.I and Format 2, item A.I)
The amount of allotted share capital and the amount of called up share capital which has been paid up shall be shown separately.

(13)   Creditors
(Format 2, items C.1 to 9.)
Amounts falling due within one year and after one year shall be shown separately for each of these items and their aggregate shall be shown separately for all of these items.

Profit and loss account formats

Format 1
(see note (17) below)

1 Turnover
2 Cost of sales (*14*)
3 Gross profit or loss
4 Distribution costs (*14*)
5 Administrative expenses (*14*)
6 Other operating income
7 Income from shares in group undertakings
   Income from interests in associated undertakings
8 Income from other participating interests
9 Income from other fixed asset investments (*15*)
10 Other interest receivable and similar income (*15*)
11 Amounts written off investments
12 Interest payable and similar charges (*16*)
13 Tax on profit or loss on ordinary activities
14 Profit or loss on ordinary activities after taxation
   Minority interests
15 Extraordinary income
16 Extraordinary charges
17 Extraordinary profit or loss
18 Tax on extraordinary profit or loss
   Minority interests
19 Other taxes not shown under the above items
20 Profit or loss for the financial year

Profit and loss account formats

Format 2

1 Turnover
2 Change in stocks of finished goods and in work-in-progress
3 Own work capitalized
4 Other operating income
5 (a) Raw materials and consumables
   (b) Other external charges
6 Staff costs:
   (a) wages and salaries
   (b) social security costs
   (c) other pension costs
7 (a) Depreciation and other amounts written off tangible and intangible fixed assets
   (b) Exceptional amounts written off current assets
8 Other operating charges
9 Income from shares in group undertakings
   Income from interests in associated undertakings
10 Income from other participating interests
11 Income from other fixed asset investments (*15*)
12 Other interest receivable and similar income (*15*)
13 Amounts written off investments
14 Interest payable and similar charges (*16*)
15 Tax on profit or loss on ordinary activities
16 Profit or loss on ordinary activities after taxation
   Minority interests
17 Extraordinary income
18 Extraordinary charges
19 Extraordinary profit or loss
20 Tax on extraordinary profit or loss
   Minority interests
21 Other taxes not shown under the above items
22 Profit or loss for the financial year

Profit and loss account formats

Format 3
(see note (17) below)

A Charges

  1 Cost of sales (*14*)

  2 Distribution costs (*14*)

  3 Administrative expenses (*14*)

  4 Amounts written off investments

  5 Interest payable and similar charges (*16*)

  6 Tax on profit or loss on ordinary activities

  7 Profit or loss on ordinary activities after taxation
     Minority interests

  8 Extraordinary charges

  9 Tax on extraordinary profit or loss
     Minority interests

 10 Other taxes not shown under the above items

 11 Profit or loss for the financial year

B Income

  1 Turnover

  2 Other operating income

  3 Income from shares in group undertakings
     Income from interests in associated undertakings

  4 Income from other participating interests

  5 Income from other fixed asset investments (*15*)

  6 Other interest receivable and similar income (*15*)

  7 Profit or loss on ordinary activities after taxation
     Minority interests

  8 Extraordinary income
     Minority interests

  9 Profit or loss for the financial year

Profit and loss account formats

Format 4

A Charges

  1 Reduction in stocks of finished goods and in work-in-progress

  2 (a) Raw materials and consumables

     (b) Other external charges

  3 Staff costs:

     (a) wages and salaries

     (b) social security costs

     (c) other pension costs

  4 (a) Depreciation and other amounts written off tangible and intangible fixed assets

     (b) Exceptional amounts written off current assets

  5 Other operating charges

  6 Amounts written off investments

  7 Interest payable and similar charges (*16*)

  8 Tax on profit or loss on ordinary activities

  9 Profit or loss on ordinary activities after taxation
     Minority interests

 10 Extraordinary charges

 11 Tax on extraordinary profit or loss
     Minority interests

 12 Other taxes not shown under the above items

 13 Profit or loss for the financial year

B Income

  1 Turnover

  2 Increase in stocks of finished goods and in work-in-progress

  3 Own work capitalized

  4 Other operating income

  5 Income from shares in group undertakings
     Income from interests in associated undertakings

  6 Income from other participating interests

  7 Income from other fixed asset investments (*15*)

  8 Other interest receivable and similar income (*15*)

  9 Profit or loss on ordinary activities after taxation
     Minority interests

 10 Extraordinary income
     Minority interests

 11 Profit or loss for the financial year

Notes on the profit and loss account formats

(14)   Cost of sales: distribution costs: administrative expenses
(Format 1, items 2, 4 and 5 and Format 3, items A.1, 2 and 3.)
These items shall be stated after taking into account any necessary provisions for depreciation or diminution in value of assets.

(15)   Income from other fixed asset investments: other interest receivable and similar income
(Format 1, items 9 and 10: Format 2, items 11 and 12: Format 3, items B.5 and 6: Format 4, items B.7 and 8.)
Income and interest derived from group undertakings shall be shown separately from income and interest derived from other sources.

(16)   Interest payable and similar charges
(Format 1, item 12: Format 2, item 14: Format 3, item A.5: Format 4, item A.7.)
The amount payable to group undertakings shall be shown separately.

(17)   Formats 1 and 3
The amount of any provisions for depreciation and diminution in value of tangible and intangible fixed assets falling to be shown under items 7(a) and A.4(a) respectively in Formats 2 and 4 shall be disclosed in a note to the accounts in any case where the profit and loss account is prepared by reference to Format 1 or Format 3.

Appendix 6

Blank forms for use in analysis

Please feel free to photocopy any or all of these forms for use as convenient.

SUMMARY OF KEY FIGURES AND RATIOS

	19	19	19	19	19
Key figures (as in 5 year summary) £m Turnover Net assets Profit after tax & minorities					
Growth annual % Turnover Net assets Profit after tax & minorities					
Economic indicators annual % change World trade UK trade Retail prices index					
Performance ratios Return on Equity (%) Tax ratio (%) Return on net operating assets Operating profit margin (%) Net operating asset turnover (times) Tangible fixed asset turnover (times) Stock (days) (COGS basis) Stock (days) (sales basis) Trade debtors (days) (sales basis) Trade creditors (days) (COGS basis) Total debtors (days) (sales basis) Total creditors (days) (sales basis)					

SUMMARY OF KEY FIGURES AND RATIOS
(Continued)

	19	19	19	19	19
Financial status ratios					
Total debt/Capital employed %					
Total debt/Equity %					
Interest cover (times)					
Current ratio					
Acid test					
Stock market ratios					
Earnings per share					
Price/earnings ratio					
Dividend yield %					
Dividend cover (times)					
Stock market indicators					
Share price					
Annual % change					
Share price					
All share index					
Industry index					

PERFORMANCE RATIOS

		19		**19**
Return on equity %	_____ = _____ =		_____ = _____ =	
Tax ratio %	_____ =		_____ =	
Return on net operating assets % (a)	_____ = _____ =		_____ = _____ =	
Operating profit margin % (a)	_____ =		_____ =	
Net operating asset turnover (a)	_____ =		_____ =	
Tangible fixed asset turnover	_____ = _____ =		_____ = _____ =	
Stock turnover (days) (COGS/stock)	_____ =		_____ =	
Stock turnover (days) (sales/stock)	_____ =		_____ =	
Trade debtor (days) (sales/trade debtors)	_____ =		_____ =	
Trade creditors (days) (COGS/trade creditors)	_____ =		_____ =	
Total debtors (days) (sales/total debtors)	_____ =		_____ =	
Total creditors (days) (sales/total creditors	_____ =		_____ =	

(a)   Exclude FA investments and related income if significant

328

FINANCIAL STATUS RATIOS

Solvency

Total debt/Capital employed %   (a) _____ = _____ = _____ = _____ =

Debt/Capital employed %   (b) _____ = _____ = _____ = _____ =

Total debt/Equity %   (a) _____ = _____ = _____ = _____ =

Debt/Equity %   (b) _____ = _____ = _____ = _____ =

Interest cover   _____ = _____ = _____ = _____ =

Liquidity

Current ratio   (a) _____ = _____ = _____ = _____ =

   (b) _____ = _____ = _____ = _____ =

Acid test   (a) _____ = _____ = _____ = _____ =

   (b) _____ = _____ =

Stock market ratios

Earnings per share   _____ = _____ =

Price earnings ratio   _____ = _____ =

Dividend yield %   _____ = _____ = _____ = _____ =

Dividend cover (times)   _____ = _____ =

Treating all interest bearing current liabilities (IBCL) as (a) capital employed (b) current liabilities

PRODUCT ACTIVITY

Product group	Sales £m					% of sales					% growth			
	19	19	19	19	19	19	19	19	19	19	19	19	19	19
Total														

Product group	Profit £m					Profit/Sales %				
	19	19	19	19	19	19	19	19	19	19
Total										

PRODUCT ACTIVITY (continued)

Product	Net assets £m					Profit/Net assets %				
	19	19	19	19	19	19	19	19	19	19
Total										

MARKET ACTIVITY

Geographical area	Sales £m					% of sales					% growth			
	19	19	19	19	19	19	19	19	19	19	19	19	19	19
Total														

Geographical area	Profit £m					Profit/Sales %				
	19	19	19	19	19	19	19	19	19	19
Total										

Geographical area	Net assets £m					Profit/Net assets %				
	19	19	19	19	19	19	19	19	19	19
Total										

RESTATED FUNDS/CASH FLOW STATEMENTS

		19	19	19	19	19
INTERNAL FUNDS/INVESTMENT						
Group operating profit						
Items not involving the flow of funds						
Depreciation						
Gross funds from operations						
Interest						
Tax						
Dividends						
Foreign exchange adjustments						
Net funds from operations						
Working capital inc./(dec.)						
Stocks (increase)						
Debtors (increase)						
Creditors increase/(decrease)						
FX on working capital						
Net funds/cash available for fixed asset investment						
Sale of fixed assets						
Other fixed asset disposals						
Total funds/cash available						
Fixed asset investment						
Fixed assets						
FA investments						
Acquisition of business						
(Financing requirement)/surplus	£m					
EXTERNAL FINANCING						
Ordinary share capital						
Minorities						
Loans						
Overdrafts						
Liquid resources						
Financing/(investment)	£m					

Insert descriptions from Annual Report

	19	19	19	19	19

Insert descriptions from Annual Report

	19	19	19	19	19

Solutions

1.5 The Acme Company Limited

THE ACME COMPANY LIMITED
Balance sheet at 30 June 1992

		£'000
Fixed assets		
Freehold shop		150
Fixtures and fittings		30
		180
Current assets		
Stock	60	
Debtors	40	
Cash	20	
	120	
Less: **Creditors due within one year**		
Trade creditors	30	
Taxation payable	20	
	50	
		70
		250
Capital and reserves		
Called up share capital		200
Profit and loss account		50
		250

Notes

1 Note the order of the items shown in current assets and in creditors due within one year.

2 Note the grouping of items and subtotals in each part of the balance sheet.

1.6 General Contractors Limited

GENERAL CONTRACTORS LIMITED
Profit and loss account
for the year ended 31 December 1992

	£'000
Turnover	1 250
Cost of sales	1 100
Trading profit	150
Interest payable	10
Profit before tax	140
Tax	40
Profit after tax	100
Dividends	60
Retained profit for the year	40

Notes

1 The heading for the profit and loss account

    (a)   includes the name of the company

    (b)   indicates that the account is 'for the year ended 31 December 1992'.

2 Turnover has to be disclosed; and deducting cost of sales determines the amount of trading profit.

3 Cost of sales is £1 050 000 plus depreciation £50 000.

4 Tax is not combined with interest payable; but separate subtotals are shown for

    (a)   'profit before tax'

    (b)   'profit after tax'.

1.7 The Marvel Trading Company Limited

THE MARVEL TRADING COMPANY LIMITED
Profit and loss account
for the year ended 30 June 1992

	£'000
Turnover	1 200
Cost of sales	1 100
Trading profit	100
Income from investments	12
	112
Interest payable	8
Profit before tax	104
Tax	26
Profit after tax	78
Dividends	40
Retained profit for the year	38

Notes

1 The whole account is normally presented as one. Strictly speaking, a separate appropriation account could be shown beginning with 'profit after tax £78 000'.

2 The 38 000 retained profit in respect of the year (that part of the profit for the year not paid to shareholders as dividends) will appear as part of the reserves in the balance sheet, under the heading 'profit and loss account'. The £38 000 retained for the year ended 30 June 1992 will, of course, be added to the balance retained on the profit and loss account at 30 June 1991.

1.8 The Fine Fare Catering Company Limited

THE FINE FARE CATERING COMPANY LIMITED
Balance sheet at 31 March 1991

	£'000			£'000
Capital and reserves		**Fixed assets**		
Called up share capital	60	Leasehold restaurant		70
Profit and loss account	12	Fixtures and fittings		10
Shareholders' funds	72			80
Creditors due within one year		**Current assets**		
Trade creditors	20	Stock	20	
Dividends	8	Cash	10	
Tax	10			30
	38			
	110			110

Profit and loss account
for the year ended 31 March 1991

	£'000
Turnover	150
Cost of sales	120
Trading profit	30
Tax	10
Profit after tax	20
Dividends	8
Retained profit for the year	12

Notes

1 We have chosen to present the balance sheet in the horizontal 'account format'. You might care to re-present it in the more usual 'vertical format' which we have used up to now.

2 Some companies might omit the 'cost of sales' line in the profit and loss account; in which case details would have to be given in a note.

1.9 Andrew Hunt Limited

ANDREW HUNT LIMITED
Balance sheet at 30 September 1992

			£'000
Fixed assets			
Leasehold factory			600
Plant and machinery, net			450
			1 050
Current assets			
Stock	330		
Debtors	470		
Cash	200	1 000	
Less: **Creditors due within one year**			
Trade creditors	320		
Dividends	150		
Taxation	145	615	
			385
			1 435
Creditors due after more than one year			
10% Debenture 1997			400
Capital and reserves			
Called up share capital		750	
Profit and loss account		285	1 035
			1 435

Profit and loss account
for the nine months ended 30 September 1992

	£'000
Turnover	3 400
Cost of sales	2 790
Trading profit	610
Interest paid	30
Profit before taxation	580
Taxation	145
Profit after tax	435
Dividends	150
Retained profit	285

3.5 Chemical Engineering Company Limited (A)

CHEMICAL ENGINEERING COMPANY LIMITED
Balance sheet at 31 ~~July~~ *August* 1991   £'000

Fixed assets
Plant at cost $a + 10$ ~~38~~ 28

Current assets
Stock $d - 18$ ~~25~~ 7
Debtors $b - 8$ $d + 15$ ~~15~~ 22
Cash $a - 10$ $b + 8$ $c - 5$ ~~12~~ 5

                                                              34 ~~52~~
                                                              72 ~~80~~

Capital and reserves
Called up share capital   50
Profit and loss account $d - 3$ 17 ~~20~~
                                                              67 ~~70~~

Creditors due within one year
Trade creditors $c - 5$ 5 ~~10~~
                                                              72 ~~80~~

Final solution

CHEMICAL ENGINEERING COMPANY LIMITED
Balance sheet at 31 August 1991   £'000

Fixed assets
Plant at cost   38

Current assets
Stock   7
Debtors   22
Cash   5
                                                              34
                                                              72

Capital and reserves
Called up share capital   50
Profit and loss account   17
                                                              67

Creditors due within one year
Trade creditors   5
                                                              72

Note

Notice that there was a *loss* on the sale of goods. Sales proceeds were £15 000 while the goods had cost £18 000. The loss of £3 000 (being a negative profit) is *deducted* from the £20 000 balance on profit and loss account.

3.8 Abacus Book Shop Limited (C)

ABACUS BOOK SHOP LIMITED
Balance sheet, ~~31 January~~ 1991   *28 February*   £

Fixed asset

Leasehold shop	*b + 6000*		6000

Current assets

Stock	*c − 2000*	*E + 2500*	~~4000~~	5000
	d − 1500	*f + 2000*		
Debtors	*d + 2000*		~~1000~~	3000
Cash	*a + 3000*	*c + 3000*	~~4000~~	1500
	b − 6000	*E − 2500*		9 500
				15 500

Capital and reserves

Called up share capital				3 000
Profit and loss account	*c + 1000*	*d + 500*	~~5000~~	6 500
			~~8000~~	9500

Creditors due after more than one year

10% Loan (secured)	*a + 3000*	3000

Creditors due within one year

Trade creditors	*f + 2000*	~~1000~~	3000
		~~9000~~	15500

Final solution

ABACUS BOOK SHOP LIMITED
Balance sheet, 28 February 1991   £

Fixed assets

Leasehold shop		6 000

Current assets

Stock	5 000	
Debtors	3 000	
Cash	1 500	
		9 500
		15 500

Capital and reserves

Called up share capital	3 000	
Profit and loss account	6 500	
		9 500

Creditors due after more than one year

10% Loan (secured)		3 000

Creditors due within one year

Trade creditors		3 000
		15 500

Note

Notice the two new balance sheet categories:

    Fixed asset: Leasehold shop

    Creditors due after more than one year: 10 per cent Loan

WHITEWASH LAUNDRY LIMITED
Balance sheet at ~~1 January~~ 1991
31 March

	£'000
Fixed assets	
Laundry and equipment	50
Current assets	
Debtors $a + 60$ $c - 55$	~~30~~ 35
Cash $b - 6$ $d - 30$	~~10~~ 14
$c + 55$ $E - 15$	
	~~49~~ ~~40~~
	~~99~~ ~~90~~
Capital and reserves	
Called up share capital	75
Profit and loss account $+ 9$ (SEE below right)	24 ~~15~~
	~~99~~ ~~90~~

Final Solution

WHITEWASH LAUNDRY LIMITED
Balance sheet at 31 March 1991

		£'000
Fixed assets		
Laundry and equipment		50
Current assets		
Debtors	35	
Cash	14	
		49
		99
Capital and reserves		
Called up share capital		75
Profit and loss account		24
		99

Profit and loss account
for the quarter ended 31 March 1991

		£'000
Turnover		60
Less: Supplies	6	
Operating expenses	30	
		36
Gross profit		24
Selling and administrative expenses		15
Trading profit		9

3.11 A Green Limited

Cash book

1 April	Balance	3 000	(d)	Operating expenses	2 000
(b)	Sales	15 000	(e)	Creditors (suppliers)	14 000
(f)	Debtors	3 000		Balance c/d	5 000
		£21 000			£21 000
	Balance b/d	5 000			

Ledger

Share capital

| | | | 1 April | Balance | 3 000 |

Profit and loss account

| | | | 1 April | Balance | 2 000 |

Trade creditors

(e)	Cash	14 000	1 April	Balance	3 000
	Balance c/d	5 000	(a)	Stock	16 000
		£19 000			£19 000
				Balance b/d	5 000

Van

| 1 April | Balance | 4 000 | | | |

Stock

(a)	Creditors	16 000	(b)	Cost of sales	12 000
			(c)	Cost of sales	4 000
		£16 000			£16 000

Trial balance, 30 June 1991

	Total		Profit and loss account		Balance sheet	
	Dr	Cr	Dr	Cr	Dr	Cr
Share capital		3 000				3 000
Profit and loss account		2 000				2 000
Trade creditors		5 000				5 000
Vans	4 000				4 000	
Stock						
Debtors	3 000				3 000	
Sales		20 000		20 000		
Cost of sales	16 000		16 000			
Operating expenses	2 000		2 000			
Cash	5 000				5 000	
Profit for quarter			2 000			2 000
	£30 000	£30 000	£20 000	£20 000	£12 000	£12 000

Debtors

1 April	Balance	1 000	(f)	Cash	3 000
(c)	Sales	5 000		Balance c/d	3 000
		£6 000			£6 000
	Balance b/d	3 000			

Sales

			(b)	Cash	15 000
			(c)	Debtors	5 000
					20 000

Cost of sales

(b)	Stock	12 000			
(c)	Stock	4 000			
		16 000			

Operating expenses

| (d) | Cash | 2 000 | | | |

A GREEN LIMITED
Profit and loss account
for the three months ended 30 June 1991

	£
Turnover	20 000
Cost of sales	16 000
Gross profit	4 000
Operating expenses	2 000
Trading profit	2 000

Balance sheet, 30 June 1991

		£
Fixed assets		
Vans		4 000
Current assets		
Debtors	3 000	
Cash	5 000	
		8 000
		12 000
Capital and reserves		
Called up share capital		3 000
Profit and loss account		4 000
		7 000
Creditors due within one year		
Trade creditors		5 000
		12 000

3.12 Precision Engineering Limited

Cash book £'000

1 July	Balance	40	(c)	Stock	250
(a)	Sales	350	(e)	Expenses	100
(g)	Debtors	130	(f)	Creditors	90
			Dec	Balance c/d	80
		520			520
1 Jan	Balance b/d	80			

Trial balance, 31 December 1991

£'000	Total		Profit and loss account		Balance sheet	
	Dr	Cr	Dr	Cr	Dr	Cr
Share capital		300				300
Profit and loss account		130				130
Trade creditors		90				90
Factory and machinery	250				250	
Stock	170				170	
Debtors	80				80	
Sales		900		900		
Cost of sales	660		660			
Expenses	170		170			
Tax	10		10			
Cash	80				80	
Profit for year			60			60
	1 420	1 420	900	900	580	580

Note

The balance shown on the profit and loss account in the ledger at 30 June, when the transactions for 1991 appear in separate ledger accounts, is the £130 balance as at 1 January 1991 not the £150 balance appearing in the balance sheet at 30 June. The difference is the £20 profit for the six months ended 30 June.

Ledger accounts

		£'000			£'000
			Share capital		
			1 July	Balance	300
			Profit and loss account		
			1 Jan	Balance	130
			Trade creditors		
(f)	Cash	90	1 July	Balance	100
	Balance c/d	90	(d)	Stock	80
		180			180
			1 Jan	Balance b/d	90
			Factory and machinery		
1 July	Balance	250			
			Stock		
1 July	Balance	200	(a)	Cost of Sales	250
(c)	Cash	250	(b)	Cost of Sales	110
(d)	Creditors	80		Balance c/d	170
		530			530
1 Jan	Balance b/d	170			
			Debtors		
1 July	Balance	60	(g)	Cash	130
(b)	Sales	150		Balance c/d	80
		210			210
1 Jan	Balance b/d	80			
			Sales		
			July	Balance	400
			(a)	Cash	350
			(b)	Debtors	150
					900
			Cost of sales		
1 July	Balance	300			
(a)	Stock	250			
(b)	Stock	110			
		660			

PRECISION ENGINEERING LIMITED
Balance sheet, 31 December 1991

	£'000	£'000
Fixed assets		
Factory and machinery		250
Current assets		
Stock	170	
Debtors	80	
Cash	80	
		330
		580
Capital and reserves		
Called up share capital		300
Profit and loss account [= £130 + £60]		190
		490
Creditors due within one year		
Trade creditors		90
		580

Profit and loss account
Year ended 31 December 1991

	£'000
Turnover	900
Cost of sales	660
Gross profit	240
Expenses	170
Profit before tax	70
Tax	10
Profit after tax	60

		Expenses	
1 July	Balance	70	
(a)	Cash	100	
		170	
		Tax	
1 July	Balance	10	

4.5 Wheeler Limited

Solution

	Trial balance Dr £'000	Trial balance Cr £'000	Adjustments Dr £'000	Adjustments Cr £'000	Profit and loss Dr £'000	Profit and loss Cr £'000	Balance sheet Dr £'000	Balance sheet Cr £'000
Cash book	201						201	
Ordinary share capital (£1 shares)		200						200
Profit and loss account b/f		283						283
12% Loan		300						300
Fixed assets: cost	942						942	
Fixed assets: accumulated depreciation		347						347
Sales ledger control	183						183	
Stock	141			(c) 12			129	
Purchase ledger control		39		(a) 5				39
Accrued charges				(b) 9				14
Tax payable				(d) 95				95
Dividend payable				(e) 80				80
Sales		1 442				1 442		
Cost of goods sold	818		(c) 12		830			
Selling and administrative expenses	299		(a) 5		304			
Loan interest	27		(b) 9		36			
Tax expense			(d) 95		95			
Ordinary dividend			(e) 80		80			
					1 345			
Profit for year retained					97			97*
	2 611	2 611	201	201	1 442	1 442	1 455	1 455

Notes on trial balance schedule solution

1 Notice that the names of accounts were included in the trial balance schedule even though there was no balance in the 'trial balance' column itself, for instance for accrued charges, tax liability, dividend payable, tax expense and ordinary dividend. In practice, of course, one would have to be prepared to write in the names of accounts if necessary.

2 Three categories of accounts sometimes give difficulty: those connected with tax, dividends and depreciation. Perhaps tax is the easiest to use as an example.

In the Wheeler case notice that *two* accounts have been opened for tax: one for 'tax expense', or more strictly tax provision, which is a debit (and appears in the profit and loss as an expense), and the other for 'tax liability', which is a credit (and appears in the balance sheet as tax payable).

In practice it is not uncommon for only a single 'tax' account to be opened. Although an experienced accountant would have no difficulty in dealing with the necessary entries on a single account, it is probably simpler for anyone else deliberately to set up *two* accounts, one for the expense and the other for the liability.

In the same way it may be best to have *separate* accounts for 'depreciation expense' and 'accumulated depreciation', and for 'dividend payable' (the liability) and 'ordinary dividend' (the debit in the appropriation account).

3 Notice how the profit for the year in the trial balance schedule (£97)* is the *excess* of the credits in the profit and loss account columns over the debits. It is therefore added to the debits, to 'balance' the columns, and the *credit* balance is extended into the balance sheet columns. The new accumulated balance on the profit and loss account is now £380 (= £283 + £97).

344

WHEELER LIMITED

Profit and loss account for the year ended 31 March 1992

	£'000
Turnover	1 442
Cost of goods sold	830
Gross profit	612
Selling and administrative expenses	304
	308
Loan interest payable	36
Profit before tax	272
Tax	95
Profit after tax	177
Ordinary dividend	80
Retained from the year's profit	97

Balance sheet, 31 March 1992 £'000

Share capital and reserves		**Fixed assets**	£'000
Ordinary share capital	200	at cost	942
Profit and loss account	380	*Less:* depreciation	347
	580		595
Creditor due after more than one year		**Current assets**	
12% Loan	300	Stock	129
		Debtors	183
		Cash	201
			513
		Less: **Creditors due within one year**	
		Creditors	39
		Accrued charges	14
		Tax	95
		Dividend	80
			228
		Net current assets	285
	880		880

4.6 Canning and Sons Limited: Writing down stock

CANNING AND SONS LIMITED

Balance sheet at 31 December 1991

		£'000
Fixed assets (net)		330
Current assets		
Stock	193	
Debtors	254	
Cash	26	
	473	
Less: **Creditors falling due within one year**		
Trade creditors	132	
Tax	31	
	163	
		310
		640
Share capital and reserves		
Called up share capital		400
Profit and loss account		240
		640

Profit and loss account for the year ended 31 December 1991

	£'000
Turnover	1 127
Cost of Sales	891
Gross profit	236
Selling and administrative expenses	113
	123
Tax	31
Profit after tax	92

4.7 Anderson Tiles Limited

		£
Closing stock valuation		
3 000 cases at £5.00	=	15 000
2 000 cases at £4.75	=	9 500
1 000 cases at £4.25	=	4 250
		28 750
Cost of sales		
Opening stock		12 000
Purchases		41 500
		53 500
Less: Closing stock		28 750
		24 750
Cost of sales identified		
3 000 cases at £4.00	=	12 000
3 000 cases at £4.25	=	12 750
		24 750

4.8 Berwick Paper Limited: see next page

4.9 Newport Machines Limited

The overhead percentage is:

$$\frac{540\,000}{300\,000} = 180 \text{ per cent on direct labour}$$

The stock will therefore be valued as follows:

	£
Direct materials	30 000
Direct labour	20 000
Overheads (180% × 20 000)	36 000
	86 000

Note
The absorption cost method defers some *period* expenses by relating them to the *products* in stock. (Not all overheads, of course, are necessarily period costs.)

4.10 Tiptop Office Supplies

Provision for bad debts at 30 September 1992 is 5% × £426 000 = £21 300. (This *credit* balance is deducted on the balance sheet from debtors, which will appear simply as £404 700 at 30 September 1992.)

Bad debt expense = £28 300. This is the amount of specific bad debts written off, plus the increase of £11 300 in the general provision.

Provision for bad debts

Sept 92	Balance c/d	21 300	Oct 91	Balance b/f	10 000
			Sept 92	Bad debts	11 300
		21 300			21 300
			Oct 92	Balance b/d	21 300

Bad debts expense

Sept 92	Debtors	17 000	Sept 92	Profit & loss a/c	28 300
Sept 92	Provision for bad debts	11 300			
		28 300			28 300

4.8 Berwick Paper Limited

BERWICK PAPER LIMITED

Date 1991	Stock	Tonnes	Average cost £	Amount £	Value of Issues £
Jan	Opening	1 200	21.00	25 200	
March	Issues	900	21.00	18 900........	18 900
		300	21.00	6 300	
March	Purchases	1 800	18.00	32 400	
		2 100	18.43	38 700	
June	Issues	1 700	18.4286	31 329........	31 329
		400	18.4	7 371	
June	Purchases	2 400	15.0	36 000	
		2 800	15.4896	43 371	
Sept	Issues	1 400	15.5	21 686........	21 686
		1 400	15.5	21 685	
Sept	Purchases	1 200	25.0	30 000	
		2 600	19.8788	51 685	
Dec	Issues	1 900	19.9	37 770........	37 770
		700	19.9	13 915	
Dec	Purchases	1 800	20.0	36 000	
	Closing	2 500	19.966	49 915	109 685

Opening stock	25 200
Purchases	134 400
	159 600
Less: Closing stock	49 915
Cost of issues	109 685

Note to 5.10 James Hillier Limited (A): *Any declining balance rate between 33 per cent and 40 per cent would seem appropriate to produce a net book value at the end of year 4 of around £1 300. Using the formula shown in the text, a rate of 36.5 per cent can be calculated (see below).

$$r = \left[1 - \sqrt[4]{\frac{1\,300}{8\,000}} \right] \times 100 = 36.5\%$$

5.9 Jonas Limited (C)

(a) The annual depreciation charge would be reduced from £1 400 (= £8 400/6) to £1 300 (= [£8 400 − £600] ÷ 6), that is by £100 (= £600/6). The net book value at the end of the year 6 (the asset's expected life) would then be £600 (the asset's expected residual value) instead of zero.

(b) The cost of the improvement (£1 200) would have to be 'capitalized' and written off over the remaining three years of the asset's life, so the depreciation charge would be increased by £400 in each of years 4, 5, and 6. The net book value would therefore be increased by £800 at the end of year 4 (= £1 200 − £400) and by £400 at the end of year 5 (£1 200 − [2 × £400]).

5.10 James Hillier Limited (A)

	(a) 50% £	33% £	(b) 40% £	36.5%* £
Cost	8 000	8 000	8 000	8 000
Year 1 Depreciation	4 000	2 667	3 220	2 920
Net book value	4 000	5 333	4 800	5 080
Year 2 Depreciation (x% of n.b.v.)	2 000	1 778	1 920	1 854
Net book value	2 000	3 555	2 880	3 226
Year 3 Depreciation	1 000	1 185	1 152	1 178
Net book value	1 000	2 370	1 728	2 048
Year 4 Depreciation	500	790	691	748
Net book value	500	1 580	1 037	1 300
Expected proceeds	750			
Expected profit on sale	250			

Note

It is not unusual to 'expect' some profit or loss on sale in advance. With declining balance depreciation it is not always easy to find a rate that will conveniently write the asset down to its expected residual value over its expected life.

5.11 James Hillier Limited (B)

(a)

	£
Year 4 Net book value	500
Year 5 Depreciation	250
Net book value	250
Year 6 Depreciation	125
Net book value	125
Sale proceeds	600
Profit on sale	475

(b) Journal entries in year 6

	Dr	Cr
(1) Depreciation expense	125	
Accumulated depreciation		125
Annual depreciation charge in year 6		
(2) Accumulated depreciation	7 875	
Disposal A/c	125	
Cost of fixed asset		8 000
Transferring net book value to disposal A/c		
(3) Cash	600	
Disposal A/c		600
Entering sales proceeds in disposal A/c		
(4) Disposal A/c	475	
Profit and loss account		475
Transferring profit on sale to P&L account.		

(c) Ledger accounts for year 6

Cost of fixed asset

Balance b/f	8 000	Disposal a/c	8 000

Accumulated depreciation

Disposal a/c	7 785	Balance b/f	7 750
		Depreciation expense	125

Depreciation expense

Accumulated depreciation	125	Profit and loss account	125

Disposal account

Cost of fixed asset	8 000	Accumulated depreciation	7 875
P & L a/c: profit on sale	475	Cash	600
	8 475		8 475

5.12 Gilbert Limited and Sullivan Limited

		Gilbert £	Sullivan £
	Cost	7 200	7 200
Year 1	Depreciation	600	2 400
	Net book value	6 600	4 800
Year 2	Depreciation	600	1 600
	Net book value	6 000	3 200
Year 3	Depreciation	600	1 067
	Net book value	5 400	2 133
Year 4	Depreciation	600	711
	Net book value	4 800	1 422
	Sales proceeds	200	200
	Loss on disposal	4 600	1 222

5.13 Talmen Limited (A)

Net book value at 31 December 1993 = £22 800 (£30 000 − 3 × £2 400).
The company needs to write off £22 800 − £2 000 (= £20 800) over the remaining 4 years of estimated life = £5 200 per year.

5.14 Talmen Limited (B)

Net book value at 31 December 1993 = £22 800 (as in case (A)).
The company needs to write off £22 800 − £10 000 (= £12 800) over the remaining 10 years of estimated life = £1 280 per year.

6.3 Northern Foods plc

Solution

Balance sheet difference

	1991	1990	Difference	Cash flow	Book entry
Intangible fixed assets	–	–	–	– 54 g'will	+ 54 g'will
Tangible fixed assets	400	346	– 54 {	– 91 additions	+ 34 depn.
			{	+ 3 nbv sales	
Stocks	54	51	– 3	– 3	
Debtors	143	139	– 4	– 4	
Cash	20	18	– 2	– 2	
Less: Creditors:					
< 1 year	(293)	(230)	+ 63	+ 23 creditors	+ 7 tax
				+ 30 s/t borr.	
> 1 year	(7)	(4)	+ 3	+ 3 s/t borr.	+ 3 divs.
Provisions	(12)	(6)	+ 6	–	+ 6 misc.
	305	314	+ 9	– 95	
Share capital + premium	117	117	–		
Reserves	16	16	–		
Profit and loss account	172	181	– 9	+ 95 P&L	– 54 g'will
					– 50 P&L
	305	314	– 9	+ 95	

Profit and loss account

PBDIT	145	+ 151	– 6 misc.
Depreciation	34		– 34 depn.
Interest payable	6	– 6	
PBT	105		
Tax	28	– 21	– 7 tax
PAT	77		
Dividends	32	– 29	– 3 divs.
Retained profit	45	+ 95	– 50

6.3 Northern Foods *Solution (cont.)*

Cash flow statement
Year ended 31 March 1991

		£m
Operations		
Operating profit		+ 111
Depreciation		+ 34
Miscellaneous		+ 6
		+ 151
Less: Interest	– 6	
Tax paid	– 21	
Dividends	– 29	
		– 56
Internally generated net		+ 95
Proceeds from disposals		+ 3
Total internally generated		+ 98
Changes in working capital		
Stocks	– 3	
Debtors	– 4	
Creditors	+ 23	
		+ 16
Investment in fixed assets		
Goodwill	– 54	
Tangible fixed assets	– 91	
		– 145
Deficit before financing		– 31
External finance		
S/T borrowings	+ 30	
L/T borrowings	+ 3	
		+ 33
Increase in cash		+ 2

7.8 Graphic Enterprises Limited

	Factory buildings £'000		Office buildings £'000		Plant and machinery £'000	
(a) (b) in the books:						
Cost b/f	280		106		184	
Additions	20	300	14	120	26	210
Depreciation b/f	105		24		142	
Charge for year	15	120	6	30	21	163
= Net book value, 31 December 1991:		180		90		47
(c) (d) For tax purposes:						
Written-down value b/f	90		106		30	
Additions	20	110	14	120	26	56
Annual allowances		12		—		14
Written-down value, 31 December 1991:		98		120		42

Notes on annual allowances:

(i) Annual allowance is 4 per cent on *cost* of factory buildings (300).
(ii) No tax writing-down allowance on office buildings.
(iii) Annual allowances on plant 25 per cent of written-down value (56).
(iv) No tax capital allowances or book depreciation on land £600.

7.9 Archimedes Kaye Limited

		£'000
(a) Tax computation:	Profit before tax	2 200
	Add back: Depreciation charged	400
		2 600
Less:	Capital allowances	1 000
	= Taxable profit	1 600

Tax payable:
CT Year 1989 75% × £1 600 000 = £1 200 000 at 35% = £420 000
CT Year 1990 25% × £1 600 000 = £400 000 at 34% = £136 000

£556 000

The 'net' dividend of 2p per share (= £200 000) represents a 'gross' dividend of £266 667* from which £66 667** is 'imputed' to shareholders as basic rate income tax 'deducted at source'.

$$*266\,667 = \frac{200\,000}{100\% - 25\%} = \frac{200\,000}{75\%}$$

$$**66\,667 = \frac{25}{75} \times 200\,000 = 25\% \times 266\,667$$

But payment of the dividend on 1 September 1990 would require the company to pay the Inland Revenue £66 667 ACT on or before 14 October 1990. The corporation tax payable on 31 March 1991 would be £556 000 less ACT on any dividends paid in the previous accounting year. The £66 667 ACT would be deducted from corporation tax payable on 31 March 1992, due in respect of the company's taxable profits for the year ended 30 June 1991 (the basis year).

(b)	(i) With deferred tax account £'000	(ii) With no deferred tax account £'000
Profit before tax	2 200	2 200
Corporation tax	748*	556
Profit after tax	1 452	1 644
Net dividends payable	200	200
Retained profits for the year	1 252	1 444

*Subject to adjustment for the change in rate during the year.

7.10 Regeneration Limited (A)

CT Year 1989 75% × £2 000 000 = £1 500 000 @ 35% = £525 000 }
CT Year 1990 25% × £2 000 000 =   £500 000 @ 34% = £170 000 } = £695 000
CT Year 1990 (nine months)   £1 500 000 @ 34% = £510 000   = £510 000
CT Year 1991 (twelve months)   £2 400 000 @ 33% = £792 000   = £792 000

The tax would be payable nine months after the end of the accounting period in each case:

On 31 March 1991	£695 000
On 31 December 1991	£510 000
On 31 December 1992	£792 000

7.11 Regeneration Limited (B)

(a) No *extra* tax would be payable as a result of the dividend, but the date of payment of part of the tax would be accelerated by ACT.

(b) Income tax @ 25/75 on £500 000 (= £166 667) would be deducted from the 'gross' dividend of £666 667. A net dividend of £500 000 would be paid to shareholders on 1 June 1992; and the company would pay the Inland Revenue the £166 667 income tax 'deducted at source' (as ACT) on or before 14 July 1992.

The 'mainstream' corporation tax liability payable on 31 December 1992 would be £792 000 less ACT on any dividends paid in the year ended 31 March 1992. The £166 667 ACT paid in the year ended 31 March 1992 would be deducted from the mainstream corporation tax liability payable on 31 December 1993 in respect of taxable profits for the year ended 31 March 1993.

	£'000
Profit before tax	2 400
Corporation tax	792
Profit after tax	1 608
Net dividend	500
= Retained earnings	1 108

8.6 Kent Traders Limited

KENT TRADERS LIMITED
Balance sheet at 30 April 1992

		£'000
Fixed assets, net		750
Current assets		
Stock	260	
Debtors	190	
Cash	670	
	1 120	
Less: Creditors due within one year	240	
		880
		1 630
Capital and reserves		
Called up share capital, 1.5 million ordinary 50p shares		750
Share premium account		450
Profit and loss account		160
= Shareholders' funds		1 360
Creditors due after more than one year		
Long-term loans		270
		1 630

Notes

1 A 1 for 4 rights issue involves issuing a quarter of the shares now in issue = 300 000. At 200p per share the proceeds will be £600 000, which must be added to the cash balance.

2 The £600 000 proceeds are split:

(a) Nominal share capital: 300 000 at 50p = £150 000.
(b) Share premium: 300 000 at 150p = £450 000.

3 Notice that, since a rights issue really increases the company's capital, in this case £600 000 is added both to shareholders' funds and to net assets.

ANTROBUS LATHES LIMITED
Balance sheet, start of 1992

	Actual £'000	With loan converted £'000
Capital and reserves		
Called up ordinary £1 share capital	2 400	3 000
Reserves	1 100	2 000
Shareholders' funds	3 500	5 000
10% Convertible loan stock	1 500	—
8% Loan stock	1 000	1 000
Capital employed	6 000	6 000
Debt ratio	$\dfrac{2\,500}{6\,000} = 42\%$	$\dfrac{1\,000}{6\,000} = 17\%$
Profit and loss account 1991		
PBIT	1 430	1 430
Loan interest payable	230	80
Profit before tax	1 200	1 350
Tax at 33%	396	445
Profit after tax	804	905
Earnings per share	$\dfrac{804}{2\,400} = 33.5\text{p}$	$\dfrac{905}{3\,000} = 30.2\text{p}$
Interest cover	$\dfrac{1\,430}{230} = 6.2$	$\dfrac{1\,430}{80} = 17.9$

Notes

1 The implied price of 250p per share gives a *premium* of 150p per share. Thus the share premium on conversion = 600 000 at 150p = £900 000.
2 Total capital employed has not changed.
3 Notice the significant reduction in the debt ratio and the increase in the interest cover. An analyst should be well aware of this *potential* change in the company's capital structure when analysing the accounts.
4 Finally, note that conversion reduces earnings per share by 10 per cent; even though profit after tax increases by 12½ per cent.

WESTERN ENTERPRISES LIMITED
Balance sheet, at 31 December 1992

	1 January 1992 £'000	Changes in year £'000			31 December 1992 £'000
Fixed assets					
Land and buildings at valuation	700	b + 800			1 500
Plant, net	1 700				1 700
	2 400				3 200
Working capital	800	a + 150	d + 380		1 060
			e − 270		
	3 200				4 260
Capital and reserves					
Called up ordinary £1 shares	700	a + 50	c + 1500	f + 150	2 400
Share premium account	350	a + 100	c − 450		
Revaluation reserve		b + 800	c − 800		
Profit and loss account	950	c − 250	d + 380	f − 150	660
			e − 270		
	2 000				3 060
8% £1 Preference shares	200				200
10% Loan stock	1 000				1 000
	3 200				4 260

Notes

1 Did you remember to change the description of land and buildings from 'at cost' to 'at valuation'?
2 The bonus issue in (c) involves capitalizing reserves. Normal practice is to capitalize the most 'permanent' reserves first, that is, first share premium, then other capital reserves, finally profit and loss.
3 The cash dividend of £270 000 in (e) is deducted from the £380 000 profit after tax, leaving retained profits for the year of £110 000.

8.9 Sadler Limited (A)

Profit and loss account extract
Year ended 31 December 1990

		£'000
Profit before interest payable and tax		48.0
10% Debenture interest		8.0
Profit before tax		40.0
Tax at 25%		10.0
Profit after tax		30.0
Dividends: 3.5% Preference	2.1	
8p Ordinary	16.0	
		18.1
Retained profit		11.9

(a) Interest cover $= \dfrac{48.0}{8.0} = 6.0$ times

(b) Profit for ordinary shareholders:

Profit after tax	30.0
Less: Preference dividend	2.1
	27.9

Ordinary dividend cover $= \dfrac{27.9}{16.0} = 1.74$ times

8.10 Sadler Limited (B)

Balance sheet extract at 31 December 1990
Capital and reserves

	£'000
Called up ordinary £1 share capital	200
Reserves	60
Ordinary shareholders' funds	260
3½% Preference share capital	60
10% Debentures	80
Capital employed	400

(a) Debt ratio = 80/400 = 20 per cent.

(b) If net assets realize — 125
debentures amount to — 80

leaving for preference and ordinary shareholders — 45
but preference share capital is — 60

Therefore preference shareholders will get only 75 per cent of the nominal amount of their shares, that is, 75p per share. Ordinary shareholders will get *nothing*.

(c) If net assets realize — 190
debentures and preference capital amount to — 140

leaving for ordinary shareholders — 50

(= 25p per share)

Notes

1 In this case net assets realize enough to pay creditors (both short term and long term) in full. If there were not enough to do that, and assuming that all creditors were 'unsecured', every creditor would be paid *pro rata* (except for certain debts, such as amounts due for wages, and taxes, which have statutory priority). There is *no* priority for current as opposed to longer-term creditors.

2 As you know, balance sheets are prepared on a going concern basis, and do not purport to show the *realizable value* of *all* the company's assets. Balance sheets show the *unexpired costs* of those assets which have cost something. (Some valuable assets, for instance goodwill, may have cost nothing.)

3 Despite the above, some analysts refer to a calculation of 'book value per share' from time to time. This simply assumes that net assets could be realized for their book value: and divides the ordinary shareholders' funds by the number of ordinary shares in issue.

For Sadler Limited, then, the 'book value per share' is 130p (260/200).

8.11 Bell Limited, Book Limited and Candle Limited

	Bell Limited £'000	Book Limited £'000	Candle Limited £'000
(a) 1990			
PBIT	180	180	180
Interest	60	20	—
Profit before tax	120	160	180
Tax at 25%	30	40	45
Profit after tax	90	120	135
(i) Return on net assets	18%	18%	18%
(ii) Return on equity	22.5%	15.0%	13.5%
(iii) Interest cover	3.0	9.0	—
(iv) Earnings per share	60p	40p	33.8p
(b) 1991			
PBIT	50	50	50
Interest	60	20	—
Profit (loss) before tax	(10)	30	50
Tax at 25%	—*	7½	12½
Profit (loss) after tax	(10)	22½	37½

*Tax refund of £2½ might be available in respect of the loss.

(i) Return on net assets	5%	5%	5%
(ii) Return on equity	(2.5%)	2.8%	3.8%
(iii) Interest cover	0.83	2.5	—
(iv) Earnings per share	(6.7p)	7.5p	9.4p

9.6 Barber Limited and Jenkins Limited

Extracts from 1991 accounts

	Barber £'000	Jenkins £'000
Net assets	3 600	3 600
Investment in subsidiary	400	500(a)
	4 000	4 100
Profit after tax	500	600
Dividend paid	300	300
Retained profit for the year	200	300(a)

(a) Including the holding company's 100 per cent share of the subsidiary's retained profits.

If the subsidiary paid a dividend of £75 000 (all to the holding company), Barber ('cost' method) would include it in the profit and loss account and add £75 000 to cash. Barber would ignore the £25 000 profit retained by the subsidiary.

Under the 'equity' method, Jenkins has already included all the subsidiary's 1991 profit of £100 000 whether or not any dividend is paid. Thus the only effect of Jenkins's subsidiary paying a £75 000 dividend would be on the balance sheet: to increase assets (cash) by £75 000, and reduce the investment in the subsidiary by the same amount.

9.7 Leach Limited and Dixon Limited

LEACH LIMITED
Consolidated balance sheet at 31 March 1991

	Acquisition £m		Merger £m
Net assets	95		95
Called up share capital (40 + 20)	60		60
Share premium account	20		—
Profit and loss account (20 − Goodwill 5)	15	(20 + 15)	35
	95		95

Notes

1 Goodwill = £40 million purchase price − £35 million net assets acquired = £5 million. This has been written off to reserves.

2 Retained profits are higher using merger accounting.

9.8 Triple Enterprises Limited

TRIPLE ENTERPRISES LIMITED
Balance sheet at 1 April 1991

	Brighton Brands £'000	Corbett Chemicals £'000	Duckham Drugs £'000		Triple Enterprises £'000
Fixed assets, net	370	420	350	=	1 140
Net working capital	280	380*	110	=	700
	650	800	460	=	1 910
Less: Long-term debt	150	200	60	=	410
	500	600	400	=	1 500
Capital and reserves					
Called up share capital	120	200	80	=	400
Revaluation reserves	110	90	140	=	340
Profit and loss account	270	310*	180	=	760
Shareholders' funds	500	600	400	=	1 500

*After deducting £30 000 written off Corbett's stocks.

Notes
1 The revaluation makes merger accounting in this case very simple: just a question of adding the numbers together.
2 What would happen if the fixed assets were *not* revalued? (Assuming the agreed valuations were the same as before.) Triple's balance sheet would simply show fixed assets, net at £800 000 (= 260 + 330 + 210); and would not include any revaluation reserves.

9.9 Chain Industries Limited

Yes, Chain Industries Limited *would* normally consolidate E Limited's accounts, on the grounds that Chain controls E (indirectly), even though the beneficial interest amounts to only 7.8 per cent. Thus 100 per cent of E's assets (and profits) would be consolidated in the Chain Group accounts, and 92.2 per cent would be shown separately as minority interests.

Chain owns 60.0% of A, so minority interests own 40.0% × £420 000 = £168 000
Chain owns 36.0% of B, so minority interests own 64.0% × £300 000 = £192 000
Chain owns 21.6% of C, so minority interests own 78.4% × £180 000 = £141 120
Chain owns 13.0% of D, so minority interests own 87.0% × £240 000 = £208 800
Chain owns 7.8% of E, so minority interests own 92.2% × £100 000 = £ 92 200

Thus, in the Chain group minority interests will stand at £802 120

9.10 Philip Limited

No profit for sales between companies within a group should be included in consolidated accounts until the goods have been sold to a customer outside the group. Only then is profit 'realized' from the group's point of view.

Arising from sales to Philip in the year ended 31 March 1991, Sidney will have incorporated the following transactions in its accounts:

Sale	£80 000
Cost of sales	£50 000 = Profit £30 000

Thus Sidney has included in its accounts a profit of £30 000 in respect of inter-company sales, one quarter of which are still 'unrealized' by the group at 31 March 1991. Group profits should therefore be reduced by £7 500 (sales turnover down £20 000, cost of sales down £12 500); and stock should be reduced by £7 500.

Any amount still owing by Philip to Sidney at 31 March 1991 will be cancelled out against the amount shown as debtors in Sidney's books.

10.5 Parkside Limited (A)

(a) Blue Moon: Profit and loss account
Year ended 31 December 1991

	R$'000	£'000
Sales	7 000	3 500
Depreciation	300	150
Other expenses	6 560	3 280
Profit	140	70

Blue Moon: Balance sheet as at 31 December 1991

	1991 R$'000	1991 £'000	1990 R$'000	1990 £'000
Fixed assets	1 200	600	1 500	500
Working capital	560	280	360	120
	1 760	880	1 860	620
(Long-term debt)	(720)	(360)	(960)	(320)
	1 040	520	900	300
Capital and reserves:				
Called-up share capital	200	50	200	50
Retained profits	840	470	700	250
	1 040	520	900	300

Exchange differences for year 1991

	£'000
Opening net assets (R$900) @ opening exchange rate (£1 = R$3.00)	= 300
Opening net assets (R$900) @ closing exchange rate (£1 = R$2.00)	= 450
Exchange differences for year 1991	= 150

Retained profits at 31 December 1991

	£'000
Opening balance at 1 January 1991	250
Profit for the year	70
Exchange differences for the year	150
Closing balance at 31 December 1991	470

(b) Using the average rate, instead of the closing rate, to translate 1991 profits would produce a profit for 1991 of £56 (R$140 @ £1 = R$2.50). The difference of £14 would be an additional exchange difference in reserves.

10.6 Parkside Limited (B)

Blue Moon: Profit and loss account
Year ended 31 December 1991

	R$'000	£'000
Sales	7 000	2 800
Depreciation	300	75
Other expenses	6 560	2 624
Exchange losses	–	56
Profit for year	140	45

Blue Moon: Balance sheet as at 31 December 1991

	1991 R$'000	1991 £'000	1990 R$'000	1990 £'000
Fixed assets	1 200	300	1 500	375
Working capital	560	280	360	120
	1 760	580	1 860	495
(Long-term debt)	(720)	(360)	(960)	(320)
	1 040	220	900	175
Capital and reserves:				
Called-up share capital	200	50	200	50
Retained profits	840	170	700	125
	1 040	220	900	175

Exchange differences for year 1991

		£'000
Profit before depreciation R$440: @ average rate R$2.50		= 176
	@ closing rate R$2.00	= 220
		+ 44

Opening net monetary liabilities R$600: at opening rate	R$3.00 = 200	
at closing rate	R$2.00 = 300	– 100
		– 56

356

11.12 Thames Manufacturing Limited (B)

All money amounts in the December 1991 CCA balance sheet need to be multiplied by 105.0/100.0, that is, by 1.05, in order to express them in 'amounts updated for the change in value of the pound'. In summary the figures are as follows:

THAMES MANUFACTURING LIMITED
CCA balance sheet at 31 December 1992

1991 original £		1992 £	1991 restated £
199 440	Fixed assets	198 720	209 412
74 267	Current assets *Less:* Creditors due	193 769	77 980
(20 000)	within one year	(65 000)	(21 000)
54 267		128 769	56 980
253 707		327 489	266 392
(20 000)	*Less:* long-term debt	(30 000)	(21 000)
233 707		297 489	245 392
233 707	Shareholders' funds	297 489	245 392

THAMES MANUFACTURING LIMITED
CPP profit and loss account
Year ended 31 December 1992

		Dec. 92 £
Sales		204 880
Cost of sales	88 098	
Depreciation	26 670	
		114 768
		90 112
Interest payable	5 122	
Loss on net monetary assets	3 182	
		8 304
Profit before tax		81 808
Tax		30 732
Profit after tax		51 076
Dividends		15 366
Retained profit for the year		35 710

Notes

1 All numbers except depreciation and loss on net monetary assets (for which see below) calculated by multiplying the HC figures by 1.0244 (that is, 105.0/102.5) − to translate from 'mid-1992' pounds to 'end-1992' pounds.

2 Depreciation is one-fifth of the adjusted 'cost' of production machinery; which is the end-1991 amount of $_{91}$£127 000 (given) × 1.05 = $_{92}$£133 350. 1/5 × $_{92}$£133 350 = $_{92}$£26 670.

3 Loss on net monetary assets is calculated as follows:

Net monetary assets at December 1991 = $_{91}$£34 000 (given) × 1.05 = $_{92}$£35 700

Net monetary assets as December 1992 = $_{92}$£98 000

Average net monetary assets for year = $_{92}$£66 850

Loss of purchasing power of pound during year = 100.0/105.0 = 4.76 per cent (notice, *not* 5.0 per cent exactly).
Loss on net monetary assets = 4.76% × $_{92}$£66 850 = $_{92}$£3 182.

THAMES MANUFACTURING LIMITED
CPP balance sheet at 31 December 1992

1991 $_{91}$£		1992 $_{92}$£	1991 $_{92}$£
105 000	Land at cost	110 250	110 250
127 000	Production machinery: Cost	133 350	133 350
34 150	Depreciation	62 528	35 858
92 850	Net	70 822	97 482
54 000	Net current assets	128 000	56 700
251 850		309 072	264 442
	Less: Creditors due after		
(20 000)	more than one year	(30 000)	(21 000)
231 850		279 072	243 442
164 474	Called up share capital	172 697	172 697
67 376	Retained profits	106 455	70 745
—	Other reserves	(80)	—
231 850		279 072	243 442

Notes

1 Called up share capital is assumed to be £150 000 on 1 January 1990; and is translated by the Retail Prices Index assumed to be standing at 0.912 on that date. Retained profits is then simply assumed to be the balance of equity at December 1991.

2 All CPP figures in December 1991 pounds are simply multiplied by 1.05 to translate them into December 1992 pounds.

3 Accumulated depreciation is $_{92}$£35 858 opening + $_{92}$£26 670 charged in year.

4 Retained profits are $_{92}$£70 745 opening + $_{92}$£35 710 retained for year.

5 'Other reserves' of $_{92}$£(80) is simply the unexplained 'difference'.

Index